MODERN SURVIVAL GUNS

THE COMPLETE PREPPERS' GUIDE TO DEALING WITH EVERYDAY THREATS

BY JORGE AMSELLE

Published by

Gun Digest® Books, an imprint of Caribou Media
Gun Digest Media, P.O. Box 12219, Zephyr Cove, NV 89448
www.gundigest.com

To order books or other products call toll-free 1-800-258-0929
or visit us online at www.gundigeststore.com

CAUTION: Technical data presented here, particularly technical data on handloading and on firearms adjustment and alteration, inevitably reflects individual experience with particular equipment and components under specific circumstances the reader cannot duplicate exactly. Such data presentations therefore should be used for guidance only and with caution. Caribou Media accepts no responsibility for results obtained using these data.

All photos by author except where noted

ISBN-13: 978-1-946267-14-6
ISBN-10: 1-946267-14-7

Cover design by Jeromy Boutwell
Designed by Dane Royer
Edited By Corey Graff

Printed in The USA

10 9 8 7 6 5 4 3 2 1

ACKNOWLEDGMENTS

There are a lot of emergency supply companies, trainers, accessory makers and firearms manufacturers and every one of them I contacted for assistance was incredibly helpful with products, advice and images for this book. There are too many, in fact, to list here but all of the companies featured in this book produce high-quality gear and provide excellent customer service. I am also grateful to my wife Megan for her help and advice.

Jorge Amselle.

ABOUT THE AUTHOR

Jorge Amselle is an NRA-certified firearms instructor, military veteran, bullseye shooter, and noted author for various national gun magazines. He routinely tests out the latest guns, ammunition, gear and holsters from large and small manufacturers around the country and the world. He is on the road observing, attending, participating in and reporting on law enforcement and self-defense training academies throughout the year. He covers prepper and emergency medical survival courses, including shelters and evacuation as well as focusing on renewable food and energy sources.

Mr. Amselle has a Juris Master from the George Mason University School of Law and more than 25 years of experience in communications and public policy. His articles on politics and firearms have appeared in *The New York Times*, *The Wall Street Journal*, *National Review*, and *The Daily Caller*. He is the author of the *Gun Digest Guide to the Modern AK* and *Gun Digest Shooter's Guide to Concealed Carry*. He has appeared on C-SPAN, PBS, MSNBC and FOX News and has testified before Congress and state legislatures. He practices what he preaches and has been carrying a concealed firearm on a daily basis for over 20 years.

More articles by Jorge Amselle can be found at his blog, www.GunsNTacos.com

FOREWORD

By Massad Ayoob

I've enjoyed Jorge Amselle's writing for many years, have met the man, and feel privileged to be asked to write the foreword for his book *Modern Survival Guns*. The timing was actually rather ironic. This is being written as I sit in Florida in the aftermath of Irma, the Category 5 hurricane that recently hit, and just after returning from Houston, which was devastated by Hurricane Harvey, within days of each other in the third quarter of 2017.

Each experience was a reminder of how thin the veneer of civilization can be, and how small any human is against so giant a force as nature itself. In the days before writing this, I've interacted with some of the courageous rescuers who saved lives in those disasters ... and have seen the utter, soul-crushing *helplessness* of the victims who were not prepared for what happened to them.

Jorge Amselle is best known for his work in the firearms field, particularly defensive firearms, but the greatest strength of this book is that he wrote it holistically. He has gone down the full list of preparedness for life-threatening disasters — medical, interpersonal, force of nature or aftermath of civil upheaval or even war. Most of us will be more likely to be able to save a life with first aid knowledge and equipment than with a gun. Something as benign and unnoticed by others as sudden loss of a job can make us awfully grateful for a substantial supply of food on hand and a source for more. And if the emergency is broader in scope, well, you'll be all the more gratified that you were prepared beforehand.

It's not just about us and our families. Preparedness allows us to be of help to others. I had been away from my Florida home between

Hurricanes Harvey and Irma, but was able to offer stockpiled food, a high capacity generator, and extra vehicles to others who needed them there on the ground during the emergency. (Didn't have to lend any weapons this time, but those were available, too.)

Yet if anyone thinks Amselle put too much emphasis on weapons in this book, they may just be whistling past the graveyard. On the one hand, emergencies bring out the best in some people, but they bring out the worst in others. In the two disasters just cited — and many that went before — the authorities flatly told the citizenry they were on their own and beyond official help. Force multipliers such as the gun are essential to survival for crime victims on any day in everyday life, and the possibility looms much larger when society and authority break down. Man is the tool-bearing mammal, which allows him to rebuild from such disasters, but that also makes him the weapon-bearing mammal, and these can sometimes be the only tools that allow him and his loved ones to survive to rebuild.

Jorge Amselle has put this book together wisely. It follows naturally that you are wise to be reading it.

Massad Ayoob has spent 45 years in the criminal justice system, is the author of some twenty books on weapons, self-defense, and related legal issues, and teaches full-time in those areas through massadayoobgroup.com.

TABLE OF CONTENTS

THE THREAT IS REAL

*A*s a kid growing up during the Cold War, I had a terrible dread that a nuclear war would wipe us all out, a sentiment shared by many in those days. Yet, I walked to school fearless of being hit by a car. I was naïve, but it's still easy to get swept up in our greatest worries while ignoring less epic (but far likelier) dangers around us.

I am not advocating being fearful of everything, but threats must be kept in perspective. This is especially the case when we are investing limited time and money to prepare for what can be potentially unlimited dangers. Focus your energies on preparing for the most likely or biggest threats. By all means, prepare for less likely scenarios, but keep these preparations proportional. The right balance is to weigh the likelihood

> ## SURVIVAL SNAPSHOT: THE THREAT IS REAL
>
> **EVALUATE:** Prepare most for the likeliest scenarios where you live.
>
> **CHALLENGES:** Limited storage space may be the biggest hurdle.
>
> **STOCKPILE:** Shelter, food and drinking water are your most valuable assets.
>
> **AUTHOR'S TOP THREAT:** Natural disasters are the most likely survival situation.
>
> **PRIORITY:** Have a plan and make sure all family members know it.

and severity of a survival situation with your personal ability, desire, and commitment to prepare for it.

When we discuss survival, it is too limiting to only think in terms of radical societal changes, wars, or natural disasters. These dangers are real, but more pressing survival challenges can include a home invasion, an armed robbery, a sexual assault, even an extended power outage. Each scenario calls for a different response and level of preparation in order to increase your chances of survival.

I discuss armed self-defense at length in this book, but I recognize that this may not be something everyone is prepared to do. I do include details on less lethal self-defense options and, better still, how to avoid confrontations in the first place. If you do chose to arm yourself, you must take proper precautions and commit yourself to getting trained and to understanding safe storage. I highly recommend arming yourself and getting trained; but, if you do not, you can still use this book to prepare and help yourself survive.

Criminals mostly victimize one another and people they know — rarely complete strangers at random, but it does happen. During a local or national crises, this danger can be expected to increase.

CRIME

As of this writing, violent crime rates in the United States are at near record lows. Criminologists will attest that many factors affect crime rates, and it is nearly impossible to single any one factor as a main culprit. Population density, law enforcement, the economy, and even the weather can cause crime rates to vary. Rural areas have lower murder rates in part because the lower population density means people have fewer interactions with each other. Violent crime is also much more likely to occur among people who are known to each other and far less likely to happen among people who are strangers. Nevertheless, the great fear when it comes to criminal assault is that some stranger will attack you. In reality, it is far more likely that a family member or acquaintance will harm you.

"Hot" home invasions in the United States are also very rare. A "hot" home invasion occurs when someone enters your home with the knowledge that you are inside. These are extremely dangerous

COOPER'S COLOR CODE SYSTEM FOR SURVIVAL

The late Col. Jeff Cooper (who started the well-known Gunsite training academy in Arizona) established a color code system of situational awareness that is still widely promoted today. He specified that this was not simply a skill to have in place in dangerous situations but also in our daily lives. In condition white, a person is completely unaware of their surroundings and has a feeling of complete safety. In Cooper's mind, it seems the only time you should be in condition white is when you are asleep. Condition yellow is the full-time preferred condition in which to live. In yellow, you don't sense any specific danger or threat, but you remain vigilant and observant of your environment. You notice people around you, movements, buildings, objects, etc. In condition orange, you have identified a potential threat and commence your contingency plans: looking for an exit, looking for cover, looking for a weapon, looking for assistance, etc. In the final condition of red, you are engaged in defensive action, flight or fight. Anytime you are out in a public place, it is important to maintain at least a minimal amount of situational awareness of the people around you.

The aftermath of a tornado. Are all of your firearms in one location where damage such as this would result in a total loss? *Photo: FEMA*

scenarios because anyone breaking into your home knowing you are present is most likely intending to harm you — and has the wherewithal to do so. Fortunately, it is more common for people to break into your home as a result of intoxication and confusion, thinking it is their home. The most common type of home invasion is for theft, and the perpetrators want to make sure you are not home to interrupt them.

One survey of prison inmates found that they were far more fearful of being shot by a homeowner than by the police. Given that one-third to one-half of U.S. households (it varies a lot by state) own a firearm, this fear is not unfounded. The irony here is that the households that have chosen to remain unarmed are benefiting from their armed neighbors, since criminals have no way of knowing who is armed and who is not.

The bottom line when it comes to crime is this: you should make every effort to distance yourself and avoid anyone who has violent or criminal tendencies, regardless of whether they are a friend or family member. They are the greatest threat to you, and ironically, you are most likely to be at the lowest level of awareness while around people who are familiar to you. In later chapters, I address the specifics of defending your home and yourself from assault, including the use of less lethal means and women's self-defense issues. For now, keep in mind that the danger of an attack by a stranger is low, albeit still higher than most of the other dangers listed in this book.

TERRORISM

We live in a world where the threat of terrorism is real. Fortunately, two vast oceans separate us from most of the world's terrorism. The actual danger of an American on U.S. soil being killed by a terrorist is infinitesimally small. There has not been an externally coordinated terrorist attack in the United States since 9/11. There have been thwarted plots, many of them amateurish. The greatest danger here comes from lone wolf-type attacks that are nearly impossible to predict or stop.

Anti-terrorism security measures implemented at large, crowded venues only shift the point of attack farther out. Security checkpoints create bottlenecks that present ripe targets. If the threat of terrorism is a real concern, then it is best to avoid crowds of any sort. That includes mass transportation, sporting and music events, large shopping centers, community fairs, or other gatherings. Clearly, for many this would be a difficult way to live, so they take their chances.

Situational awareness (see sidebar this chapter) is important but complicated by the sheer volume of information you need to track. In a large crowd with lots of movement, noise, and distractions, it is impossible to be completely aware of everything. Obvious things to avoid include packages or bags left unattended and suspicious people. In many of these larger venues, it is unlawful to be armed, so your ability to defend yourself is very limited.

The threat of terrorism is statistically small but ever present. Nations with strict gun control laws such as the UK have had to deal with more of it. *Photo: David Holt*

Here, the best and possibly only option is to identify clear avenues of escape or cover should the need arise.

There are two basic types of mass casualty events: bombings and mass shootings. As we saw with the Boston bombing, explosives can be ridiculously easy to manufacture, and even if the number of casualties is not large, the disruptive effect can be significant with long-lasting trauma for survivors and witnesses. This is the entire goal of terrorism — to sow fear in a population in order to achieve a political objective. Acquiring low-grade radioactive material (from old medical devices, for example) and adding it to the bomb can create an even bigger sense of fear, even if the danger of radiation poisoning is small.

SURVIVAL GUNS AND THE LOS ANGELES RIOTS

In 1992, following the jury's not guilty verdict in the case of five Los Angeles police officers who were caught on tape beating a black suspect, the city of Los Angeles erupted in days of rioting. Looting, assault, and arson soon followed. The center of the firestorm was known as Koreatown in South Central Los Angeles. Although the neighborhood was mostly African American, many of the small shops and stores were owned by Korean immigrants. These quickly became targets of opportunity for looters and vandals.

In the chaos that ensued, 50 people died, over 2,000 were injured and over 1,000 buildings and businesses were damaged. The police completely lost control of entire parts of the city and abandoned them to rioters. This left business owners little choice but to protect their property themselves as many of them lacked insurance for this type of occurrence.

NBC news interviewed Sonny Kang, who helped organize the community to help storeowners protect their businesses from armed assailants and gang members. The only way for them to do so, said Kang, was to be armed. Soon, rooftops and store fronts filled with images of merchants, employees, friends and family armed with whatever they had, from shotguns to rifles to pistols.

Mass shootings are even easier to carry out, as we have sadly seen time and again. Depending on the target, these types of events can reach even higher casualty rates than bombings. Even vehicles can be used for mass casualty attacks, and we have seen this happen in Europe. The indiscriminate and unexpected nature of terrorist attacks increases our fear of them. The best defense is to always maintain a situational awareness of avenues of escape. Even if you are armed when such an event occurs, shooting back must take place only if you have no other options of escape and have become an "unwilling participant."

Terrorists take advantage of the chaos and confusion they cause. Remain aware, have a plan, and know the exits. It is easy to become complacent and assume a disturbance is nothing to worry about (just a car backfiring!). We want to feel comfortable and tend to excuse or ignore things that disrupt that feeling — until it is too late. Rely on your instincts and be prepared to move out of the area.

NATURAL DISASTERS

Up to this point, I have mainly addressed situations that can affect you personally. However, the danger of a wide-scale situation dramatically increases your risk because it places stress on your usual sources of help. If everyone around you needs help at the same time, your chances of getting the help you need decrease due to the strain on first responders and emergency resources. Therefore, a certain amount of self-reliance is essential.

Natural disasters, including blizzards, hurricanes, fires, earthquakes, tornadoes, flooding and landslides, can leave you stranded at home or work, without electricity and with limited supplies. Communications networks can be knocked out. Food and drinking water may run short, and this situation could last for days or longer.

Floods can force evacuations, cause significant property damage, and compromise the safety of municipal water treatment systems. *Photo: Eric Hamlter*

The danger is further complicated because, in some cases, you may need to evacuate to a safer area whereas in others, it is best to stay home. A plan of action must be established with family members to designate one or more rally points in case communications break down. Your plan must include both hunker down and evacuation scenarios. Also, write down family and emergency contact numbers and keep them with you. Do not rely on your memory or electronics.

If you need to evacuate, you must prioritize what to take with you, since you can carry relatively little. You must also think of evacuation routes. Keep paper maps in your car in case the main roads become gridlocked. Keep an emergency "bug-out" kit in your vehicle with at least three days' food and water for one person plus something to keep you warm. Keep all vehicles at least half full of gas at all times.

If you hunker down at home, you need access to food and water for all family members — at least a 30-day supply. You may need to be able to seal the doors and windows. You will need

Protests can quickly morph into violent civil disturbances. *Photo: Josephine Pedersen*

emergency lights, heat, bathroom facilities, and alternate means of communication, an emergency radio, and medical supplies. How you prepare depends heavily on where you live and what types of natural disasters are most likely to affect you. In a worst case scenario, you must be prepared for a longer period of isolation and must consider sustainable sources of food, water, and energy.

In some cases of natural disaster, emergency services can be insufficient, unreliable, or even work against your interests. During the aftermath of Hurricane Katrina in New Orleans, some law enforcement agencies went door to door, disarming civilians, leaving them defenseless. The Louisiana Superdome, which is a designated shelter and emergency assistance area, was completely unprepared and short on supplies and sanitation. For some, the shelter was a source of danger. Use the assistance provided to you by emergency services, but be prepared to go it alone if these services are inadequate or even become hostile.

Crowded and unsanitary conditions can lead to the spread of disease in very short order. Combine this with a lack of access to medical care and the situation is ripe for major health crises that only increases panic. The Spanish flu, which was a worldwide contagion in the early part of the 20th century, infected nearly 30 percent of the population of the United States, and over 500,000 people died; in total, 3-5 percent of the world's population perished. Today, we have improved medical care and have better access to antibiotics and vaccines. However, new antibiotic resistant superbugs and fresh, more virulent strains of the flu continue to threaten us. A good survival strategy must include ways to limit exposure to disease.

SOCIETAL UPHEAVAL

A friend once told me that if you went to the grocery store one day and the shelves were empty, it would strike you as strange. If you returned the next day and the shelves were still empty, you might start to panic. By the third day, things could get very ugly. That may be overly generous — a single day's loss of stocked shelves would more than likely bring out the worst in people. In our modern world, we rely on just-in-time delivery of everything we need. No business wants to have warehouses full of unsold items. They order and ship as needed. All of this relies on a national transportation network of ships, trains, and trucks to keep the store shelves full.

The electrical grid is absolutely essential but is sadly vulnerable to attack by everyone from saboteurs to hackers. A teenage hacker recently planted malware on a link to a website that was widely shared on social media accounts. The Malware caused phones to repeatedly dial 911 and hang up without the owner's knowledge. This in turn caused 911 systems to become overwhelmed in several cities across the country. Imagine the harm that a determined hacker or group of hackers could do with the assistance and protection of a hostile foreign government. And they could do it anonymously.

Extended emergency situations can quickly empty store shelves of food and other necessities. As people panic, they can become violent. *Photo: Aleksi Pihkanen*

A long-term shutdown of the grid would mean you couldn't get online, couldn't use your credit card to make purchases, couldn't get paid via electronic payroll, and couldn't charge your cell phone or other devices. People once lived without electricity, but how many of us are prepared to return to that lifestyle with no warning? The Amish can't take care of all of us. Again: to be fully prepared, you must consider alternative and renewable fuel and electricity sources.

Economic disruptions can also cause mass panic. For example, if our banking system were shut down for even a short period of time, commerce would come to a standstill. This would lead to severe economic harm and a panic. We have already been through a great depression and a great recession. We survived both, but not without great social upheaval. Hyperinflation and the suffering caused by economic mismanagement in other countries such as Venezuela and Zimbabwe dwarf our experiences in America. Even so, it can happen here with a vengeance as it has in other developed countries, like the German Weimar Republic after World War I.

There is also the danger of rioting and looting, which is mainly an issue in larger cities, but can occur in smaller towns as well (see sidebar on the Los Angeles riots). Fortunately, this type of situation tends to be short-lived, but it does require a level of preparation.

The worst case scenario is one of civil war or the complete collapse of government authority. We have seen this type of situation occur around the globe with tragic consequences and intense mass civilian casualties and suffering. Entire populations have been displaced. Such a situation seems highly unlikely to occur in our modern and powerful country, but short-term or regional disruptions could happen. A deterioration of the political situation is not likely to happen all at once, which affords some time to develop a longer-term evacuation plan.

GUN CONTROL & DISARMAMENT

*I*t may be my bias, but I strongly advocate for any survival plan to include being armed. This is not simply a precaution against two-legged predators, but also an essential part of long-term survival that may include hunting for your food. We are fortunate that, in the United States, access to firearms is not difficult (at least if you aren't picky).

Firearms can be purchased from licensed dealers with a simple background check in the vast majority of the country. In about 10 states, the types of firearms you can buy may be restricted, or there may be additional hurdles beyond a basic background check. For handguns, some states have licensing and training requirements; others restrict certain types of handguns. Some states limit the ammunition capacity of magazines, or they make it difficult to buy ammunition. Some restrict or outright ban certain semi-automatic rifles or shotguns due to their appearance.

The excuse for these types of restrictions is always the same: to fight crime and keep guns out of the wrong hands. Some guns are simply considered too dangerous for regular people to own (which begs the question: too dangerous for whom?) For every accessory or gun, it seems someone tries to come up with an excuse why it should be illegal. Small, cheap guns are mislabeled "Saturday Night Specials" that are allegedly preferred by criminals. Rifles with scopes are vilified as so-called "Sniper Weapons." Guns are

OVERVIEW: There is nothing good to be said about gun control. Constant anti-gun legislation does remind us that politicians are eager to exploit catastrophe to introduce legislation to restrict gun ownership.

BIGGEST THREAT: State and local efforts to impose training, licensing, registration and restrict or outlaw magazine capacity or specific categories of firearms.

WORST/BEST STATES: The most restrictive states include CA, HI, NY, CT, MD, NJ, MA, RI, and IL (conditions tend to be worse in the cities). The rest of the country is relatively free.

AUTHOR'S TOP PICK: Virginia. Good gun laws, temperate climate, plenty of tree cover, sources of water, land, hunting, farming.

labeled as "bad" for simply being too powerful, not powerful enough, too big, too small, too accurate, too cheap, etc.

When it comes to survival, there is another dangerous wrinkle in the gun control game. Most states and localities ban guns from emergency shelters, assuming that people crowded together in a high-stress situation cannot be trusted. There is no need to delve into dark corners to dig up paranoid fantasies of government thugs rounding people up and/or confiscating their firearms in order to subjugate them. There are plenty of real world examples of this type of behavior.

Firearms have been a common sight throughout America's history, used by hunters, farmers, target shooters, law enforcement, and the military. We have been fortunate; in many other countries, weapons (including swords, crossbows, and other weapons of war) were illegal for the peasants to own. It was a system of control to subjugate the masses. This is why many martial arts weapons we see today started out as perfectly legal farm tools.

The first state to aggressively regulate firearms was New York, with the passage of the Sullivan Act in 1911. It mandated that anyone seeking to own a concealable handgun had to first obtain a permit, with further regulations for carrying a firearm. Yet, as far as rifles were concerned, even places like New York City remained pretty much unregulated until the 1960s.

A broad selection of modern survival guns is available in most states. *Photo: Michael Saechang*

FEDERAL LAWS

In the past, the Second Amendment to the Constitution protecting the right to keep and bear arms was seldom brought up, because the federal government had not taken any steps to restrict firearms; laws that did so were left up to the states. That changed in 1934 with the passage of the National Firearms Act, which implemented restrictions on machine guns, sawed-off shotguns, short-barreled rifles, suppressors, and various other uncommon guns (like pen guns and cane guns).

These were not outlawed completely, but they had to be registered and a tax paid. At the time, the $200 tax was astronomically high and intended to dissuade ownership of these weapons. Fortunately, the tax has remained unchanged, and $200 is far more affordable today. The federal government seemed to understand at the time that the Second Amendment would not allow for an outright ban on any firearm, even a fully automatic machine gun. That understanding has waned significantly over the years.

In 1938, the Federal Firearms Act mandated licensing of gun dealers, importers, and manufacturers, and required that a record be kept of each sale. It also included prohibitions against selling firearms to prohibited individuals, mainly felons. This law was supplanted by the 1968 Gun Control Act, which contained many of these same provisions.

The Gun Control Act of 1968, which was enacted following several high-profile political assassinations, came next and resulted in most of the restrictions we see today. In addition to the restrictions it carried over from the 1938 Federal Firearms Act, this new bill also restricted the ability of private individuals to buy guns directly across state lines. It implemented importation restrictions on "non-sporting" firearms. It is still legal in most states for individuals "not engaged in the business" to buy and sell guns to each other unrestricted, as long as they are both residents of the same state and the transaction occurs in that state. The 1968 gun control act did not ban any guns completely.

In 1986, the Firearm Owners' Protection Act was enacted to help clean up some of the abuses gun owners were suffering at the state and federal level. This act established protections for federally licensed firearms dealers from abusive regulations and oversight. It protected the rights of people traveling with firearms across state lines (cased and unloaded as long as the firearm is legal to possess at the destination). It prohibited the federal government from maintaining a national registry of firearms. Sadly,

The Bureau of Alcohol Tobacco and Firearms (ATF) is an entire federal agency dedicated to enforcing our nation's gun control laws. *Photo: Public Domain*

it also prohibited the registration of any new machine guns, freezing the supply of legally transferable machine guns and causing prices to skyrocket.

The next significant federal firearms law was the 1993 Brady Handgun Violence Prevention Act. Licensed dealers were already required to keep records and forbidden from selling guns to prohibited people (a list that keeps getting longer), but now background checks and waiting periods were also mandated. The waiting period expired once the National Instant Check System

Most all emergency shelters, hospitals, and many private businesses ban guns on their premises. This is something you'll need to anticipate and plan for accordingly. *Photo: Cory Doctorow*

was in place a few years later. Now, the FBI can run background checks instantly. States have the ability to access the system and run their own background checks instead.

It should be noted that, in 1989, one of the most objectionable aspects of the 1968 Gun Control Act became even worse thanks to George H. W. Bush. One of the stupider aspects of the 1968 law was to apply a "sporting test" to imported firearms. This largely killed the military surplus rifle market and created a "point" system for handguns that effectively outlawed the importation of very small handguns. Some manufacturers have to add tiny bumps on the side of the grip (thumb rests) to add the necessary points to import their handguns, as well as a host of other silly features.

Congress left the specifics up to the administration and their regulatory agency, the Bureau of Alcohol, Tobacco, and Firearms (ATF). Military surplus firearms were eventually allowed to be imported, especially older guns from the two World Wars. Modern semi-automatic rifles, based on military designs, could also be imported for several years until 1989, when the first Bush administration decided to ban the importation of these mislabeled "assault rifles" as "non-sporting." In order to own one of these banned guns (that had not been previously imported and thus grandfathered), it had to be "Made in the USA," so at least it wasn't a complete ban.

The first real gun ban in this country was the 1994 Assault Weapons Ban, which sunset in 2004 and is no longer applicable. That law — which has been copied in several states — outlawed any semi-automatic rifle that used a centerfire cartridge, could accept detachable magazines, and had more than two of the following features: collapsible or folding stock, bayonet lug, flash hider, grenade launcher, or a pistol grip. The law banned the sale of new magazines with a capacity of over 10 rounds, making the existing legal mags more expensive. People were literally paying five times the normal price for regular capacity pre-ban magazines leading up to the ban.

The obvious result was that manufacturers simply made the exact same guns minus three of the offending features. Semi-automatic rifles with detachable magazines and pistol grips were perfectly legal and just as effective. What you could not do was mount a bayonet, a grenade launcher, or a flash hider (although you could use a recoil compensator on the muzzle, which looks and functions in a similar fashion). You also could not fold or collapse the stock. For some rifles like the civilian AR-15, there were plenty of 20- and 30-round magazines, but for some newer guns like the Glock, magazines were at a premium. Again, this stupid law died in 2004, but not before several states enacted copycat legislation on their own. If you live in one of these states, your ability to own the most effective self-defense tool, especially for extreme survival situations, is now compromised.

There is one bright spot in terms of federal laws. Gun control advocates, upset that they had failed to enact any meaningful gun bans and even more upset at the spread and popularity of concealed carry laws at the state level, decided to go after the gun manufacturers themselves. They devised a plan to sue them out of business. The premise was that guns are inherently dangerous, and when someone is hurt with a gun, the manufacturer has automatic liability.

The firearms business is not especially lucrative, and while there are a few large manufacturers, most are very small. Even if they could easily win these lawsuits in court, the attorneys' fees would drive them out of business (and that was the intent). As a result, Congress enacted the Protection of Lawful Commerce in Arms Act in 2005, giving gun manufacturers and dealers immunity from liability for crimes committed with their products. As long as their product functioned as designed, they could not be held liable for negligence.

STATE LAWS

At the state level, we have a mixed bag. On the positive side, all 50 states now have laws that provide for residents to apply for a permit to carry a concealed handgun. In the vast majority of the states, the law stipulates that the issuing authority (the state or local police, local sheriff, or judge) has no discretion. They must issue concealed handgun permits to all applicants who meet the standards set by the state. Applicants do not have to provide a reason for carrying, or if they do, self-defense is accepted without question. This policy is known as "Shall-Issue."

In a small handful of states, concealed carry licenses are left to the arbitrary discretion of the issuing authority, the state or local police, county sheriffs, or judges. These are known as "May-Issue" states. In those places where the state police are in charge of permits, there

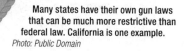

is at least some uniformity and guidelines that residents can clearly learn and follow. In Maryland, for example, the state police issue permits, and while it is extremely difficult to get one and applicants have to show a compelling reason, at least the system is transparent and uniformly applied.

Many states have their own gun laws that can be much more restrictive than federal law. California is one example.
Photo: Public Domain

In states where local authorities issue permits, you get a complete hodgepodge. In California, getting a concealed handgun permit is left to the arbitrary discretion of the county sheriffs. If you live in a small rural county and are best buds with the sheriff, then there's no problem. However, if you reside in one of the state's more populous and urban counties (where you might feel more inclined to need a gun to protect yourself), tough luck. Each county establishes their own criteria for issuing permits, or the sheriff may decide that he or she doesn't want to issue any permits, period.

From a survival standpoint, this is incredibly significant. With a concealed carry permit, you can be armed almost everywhere (exceptions typically include schools, churches, some government buildings, private property marked as no guns, etc.). It also means that you can keep a loaded gun in your vehicle readily accessible. Many states recognize each other's permits — known as reciprocity — and issue non-resident permits. So if you live in a restrictive state, at least you can be free to protect yourself when you travel. There is an effort underway at the federal level to require all states to honor each other's permits, basically establishing national concealed carry.

On the downside, some states have chosen to make firearm ownership more difficult even for very common guns such as handguns. These states are in the minority, but they typically ban "high-capacity" magazines, "assault rifles," or impose licensing, registration, and training requirements for the mere possession of some types of firearms. Some require local law enforcement's approval for purchase, restrict online ammunition purchases, and have extensive ID requirements, even for ammunition purchases. Furthermore, some states maintain a list of "approved" guns that can be bought, and getting on the approved list is no easy task. Some states and localities apply a criminal standard to anything they consider to be "improper" firearms storage and have "approved" storage devices.

California is an especially egregious example of how gun control laws can be used to gradually deny citizens the right to own certain guns altogether. California first tried to outlaw "assault" weapons by name, so the manufacturers changed the names of their guns. Then they tried to ban them by a specific description (as in the federal ban) and told existing owners that they could keep their guns only if they registered them. Then manufacturers made other changes to keep the guns legal. California responded by extending their definition of "assault weapons" and by telling all those law-abiding people who had dutifully registered their grandfathered gun that these were also no longer legal and had to be disposed of. Old grandfathered normal capacity magazines were also outlawed, and now it is illegal to possess a magazine with over 10 round capacity (no matter when you bought it).

This is exactly the reason so many gun owners are so resistant to any registration scheme. They do not trust the government not to use those registration records to threaten gun owners when they decide to no longer allow the grandfathered guns. It is the same reason I refuse to participate in the national Census. Those census records were used during WWII to identify Japanese Americans, illegally round them up, and place them in prison camps for the duration of the war.

Justice is blind, especially when it comes to gun laws. Courts generally uphold gun control laws with few exceptions. *Photo: Matt Wade*

People are well aware that information is power and that the more power you give to government, the greater its ability to cause you harm. I do not advocate law breaking or any illegal behavior, but many people have chosen this path over abiding by gun registration laws. In Canada, the national firearms registry law was ignored by as many as 70 percent of gun owners. In Connecticut, a law that made it a felony to fail to register grandfathered "assault" weapons was ignored by as many as 50 percent of gun owners. To date, only 50,000 such weapons have been registered in that state. Interestingly, "high-capacity" magazines were also supposed to be registered (although magazines don't have serial numbers and are federally unregulated).

COURT CASES

Until recently, court cases on Second Amendment grounds had very little luck. Back in 1939, the Supreme Court looked at the matter in United States v. Miller. That case had mixed results and upheld the National Firearms Act (NFA) as constitutional. The question was over a sawed-off shotgun, and the Court found that there was no constitutional right to own one because it was not a suitable militia weapon. It should be noted that the NFA did not outlaw possession of sawed-off shotguns or machine guns, rather it just said you had to register them and pay a tax.

Then in 2008, everything changed. The Supreme Court agreed to hear a challenge to the gun laws in Washington D.C. The District of Columbia falls directly under federal jurisdiction but was granted "home rule" in 1973. The new DC government immediately set out to impose gun restrictions and an onerous licensing and registration scheme for gun owners living in the city. In 1976, they simply stopped accepting applications for new handguns. They also mandated that all firearms stored in the home had to be kept unloaded and locked away or disassembled. While difficult to prove causation, in the 1980s Washington, D.C. nonetheless became known as the murder capital of the United States.

A DC resident named Dick Heller sued the city on Second Amendment grounds and in District of Columbia v. Heller

(2008), the Supreme Court ruled in his favor. For the first time, the Court declared that the Second Amendment guarantees an individual right to own a gun and that self-defense is a legitimate use and reason for gun ownership. The Court required that the city allow residents to register and possess handguns again, and specifically threw out the city's laws against keeping a loaded and accessible gun in the home. This decision applied only to federal areas like DC however, not to the states.

In 2010, the Supreme Court again revisited this issue in McDonald v. Chicago. The city of Chicago, Illinois had banned handgun possession in the early 1980s. After the Heller decision, Chicago resident Otis McDonald sued the city. The Court agreed and extended the holding in Heller to the states. Now states had to honor the same Second Amendment right as the federal government.

As a direct result of these decisions, more lawsuits were brought and continue to be litigated that challenge all sorts of firearms restrictions at the local and state level. The most notable example is that of Moore v. Madigan (2013) decided by the U.S. Court of Appeals, 7th Circuit, against the State of Illinois. Illinois was the

Nationwide efforts to demand more gun control and enact far-reaching gun bans continue.
Photo: Wikimedia Commons

last holdout with no provision to allow for concealed carry for any reason. The court ordered the state to come up with a law that would allow concealed carry, and now Illinois is a shall-issue state where any law-abiding person who meets the requirements will receive a concealed carry permit.

Sadly, there have been many more cases in which the courts did side with gun control proponents. In two recent examples, courts did not support the notion that the Constitution enumerates your right to own an "assault rifle" or to openly carry a gun. Even in the landmark Heller case mentioned above, the Supreme Court said that certain types of firearms could be banned and certain types of restrictions would pass Constitutional muster.

THE DANGER

In 1996, following a mass shooting, Australia imposed very strict gun controls. All firearms had to be registered and owners licensed. Training, waiting periods, and a reason for ownership were required, and semi-automatic rifles and shotguns (including pump-action shotguns) were banned outright and had to be turned in. Handguns were severely restricted only to recognized and active competitive shooters. A compensation fund was established to pay the gun owners who were forced to surrender their guns. In the first year, about 750,000 firearms were turned in and destroyed. In a subsequent amnesty years later, another 250,000 or so were turned in to be destroyed. No one believes that this was the sum total of the banned guns. An estimated 20-30 percent were never registered or surrendered.

Also in 1996, following another mass shooting, Great Britain enacted even stricter gun control than Australia. They banned all handguns and many types of rifles and shotguns. Firearms that were permitted had to the registered and the owners licensed. All banned guns had to be turned in. There is a great deal of irony in such a large-scale disarmament in the UK. At the start of World War II, the British sent a force into France that was overwhelmed by the Germans and had to retreat back to England, abandoning much of their weapons and equipment. The British feared an invasion by Germany and were woefully unprepared. The British government sent a distress call to American gun owners to send any working firearms that could be distributed to home guard units to use in the event of an invasion. Americans responded, but after the war these guns were rounded up and disposed of.

This type of large-scale registration and confiscation could certainly happen in the United States, but is not likely to be successful. Given the number of firearms privately held (more guns than people) and the number of gun owners (approximately 40 percent of all households), any attempt at nationwide confiscation would be prohibitively expensive and logistically impossible. There would also be significant civil disobedience. That is not to say that this has not happened at the local and state level. I have already mentioned states like Connecticut and California that have banned entire classes of firearms. However, they don't need to confiscate them or buy them back; they only require you to dispose of them. Owners are welcome to turn their guns over to the authorities voluntarily for no compensation, or they can sell them to out of state dealers.

This can be especially problematic following a serious event such as a natural disaster. In the days and weeks after Hurricane Katrina, New Orleans was in complete chaos. Many had not evacuated due to illness, poverty, stubbornness, or nefarious intent. After the storm, emergency services were overwhelmed. People were trapped on their rooftops and needed rescue. Food and clean water were in short supply. What was not in short supply were the looters and the criminals.

Law abiding people took up arms to defend themselves, but from the perspective of some in law enforcement, this was unacceptable. Police were already forcing people to evacuate to emergency shelters and had started to confiscate any guns they found from people in their own homes. A lawsuit brought the practice to a stop, and the confiscated guns were eventually returned to owners, but not until years later.

RIMFIRE GUNS

Rimfire refers to a specific type of ammunition cartridge in which the primer compound (which ignites the powder charge) is embedded along a rim at the rear of the cartridge case. The firing pin can strike this rim at any location for the round to go off. Obviously, the brass rim and case has to be thin enough so that the firing pin can detonate the primer compound. This means that rimfire cartridges are limited in how much pressure they can handle and thus the power of the bullet they can fire.

Historically, there have been large-caliber rimfire cartridges, but these used low-pressure powder. Modern rimfire cartridges are typically .22 caliber, and the most common by far is the .22 LR (or Long Rifle), so I will limit this chapter to that specific round.

RIMFIRE CARTRIDGES

The .22 Long Rifle (LR) cartridge as it exists today first appeared in 1887 and has been adopted for use in a multitude of rifles and pistols. Unless you started shooting later in life, you probably began shooting real guns with a firearm chambered in .22 LR. In the minds of many shooters, this is where the .22 remains — a basic cartridge for kids and beginners, relegated to high-end competition, for hunting pests and squirrels, or the fun option for occasional lazy Saturdays spent plinking cans.

In a survival situation, if you need to hunt, small game is far more plentiful and manageable. You don't have to worry about long-term preservation of the meat, unless you are stockpiling for winter. One rabbit or squirrel can be cleaned, cooked, and eaten with no spoilage, and the .22 is perfect for this type of small game hunting.

If you need to train a new shooter, the .22 is ideal thanks to its low cost and light recoil. It represents an excellent training aid that is more cost effective, easier to accommodate on small ranges, and can even be used for self-defense and survival if need be. The .22 LR cartridge is far cheaper than standard centerfire ammunition, which means more shooting and practice time; it has minimal recoil, which translates to a greater focus on the fundamentals of proper grip, sights alignment/picture, and trigger control, and less fatigue for the shooter. Today, firearm manufacturers are responding to this training aspect by developing conversion kits as well as dedicated guns that mimic full-caliber versions but are chambered for .22.

Because of its small footprint, it is also possible to purchase and store a large quantity of .22 LR ammunition for relatively low cost, assuming you can find it. I never in my life thought that .22 ammunition would be difficult to find, but in recent years people have been hoarding it like crazy. The situation has finally improved somewhat, but you still see stores limiting how much they allow each customer to buy at a time.

SURVIVAL SNAPSHOT: RIMFIRE GUNS

PROS: Less expensive to own and shoot.

CONS: Low power cartridge not suitable for self-defense.

AMMO TO STOCKPILE: Keep a minimum of 2,000 rounds.

AUTHOR'S TOP PICK: Walther Colt M4 OPS AR.
MSRP: $639

SPARE PARTS TO STOCK: Magazines.

REQUIRED ACCESSORIES: Scope, sling, magazine holder.

OPTIONAL ACCESSORIES: Lights, laser.

From left to right: .22 Short, .22 LR, and .22 Magnum. The .22 LR is the most common and popular.

THE .22 LR FOR SELF-DEFENSE?

Everyone agrees that the best gun to have in a fight is the gun that you have with you, and if a .22 is all you have, then you need to know how best to make it work to your advantage. Unlike centerfire ammunition, rimfire has a tendency to be very finicky, and different types and brands should be tried out to find the most reliable for your particular gun. Also, .22 guns don't operate well when dirty, so keeping yours clean is of paramount importance.

When using a sub-caliber firearm for self-defense, you can't rely as much on so-called stopping power. It takes five shots from a .22 to roughly equal the force of one round from a .45 ACP. Focus on placing as many shots as possible in the critical area of the target (meaning center mass) as quickly as possible. When choosing a rim-fire, remember that longer barrels will produce higher velocities, and many semi-automatic rifles have higher capacity magazines.

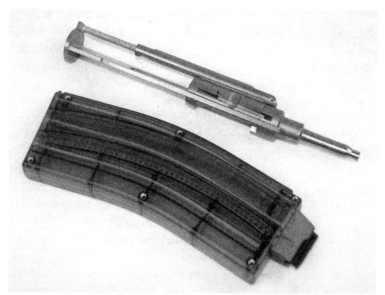

AR conversion kits like this one from WMD Guns allow an AR to fire standard .22 LR ammunition just by replacing the bolt carrier group and magazine.

RIMFIRE RIFLES

The longer barrel of a rifle gives the powder in the bore more time to burn and adds velocity to the bullet. For a low-powered round like the .22 LR, this extra velocity adds more energy, which can be applied to hunting and self-defense situations. The longer barrel and stock add stability, enhancing accuracy and long-range shooting.

AR CONVERSION KITS

Being able to shoot more than one caliber out of the same gun is certainly handy, and if that second caliber is the cheap, low recoiling, and easy-to-find .22 LR, then all the better. AR owners have the distinct advantage that the diameter of the .223 Remington/5.56mm NATO round is close enough to the .22 LR that the change can be completed simply by swapping out the bolt and bolt carrier and replacing the magazine.

I first encountered one of these quick and easy conversion kits in the military, and we used them extensively for cheap training and practice on indoor ranges when access to a standard range was limited. The kit bypasses the gas system altogether and turns the AR into a simple, straight blowback system. All of your rifle's familiar controls and optics remain in place while you train at a much lower cost.

Of course, the .22 LR cartridge tends to create a fair amount of fouling, and some of the conversion kits offered provide iffy reliability once they start to get dirty. This is not the case with the "Little Beast" conversion kit from WMD Guns, however. This company, which specializes in NiB-X coatings, has covered the unit in nickel boron, which provides excellent corrosion resistance and natural lubricity to the metal parts. This keeps the kit running reliably shot after shot and makes clean up much easier. The Little Beast comes with one polymer 26-round magazine. To learn more visit wmdguns.com or call 231-421-4867.

WALTHER COLT M4 OPS

The advantage of conversion kits for your standard AR is that they are cheap and essentially give you two guns. However, the rifling on the AR is not standard for the .22 LR nor is the sizing of the barrel exact. The kits work, but many people prefer a dedicated AR-style rifle exclusively chambered in .22 LR, which improves the rifle's function and accuracy.

Among ARs, the most popular are the carbine versions, and if you want a real M4, you have to get a Colt. The problem is that Colt only sells the M4 to the military and law enforcement, and they don't make one in .22. Colt does make other AR carbines for the civilian market but not in .22. Fortunately, Walther Arms has a fully licensed Colt M4 replica in .22 LR.

Walther Arms is a renowned German firearms manufacturer with more than 125 years of history and a solid reputation for quality and innovation. The company produces several licensed versions of famous firearms that they dub Tactical Rimfire Replicas. These full-sized replicas are made in Germany and come with all

The Walther-made Colt M4 OPS tactical AR carbine is a fully licensed reproduction of the original Colt M4, only chambered in .22 LR.

the details, weight, and handling characteristics of the originals.

The Walther-made Colt M4 OPS tactical AR carbine is a blowback-operated semi-automatic and is designed to be as close in appearance to the full-auto carbine currently issued to the U.S. Special Forces. The controls function just like on the original, which makes this an excellent rifle to use as a low-cost trainer.

The Colt M4 OPS looks very authentic on the outside, but it's a completely different animal on the inside. The rifle comes with a 16-inch steel match-grade barrel that is actually located inside the Parkerized metal barrel sleeve that replicates the contours of an M4 barrel. The barrel is topped off with an A1-style flash hider that is one of the few steel components in the rifle.

The front sight is a standard A2 gas block, and it is properly "F" marked for a carbine. It includes the bayonet lug and the front sling swivel. Carbines have a slightly different elevation of the front sight than rifles and should be F-marked. The front sight is adjustable for elevation as well.

One thing that distinguished the M4 OPS rifle from the other Colt AR replicas that Walther offers is the free-floated quad rail handguard. This handguard offers 6 inches of Picatinny rail space at the 12, 3, 6 and 9 o'clock positions and features Knight's Armament-style one piece polymer-ribbed rail panels for improved comfort while handling. They come off easily with a simple spring steel push lever and allow for the easy addition of any desired accessories such as lights, lasers, bipods, or forward vertical grips.

The upper and lower receivers are both made from aluminum like the original. The left side of the lower receiver carries all of the proper markings with the Colt rampant horse logo and is labeled "M4 Carbine" above the serial number. It is marked "Hartford, Conn. USA" as appropriate. It does differ in listing the caliber designation as .22 LR. The real manufacturing information from Walther is on the right side of the lower receiver.

I was impressed with the attention to detail in this replica. The trigger guard has the detent tab and hinges down for use with mittens or gloves, as the original. The upper and lower receivers look and feel just like on a real AR. The magazine release button works the same way, and the safety selector rotates 90 degrees from safe to fire (there is no full-auto marking, however) with the same resounding click and feel as the original.

The bolt release/hold is a separate piece and, rather than simply molded on, it is made from polymer instead of metal and is not functional. There is a steel forward assist that looks and feels real and moves as designed, but it too is for looks only. The dust cover is made of steel but remains fully functional, although the latch itself is polymer. The metal charging handle has a functional latch and retracts to load and operate the rifle, but only about one-third of the distance as on an actual .223-chambered AR.

The furniture on the Colt M4 OPS is very accurate as well, with the polymer pistol grip and collapsible stock that includes a rear sling swivel. These did not seem quite as sturdy as on the real thing, but they don't need to be. I also noticed that the adjustable length of pull on the stock provided five positions instead of six.

The upper receiver has a flattop design with Picatinny rail that forms a continuous length with the quad rail handguards. This provides 13 inches of uninterrupted space on which to mount optics. An A2 removable rear sight is included, allowing for both

The Walther Colt M4 OPS is true to the original in most every detail and allows for low cost training and practice.

windage and elevation adjustments and includes dual aperture peep sights with the larger opening for shorter distances and the smaller opening for distances greater than 200 meters. This may be slightly optimistic, given the rifle's chambering.

Disassembly of the Colt M4 OPS starts off very similarly to a standard AR. The takedown pins at the front and rear are fully functional but not captive. I found them to be very stiff and used a punch and a few taps from a light hammer to remove them. At that point, the upper and lower receiver halves came apart easily, and the guts of the rifle were exposed. There is nothing AR-like about the internals here. You get all zinc metal alloy construction that is housed inside an aluminum cover.

At the rear of the zinc receiver, inside the false upper receiver and just below the charging handle, there is a screw that can be turned to tune the bolt speed to correspond with the types of ammunition being used. For high-velocity ammunition, the bolt speed can be increased by turning the screw clockwise. For low velocity, the bolt speed can be slowed by turning the screw counterclockwise. This should only be done if the rifle is experiencing cycling problems with the ammunition you are using. I tested three different types of ammunition and found that the rifle functioned just fine and no adjustment was necessary.

Operation on the Colt M4 OPS is almost identical to the real thing. From a training perspective, this is close to ideal, as the manual of arms will not significantly change. The 30-round magazine loads easily with dual side tabs that help the process along by allowing the operator to lower the follower and drop the rounds in. The bolt hold open device is internal and will only lock open on an empty magazine. This is not ideal, but not uncommon for rimfire rifles. Once a full magazine is inserted, simply retract and release the charging handle to chamber a round, flip the safety selector to the fire position, and squeeze the trigger.

There are 10- and 20-round magazines available, but most people will opt for the 30-round mag. These are solidly built and not at all flimsy, but I actually found it to be too long for comfortable prone or benchrest shooting. It is in fact 2.5 inches longer than a standard AR 30-round magazine. I believe that the 20-round mag would be more comfortable and look more authentic. Also, the reader should be aware that most dedicated .22 ARs use proprietary magazines, and they don't often interchange between manufacturers. If purchasing aftermarket .22 AR magazines, check with the manufacturer beforehand to ensure proper fit and functioning.

The single-stage trigger had a fair amount of creep and a mushy yet heavy feel at the same time. I measured it at 8 pounds and found it to be a challenge in precision shooting. However, bad triggers are very common in real ARs and a creepy, mushy, heavy trigger is entirely Mil-Spec. Of course, with a standard AR, you can change the trigger, but not here.

The rifle weighed 6 pounds, 3 ounces when empty, which places it very close to a real AR carbine. It was sized and weighted properly, and the extensive use of metal and aluminum gave it a very real feel. It was light and easy to handle on the range, and I experienced no malfunctions firing offhand or from the bench.

Given the rifle's tactical design, I opted for a red-dot sight with no magnification for accuracy testing at 50 yards from an improvised benchrest position. I say 'improvised' because the length of the magazine necessitated it. I mounted a Bushnell TRS-25 HiRise red-dot sight, which fit perfectly and features a 3 MOA dot. The 11 brightness settings make the dot visible in all light conditions and helped wring out the rifle's accuracy potential.

Buyers of ARs chambered in .22 LR have a lot of options. You can buy a conversion kit that replaces the bolt carrier, or you can purchase a dedicated .22 upper receiver for your standard AR lower. But for many, there is nothing better than an entirely dedicated rimfire AR rifle, and if you want one that looks and feels as close to the real thing as possible, you are only going to get it from Walther Arms. The licensed Colt M4 OPS is an accurate rifle that pays homage to America's Special Forces and provides you with cheap, fun, and reliable operation.

SPECIFICATIONS
WALTHER COLT M4 OPS

CALIBER: .22 LR
BARREL: 16.1-in. match
OA LENGTH: 31.1 in. collapsed, 34.4 in. extended
WEIGHT: 6.2 lbs. empty
STOCK: Polymer-adjustable
SIGHTS: Adjustable iron sights
ACTION: Semi-auto blowback
FINISH: Blued
CAPACITY: 30, 20, 10 rounds
PRICE: $639
WWW.WALTHERARMS.COM
479-242-8500

AK-47 IN .22 LR

Just as the AR has become possibly the most popular semi-automatic rifle in America, the venerable AK-47 is starting to catch up, and manufacturers are stepping into the competition with a dedicated .22 AK ideal for training use. The value in training

GSG's (German Sport Guns) Rebel AK, distributed in the U.S. by ATI (American Tactical Imports) is a semi-automatic, blowback-operated replica rifle chambered in .22 LR.

with an AK is that it has been produced more or less continuously in two dozen countries for over six decades and in numbers of over 100 million. It is the most ubiquitous firearm ever produced. The simplicity of the design, low cost of manufacture, ease of use after limited training, and the rifle's incomparable reliability only add to its popularity.

From a survival perspective, the AK is frequently encountered in foreign countries, especially the ones with more complicated political situations. Knowing how to operate and use the AK can be extremely helpful, and while some AKs found in "conflict zones" may appear to be in poor condition, they most often still function.

GSG's (German Sport Guns) Rebel AK, distributed in the U.S. by ATI (American Tactical Imports) is a semi-automatic, blowback-operated replica rifle chambered in .22 LR with a wooden stock, pistol grip, handguards, and intentionally distressed metal to simulate years of hard use.

GSG has been making .22-caliber replicas of famous and popular full-sized combat rifles for over a decade, including a rifle that resembles a suppressed H&K MP5, a 1911, and a very accurate reproduction of the WWII German StG44. The company also makes airsoft versions of popular guns. The reasons behind the popularity of the company's offerings lies in the less restrictive ownership laws in Europe concerning rimfire firearms and the significantly lower cost of .22 ammunition.

As with all its offerings, German engineering and a commitment to authentic detail are evident throughout the Rebel AK. The outward appearance of the rifle is a mix of the AK-47 and the AKM with the addition of an optics rail on the left side of the receiver. GSG does offer an optional scope mount that fits this rail. The rifle uses a receiver made from a zinc alloy — in fact, most of the rifle is either wood, polymer, or zinc alloy. Only the springs, bolt, screws, barrel, and barrel sleeve are steel, as are the receiver dust cover and the cleaning rod.

The metal parts have been Parkerized and then hand weathered for a worn look. The wooden stock does appear in good condition, however GSG added medical tape around the handguard and at the bottom of the 24-round capacity magazine for each of the two provided. In addition, the stock has a red bandana "tied" onto it. The bandana is just wrapped around the stock and secured with staples.

The 16.3-inch six-groove steel barrel sits inside a barrel sleeve that closely matches the contours of the original. Of course, the gas tube and gas block are just for looks. The front of the barrel does have a removable nut that can be replaced with a flash hider or suppressor adapter. GSG provides an optional folding stock kit with a polymer stock to match their polymer non-Rebel AK, and it will fit this rifle as well. There is already a stock catch on the left side of the receiver.

The sights are fairly standard AK, with both the front and rear being elevation adjustable but not adjustable for windage. The controls are standard AK, with the reciprocation bolt charging handle, ambidextrous paddle magazine release, and a right-side safety lever with up for safe and down for fire. This lever is longer than that on the actual AK and includes a bolt hold open device. The operation of the Rebel AK is very straightforward with magazines rocking into place like on the original and reliable functioning.

The controls on the Rebel AK operate in the same fashion as on a real AK. The Rebel allows for inexpensive training with less recoil.

The magazines are heavy polymer and match the contours of the original steel mags down to the rear strengthening rib. On the last shot, the bolt locks open, but to engage the safety, it must be pulled farther to the rear. When you load a fresh magazine, simply press the safety down to the fire position, and the bolt will release to chamber a round. The rifle is ready to fire, but the safety can be put back into the 'on' position if desired. There is a magazine disconnect safety that will prevent the rifle from firing with no magazine inserted. GSG does include a magazine coupler so the two mags can be placed side-by-side with the rounds on opposite ends for faster reloads.

While the Rebel AK certainly looks like an AK on the outside, the similarities are only skin deep. The original AK has a very simple system for disassembly and cleaning; the GSG version, not so much. You first have to make sure the gun is empty and de-cocked, so inspect the chamber, insert an empty magazine, and then dry fire. Next, remove the stock by removing the two top and bottom stock screws. Next remove the dust cover, which is done exactly like on a real AK. Then unscrew and remove the rear trunnions and stock adapter so the whole pistol grip firing mechanism assembly drops out. Finally, the bolt carrier and bolt can be removed to provide access to cleaning the barrel.

Overall, disassembly is not complicated, but it does involve a lot of small parts and screws you do not want to lose. GSG does include a screwdriver with multiple bits for all the different screws and to adjust the front sight elevation. There is a wrench for removing the original AK-style muzzle device. The handguards can be removed with the original AK-style handguard latch at the rear sight block. You do have to loosen a retaining screw at the front of the mock gas block. Also, the handguard band can be loosened and the lower handguard removed. Keep in mind that on the Rebel AK the handguards are taped together so you will have to cut or remove the tape to do this.

One thing I did like is that the cleaning rod is fully functional and not just for looks, plus it is screwed into the receiver — not snapped on like the original — which provides a much firmer and more secure hold. There is no bayonet lug, however.

On the range, the Rebel AK performed very well and handled easily. Given its weight, which closely matches that of a real AK, the .22 LR cartridge kicked even less than normal, and there was no muzzle rise, making it very easy to stay on target during fast offhand shooting. In true AK fashion, I did not experience any malfunctions, but I did stick with high-velocity ammunition as the manual suggested. As a scope mount was not included, I could not mount an optic, so all accuracy results are tested using iron sights from a bench rest at 50 yards.

The lack of adjustment did necessitate about three inches of Kentucky windage hold to the left, but once I got my hold figured out,

SPECIFICATIONS
GSG REBEL AK47

CALIBER: .22 LR
BARREL: 16.5 in.
OA LENGTH: 36.25 in.
WEIGHT: 7 lbs. empty
STOCK: Wood
SIGHTS: Iron adjustable
ACTION: Semi-auto
FINISH: Black distressed
CAPACITY: 24+1
PRICE: $482.95
800-290-0065
WWW.AMERICANTACTICAL.US

accuracy results were fairly good with averages across three different types of ammunition remaining under 2 inches, and my best five-shot group at just 1 inch. The long and mushy trigger, while certainly AK-like, was heavy at over 10 pounds and not conducive to good accuracy. I imagine with a good optic and a better trigger this rifle would be capable of significantly better results. My only other complaint is that there is a real AK-type sling attachment point at the front but no provision for one at the rear.

When all is said and done, GSG and American Tactical Imports have done an excellent job of providing American shooters a very impressive historical rifle that is both accurate and easy to shoot a lot.

ANSCHÜTZ MSR RX22

Anyone who's interested in low-cost training with a military rifle has a lot of options. In U.S. Special Forces operations, one rifle that you may encounter is the FN SCAR. The MSR RX22 Tactical Trainer is a dedicated .22 LR version of this rifle, which is made by Anschütz, best known for manufacturing the ultimate precision rifles for competition.

The MSR RX22 Tactical Trainer is, however, not purely an Anschütz endeavor. In producing this blowback-operated, semi-automatic, magazine fed .22 LR rifle, the company teamed up with another well-regarded German arms maker, German Sport Guns or GSG.

Although perfectly capable of fulfilling the role of a fun plinker, the RX22 is built as a precision rifle and is capable of outstanding accuracy suitable for hunting small game or precision shooting. Anschütz designed this rifle as they do most of their guns: with the competitor in mind, specifically German sport shooting competitors. The rifle was tested extensively to the same standards as the company's hunting and Olympic biathlon rifles for functional performance in varied weather conditions. It was also put through its paces in the development stage by German shooting champion Dirk Frey for tactical applications.

The key factor in the rifle's accuracy is in the Anschütz custom target steel sports barrel with button rifling. As opposed to cut

The Anschütz MSR RX22 Tactical Trainer is a reproduction of the U.S. Special Forces operations FN SCAR in a dedicated .22 LR.

rifling, which cuts the grooves into the barrel bore, or hammer forging, which hammers a barrel blank around a mandrel, button rifling pushes or pulls a shaped button through the barrel blank. This process does not remove any material but instead forces the shape of the rifling into the bore, providing improved accuracy.

At the muzzle, the barrel features a very slight recessed target crown, designed to protect the rifling. As this is the last bit of rifling that is making contact with the bullet before it exits the barrel, preserving its integrity is very important, which is why it is best to clean a barrel from the chamber rather than from the muzzle end.

Anschütz added a competition single-stage adjustable trigger. By using "hardened finely ground components," the RX22 achieves a very crisp trigger with a clean break, allowing you to achieve maximum accuracy. The trigger weight is adjustable from 3.3 to 5.5 lbs. but comes set from the factory with a 4-lb. trigger. To adjust the trigger, simply remove the lower receiver/trigger group. There is a set screw in front of the hammer; turn clockwise to reduce weight, and counterclockwise to increase trigger weight.

The Anschütz MSR RX22 features a folding and collapsible stock for ease of transport.

Ergonomically, the rifle is very well designed. There is a non-reciprocating forward charging handle that can be placed in any one of three positions, from just above the ejection port to 3 inches and 5.5 inches forward of the ejection port. The charging handle can be mounted on the right or left side of the rifle, providing six possible placement options for full ambidextrous use and shooter preference.

The magazine release, located within easy reach just above and forward of the trigger guard, is fully ambidextrous and features a protective frame to prevent unintentional release. The safety selector is ambidextrous and clearly marked on both sides with color coded safe and fire modes. It rotates easily up for safe and down for fire with a sturdy click, but it felt a bit high to reach comfortably for me.

The lower receiver/trigger group is made from a tough polymer and has an enlarged trigger guard for easy use with gloves. The integral pistol grip has a good amount of internal storage space for spare batteries or a small cleaning kit. The polymer stock is extremely well designed and folds easily to the right, locking in place while still allowing the rifle to be fired in this condition. With the stock folded, the rifle's length comes down to a very portable sub-25 inches.

The folding stock is collapsible, with three positions of adjustment for length of pull. The comb height can be adjusted up for use with optics if needed, and there are ambidextrous quick detach sling swivel attachment points as well as a more traditional sling loop at the toe.

The upper receiver is aluminum with an extremely well-done matte black finish. There is a full-length Picatinny rail on top, providing 15.5 inches of usable real estate for optics or lasers. On the standard model, the upper receiver comes standard with 6.5-inch Picatinny rails on the handguard at the 3,

The Anschütz MSR RX22 has a match-grade target barrel and exhibits superior accuracy, making it well-suited for hunting as well as training.

6, and 9 o'clock positions. These are not overly sharp and do not hurt the hand while handling or shooting; still, some may prefer to add rail guards. These rails are also very handy for adding a bipod, lasers, lights, vertical foregrip, or other accessories.

The rear of the upper receiver features two sling attachment points — one right above the other on the left side — while the front of the receiver has two more sling attachment points, one on either side. Removable backup iron folding sights come standard on the RX22 and are fully adjustable for windage and elevation. I found that the only way to install or remove them, however, was to slide off the front of the rail, which was only a slight inconvenience. The rifle comes standard with 10- and 22-round polymer magazines.

The operation of this rifle is very straightforward. Simply insert a loaded magazine and retract the charging handle to chamber a round. The bolt will stay open on an empty magazine; but otherwise, there is no way to lock the bolt to the rear. To disassemble the RX22, simply remove the screws at the front and rear of the lower receiver and separate the trigger group from the upper receiver. No further disassembly is recommended, and the manual states that cleaning should be conducted between every 1,000 to 5,000 rounds fired.

On the range, the RX22 handles very easily given its compact dimensions and lightweight. Over several days of range testing the rifle consumed hundreds of rounds of mixed .22 ammo with only two failures to feed — well within the break-in period.

Given Anschütz's reputation for making Olympic target rifles, I was eager to test for accuracy. From a stable bench rest, I mounted the Trijicon TR20-2 AccuPoint scope with 3-9x40 power and a Mil-Dot crosshair reticle with amber dot. The variable power allows you to have a wider range of view for observation and then easily zoom in for targeting. The excellent fiber optics on the Trijicon scope gather ambient light to illuminate the center amber dot without batteries.

At 50 yards, the RX22 performed admirably, with my best group measuring just over a half-inch using CCI ammunition. What was most impressive, however, was the sheer consistency of the Anschütz barrel, for every five-shot group was under 1 inch.

The RX22 is being imported to the U.S. by Steyr Arms and comes standard in a hard case with extra magazines, manual, sights, and tools. It's available in four versions, including tactical models in black and desert tan as well as target versions that feature a smooth handguard and non-folding wooden stock.

SPECIFICATIONS
ANSCHÜTZ MSR RX22

CALIBER: .22 LR
BARREL: 16.5-in. target
OA LENGTH: 25 in. folded, 32.8 in. collapsed and 34.2 in. extended
WEIGHT: 6.94 lbs. empty
STOCK: Polymer adjustable/folding
SIGHTS: Flip-up iron sights
ACTION: Semi-auto
FINISH: Blued
CAPACITY: 22-round magazine
PRICE: $895
205-655-8299
WWW.ANSCHUETZ-MSR.COM

As a tactical trainer, the RX22 has significant practical applications, especially for those who may already own an FN SCAR rifle. The controls on both rifles function in the same manner, so by using low cost .22 LR ammunition, you can increase familiarity and training time while reducing fatigue, building muscle memory, and mastering trigger control.

Anschütz has clearly raised the bar for all tactical .22 rifles and produced an incredibly accurate and reliable gun. Its light weight, easy handling and compact size make it ideal as a hunting or target rifle, or simply a backcountry or trunk gun. Its small dimensions and low recoil also make it well suited for young and smaller-statured shooters as well as for beginners and when combined with a quality optical sight, makes for easy hits.

RUGER 10/22 TACTICAL

Arguably the king among .22-caliber rifles is the Ruger 10/22 semi-automatic. This light little rimfire rifle has been in continuous production since 1964 and has lost none of its popularity, that thanks to its well-designed versatility and the gift of aftermarket parts and accessories.

Recently, interest in tactical rifles has increased dramatically, and now Ruger has introduced its own Ruger 10/22-FS Tactical Rifle. The 10/22 is a standard blowback-operated, semi-automatic .22 LR rifle. The gun features an innovative (if boxy) 10-round rotary magazine, which ensures reliable feeding.

Designed from the ground up as an adult-sized .22 rifle with a 13.5-inch length of pull, the 10/22's ergonomics are comfortable, but the rifle remains light and handy enough for junior shooters as well. In addition, Ruger offers variations of the 10/22 with shorter lengths of pull, designed specifically for junior shooters, as well as a handy takedown model that separates into two equally sized parts for easy transport.

The Ruger comes standard with a carbine-length precision-rifled, cold hammer-forged, alloy steel barrel with black matte finish. The barrel has no sights and is topped off with a removable Ruger SR-556 Mini-14-style flash hider, which adds about 1.5

The Ruger 10/22-FS Tactical comes standard with a carbine length and precision-rifled, cold hammer-forged barrel with black matte finish.

inches to the 16 1/8-inch barrel. The barrel is threaded to a standard 1/2-28, which allows you to add custom muzzle accessories, breaks, flash hiders, or suppressors.

Since the 10/22-FS has no iron sights, the included scope base is a necessity, and happily it accepts both standard Weaver style and .22 "tip-off" scopes. Another very handy feature of 10/22s is that the receivers come ready to install a scope base. I must add that, for a survival situation, being able to have backup iron sights is very helpful and you should consider the other 10/22 models as well.

The FS includes a standard black synthetic stock, which makes this the lightest weight 10/22 that Ruger makes at only 4.3 lbs. Other features include an extended magazine release, push button cross-bolt manual safety, polymer trigger housing, and aluminum alloy receiver. My only complaint, albeit a minor one, is that there is no provision for attaching a sling to the stock.

The Ruger 10/22 is a very easy gun to use. First, ensure that the safety is activated by pushing the cross-bolt safety button, located toward the front of the trigger guard, to the right. Next, lock the

Although designed as an adult-sized .22 rifle, the Ruger 10/22-FS remains light and handy enough for junior shooters as well.

bolt open by pulling back on the bolt handle and up on the bolt lock, located in front of the trigger guard and behind the magazine release, simultaneously. The magazine loads like a standard box magazine except that the force needed for the last round is about the same as for the second, thanks to its rotary design.

To load, insert the magazine, pull back on the bolt handle while simultaneously pushing up on the bolt close latch (which is the same as the bolt hold open latch), and then release the bolt handle. The bolt works in this fashion as a safety device to prevent the accidental release of the bolt. If the bolt is already in the forward position when a full magazine is inserted simply pull back and release the bolt handle. To fire, simply depress the safety button to the left, which for most right-handed shooters can be easily accomplished using the trigger finger, and squeeze the trigger. The bolt does not lock open on the last shot.

The extended magazine release is a big improvement over the old push button style, but to remove the magazine it must still be gripped with the thumb and forefinger of the other hand. This prevents the magazine from being accidentally removed if the magazine release lever should be unintentionally pushed. With a small amount of practice, magazine changes can be done fairly quickly. The rifle can shoot without a magazine by loading the rounds individually into the chamber.

One of the great benefits of the Ruger 10/22 design is how easily it can be disassembled and its parts replaced. The procedure is straightforward and begins, as always, with ensuring that the gun is unloaded. With the bolt in the closed position, first loosen the barrel band screw and remove the barrel band, which secures the barrel to the forward part of the stock. Next, loosen the takedown screw located underneath the rifle on the stock, forward of the magazine well.

To remove the receiver/barrel assembly from the stock, position the cross-bolt safety button so that it is halfway, with an equal amount showing on either side of the trigger guard. Next, swing the barrel assembly and receiver up and away from the stock, keeping the whole assembly even with the ground. If it comes out tilted, the two receiver cross pins and the bolt stop pin may fall out of the receiver. The trigger guard and trigger assembly can then be removed from the receiver by pushing out the two receiver cross pins.

It is not necessary to remove the bolt for cleaning, but if so desired, it is easily accomplished. With the receiver upside down, remove the bolt stop pin at the back of the receiver. Next, pull back the bolt handle and lift the front of the bolt until the handle disengages, and then pull the complete bolt handle assembly out through the ejection port. The bolt will now easily lift out of the receiver from the back. It may also help to turn the receiver right side up and shake the bolt lose.

The bolt itself is a well-machined, solid chunk of steel, and the machining marks are clearly visible on the left and top of the bolt. The part that can be seen through the ejection port is polished to a mirror finish.

To reassemble the rifle, first place the bolt handle assembly back into the receiver so that the rear of the recoil spring guide rod fits into the recess at the rear right of the receiver. The recoil spring must then be fully compressed and the bolt handle held to the rear. This is best done using a screwdriver to compress the guide rod spring while pulling back on the bolt handle simultaneously.

Holding the bolt handle all the way to the rear, insert the bolt front first and press down on the rear portion of the bolt until it clicks where the catch on the bolt handle assembly fits into the recess on the top of the bolt. Reinstall the bolt stop pin and turn the receiver right side up to install the trigger assembly, making sure that the ejector is in its proper forward position. Then, reinstall the two receiver pins and place the entire assembly back into the stock, securing it with the takedown screw and barrel band.

The barrel on the 10/22 can be easily removed and replaced simply by removing the two retainer screws and retainer v-block located underneath the barrel toward the back. This is a feature that aftermarket parts makers have taken to heart, and it has greatly increased the rifle's popularity and versatility. With little more than a set of screwdrivers, a hammer, and a punch, you can customize your 10/22 and make it a really unique and personalized gun.

The Picatinny rail on the Ruger 10/22-FS makes it easy to add red-dot sights or other optics such as the EOTech Holosight.

Installing a new heavy bull barrel is a popular upgrade that can turn this already accurate rifle into a true tack driver. The heavier bull barrel does require the use of a replacement stock with a larger channel, a great excuse to upgrade the stock. For a more tactical look to match the flash-hider, replacement pistol grips and collapsing stocks are available from a variety of manufacturers at reasonable cost.

On the range, the Ruger was a pleasure to shoot, especially given its crisp, 5-pound trigger with no take-up. I fired a mix of ammunition, and the Remington Thunderbolt produced no malfunctions of any sort. The CCI Blazer ammunition did produce two failures to feed and one failure to eject but also printed the best group at under 1 inch. Aguila's Hyper Velocity ammo yielded mixed results with one failure to feed and one dud round. Aguila shot 2 inches higher than the other ammunition and had the largest average groups.

While the rifle handles and shoots very well, there is a bit of a learning curve with the magazine, and it takes practice to easily tell the front from the back. It also does not always eject easily, but it got better the more I used it. In my experience, it is easier to eject the longer after-market mags than the standard factory flush mag.

The Ruger 10/22-FS Tactical Rifle makes for an excellent platform for anyone seeking to build a truly custom tactical .22 survival rifle. Of course, it fills that function out of the box as well, especially when fixed with an outstanding tactical scope like EO Tech's XPS2-RF Rimfire scope. The bottom line is that, when it comes to survival guns, you simply can't go wrong with a Ruger.

SPECIFICATIONS
RUGER 10/22-FS TACTICAL RIFLE

CALIBER: .22 LR
STOCK: Black synthetic
FINISH: Black matte
BARREL LENGTH: 16.12 in.
OVERALL LENGTH: 36.25 in.
LENGTH OF PULL: 13.50 in.
SIGHTS: None (3/8 in. Dovetail/1 in. Weaver rail included)
WEIGHT: 4.30 lbs.
GROOVES: 6
TWIST: 1:16 RH
CAPACITY: 10
SUGGESTED RETAIL: $316
603-865-2442
WWW.RUGER.COM

MARLIN CLASSIC MODEL GOLDEN 39A

A semi-auto rifle may not be for everyone, and they may be restricted in some jurisdictions (although typically there are exceptions for .22 LR guns). One solution is the tried and true lever action. The lever-action Marlin Golden 39A is no kid-sized gun but an adult rifle with a rich history. It is capable of shooting not just .22 LR but also .22 Short and .22 Long. The Model 39 has been in continuous production in its current form since it was named the Model 1897 (a record). It was the first solid top receiver lever-action rifle with side ejection and was extremely popular with exhibition shooters around the turn of the 20th century, including Annie Oakley.

This easy takedown lever action features a tubular magazine, blued steel construction and American black walnut stock. The tubular magazine is made from stamped steel and extends almost the full length of the barrel for maximum magazine capacity. Inside the magazine tube is a spring-loaded brass inner tube that

The lever-action Marlin Golden 39A is not a small gun, and it's capable of shooting not just .22 LR but also .22 Short and .22 Long.

forces any rounds down into the receiver for proper feeding. The rounds actually ride inside this brass tube, and a red polymer tip seals in the internal spring. That design allows you to load .22 Short, .22 Long, or .22 Long Rifle ammunition, and the magazine capacity adjusts accordingly, from 26 rounds for the Short ammo to 21 rounds for Long and 19 rounds for LR.

Loading is a very simple matter. The top of the inner brass tube has a knurled locking end knob that unlocks by pressing down, turning it out of the locking tab and lifting up. It is not necessary to completely remove the inner tube to load, as there is a cartridge-shaped opening about 6 inches from the top. With the rifle oriented upward, simply drop the desired number of rounds in one at a time and push down the inner tube to lock it. The tube will not close or lock if the maximum number of rounds has been exceeded.

To unload, the action should be cycled until the rifle is empty. There is a handy viewing port on the left side of the receiver. Through this port, you can see if there are rounds present, or if the rifle is empty. Moreover, you can see the red polymer magazine tube follower when empty for further verification. With the magazine in place, you can see the brass coloring of the inner tube outlining the image of a cartridge case at the loading port.

The 24-inch round contour barrel is very heavy and features Marlin's micro groove rifling. This process was first developed for rifles by Marlin and features multiple small grooves in the barrel, as opposed to more traditional rifling known for leaving fewer and larger grooves. The advantage is that the shallower grooves provide less bullet distortion and improved accuracy. Indeed, the 39A has a well-deserved reputation for accuracy.

The rifle's sights are of a very traditional style. The rear sight is attached to a spring steel sight base that is dovetailed onto the top of the barrel. It folds down to stay out of the way for scopes and is of the semi-buckhorn variety. This is a softly sloping 'U" shape with a center notch and is easily elevation adjustable with a simple sliding sight elevator. With your fingertips, just lift the rear sight slightly and move the sight elevator forward or back to lower or raise the sight.

The easy takedown Marlin 39A features a tubular magazine, blued steel construction and American black walnut stock. Don't overlook the lever actions when it comes to today's survival guns!

To adjust for windage, the rear sight base must be tapped slightly right or left for proper adjustment. The front sight is of the post and dot type, with a bright brass bead that offers good contrast against the rear sight. It is protected with a spring steel hood in what Marlin calls a "Wide-Scan" style, which is almost oval in shape to give a wider field of view on target.

With a flat, solid top receiver and side ejection, the Model 39A is perfectly well-suited for mounting a scope, and that helps wring out the rifle's maximum accuracy potential as a plinker and hunting arm. The top of the receiver is pre-drilled and tapped and will accommodate several aftermarket scope bases and mounts. Marlin ships each rifle with an offset hammer spur, reversible for left or right-hand use. This spur provides you with sufficient access to operate the hammer with a scope mounted.

The all-wood stock is made from a very nice grade of American black walnut and has a deep matte finish. The fore-end and pistol grip are both well checkered with a traditional diamond pattern. It has a nicely blued steel cap, which also houses the front sling

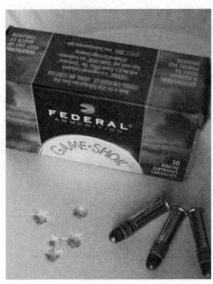

Solid accuracy is achieved in the Marlin 39A thanks to its 24-inch round contour barrel, which is very heavy and features Marlin's micro groove rifling.

swivel. The comb is fluted and raised for an improved grip and better cheek weld. The bottom of the pistol grip has a black cap held with a brass screw. At the back of the stock, there is a comfortable rubber butt pad with the company's distinctive Marlin man on horseback logo. The buttstock has a well-placed rear sling swivel at the bottom.

The Marlin 39A abounds with safety features. The rebounding hammer has a built-in hammer drop safety where the hammer position remains in a standard "half cock." The hammer can only go forward to strike the firing pin when the trigger is depressed and the cross bolt safety is in the fire position. As soon as the gun fires, the hammer returns to the rebound position.

The cross bolt safety is a round button located at the rear of the receiver toward the top, and acts as a hammer block. To activate it, simply push it in from left to right, and a button that reads "safe" pops up on the right side of the receiver. To deactivate the safety, push the button in from right to left, and it pops up with a red circle on the left side of the receiver.

The hammer must be cocked either manually or through the cycling of the action in order for the rifle to fire. The hammer can be safely lowered on a live round by placing the gun on safe and depressing the trigger while manually holding the hammer and slowly lowering it to the rebound position. When ready to fire again, simply cock the hammer.

One of the most welcome features of this rifle is its ability to be easily taken down into two parts for transport and cleaning. On the right side of the receiver, there is a distinct knurled and good-sized takedown screw. It is usually torqued on a bit too tight to unscrew it with just the fingers, but most any size coin will do nicely. Once the screw is loosened, the two halves of the receiver split cleanly, with the right side retaining the hammer and buttstock and the left side retaining the bolt and barrel assembly.

Fit and finish on the Marlin Model 39A is very well done. All of the major parts are machine forged from solid steel and heat treated. All the metal parts feature what Marlin calls "Mar-Shield," which leaves a deep blue finish that is tough and corrosion resistant. Of course, the 39A features a very distinct gold plated trigger, thus the rifle's name.

SPECIFICATIONS
MARLIN MODEL GOLDEN 39A

CALIBER: .22 Short, .22 Long or .22 LR
BARREL: 24 in.
OA LENGTH: 40 in.
WEIGHT: 7.1 lbs. empty
STOCK: American black walnut
SIGHTS: Adjustable iron sights
ACTION: Lever action
FINISH: Blued
CAPACITY: 26 Short, 21 Long or 19 LR
PRICE: $702.22
800-544-8892
WWW.MARLINFIREARMS.COM

The rifle is a bit of a heavyweight, just over 7 pounds on my scale, and at 40 inches in length, it has a full-sized feel. With the long and heavy barrel, the weight seems to carry mostly in the front, and the 14-inch length of pull shows that this was always intended as an adult-sized rifle.

On the range, the Model 39A handled extremely well, and there were no malfunctions of any sort. It was easy to load and easy to shoot with virtually no recoil. I did not have the opportunity to mount a scope on the gun and fired it using the iron sights alone. Testing three different types of ammunition including hollow-points and round nose, my best result of the day was a five-shot group measuring just over half an inch. With a proper scope, this rifle is clearly capable of outstanding accuracy.

The Marlin Model Golden 39A is not an inexpensive rifle or one ideally suited for a small child, but it is a rifle that carries a lot of history, tradition, and quality.

The M&P 22 Compact is a blowback-operated semi-auto. It is 15 percent smaller than the standard M&P pistol, but retains the look and feel of its larger centerfire version.

The M&P 22 has the same controls as the larger M&P, with the addition of a threaded barrel for suppressor use and an accessory rail for this Crimson Trace laser.

RIMFIRE HANDGUNS

In a survival situation, you need to be comfortable with all types of firearms. While the .22 LR performs best in long-barreled rifles, there are many pistols chambered in the round that provide excellent training opportunities, and if needed, hunting and self-defense options. The obvious advantage of a handgun over a rifle is its size. Pistols are easier to store and transport. Here is a look at some of the best contenders for .22 handguns for survival.

SMITH & WESSON M&P 22 COMPACT

The M&P 22 Compact is a semi-automatic blowback-operated pistol. It is 15 percent smaller than the standard M&P pistol, but retains the look and feel of its larger centerfire version. Ergonomically, it fits the hand very well and is a pleasure to shoot. It is a polymer-framed pistol, but uses a single-action only, internal hammer-fired method of operation, as opposed to a striker-fired system. It is very lightweight, just over 15 ounces, thanks to its aluminum alloy slide.

The 3.56-inch carbon steel barrel makes the accuracy on this little pistol outstanding as long as you do your part. The barrel is threaded so you can easily add a suppressor. The high profile three white dot sights are very easy to acquire, and the rear sight is fully adjustable for windage and elevation. The polymer frame sports a Picatinny rail section at the dust cover, making it very easy to attach a light or laser.

The S&W M&P 22 features a magazine safety so

SPECIFICATIONS
S&W M&P 22 COMPACT SUPPRESSOR READY

CALIBER: .22 LR
BARREL: 3.56 in.
OA LENGTH: 7.25 in.
WIDTH: 1.48 in.
HEIGHT: 5.3 in.
WEIGHT: 15.3 oz. empty
SIGHTS: Three white dot
GRIPS: Polymer
ACTION: Single-action hammer fired
FINISH: Black
CAPACITY: 10+1
ACCESSORIES: Two magazines, manual, box
PRICE: $409
WWW.SMITH-WESSON.COM

The Colt Government 1911 in .22 L.R. is a licensed reproduction made by Carl Walther in Germany and imported by Umarex USA. *Photo: Walther*

The steel frame of the Colt-Walther .22 includes fully functional slide lock/slide release, right-side thumb safety and grip safety. *Photo: Walther*

that the pistol will not fire without a magazine securely inserted. Given its single-action operation, I understand why this extra safety feature is included, and although it is a common feature in many semi-automatic pistols, I am not a fan. In a scenario where you have lost your magazines, the pistol becomes completely unusable. In a survival situation, where magazines are easy to lose or damage, this could be a big problem.

There are ambidextrous thumb safeties on the gun that are very easy to operate, and the magazine release is reversible for left-handed shooters. The slide stop/release is rather smallish and best relegated to the slide stop function. Unlike some other .22 pistols, disassembly of the S&W M&P 22 is a breeze with a convenient takedown lever on the left side of the frame and a captive recoil guide rod and spring. You will have to remove the thread adapter, however.

COLT GOVERNMENT 1911 IN .22 LR

As with rifles, many manufacturers are making dedicated .22 LR versions of popular handguns, and there is perhaps no more popular handgun in the U.S. than the 1911. There are conversion kits available for a standard .45 ACP 1911, but for about the same price you can buy a dedicated .22 LR pistol.

When it comes to 1911s, there is no more famous name than Colt, and they are licensing blowback-operated, single-action only semi-automatics manufactured by Carl Walther in Germany and imported by Umarex USA. These pistols feature the same familiar weight, feel, and handling of the classic 1911 with 12+1 capacity.

The Colt Government Model features all-steel construction with an even flat black finish and black rubber grips. The slide has traditional blacked out iron sights that are dovetailed into the slide and include a set screw. By loosening the set screw, both front and rear sights can be adjusted for windage. Both sides of the slide have a distinct white engraving, which includes the Colt name and rampant horse logo. The rear slide serrations are sharp and close together, again following the traditional pattern.

The steel frame includes fully functional slide lock/slide release, right-side thumb safety, and grip safety. The grip safety

is of a similar pattern to the slightly elongated style found on the 1911-A1 to help avoid hammer bite on the hand. The hammer is of the traditional spur design and includes a half-cock feature. At the top of the ejection post and the rear of the chamber, there is a small window that serves as a loaded chamber indicator, showing the rim of a cartridge case if one remains in the chamber.

The right-side magazine release allows the 12-round steel mag to drop free. The magazine's polymer baseplate sits fits flush with the frame. The rear of the frame has a flat mainspring housing like the original 1911, and there is no checkering on this part or on the front of the grip. The black rubber grips feature a well-executed diamond checkering pattern and are interchangeable with standard 1911 grips.

While the Colt 1911 .22 LR is almost identical to a standard 1911-A1 on the outside, internally there are key differences — most notably the frame-mounted and fixed 5-inch barrel and the gun's blowback operation.

The method of disassembly is very similar to a standard 1911. Ensuring the pistol is unloaded, simply depress the recoil spring plug and turn the barrel bushing to remove it. Then the plug and recoil spring can be removed followed by the slide stop. The slide must be retracted and lifted up off the frame and forward from the barrel assembly. The barrel, which actually rides inside a sleeve, can be removed from the frame by removing the barrel nut at the front. As the barrel itself is threaded, it is a simple matter to equip the pistol with a suppressor or other muzzle device with the use of

This Colt-licensed Walther .22 LR pistol features the same familiar weight, feel and handling of the classic 1911 but with 12+1 capacity. *Photo: Walther*

SPECIFICATIONS
COLT GOVERNMENT 1911 IN .22 LR

CALIBER: .22 LR
BARREL: 5 in.
OA LENGTH: 8.6 in.
WIDTH: 1.25 in.
HEIGHT: 5.4 in.
WEIGHT: 36 oz. empty
SIGHTS: Adjustable
GRIPS: Polymer
ACTION: Single-action hammer fired
FINISH: Black
CAPACITY: 12+1
ACCESSORIES: One magazine, manual, box
PRICE: $375
WWW.UMAREXUSA.COM

an aftermarket thread adapter.

On the range, there were no malfunctions of any kind using a mix of ammunition over two range sessions with no break-in or maintenance. Recoil was negligible, thanks in large part to the .22 LR cartridge and the pistol's full-sized grip, weight, and feel.

Accuracy from a benchrest at 25 yards was very good, aided by the inherent accuracy of a fixed barrel design and the clean, single-action trigger, which broke at 4 lbs. with virtually no creep and zero stacking or overtravel. The trigger itself is of the longer 1911 variety and not the shorter 1911-A1 style, although the frame does have the 1911-A1 frame cutouts to help you reach the trigger more easily.

The Colt Government Model 1911 may not be an original, but it is made under license to Colt's demanding specifications by Carl Walther, which itself has a long reputation for manufacturing very high-quality firearms. The end result is an interesting mix between the original 1911 and the WW2 1911-A1, with all the weight, feel and manual of arms. Even the disassembly procedure largely mirrors the original, and there is the added benefit of a threaded muzzle for versatility.

Umarex offers three variants of the Government 1911, including a tactical model with an accessory rail on the dust cover and a competition version. Each pistol ships in a hard plastic padded case with one magazine, owner's manual, magazine loading tool, and barrel wrench. Parts interchangeable with standard 1911 pistols include the grips, sights, trigger, grip safety, thumb safety, and hammer. Those seeking a low-cost training alternative that retains the look and feel of a full-sized 1911 are sure to be pleased with this offering.

WALTHER P22

The Walther P22 is a polymer-framed, semi-auto 10-shot pistol chambered in .22 LR. This hammer-fired pistol fires with a traditional single- and double-action operation. It has a slide-mounted safety on both sides that blocks the firing pin so the hammer can be manually lowered safely. It also has a magazine disconnect safety (so the gun won't fire without the magazine inserted) and a paddle-style mag release that can be used by right- or left-handed shooters. There is an accessory rail at the front for installing a light or laser.

Like many of the other pistols listed here, the P22 is a 3/4 copy of Walther's full-sized P99 pistol. This blowback semi-auto comes with interchangeable backstraps to adjust the gun to your hand. The three dot sights are easy to adjust, although to adjust the front one for elevation, it must be completely removed and replaced with one of the included replacement sights, of a different height. The magazine release is of the European paddle variety, but it works well and is ambidextrous.

The gun has a threaded barrel, but it is covered by a simple

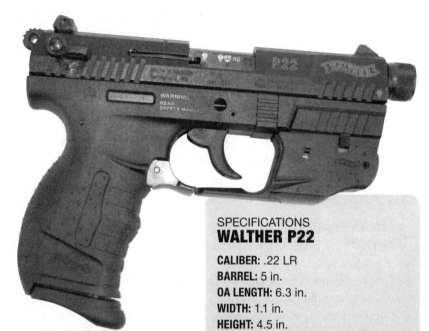

The Walther P22, a polymer-framed semi-auto 10-shot chambered in .22 LR and a ¾-sized copy of Walther's full-sized P99 pistol.

SPECIFICATIONS
WALTHER P22

CALIBER: .22 LR
BARREL: 5 in.
OA LENGTH: 6.3 in.
WIDTH: 1.1 in.
HEIGHT: 4.5 in.
WEIGHT: 17 oz. empty
SIGHTS: Adjustable
GRIPS: Polymer
ACTION: Single-action/double-action hammer fired
FINISH: Black
CAPACITY: 10+1
ACCESSORIES: One magazine, manual, box
PRICE: $410
WWW.WALTHERARMS.COM

thread protector and looks completely unthreaded with this in place. An adapter is included for suppressor use. The small size and low recoil make it easy for anyone to shoot, and accuracy was very good for my informal testing against a small army of plastic bottles. You really have to focus on your fundamentals to get good hits, and with the Walther P22, this is both fun and cheap.

NORTH AMERICAN ARMS POCKET PISTOLS

Revolvers were among the earliest pocket pistols, and many of these early wheelguns were rimfire. Small, short-barreled revolvers are still very popular for personal protection and concealed

but if you want something that is truly small and conceal-
check out the mini revolvers from North American Arms.
..ese almost-too-small-to-be-believed guns are chambered in
.22 rimfire calibers, which in all honesty is not ideal for self-defense, especially from extremely short barrels. Nevertheless, if it
is what you have, it will at the very least dissuade most aggressive
dogs or people. Among these, the most effective are the revolvers
chambered in .22 Magnum.

NAA BLACK WIDOW .22 MAGNUM

The NAA Black Widow.22 Magnum is designed for serious use and
not as a novelty. It features single-action firing and a five-shot heavy
bull cylinder with no flutes. Between the chambers, there are notch-
es cut to hold the hammer in place. This allows the revolver to be
carrier loaded with the hammer down safely so that it will not fire
if dropped. The spur trigger is semi-shrouded until the hammer is
cocked, and there is no trigger guard. This keeps the gun extremely
compact, but caution should be exercised when firing.

On top, you have a choice between Millet fixed or adjustable
sights, either of which are very visible and easy to use. The gun
features a 2-inch heavy vent barrel and oversized rubberized black
grip with a distinctive red and black hourglass black widow spider logo.
The grip is still very small but is significantly larger and easier to hold
than those found on the company's other revolvers, all of which feature
stainless steel construction that makes them extremely durable and corrosion resistant.

Out of such a short barrel, the .22 Magnum does lose a lot of its punch,
but still the performance (depending on the ammunition) is 1,000 feet
per second or more. This places the diminutive pistol in the same league

SPECIFICATIONS
NAA BACK WIDOW .22 MAG

CALIBER: .22 Magnum
BARREL: 2 in.
OA LENGTH: 5.87 in.
WIDTH: 0.875 in.
HEIGHT: 3.62 in.
WEIGHT: 8.8 oz. empty
GRIPS: Rubber
SIGHTS: Fixed or adjustable
ACTION: Single action
FINISH: Stainless
CAPACITY: 5
PRICE: $274

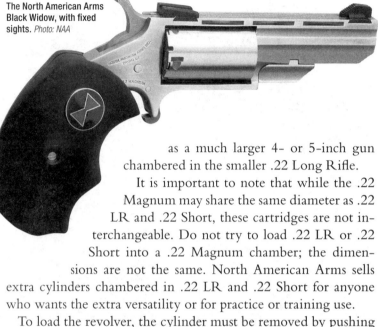

The North American Arms Black Widow, with fixed sights. *Photo: NAA*

as a much larger 4- or 5-inch gun chambered in the smaller .22 Long Rifle.

It is important to note that while the .22 Magnum may share the same diameter as .22 LR and .22 Short, these cartridges are not interchangeable. Do not try to load .22 LR or .22 Short into a .22 Magnum chamber; the dimensions are not the same. North American Arms sells extra cylinders chambered in .22 LR and .22 Short for anyone who wants the extra versatility or for practice or training use.

To load the revolver, the cylinder must be removed by pushing the cylinder pin out of the front. Cartridges are loaded singly, and the cylinder is then placed back into the gun. To unload, the cylinder is again removed, and the cylinder pin can then be used to push the spent brass out one at a time. Clearly, this is not a system that lends itself to fast reloads, but the revolver finds its niche as a deep cover backup gun.

The manufacturer warns against dry firing, as it can damage the firing mechanism. Instead, use a spent or dummy case if you want to practice dry firing. For hiking or camping, the revolver can be loaded with bird shot loads to ward off snakes.

AA .22 LR

The NAA .22 Long Rifle is the gun that started it all and is the most popular mini-revolver in existence. You can shoot both .22 LR and .22 Short cartridges, and over the years, a plethora of accessories have been developed including laser sights and various holsters and grips. The company does warn against firing the

The NAA .22 Long Rifle Snub is a handy little backup gun. *Photo: NAA*

SPECIFICATIONS
NAA .22 LR

CALIBER: .22 LR or .22 Short
BARREL: 1.12 in.
OA LENGTH: 4 in.
WIDTH: 0.812 in.
HEIGHT: 2.37 in.
WEIGHT: 4.5 oz. empty
GRIPS: Wood
SIGHTS: Fixed
ACTION: Single action
FINISH: Stainless
CAPACITY: 5
PRICE: $209

gun with mother of pearl grips, as these may crack under recoil. One extremely cool holster is the belt buckle holster that makes the gun look like it is just a fancy, large western style buck (and not actually a gun) but in reality, a quick flick of a switch allows the gun to be drawn. Another holster option is actually a larger folding grip that includes a belt or pocket clip for convenience.

NAA SIDEWINDER

If you prefer a more traditional-style revolver, the North American Arms Sidewinder features a swing out cylinder. It does swing out to the right instead of to the left, but it includes an extractor that makes loading and reloading much easier and faster. The cylinder release is actually part of the cylinder rod/ejector rod instead of a separate latch. This feature adds a bit in terms of length and weight, and it is only available with the .22 Magnum-length cylinder, although replacement cylinders

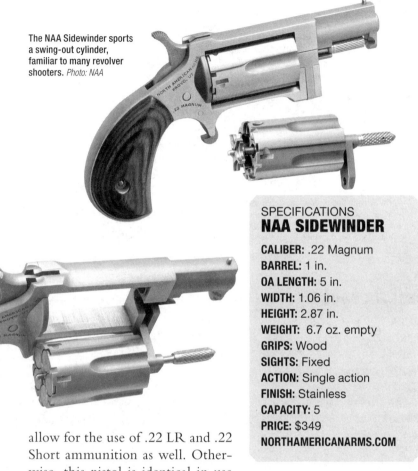

The NAA Sidewinder sports a swing-out cylinder, familiar to many revolver shooters. *Photo: NAA*

SPECIFICATIONS
NAA SIDEWINDER

CALIBER: .22 Magnum
BARREL: 1 in.
OA LENGTH: 5 in.
WIDTH: 1.06 in.
HEIGHT: 2.87 in.
WEIGHT: 6.7 oz. empty
GRIPS: Wood
SIGHTS: Fixed
ACTION: Single action
FINISH: Stainless
CAPACITY: 5
PRICE: $349
NORTHAMERICANARMS.COM

allow for the use of .22 LR and .22 Short ammunition as well. Otherwise, this pistol is identical in use and operation to the other NAA revolvers.

BERETTA BOBCAT

For more than three decades, the Beretta Bobcat, a traditional double action/single action exposed-hammer pistol, has been keeping its users safe. Available in the venerable .22 LR or the classic pocket pistol .25 ACP chambering, it features a tip-up barrel design that makes loading and unloading (as well as cleaning) a very simple affair, especially for those who may have difficulty with slide manipulation.

The Beretta Bobcat is a traditional double action/single action exposed hammer pistol available in.22 LR or.25 ACP. It has a tip-up barrel and 7+1 capacity. *Photo: Beretta*

SPECIFICATIONS
BERETTA BOBCAT

CALIBER: .22 LR/.25 ACP
BARREL: 2.4 in.
OA LENGTH: 4.92 in.
WIDTH: 1.1 in.
HEIGHT: 3.7 in.
WEIGHT: 11.8 oz. empty
GRIPS: Polymer
SIGHTS: Fixed
ACTION: Single/double
FINISH: Black or stainless
CAPACITY: 7+1
PRICE: $410
WWW.BERETTAUSA.COM

With a 7+1 capacity, the Bobcat has a left-side grip-mounted magazine release and an easy to use thumb safety in its all-metal design. The post and notch sights are diminutive but snag-free for a smooth and comfortable draw. At less than 12 ounces empty, this pistol is very easily carried, and a new stainless steel version is now available with superior corrosion resistance.

CHIAPPA 1873 SAA-22 REVOLVER

The classic single-action revolver may be a bit dated when it comes to modern day survival situations, but it served well during a period of Western expansion in America that involved some dramatic real life struggles. These types of revolvers may be slow to load, have limited capacity, and lack in features and ergonomics, but if it is all you have access to when you need it, better learn how best to use it.

One easy and inexpensive way to learn is with a .22 LR replica like the Chiappa 1873 SAA-22 Revolver. The main advantages

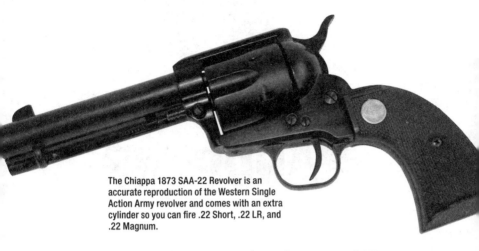

The Chiappa 1873 SAA-22 Revolver is an accurate reproduction of the Western Single Action Army revolver and comes with an extra cylinder so you can fire .22 Short, .22 LR, and .22 Magnum.

of this handgun are that it accurately replicates a real Western Single Action Army revolver, is very inexpensive, and comes with an extra cylinder so you can fire .22 Short, .22 LR, and .22 Magnum.

Largely made of zinc alloy to reduce cost, the Chiappa has steel where it is needed to handle the .22 LR cartridge. It is limited to six rounds (like the original) and uses a right-side loading gate to load one round at a time. The hammer must be in the half-cocked position to load and unload. Unloading is done via the ejector rod one empty case at a time. Again like the original, there is no safety, and it should be carried with an empty chamber underneath the hammer, as dropping the gun could cause it to fire. This further limits your initial round count to five.

Finally, don't expect superior accuracy. The sights are as rudimentary as on the original, but it did function flawlessly, and it was fun to shoot. After all, what's the point of surviving if you can't occasionally have some fun?

SPECIFICATIONS
CHIAPPA FIREARMS 1873 SAA-22

CALIBER: .22 LR/.22WMR
BARREL: 4.75 in.
OA LENGTH: 10.25 in.
WIDTH: 1.6 in.
HEIGHT: 5 in.
WEIGHT: 35.2 oz. empty
GRIPS: Polymer
SIGHTS: Fixed
ACTION: Single/double
FINISH: Black
CAPACITY: 6
PRICE: $229
WWW.CHIAPPAFIREARMS.COM

HANDGUNS

*H*andguns are the cornerstone of your survival guns battery, and can be used for self-defense, hunting, and survival. Everything from a single-shot small-caliber derringer to an AR or AK pistol is considered a handgun. Yet, on the other hand, a handgun is not the best tool for hunting or self-defense with a few notable exceptions. While a handgun can be used very effectively for these tasks, it is not the ideal firearm for either.

The main advantage of the handgun is its size, which allows easy one-handed operation and the convenience of portability. I carry a handgun every day and everywhere it is legal for me to do so. I choose to be prepared. Part of that preparation is understanding the

There are many reasons to carry a concealed handgun. Pick the sidearm that best suits your needs.

limits of the handgun, and this is the best way to immediately start an argument among gun owners. Which handgun is best to carry?

To even begin to answer that question you have to select a caliber, then size and type of handgun (pistol or revolver). Every one of these decisions carries repercussions. The common refrain is that the best handgun is the one you have with you when you need it. My own view is that: I want to keep my handgun concealed at all times so as not to alarm or raise someone's awareness of it. I want to use a caliber that is effective but at the same time minimizes recoil and provides me maximum magazine capacity. I want to be comfortable.

The Taurus Millennium G2 is typical of modern polymer-framed striker-fired semi-autos we see today, chambered in 9mm with 12+1 capacity.

Given that I recognize that the likelihood of me having to use my handgun is extremely small (but not nonexistent), I take a conservative approach and carry either a compact 9mm pistol or a sub-compact pocket pistol, depending on my clothing and the weather. I also carry one spare magazine.

I know people who consider such a setup completely inadequate, who carry a full-sized handgun with two or three spare magazines and insist on using the largest practical caliber they can find (.45 ACP or 10mm) … plus carry a spare backup gun. This is all in addition to a sizable knife, pepper spray, cell phone, flashlight, and a tourniquet. If this describes you, congratulations — you are Batman. All you need is a grappling hook.

A friend once explained his theory of the proper use of the handgun. He described it as, "Simply a tool to help me survive until I get to a proper firearm." By that, he meant a rifle or shotgun.

A handgun has limited range, power, and accuracy, despite some impressive feats of long-range shooting.

People carry handguns because they can do so comfortably and discreetly. It is the gun you will have with you when bad things happen. Understanding how best to use your handgun and its limitations will help you survive. I list here reviews and information for many of the best and most popular survival handguns that I have personally experienced.

Which handgun is right for you? My advice is: don't scrimp. Buy a good quality, name brand handgun from a well-known manufacturer with a solid reputation. Rather than acquiring a lot of guns, spend your time and money on ammunition and training. Keep a stockpile of small parts in case you need to do repairs in the field. Keep a set of basic gunsmithing tools and cleaning supplies. Buy a handgun that you can operate effectively and easily, that fits your hand, has manageable recoil and is chambered in a caliber that is common and easy to find.

SEMI-AUTOMATIC HANDGUNS

There is a good reason that police departments across America made a determined switch from revolvers to semi-automatics: firepower. In a full-sized pistol, magazine capacity can be as many as 17 rounds or more plus one in the chamber. An officer usually carries two spare magazines as well, and the pistol can be easily and very quickly reloaded simply by pressing the magazine release button (and dropping the empty magazine) and inserting a full magazine.

Semi-automatic pistols can be found in single action, double action, or both. The key difference is that a single-action pistol only needs to be cocked for the first shot. The slide operation automatically cocks the hammer for each subsequent shot. A double-action only pistol may have a hammer (which can be either visible or internal) or may be striker-fired. The advantage to both single-action only and double-action only pistols is that the trigger pull is always the same for every shot.

The Remington 1911 R1 Enhanced Suppressor Ready .45 ACP pistol is a serious survival handgun but has more limited magazine capacity. *Photo: Remington*

Many semi-automatic pistols use both double- and single-action operation. Typically, the hammer will be in the down position for the first shot, making it a longer and heavier double-action trigger squeeze, and then it will fire in the single-action mode for all of the following shots. The advantage with this system is that you have the safety of a long, heavy trigger pull for the first shot and the accuracy and speed of a single-action trigger squeeze for the remaining shots. You do need to get used to two different trigger pulls, however.

The main disadvantage of the semi-automatic pistol is that there is a steeper learning curve for beginners. Each pistol may have different controls than others. The magazine release, which allows you to remove the magazine, may be in different places and located on different sides of the gun. Many semi-automatics (less so on small pocket pistols) will have a slide lock/release lever that locks the slide to the rear. Each will have its own method of disassembly for cleaning and maintenance, and some of these can be a bit complicated.

Different semi-automatic pistols will have varying safety mechanisms, ranging from grip safeties that require a firm hold to operate to thumb safeties that must be manually deactivated. Some pistols will have trigger safeties that help prevent the trigger from moving rearward unless squeezed from the middle. Many others will have various internal safeties that are always activated until the trigger is squeezed.

The grip size on a pistol is largely fixed, although there are replacement grips and other accessories that can help adjust it to suit you better. Many pistols include replaceable panels, but this is mostly found on the mid-size and larger handguns. Operating the slide may be difficult for someone with smaller hands, hand injuries, or poor hand strength, although some manufacturers do make pistols with easier to manipulate slides. With practice, most people can handle slide manipulation.

Reliability can also be a concern. If anything obstructs the movement of the slide (such as clothing), it likely will not cycle properly. Pistols are much more sensitive to ammunition selection, and some types of ammo may not function reliably in certain handguns. With certain types of pistols, it is possible to inadvertently hit the magazine release and then be left with one shot in the chamber and a magazine on the ground when you need it most.

1911 .45 ACP

To the true firearms aficionado, there is no more perfect handgun than the John Moses Browning 1911. This classic represents everything we think a pistol should be — big, slab-sided, a powerful piece of steel and wood that has served American fighting men longer than any other firearm. While some would say that the design is dated, others would argue that it is time-tested. Certainly, there are plenty of more modern guns that are easier to operate,

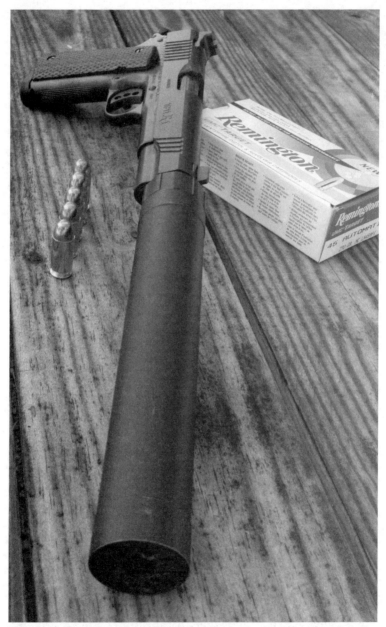

With a suppressor attached, the overall length is doubled, but the effect is to reduce noise and recoil significantly in this powerful pistol.

have higher magazine capacities, and are smaller. Regardless, there are still plenty of folks who swear by this pistol and carry it on a daily basis.

It should be noted that the 1911 is a single-action only pistol, meaning that the hammer must be cocked for the gun to function. For this reason, the 1911 has both a thumb safety and a grip safety. People who carry a 1911 defensively often do so in what is known as Condition One — also known as "cocked and locked" — meaning a round in the chamber, the hammer cocked and the thumb safety on. Some people are not comfortable with this method of carry, but in a properly operating pistol, it is perfectly safe.

Most 1911 pistols are chambered in .45 ACP, which is a big cartridge, but I have never found it uncomfortable to shoot. Some 1911s are available in other cartridges, though, including 9mm, which offers the advantage of a slight increase in magazine capacity over the standard 7- or 8-round mags of .45. Also popular these days are 1911s chambered in the powerful 10mm cartridge, popular with big and dangerous game hunters. Regardless of what caliber 1911 you choose, its operation and design presents a slightly steeper learning curve to master, in terms of its use and maintenance. Make sure to keep all manuals that come with your pistol or request one from the manufacturer.

There are a multitude of manufacturers making 1911 pistols, and some have more modern features that are worth considering.

REMINGTON 1911 R1 ENHANCED SUPPRESSOR READY
During the First World War, Remington-UMC, which represented the merger of Remington Arms and the Union Metallic Cartridge Co., produced over 20,000 Model 1911 pistols for the U.S. military. They are rare and collectable guns today. In World War II, Remington Rand, a typewriter manufacturer that was a spinoff from Remington Arms, was the largest producer of 1911 pistols, with nearly 900,000 delivered by war's end.

In recent years, Remington announced that it was back in the handgun business and resurrected their own 1911 pistol on the cusp of the 100th anniversary of its adoption by the U.S. military.

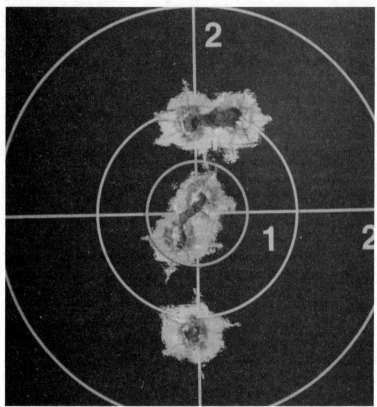

The Remington 1911 R1 performed extremely well on the range and displayed very good accuracy.

The Remington R1 is a classic, full-sized semi-automatic 1911 pistol chambered in the classic and hard-hitting .45 ACP cartridge. Within a very short period of time, Remington also introduced stainless steel versions and an Enhanced tactical model. The latest example of this is the Remington Model 1911 R1 Enhanced Threaded Barrel.

This new pistol is designed to take full advantage of the growing interest in suppressors, which are legal for civilians to own in most states. The 5-inch match-grade stainless steel barrel extends past the slide to expose the threads for attaching a suppressor. The barrel includes a knurled thread protector for use without a suppressor.

The slide features blackened fixed raised sights to allow for aimed fire over an attached suppressor. The sights are dovetailed and drift adjustable if needed, although they come factory sighted. This is quite distinct from the standard sights on the Enhanced R1, which feature a red fiber optic front sight for faster target acquisition. The slide has sharp and squared serrations at the front and rear for a more secure hold during slide operation. The ejection port has been flared and lowered for more reliable ejection of spent rounds. The raised rear sight aids in getting a firmer hold for slide operation and could be used to cycle the action one handed if pressed against a flat, hard surface such as a wall or table edge.

The frame includes many significant tactical upgrades that survival-minded shooters will appreciate. Vertical serrations at the front of the grip help secure a firm hold while at the same time remaining very comfortable. The rear of the grip features a flat mainspring housing with 20 lines per inch of sharp checkering. The aggressive beavertail grip safety sweeps upward to protect the web of the hand from hammer bite and allows a high handhold. The grip safety avoids any sharp angles for improved comfort and features an extended memory bump that ensures the safety is properly deactivated when the pistol is gripped. The memory bump on the grip safety has the same 20 line per inch checkering as the mainspring housing.

The R1 Enhanced sports an extended thumb safety for ease of use and clicks from the safe to the fire position and back with a comforting 'click' sound. Some may prefer to carry Condition 3, which is safety off, hammer down, and an empty chamber but a full magazine. In this condition, all that is required to fire is to first rack the slide. It is not common, but some foreign military units have (at least in the past) adopted this method with single-action semi-automatic pistols.

The Remington R1 uses the Colt Series 80 safety system. This is a firing pin block that was added in the 1980s by Colt to the standard 1911 design. On a standard 1911, if the gun is dropped with a round in the chamber and the hammer down, it could cause the hammer to strike the firing pin with enough force to set off the primer and fire a round. Likewise, if the gun falls barrel first and hits a hard surface, the force of inertia could be sufficient to drive the firing pin forward and set off a live round in the chamber.

The Series 80 safety system adds a firing pin block that prevents the firing pin from moving forward unless the trigger is depressed. Pressing the trigger raises a bar inside the frame that contacts a pin at the back of the firing pin, raising it and unblocking the firing pin so it can move forward when the hammer strikes it. Some feel that this system changes the trigger feel of the classic 1911 pistol, but most find the change imperceptible.

At the rear of the pistol is a combat commander-style hammer that is easy to cock. The anodized aluminum match trigger is skeletonized and includes an adjustment screw to eliminate over-travel. The front of the trigger is curved and serrated and the magazine release is extended for ease of use. The magazine well is slightly beveled to aid in faster reloads.

The R1 Enhanced comes with very attractive custom grips made from a laminated dark colored wood and well checkered with a diamond pattern. On the left side, there is a smooth cutout for easier access to the magazine release, which really helps display the detail on the lamination. The magazine (Remington includes two as standard) holds eight rounds and features a polymer follower and thick polymer bumper pad. The body of the magazine has an anti-friction coating for a smooth feel that drops free and feeds easily. With or without the bumper pads, the magazines do extend slightly past the bottom of the grip to accommodate the higher than normal capacity.

The fit and finish on the Remington R1 Enhanced I tested was excellent and the bushing was very tightly fit onto the slightly

SPECIFICATIONS
REMINGTON R1 ENHANCED THREADED BARREL

CALIBER: .45 ACP
BARREL: 5.25 in.
OA LENGTH: 9 in.
WEIGHT: 42 oz. empty
GRIPS: Enhanced wood laminate
SIGHTS: Tall dovetail front & rear, black, fixed
ACTION: Semi-auto
FINISH: Satin black oxide
CAPACITY: 8+1
PRICE: $1,140
877-801-1911
WWW.REMINGTON.COM OR WWW.1911R1.COM

flared barrel. The included disassembly tool comes in very handy at this point. The all steel pistol is finished in a matte black satin oxide, which is very well applied and provides corrosion and wear resistance.

I test fired both the standard R1 Enhanced and the threaded model with and without a suppressor. With an Advanced Armament Ti-RANT .45 suppressor, the R1 gains almost 12 ounces to its already full-sized 42 ounces, not including a full magazine. The weight alone does a good job of taming the recoil of the pistol and will give your arm a good workout on an extended range session. The Ti-RANT .45 suppressor does an excellent job, reducing the noise of the pistol by 30 decibels when fired dry and 41 decibels when fired wet.

The suppressor adds more than 8 inches to the R1, nearly doubling its overall length. It certainly gives the pistol a distinct feel when firing, as there is a bit of a backward pressure that you encounter. The elevated sights are much appreciated and make it possible to see the target over the suppressor.

After a full day of shooting the R1 Enhanced, I grew to distinctly appreciate the checkering on the back of the frame and grips, which are a bit on the sharp side and tend to bite into the hand somewhat (but not in an unpleasant way — just enough to let you know they are there). They do keep the pistol firmly in the hand and prevent any shifting due to recoil. The trigger itself is excellent with just a bit of creep and a very crisp break at slightly less than 4 pounds. This, and the match-grade bushing and barrel, contributed significantly to the excellent accuracy results. In testing the R1 Enhanced, I used a mix of ball and hollowpoint ammunition with zero malfunctions experienced over several days of shooting.

MAC 1911 BOBCUT .45 ACP HARD CHROME

The MAC 1911 Bobcut fits the bill perfectly as a customizable and feature-laden pistol for everyday carry, or EDC. The pistol itself is manufactured in the Philippines by Metro Arms Corporation (MAC), based in Manila. MAC is one of the top three largest gun makers on the island that specializes in 1911s and was started

The MAC 1911 Bobcut .45 ACP Hard Chrome is a compact pistol designed for comfortable concealed carry.

Note the "bobcut" on the mainspring housing. This is designed to make the gun more comfortable to carry and help prevent "printing" through clothing. *Photos: MAC*

by a competitive shooter to offer reliability and quality.

There is a bit of irony in a Philippine-made 1911, since it was America's involvement in an insurrection in that country that directly led to the creation and adoption of the 1911 — and the .45 ACP round. Following the Spanish-American War of 1898, the U.S. came to possess several former Spanish colonies including Cuba, Puerto Rico, and the Philippines. People in the Philippines had a different notion, however, and U.S. troops ended up facing off against highly motivated Moro guerrillas in the Philippine-American War. These insurgents did not react in the way troops wanted when hit with the then-standard .38 Long Colt. The Army determined that a larger round was needed and thus the 1911 .45 ACP was developed and first used in combat there.

The MAC 1911 Bobcut is a single-action, hammer fired, semi-automatic, recoil-operated pistol with a single column detachable box magazine and chambered in the .45 ACP cartridge. The pistol will accept any standard length 1911 magazine but ships with an 8-rounder.

On the range the MAC 1911 performed well and produced good accuracy. Recoil was stout but manageable.

As a single-action pistol, the 1911 has a thumb safety, which locks the sear to the hammer so that the trigger cannot release it, and a grip safety that likewise blocks the sear from being able to release the hammer. It does not have the Series 80 drop safety.

The MAC 1911 Bobcut is a commander-length 1911 with a 4.25-inch barrel instead of the traditional 5-inch barrel. This makes the pistol shorter, handier, and easier to conceal. As the name implies, the lower portion of the mainspring housing as well as the frame of the pistol have been cut back giving this portion of the gun a rounded profile. Given the full/standard length of the pistol grip, this cut significantly helps reduce obvious printing and reduces the gun's overall dimensions in this area. You can certainly install standard 1911 grips, but they will need to be trimmed in this area for a proper fit.

The sides of the slide and frame feature a semi-high gloss polish while the front, back, bottom, and top all have a matte finish. The left side of the slide is very nicely engraved with the company logo and the pistol's model. This helps prevent glare against the sights. The steel front sight has been dovetailed into the machined slide and is outfitted with a bright red fiber optic insert providing high-visibility and fast target acquisition. It gives you significant contrast against the white dot rear sights. The Novak-style low profile rear sights are fully adjustable for windage and elevation. Both front and rear sights are serrated to prevent glare.

The ejection port has been lowered and flared to ensure reliable ejection of spent cartridges. The slide serrations at the rear of the slide have been slightly enlarged for a better grip and easier slide manipulation. The forged steel barrel is throated in order to assure reliable feeding into the chamber of different types of ammunition. There is a full-length steel guide rod

SPECIFICATIONS
MAC 1911 BOBCUT

CALIBER: .45 ACP
BARREL: 4.25 in.
OA LENGTH: 7.88 in.
WEIGHT: 34.5 oz. empty
GRIPS: Wood
SIGHTS: Dovetail front and rear, adjustable
ACTION: Semi-auto
FINISH: Chrome
CAPACITY: 8+1
PRICE: $978
732-493-0333
WWW.EAGLEIMPORTSINC.COM

for smoother cycling, extended recoil spring life, and improved slide to frame fit for better accuracy. At the rear is a skeletonized commander-style hammer.

The frame of the MAC 1911 has a standard-sized slide release/lock, which is better for concealed carry than an extended one, as it is less likely to be inadvertently activated. The front and rear straps have aggressive stippled serrations to ensure a firm grip. The skeletonized combat trigger is adjustable for travel and has a well-checkered non-skip trigger face. The custom hardwood grips have a snakeskin checkering that is simultaneously very attractive, distinct, and effective at helping to secure a firm hold. The checkered magazine release allows the magazines to drop free.

The Mac 1911 Bobcut is available in three styles: deep blued, hard chrome (tested here), and black chrome (essentially a combination of the first two). I found the fit and finish on this pistol to be outstanding — far better, in fact, than pistols commonly seen from other larger manufacturers. There was significant attention to detail paid in the build quality, and the features were all well designed. Not only is this a very attractive pistol, but the tolerances were extremely tight, indicative of a quality build. Users will mostly notice the tight tolerances during the disassembly process, which is altered slightly from the standard procedure due to the full-length guide rod that must be captured with a pin in order to disassemble and maintain the pistol.

In handling the pistol on the range, it was very comfortable to shoot but still a .45 ACP with the expected recoil and muzzle flip. I did experience frequent malfunctions with the first one or two rounds from a full magazine. Using a replacement magazine fully resolved these issues, and the pistol functioned flawlessly thereafter. Anytime I experience malfunctions with a semi-automatic firearm, the first thing I check is the magazine. More often than not, this resolves the problem.

For function testing, I used three different types of ammunition, mixing both FMJ and defensive rounds in different weights. MAC provides a full lifetime service warranty for the original purchaser.

For those who prefer a classic 1911, Springfield Armory offers the Mil-Spec 1911, a close copy of the original World War II M1911A1. *Photo: Springfield Armory*

The Glock 19 in 9mm is a great combination of small size for concealed carry but powerful enough for serious business with a 15-round magazine. Shown here with a green Crimson Trace grip laser. *Photo: Crimson Trace*

SPRINGFIELD ARMORY MIL-SPEC 1911

When it comes to American military handguns, the 1911 .45 ACP is king. This pistol served American fighting men for more than 70 years, and I was lucky enough to be issued one toward the tail end of that run. More than 2.5 million 1911 pistols were made for the military, and many still miss them.

If you do get an original U.S.-issue 1911, you may not want to shoot it too much to preserve its collector value, but thanks to Springfield Armory, you can get a brand new American made gun that is a close copy of the original World War II M1911A1 — one that you can shoot to your heart's content. Their new Mil-Spec pistol features a Parkerized finish, arched mainspring housing, and larger grip safety like the original, and some practical improvements that make it appealing for modern use.

Springfield has updated the 1911 with larger three dot sights, a lowered and flared ejection port, polished feed ramp, and a throated barrel, as well as a beveled magazine well and angled (instead of straight) slide serrations. The pistol is available in stainless steel.

SPECIFICATIONS
SPRINGFIELD ARMORY MIL-SPEC 1911

CALIBER: .45 ACP
BARREL: 5 in.
OA LENGTH: 8.5 in.
WEIGHT: 39 oz. empty
GRIPS: Wood
SIGHTS: Fixed combat, 3-dot
ACTION: Semi-auto
FINISH: Parkerized
CAPACITY: 7+1
PRICE: $768
800-680-6866
WWW.SPRINGFIELD-ARMORY.COM

GLOCK

Glock makes one gun and one gun only: The Glock. They make it in different sizes and calibers, but fundamentally they are all polymer-framed, striker-fired pistols with a safe action trigger and multiple internal safeties as well as a polygonal rifled barrel. They are ubiquitous, the most popular sidearm in law enforcement in fact, and utterly reliable.

I have a Glock 19 — the mid-sized compact 9mm — and have put thousands of rounds through it. I use it to teach beginners, and they have shot and abused this gun to no end. Despite this

SPECIFICATIONS
GLOCK MODEL 19

CALIBER: 9mm
BARREL: 4 in.
OA LENGTH: 7.28 in.
WEIGHT: 23.65 oz. empty
GRIPS: Polymer
SIGHTS: Fixed
ACTION: Semi-auto
FINISH: Tennifer
CAPACITY: 15+1
PRICE: $629
770-432-1202
US.GLOCK.COM

abuse, it keeps running and remains my bedside home defense handgun regardless because I know I can count on it. Indeed, when the Austrian military adopted the Glock as their issue sidearm, it first had to pass several endurance and torture tests involving tens of thousands of rounds.

One of the most attractive features of the Glock is its simplicity of operation. I learned to drive on a manual transmission, and the extra pedals and levers didn't make things any easier. This is one reason I enjoy using the Glock pistol with beginners; it is like the automatic transmission of guns. The straightforward design keeps the mechanics simple and easy to understand. There is one lever on the side, the slide lock, and the Glock Safe Action system that makes the gun safe and engages automatically.

The striker-fired mechanism delivers a smooth and consistent trigger squeeze, making it far easier to hit the target. The new Gen4 Glock conveniently features interchangeable backstraps so it can be adjusted for your hand size. The cold hammer-forged steel barrel features distinct polygonal rifling for improved service life and accuracy and a nitrite finish that provides exceptional hardness and corrosion resistance. Disassembly and maintenance are very easy, and the newer Glocks feature an accessory rail for mounting lights or lasers.

BERETTA M9

Beretta's most famous firearm may well be its Model 92 pistol, first offered in 1975 in 9mm and now available in a host of calibers and configurations. Several different designs and features have followed, but one of the most significant was incorporating a hammer drop safety, which involved moving the safety from the frame to the slide.

The U.S. Military first adopted the Beretta Model 92 in 1985 as its official sidearm (designating it the M9), replacing the storied .45-caliber Model 1911. The M9 is a short-recoil, semi-automatic, hammer-fired pistol with a standard 15-round capacity magazine firing in the double-action first shot, single action for all subsequent shot mode now familiar to most American shooters. The M9 has a 4.9-inch barrel and sturdy plastic grips with aggressive checkering and Beretta's famous "trident" logo. The frame has a traditional squared trigger guard, and an extended slide release/catch on the left side. The gun's locking mechanism uses a separate locking block very similar to those found on the Walther P38 of World War II fame. This sets the M9 apart, since most recoil-operated semi-auto pistols use a block integral with the barrel that operates by causing the barrel to tip up when the slide moves rearward. This is not the case on the P38 or the M9.

The open top design isn't for looks either, although it does help reduce the pistol's weight, as does the aircraft quality 7075-T6 aluminum alloy frame. This slide design provides for easier, trouble-free feeding of rounds from the magazine to the chamber, reduces the likelihood of jams and malfunctions, and makes them easier to clear when they do occur. The M9's disassembly latch is a nice feature that makes it an extremely easy gun to disassemble for maintenance.

All M9s feature Beretta's special Bruniton finish, a Teflon-based paint finish that provides far superior corrosion resistance over bluing or Parkerizing, a reversible magazine release button (a valuable feature for left-handed shooters), as well as hard chromed bores and chambers. Chrome-lined barrels have long been known to reduce wear and prevent corrosion. They are what turned early M16s into much more reliable rifles and are also featured in AK-type rifles, which is very valuable since corrosive ammunition is not infrequently encountered in countries that use the AK.

The M9 was a radical change for a military that had relied on the single-action, single-stack .45-caliber 1911 for over 70 years. It placed the U.S. within NATO handgun caliber specs and provided our forces with the next generation of pistol design. This happened to be the same time that many police departments were phasing out revolvers for high-capacity 9mm pistols, and Beretta was no slouch in picking up several law enforcement contracts as well.

To win the U.S. military contract, however, Beretta had to beat out top industry names, including Colt, FN, HK, Sig, Smith & Wesson, Steyr, and Walther, in a grueling series of tests, which included exposure to temperature extremes, submersion in water, dirt, sand, etc., drop tests, and a lot of endurance shooting. The military expects any handgun to be able to withstand at least 5,000 rounds before any significant failure; the Beretta lasted more than six times that amount.

From the beginning, the M9 had its critics, and the biggest complaint has always been over the anemic performance of the 9mm round as a man stopper. To many, it was nonsensical to replace the battle proven and hard-hitting .45 ACP, despite what our European allies were doing. Of course, the 9mm has been in combat use longer than the .45 ACP and, with proper defensive loads and expanding bullets, it is an effective round in the vast majority of situations. However, militaries worldwide are stuck with non-expanding or full metal jacket ammunition because of international agreements.

It was perhaps in response to this criticism that the 9mm ammunition the U.S. military procured for the M9 was, unbeknownst to Beretta, loaded to a higher-than-standard chamber pressure. Early in its introduction phase, the M9 started showing troublesome signs of premature wear in the chambers, micro cracks in the slides, and even reports of broken slides that caused injury to some shooters. The military initially blamed the problem on a design flaw with the Beretta pistol, but further testing of the ammunition showed that it was producing nearly 40 percent higher chamber pressure than standard 9mm.

Once the cause of these malfunctions became apparent, the military changed the specs on their ammunition to lower the chamber pressures. In a belt and suspenders sort of move, Beretta modified the M9's design by enlarging the hammer pin, extending it into a groove in the slide. Even in the worst-case scenario of a catastrophic failure, this new safety feature prevents a broken slide from flying back and injuring the shooter. The M9 has a

Beretta 92 series pistols have always performed well for the author with zero malfunctions across several variants and over many years of testing.

chamber-loaded indicator that causes the extractor to protrude when there is a round in the chamber, providing visible and tactile warning. This is in addition to two other standard safety features.

The first safety feature is the automatic firing pin catch, a bar that blocks the firing pin from going forward unless the trigger is fully depressed. This prevents the gun from firing from inertia (i.e. being dropped). The top of the bar can be seen at the top rear of the slide just forward of the rear sights, and it sticks up when the trigger is depressed all the way to the rear (which unblocks the firing pin, allowing the gun to fire). The second feature is the spring-loaded, slide-mounted, ambidextrous safety-decocking lever that rotates the rear of the two-piece firing pin out of alignment so that the hammer cannot strike it and lowers the hammer. There is no cocked and locked carry possible with the M9.

The U.S. Military first adopted the
9mm Beretta Model 92 in 1985 as
its official sidearm (designating it the
M9), replacing the .45-caliber Model 1911.

The Beretta M9A1 is an improved
version that adds a Picatinny rail to the
frame, high-profile three dot sights, heavy
checkering, and a beveled magazine well.

Recently, Beretta introduced the use of polymer parts, which reduces both manufacturing costs and weight. Polymer parts include the recoil spring guide rod, magazine release, trigger, lanyard ring, magazine floorplate, and follower.

M9A1

A later iteration is the M9A1, the result of our experiences in the rough and sandy terrain of Iraq and Afghanistan and requests from the Marine Corps for more modern features to meet mission critical needs. The most distinct feature on the M9A1 is a MIL-STD 1913 (Picatinny) rail integral to the frame.

Other new features include high-profile three dot iron sights (as opposed to the dot and post system seen on standard M9s), heavy checkering of the front and backstraps for improved grip under a variety of conditions, and a beveled magazine well to aid in faster reloads. The most significant innovation in the M9A1, however, may well be the PVD-coated magazines, which were specially designed with an indentation along their entire length to ensure reliability and proper magazine function. Even if sand or other particulates enter the magazine body, this groove keeps ammunition from excess contact with the sides of the mag.

The PVD coating certainly feels quite slick in the hand and is designed to be sand resistant and reduce friction when conducting magazine changes. The actual coating is a very hard, durable, and wear resistant metallic compound, designed to increase the lubricity of the mag so fine sand doesn't adhere to its surfaces. This eliminates the need to lubricate the inside of the magazine, which could attract sand.

Like all Beretta firearms, the M9A1 exhibits excellent fit, finish, and superb ergonomics. However, at 33.9 ounces empty, this is the heaviest of the standard Model 92 variants offered. And at 8.5 inches in length and 5.4 inches in height, it's not a small gun. Shooters with smaller hands may find the grip overly large. The slide-mounted safety (while extremely effective and spring loaded for positive engagement) is located higher than the standard frame-mounted safety most shooters are used to on other guns. Of course, no single gun is perfect for every shooter, and the M1911 (which the M9 replaced) was no small gun, either.

M9A3

Of course, military missions and doctrine change over time, and the Beretta M9 has kept pace. Now, they have developed the M9A3 with even further significant changes. This pistol has been submitted for consideration via an Engineering Change Proposal (ECP), but civilians can purchase it now.

The M9A3 is a short-recoil, semi-automatic, hammer-fired pistol with a standard 17-round capacity magazine firing in double action for the first shot with the trigger pull both cocking and releasing the hammer, and single action for all subsequent shots.

The latest Beretta is the M9A3 (not officially adopted by the military), which features a desert tan finish, threaded barrel, night sights, and a smaller grip with interchangeable panels.

The tilting locking block has been redesigned for a longer service life. The 17-round magazine itself is one of the many improvements, adding two extra rounds from the original mag design and a PVD coating.

To further appeal to combat troops in arid environments, the M9A3 has a two-tone earth Cerakote finish on the slide and barrel, which provides improved lubricity, corrosion resistance, and durability. This finish creates a reduced IR signature, too. The steel components that are left in black feature Beretta's special Bruniton finish, a Teflon-based paint finish that provides far superior corrosion resistance over bluing or Parkerizing. Tritium night sights are standard on the M9A3.

The M9A3's barrel has a chrome-lined bore and chamber and has been extended to 5.1 inches and threaded with a 1/2 x 28-inch thread pattern to use with standard suppressor devices. A knurled thread protector is included as well. The earth color anodized frame on the M9A3 has been significantly upgraded to respond to changing military needs. At the front dustcover, Beretta has added a three slot MIL-STD 1913 accessory rail, a big improvement over the M9's lack of any rail and the M9A1's single slot rail. The traditionally squared trigger guard has been machined much flatter in the front to more easily accommodate rail mounted accessories.

Another improvement is the grip, with the backstrap now featuring a flat mainspring housing instead of the traditional bulged type. This significantly reduces the size of the grip, which was sometimes hard to handle for smaller statured shooters. To further reduce grip size, the M9A3 uses slim Vertec Thin Grip panels that feature distinct and aggressive checkering. Beretta does include Hogue rubber over-molded replacement grips that provide an original grip size and feel.

SPECIFICATIONS
BERETTA M9A1

CALIBER: 9mm
BARREL: 4.9 in.
OA LENGTH: 8.5 in.
WEIGHT: 33.9 oz.
SIGHTS: White three-dot
GRIPS: Plastic
ACTION: Double action/ single action
FINISH: Bruniton black
CAPACITY: 15 rounds
PRICE: $750
WWW.BERETTA.COM

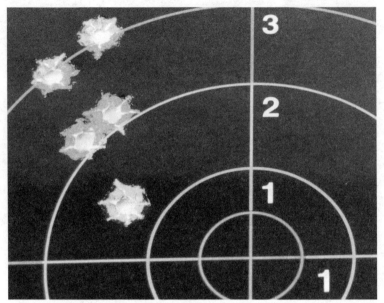

At 25 yards this full-sized Beretta pistol is capable of solid combat accuracy.

Left-handed shooters will appreciate the reversible magazine release button, which has been enlarged for easier and faster manipulation. The rest of the controls on the M9A3 remain standard, with a left-side slide lock/release and the takedown lever directly in front of it on the left side of the receiver. The use of polymer parts, reducing both manufacturing costs and weight, is minimal on the M9A3 and limited to the recoil spring guide rod, lanyard ring, magazine floorplate, and follower.

Beretta was established in 1526 and is the oldest continuously operating firearms manufacturer in the world. It is family owned, having been passed down through 16 generations. This gives Beretta a level of tradition and pride in manufacturing that is unparalleled. The M9A3 continues this tradition and is made entirely in the United States. Today, after 30 years, the M9 is still serving the needs of our military both at home and overseas, and the new M9A3 shows no signs of slowing down.

The FNS is a striker-fired pistol with many improvements, though it lacks the second-strike capability of the FNX. *Photo: FNH*

FNS 9MM

Fabrique Nationale d'Herstal, more commonly known as FN Herstal, produces the polymer-framed FNS, a recoil-operated, semi-automatic, striker-fired pistol with 17+1 capacity. The S in the name in fact stands for 'striker.' FN has been making high-quality firearms for over 120 years and is responsible for some of the most successful and famous guns ever made. This was in no small part due to their partnership with one of the most well-known names in firearms design, John Moses Browning. FN has also been relied upon and trusted by militaries worldwide, including our own, to produce firearms that are ultimately reliable and effective.

The FNS uses a double-action method of operation, but it does lack a double strike capability. On the FNS the movement of the slide must reset the striker, either under recoil or manually. If you squeeze the trigger on a dud round, there is no opportunity to squeeze it again (double strike it); the action/slide must be cycled manually to eject the bad round, feed a fresh one, and recharge the striker to be able to fire again.

This pistol is very similar in look and feel to FN's current FNP and FNX series of pistols, which use a traditional hammer-fired

The FNX pistol stands out in that it is a polymer-framed, hammer-fired pistol in the traditional single- and double-action mode.

single-/double-action method of operation. In fact, the FNS is simply an FNP/FNX with a striker. Like the FNX pistol, the FNS features blackened steel ambidextrous controls, including the frame-mounted thumb safety. This safety works in the traditional up for safe, down to fire style and shows a small red dot when it is in the fire condition. It works by physically blocking the trigger bar from moving rearward to release the striker. The safety is serrated and protrudes slightly for ease of use.

Ambidextrous slide stops are not at all a common sight on most pistols, but they are much appreciated by many left-handed shooters as well as those who train to fire with the support hand or with an injured hand that limits slide manipulation. The FNS, like the FNX, has a fully ambidextrous slide stop/slide release conveniently located right above the thumb when using a proper grip.

Since under recoil there exists the possibility that the shooter will engage the slide stop and cause a malfunction, FN has added a slight bump around it to protect it, molded right into the pistol's

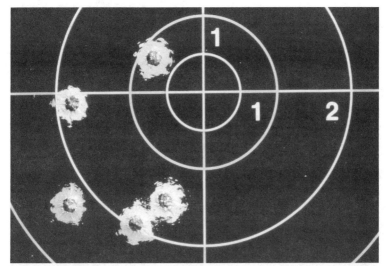

Both the FNS and FNX are extremely reliable pistols with great combat accuracy at 25 yards.

polymer frame. On the original FNP, this protective barrier covered the sides and bottom of the slide stop, which actually made it a bit difficult to engage. Someone must have complained, since the bottom portion of this barrier has been almost entirely eliminated on the FNS, making it much easier to engage the slide stop. The FNS has a fully ambidextrous magazine release that does not require you to switch it from one side to the other.

Additional safety features include a loaded chamber indicator that constitutes the front of the exposed extractor. Located on the right side of the pistol at the rear of the ejection port, the extractor has an extra bit of steel that protrudes when there is a cartridge case in the chamber, offering both visual and tactile confirmation. It has a small amount of red paint on the top to offer further visual confirmation.

Internally, the FNS has a hammer drop safety (that can be seen when the pistol is disassembled) on the bottom of the slide next to the striker firing pin. When the trigger is depressed, a metal tab on the frame pushes this safety tab up, unlocking the pin and allowing it to move forward to fire the gun. In this manner, you can

The latest version of this pistol is the FN 509, which adds interchangeable backstraps, night sights, improved slide serrations, and fully ambidextrous controls. *Photo: FNH*

be assured that the gun will not fire unless the trigger is depressed — for example, from inertia as a result of being dropped. The trigger itself has a rotating link that prevents it from moving rearward to fire unless the trigger is fully engaged.

The slide is made from all stainless steel with slide serrations at the front and rear for maximum purchase during manipulation. On top of the slide, Trijicon night sights are standard and dovetailed into the slide. They are drift adjustable for windage if needed, but the gun comes factory sighted. In daylight conditions, they appear as somewhat standard three dot sights with the front post appearing larger thanks to its distinct white outline. This allows faster front sight focus under duress, and in low light conditions it really stands out. The glow on these types of sights can be expected to last 20 years or longer.

The stainless steel 4-inch barrel has a polished chamber and feed ramp and is cold hammer forged. This is a process in which a steel blank is hammered around a mandrel, creating the lands and grooves as well as the chamber. It tends to produce longer life and improved accuracy. This is mated with a full-length captive steel guide rod with a flat-coil recoil spring for longer life.

Both the slide and barrel are finished in a matte black Melonite coating for extra hardness, durability, and corrosion resistance. This is a process that leaves a nitride finish directly on the metal that is much thicker and tougher than traditional bluing. The black color is applied on top of the Melonite finish.

The tough polymer frame has steel slide rail inserts that firmly retain the slide during operation. These can be factory replaced if needed, further extending the service life of the pistol. The frame includes two interchangeable polymer backstraps, one flat and one outwardly curved in order to better accommodate shooters with different sized hands. While I have large hands, I still prefer the flat backstrap and find it allows me a more complete grip on the pistol. The trigger guard is quite large for ease of use with gloves and includes checkering on the front.

Each backstrap has a lanyard hole, should that be needed, and is changeable with a pin hole in the back. The dustcover on the frame features a sizable MIL-STD 1913 accessory mounting rail that will allow you to mount any number of aftermarket tactical lights or laser units. The pistol's grip is aggressively checkered to ensure a secure hold even in inclement conditions. The base of the grip comes with a wide bevel that makes it easier to insert magazines for faster reloading. Also, both the slide and frame narrow toward the front for ease in holstering.

Disassembly of the FNS is a bit different than some other striker-fired guns but is still fairly straightforward. Ensuring the pistol is unloaded and pointed in a safe direction, remove the magazine, lock the slide to the rear, rotate the left-side takedown lever down, ride the slide forward and hold it even with the frame at the back so that the trigger can be squeezed to release the striker tension, and finally push the slide forward off the frame. To reassemble, simply

SPECIFICATIONS
FNS PISTOL

CALIBER: 9mm (tested) and .40 S&W
BARREL: 4 in.
OA LENGTH: 7.25 in.
OA HEIGHT: 5.5 in.
OA WIDTH: 1.55 in.
WEIGHT: 25.2 oz. empty
GRIPS: Reinforced polymer
SIGHTS: Three-dot night sight
ACTION: Semi-auto, double-action striker
FINISH: Black Melonite
CAPACITY: 17+1
PRICE: $699
703-288-1292
FNHUSA.COM

The HK P30L pistol (the L stands for Long) is available in 9mm and .40 S&W. It is a polymer recoil-operated pistol with a 15+1 magazine capacity in 9mm and 13+1 in .40 S&W. *Photo: HK*

HK's P30L is an altogether excellent choice for survival use and personal protection, offering accuracy and customization beyond routine expectations. *Photo: Koalorca*

make sure the trigger is in the rearward position and replace the slide on the frame.

On the range, the FNS handled well, and there were only two failures to feed with the first magazine of ammunition tested. After that, there were no issues and, as with any pistol, a good 200-300 round break-in period is always recommended. The trigger measured at 7 lbs. and had a distinct two-stage feel to it with a fair amount of creep but no over-travel and a fast reset. Accuracy from a sandbag rest at 25 yards produced good results.

The FNS, available in 9mm and .40 S&W, offers all the features shooters could want in a full-sized pistol, including high-capacity in two powerful cartridges and reliable performance.

HECKLER & KOCH P30L

The HK P30L (the L stands for Long) is available in 9mm and .40 S&W. It is a polymer framed semi-automatic recoil-operated pistol with a 15+1 magazine capacity in 9mm and 13+1 in .40 S&W available in either double-action only, or standard single action/ double action.

HK calls their double-action only design a Law Enforcement Modification, or LEM that operates like a striker-fired gun where the action is partially pre-cocked on closing but retains its hammer-fired mechanism so a second strike capability is possible. The sample received for evaluation, however, used a more traditional SA/DA method of firing, with some of its own unique elements as well.

Designed primarily to meet the needs of law enforcement officers for duty carry, the P30L adds over half an inch to the standard P30 and about an ounce and a half in weight (with an empty magazine). Of course, any handgun designed for law enforcement use will also serve civilian shooters looking for good quality pistols for personal protection.

While HK does offer many pistol models designed for concealed carry, this is not one of them. A gun meant for duty carry or home protection can and should be larger, and the P30L offers many features that users will find attractive, particularly in the new .40 S&W chambering.

The HK P30L proved to be a very accurate pistol firing offhand at 25 yards.

Among its many features, the P30L comes standard with three interchangeable backstraps that allow you to increase or decrease the length of the grip and determine how the gun fills your palm. Three sets of side panel inserts are included and are easily changed to provide a variety of grip thicknesses based on your hand size and preferences. In all, there are 27 possible different grip configurations for a truly custom fit.

The grip itself is extremely ergonomic and includes finger grooves, an excellent grip angle with natural pointability, and very aggressive stippling with a sand paper-like texture (but without the roughness), which really helps the gun stick in the hand. Left-handed shooters can certainly appreciate that more and more pistols now feature ambidextrous controls, but very few have ambi slide lock/slide release. The P30L is one of the few that does, and adds an ambidextrous magazine release and — on the DA/SA model — an ambi thumb safety as well.

The manual decocker, only available on the DA/SA model, is a serrated button located at the rear of the frame to the left of the hammer. While it seems unusual at first, either right- or left-handed shooters can actuate it easily. A full Picatinny rail at the front of the frame provides a significant amount of space for mounting accessories, while the slide has a slim angled profile that rides low on the frame and is topped off by luminous three dot sights for accurate shooting in low light conditions.

The pistol exhibited excellent fit and features an HE (Hostile Environment) finish, which according to HK is an "extremely hard, nitro-gas carburized black oxide coating" that will resist wear, corrosion, and even exposure to salt water, albeit limited.

The P30L includes several safety features. The thumb safety on the DA/SA models allows for cocked and locked carry (round in the chamber, hammer back, and safety on), if so desired. An internal firing pin block prevents the gun from discharging unless the trigger is fully depressed, and the low profile hammer has a rubberized coating to improve drop safety.

In addition, the sample received for evaluation included a loaded chamber indicator located on the extractor and colored bright red to offer both visual and tactile confirmation of a cartridge in the chamber. There is a "lockout device" that replaces the lanyard loop and is accessible through the magazine well. By turning the supplied key, the action is locked, and the trigger, hammer, and slide cannot move.

The cold hammer forged barrel features polygonal rifling, a

SPECIFICATIONS
HECKLER & KOCH P30L

CALIBER: 9mm and .40 S&W
BARREL: 4.45 in.
OA LENGTH: 7.56 in.
WEIGHT: 1.81 lbs. empty
WIDTH: 1.37 in.
HEIGHT: 5.43 in.
SIGHTS: Three-dot luminous fixed
GRIP: Polymer
ACTION: Semi-auto, DAO or DA/SA
FINISH: Black hard anodized
CAPACITY: 15+1 in 9mm
    and 13+1 in .40 S&W
PRICE: $1,059
HK-USA.COM

method pioneered in modern small arms by Heckler and Koch. Unlike traditional rifling with its well-defined lands and grooves, polygonal rifling appears very smooth upon inspection and has multiple flat sides that spin down the barrel. This type of rifling is not cheap, but it does provide a better bullet fit and thus higher velocity, longer barrel life, less bullet deformity, and greater accuracy. It makes barrel maintenance easier with less fouling, too.

Disassembly on the HK is a bit of a departure from what many may be used to, but it's simple enough. Start by removing the magazine and making sure that the gun is unloaded, then retract and hold the slide so that the second groove on the left side of the slide is directly above the front of the slide lock. Next, depress the pin on the front of the slide lock on the opposite side of the gun until the slide lock pops out far enough so that a red tab is visible at the top. This was a bit stiff, and I found it easier to use a punch than to try to pull the slide lock out while holding the slide back. Shooters with weaker hands may find this procedure to be a bit of a challenge.

Stopping power is a key element in choosing a sidearm for personal protection, which is a large reason to choose the .40 caliber for a survival gun. The extra weight and length of the P30L helps significantly in reducing the perceived recoil of this caliber. The sight radius is extended to almost 6.5 inches, further helping in accurate shooting. Internally, the captive flat recoil spring and guide rod include a polymer buffer tube at the back to help reduce perceived recoil.

HK's P30L is an altogether excellent choice for law enforcement use and personal protection, offering accuracy and customization beyond routine expectations. The longer slide goes a long way toward taming the recoil of the .40 S&W cartridge, and the gun proved comfortable to shoot for men and women, beginners and experienced shooters alike.

The Ruger SR series, originally introduced in 2007, is available in .45 ACP, 9mm and .40 S&W. This excellent survival gun can be had in full and compact sizes. *Photo: Ruger*

RUGER SR45

Over the past 60-plus years, Sturm, Ruger & Company has established an enviable reputation for manufacturing innovative and well-built pistols, rifles, and shotguns. Founder Bill Ruger was known for building his guns tough, but he was also a gifted gun designer. Carrying on that tradition, the company that Bill Ruger and Alexander Sturm founded continues to introduce new designs as well as regular improvements on existing popular guns.

My first experience with Ruger handguns was not with the .22 LR Standard MK I, the very first gun the company produced, but rather with the 9mm P85, the company's first center-fire semi-automatic pistol. That gun was built like a tank and sort of looked like one with all of its angular surfaces. Today's Ruger pistols have lost that tank look but not that tank-like toughness, and the Ruger SR45 is no exception.

The SR series, which was originally introduced in 2007, is available in .45 ACP, 9mm, and .40 caliber and in full and compact sizes. The SR45 is a polymer framed, full-sized, striker-fired, recoil-operated, semi-automatic chambered in the powerful .45 ACP cartridge and featuring 10+1 capacity. Ruger first developed

The SR45 is a polymer-framed, full-sized striker-fired pistol chambered in the powerful .45 ACP cartridge with 10+1 capacity on board. *Photo: Ruger*

their line of polymer (actually glass-filled nylon) frames to more easily reduce the dimensions of the pistol and make it lighter, slimmer, and more convenient for lawful concealed carry.

In this regard, Ruger succeeded. The grip on the SR45 is exceedingly thin to the point that it feels in the hand like a single stack gun, despite accommodating a 10-round double stack magazine of fat .45 ACP cartridges. The grip is very well checkered on the sides and front and stays in the hand well. The grip sides feature Ruger's distinct heraldic eagle logo.

The grip's backstrap has a rubberized insert that is removable and reversible. One side provides an arched profile while the opposite gives a flat profile. While the SR45 is incredibly thin, I found it to be on the long side from front to back, even with my good-sized hands. The flat backstrap was much more comfortable for me, but it is certainly nice to have other options. The backstrap is held in place with a steel cross-pin that does double duty as an attachment point for a lanyard.

The frame's dust cover features an integral accessory rail for mounting lights or lasers, and the trigger guard is nicely oversized for comfortable gloved use. All of the controls on the pistol seemed on the smallish side to me, but that is simply a matter of personal preference. The magazine release is ambidextrous, as is the thumb safety, a feature that will be appreciated by southpaws. The slide catch seemed very small to me, but it was fully functional, and a small slide catch helps prevent accidental activation, especially when shooting with a firm two-handed grip.

The pistol comes standard with two steel 10-shot magazines featuring a polymer follower and baseplate. The magazines include convenient witness holes to account for all 10 rounds. The baseplates feature a slightly extended finger rest and gripping grooves to make removal easier and faster, although the magazine does drop free under normal circumstances. A metal mag loading tool is included, but take note of the instructions, since it works differently than most I have tried and required manually loading the first round.

This is certainly no pocket pistol, and the brushed and matte stainless steel slide seems massive. As another option, the SR45 is available with a black nitride finished slide. Atop the slide, the three steel white dot sights are dovetailed and drift adjustable for windage. The rear sights can be adjusted for elevation with an easy-to-use screw adjustment on top. A windage lock screw must be loosened to make drift adjustments, however. The front white dot is larger than the two rear ones, making for easier front sight focus and sight alignment when speed is a concern.

The rear of the slide has a good length of well-spaced and aggressive slide serrations for easier slide manipulation and operation, and the massive external extractor does a reliable job of pulling cases from the chamber. The full-length captive guide rod uses a single spring and is polymer but functioned flawlessly.

As stated, this is a striker-fired pistol. When the action is cycled, the striker is partially charged. When the trigger is depressed, this completes the charging of the striker and then releases it. Once the striker is released, the trigger does not reset unless the action is again cycled, so there is no second strike capability. At the rear of the slide, the back of the striker is visible when the mechanism is

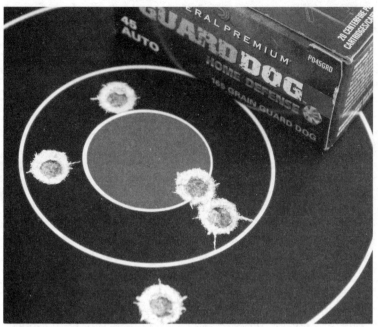

On the range, the Ruger SR45 performed flawlessly with zero malfunctions firing a mix of hollowpoint and ball ammunition.

charged and ready to fire. The two-part striker itself is primarily steel, but the rear portion that the shooter sees is actually polymer. When the trigger is depressed, you can actually see the rear of the striker retract and then fall.

Internally, as well as externally, the Ruger SR45 has multiple safety features. The ambidextrous thumb safety locks the trigger and trigger bar from any rearward movement. It clicks down to the fire position easily, but placing the thumb safety to the 'on' position requires a bit more effort. In my opinion, the thumb safety is unnecessary but meets certain state requirements and will offer many an extra peace of mind.

There is a trigger safety in the form of a tab on the face of the trigger. This tab must be depressed and rotated out of the way for the trigger to be depressed. Internally, a firing pin block works to stop the striker from moving forward unless the trigger is fully depressed. In addition, the SR45 has a magazine disconnect safety, meaning that the pistol will not fire with the magazine removed. The magazine disconnect addresses the concern that ill-trained people may assume the gun is unloaded simply because the magazine is out of the gun and not realize that there is still a round in the chamber. To the well-trained however, this feature is considered a detriment, since it renders the gun useless without the magazine.

Finally, the SR45 features a loaded chamber indicator located at the top of the slide at the rear of the chamber. When there is a cartridge case in the chamber, this indicator protrudes conspicuously, is labeled "loaded when up" all in caps, and has bright red paint on both sides. It offers immediate visual and tactile indication from either side of the pistol that there is a cartridge case in the chamber. Ruger has certainly taken every step possible to make this pistol as safe as it can be.

The magazine disconnect safety does present an interesting dilemma which I had not previously encountered. At first, it seemed odd that the trigger squeeze when dry firing felt gritty and heavy but was actually quite pleasant when live firing. I should have read the manual first, as it clearly states that the pistol should only be dry fired with an empty magazine inserted. Dry firing without the magazine in the gun increases the friction the striker experiences as it rides along the magazine disconnect safety, producing a gritty feel. Dry firing with the magazine inserted provides the proper feel for the trigger of actual live fire.

Maintenance on the SR45 is easily accomplished, and the pistol breaks down into its component parts quickly. Simply remove the magazine, ensure the pistol is unloaded, and lock the slide to the

SPECIFICATIONS
RUGER SR45

CALIBER: .45 ACP
BARREL: 4.5 in.
OA LENGTH: 8 in.
WIDTH: 1.27 in.
HEIGHT: 5.75 in.
WEIGHT: 30.15 oz.
GRIPS: Glass reinforced nylon
SIGHTS: Adjustable three-dot
ACTION: Semi-auto
FINISH: Blued
CAPACITY: 10+1
PRICE: $529
603-865-2442
WWW.RUGER.COM

rear. Next, reach into the top of the open slide and push the ejector down or the slide will not be able to go forward off the gun. Press the takedown pin on the right side of the gun and pull it out; do the same with its baseplate from the other side. Ride the slide forward and squeeze the trigger to release the striker tension, and the slide will be free to go forward off from the frame. The captive recoil spring and barrel are then easily removed from the slide for cleaning and maintenance. Assembly is in the reverse order, but make sure to return the ejector to its upward position.

On the range, the Ruger SR45 performed flawlessly with zero malfunctions experienced with a mix of hollowpoint and ball ammunition used. Recoil was extremely manageable and pleasant offhand but was more pronounced from the bench. With all of the pistol's weight located on top, and the ergonomic grip allowing for a very high hold that places the shooter's hand much more in line with the axis of the barrel, muzzle flip when shooting offhand was a non-issue, and it was easy to stay on target for faster follow-up shots. The trigger broke cleanly at a consistent 8 pounds but felt lighter than that with a medium amount of travel. The reset did require the trigger to move completely to its forward position, however.

The SR45 is unquestionably a solidly built, tough as nails, reliable handgun that is made to last and is loaded with many safety features. Its design, size, low recoil, and full power loading will certainly appeal to those interested in personal protection inside the home. Its slim profile and relatively low weight make it ideal for those who want to concealed carry a full-sized gun.

SIG SAUER P226

The SIG P226 pistol has a reputation that is the envy of just about every other handgun manufacturer on the market today. Originally designed in 1984 to compete as the replacement to the U.S. Military's 1911 pistol, the P226 was one of only two to make it to the final round of consideration. While it did not become the standard U.S. military issue sidearm, numerous units, including

Numerous military units, including the U.S. Navy Seals, have adopted the SIG P226 pistol. *Photo: SIG Sauer*

the U.S. Navy SEALs, have adopted it — and it remains a top choice for U.S. federal law enforcement.

One big advantage that hammer-fired pistols have over striker-fired ones is second-strike capability. Especially with foreign military surplus ammunition, one may occasionally encounter a recalcitrant or otherwise "hard" primer. In a survival situation, the first and correct instinct is to squeeze the trigger a second time in the hopes the round goes off before racking the slide, clearing the bad round, and loading a new one. This can be done on any double- or double/single-action pistol. It cannot be done on most striker-fired pistols. Note: immediately racking the slide on a bad cartridge is for emergencies only. You could have a hang fire, where there is a delay in the cartridge detonating. You do not want your hand over the ejection port when that happens. On the range, keep the gun pointed in a safe direction and wait 30 seconds before clearing the misfire.

As a hammer-fired double-action/single-action the SIG P226 has second-strike capability.

This full-sized, semi-automatic pistol operates with a locked breech, short recoil system and a traditional hammer-fired, double-action/single-action mechanism. The staggered column magazine provides 15+1 capacity in 9mm NATO and 12+1 capacity when chambered in either .40 S&W or .357 SIG.

Over the years, SIG has produced multiple variants of the P226 with different trigger mechanisms, compact versions, different finishes, competition and tactical models, threaded barrels, with or without accessory rails, and a choice of standard and night sights. Indeed, the P226 has something to offer every shooter.

The P226 is designed for carry and features the elements most conducive for personal protection. The steel, high profile sights are factory zeroed and include tritium inserts for clear visibility in low light conditions. The sights are dovetailed into the slide and are drift adjustable for windage. For elevation adjustments, different height sights are available, and this adjustment does require replacing the sights.

The slide is stainless steel for durability and natural corrosion resistance. On the sample pistol I received, the slide was finished in Nitron, a proprietary finish that is both extremely tough and corrosion resistant. The P226 Tribal is available in a two-tone variant with a natural stainless steel slide. This version has black tribal patterns, which stand out even more against the stainless color.

The entire length of the slide has been thoroughly dehorned with all the sharp edges and corners removed. What is left behind is a slightly melted look and feel that is far more comfortable for concealed carry with the pistol riding against your body. The one area that has been left sharp is the slide serrations, which are features at the front and rear of the slide that are well spaced with a slight forward angle. These make slide manipulation an easy matter and would likely prove very beneficial when used in inclement weather or under less than ideal conditions.

On the right side of the slide, there is a large external extractor with significant spring pressure to ensure fired cases are aggressively removed from the chamber. The extractor does not act as a loaded chamber indicator, and visual inspection of the chamber is a must for safety. To further aid in cartridge extraction and ejection, and to ensure reliable functioning, the ejection port at the top of the slide is lowered.

At the rear of the slide, the external hammer is plainly visible and can be manually operated with the serrated hammer spur to place the pistol into the single-action mode. Despite the advent of so many successful striker-fired pistols and their advantage in providing a consistent trigger

SPECIFICATIONS
SIG SAUER P226
CALIBER: 9mm NATO
BARREL: 4.4 in.
OA LENGTH: 7.7 in.
WIDTH: 1.5 in.
HEIGHT: 5.5 in.
WEIGHT: 34 oz.
GRIPS: Black aluminum
SIGHTS: SIGLITE Night Sights
ACTION: Semi-auto DA/SA
FINISH: Black Nitron
CAPACITY: 15+1
PRICE: $899
WWW.SIGSAUER.COM

The SIG P226 is designed for carry and features the elements most conducive for personal protection, including night sights. There is no external safety but several internal safeties.

squeeze, many still prefer the traditional hammer-fired comfort of a single-/double-action handgun.

The hammer helps ensure a strong, reliable strike against the firing pin and subsequently against the cartridge primer. The condition of the pistol is immediately visible, and the double-action design affords a quick second strike capability in the case of a tough primer. There is also a safety advantage. The SIG P226 does not have an external thumb safety. The safe condition for carry is with a full magazine, a cartridge in the chamber and the hammer in the down position.

The long and relatively heavier trigger squeeze, which I measured at 10.5 lbs., helps ensure that the pistol will not fire unintentionally. Subsequent shots are in the single-action mode, a much lighter 4.5 lbs., and the shorter trigger squeeze with a short reset

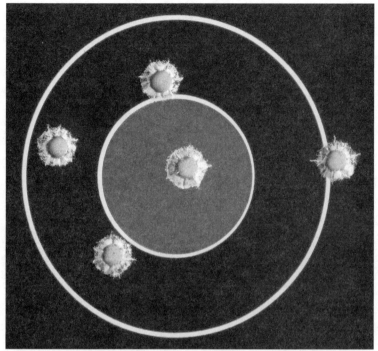

On the range the SIG P226 performed flawlessly and produced solid combat accuracy at 25 yards.

helps to improve both accuracy and speed.

The frame is a black, hard anodized aluminum alloy that helps to significantly reduce weight. The controls are all on the left side of the handgun and are set up for a right-handed shooter. The lever farthest to the rear is the slide catch, which is prominent enough to easily activate but small enough to remain unobtrusive. By being placed so far back on the frame, near where one might find the thumb safety on a different pistol, this design ensures against accidental engagement while firing when using a thumbs forward two-handed hold.

The middle lever, located in a straight line above the magazine release, is the decocker. When the pistol is in the single-action mode with the hammer in the cocked position, the decocker is the only safe and appropriate way to lower the hammer to the double action or carry mode. Attempting to manually lower the hammer by depressing the trigger and holding onto it is a very bad idea, as this deactivates the internal safety mechanism and risks an unintentional discharge.

The decocker functions in a distinct way. Unlike other decockers, which immediately and aggressively let the hammer drop, the SIG system releases the hammer on the down stroke and allows you to slowly lower it as the decocker is returned to its upward position. I personally found this to be comforting, as I once experienced a broken decocker (not on a SIG) that fired the pistol when activated, reinforcing the importance of always keeping firearms pointed in a safe direction.

The P226, however, is an extremely safe pistol. An internal firing pin block completely prevents the firing pin from any forward movement unless the trigger has been depressed. The hammer itself has a rebounding block feature that keeps it from making contact with the firing pin unless the trigger has been depressed.

The forward most lever on the frame is the takedown lever, which makes disassembly and maintenance a very simple affair. Simply remove the magazine and lock the slide to the rear. Ensuring the pistol is unloaded, rotate the takedown lever down and ride the slide assembly off of the frame. The captive, full-length, steel guide rod and barrel are then easily removed for cleaning. Re-assembly is in the reverse order.

The squared trigger guard is very well sized and easy to use with gloves. The P226 was clearly designed for duty use, for when conditions get difficult and the weather doesn't cooperate, being able to use your pistol comfortably with gloves is much appreciated. The front of the trigger guard and grip has horizontal grooves that provide excellent resistance against recoil but not much side to side retention assistance.

The steel magazine includes a flat steel baseplate and a polymer follower. It accommodates 15 rounds of 9mm NATO ammunition. Loading and firing the P226 on the range was very easy and the handling characteristics were excellent. The trigger was extremely smooth with only a slight amount of take-up and a clean, consistent break. The wide grip and weight of the steel slide kept recoil at an enjoyable minimum, while the sights were easy to acquire and produced outstanding accuracy.

Accuracy testing was conducted from a stable benchrest off of sandbags at a distance of 25 yards for three 5-shot groups using three types of ammunition. Over two days of testing, the P226 experienced zero malfunctions of any sort and was eminently reliable.

I must admit that, until I received this sample pistol from SIG, I had virtually no experience with their handguns and had some difficulty understanding their almost cult-like following. However, combining Swiss precision and German engineering has produced a handgun that is most certainly greater than the sum of its parts. There is good reason the SIG P226 is the choice of the experts from several state police agencies and the Federal Bureau of Investigation, plus special operations forces with every branch of the military.

SMITH & WESSON M&P

The M&P M2.0 represents an upgrade on S&W's duty pistol. This is a polymer framed, striker-fired pistol available in 9mm, .40 S&W and .45 ACP that has been extremely popular. In the 2.0 version, several design elements have been improved, including the trigger, grip, frame, and finish.

The M&P M2.0 features an extended and internal stainless-steel chassis. The barrel and slide are made from stainless steel and receive a corrosion resistant Armornite finish. The frame has a grip with a high angle that allows you to place your hand higher and closer to the bore axis. The advantage here is that recoil is better controlled, and the recoil impulse is rearward as opposed to upward. This helps keep the muzzle on target for faster follow-up shots.

The texturing on the grip is very aggressive, helping maintain a firm hold,

SPECIFICATIONS
SMITH & WESSON M&P 9 M2.0

CALIBER: 9mm
BARREL: 4.25 in.
OA LENGTH: 7.4 in.
WEIGHT: 24.7 oz.
GRIPS: Polymer
SIGHTS: Three dot
ACTION: Semi-auto DA/SA
FINISH: Black Armornite
CAPACITY: 17+1
PRICE: $599
800-331-0852
WWW.SMITH-WESSON.COM

The Smith & Wesson M&P M2.0 features an improved trigger, grip, frame, and finish.
Photo: Smith & Wesson

and there are four interchangeable backstrap inserts for a custom fit to your hand. The trigger has been improved and now features a lighter pull and distinctive reset. In the 9mm model, the standard magazine capacity is a pleasing 17 rounds.

SMITH & WESSON SD9 AND SD40

Smith & Wesson also offers their popular SD line in a complete beginner's kit. The SD9 and SD40 Self Defense Pistols (chambered 9mm and .40 S&W respectively) come complete with a readymade home defense kit. This includes just about everything a first time gun owner needs (minus the ammunition) for only a few dollars over the standard price and takes a lot of the headache and guesswork out of the equation.

The first purchase many first-time gun buyers make (or should) after their pistol is a suitable storage device, preferably one that allows for both security at home and on the road — one that adds fast access should the gun be needed quickly. With this consideration in mind, the Smith & Wesson Home Defense Kit includes a NanoVault 200 gun safe made by GunVault.

This compact 21-gauge steel safe is approved for interstate and

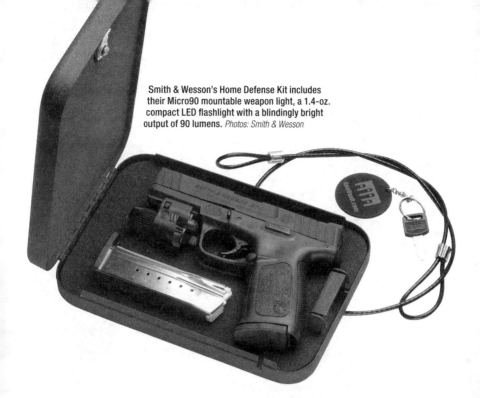

Smith & Wesson's Home Defense Kit includes their Micro90 mountable weapon light, a 1.4-oz. compact LED flashlight with a blindingly bright output of 90 lumens. *Photos: Smith & Wesson*

air travel and can easily fit inside a drawer or range bag. The vault features easy key lock operation for fast access with two keys provided and is foam-lined to protect the pistol. It includes a 1,500 lb. steel cable that allows you to secure the safe to a stationary object. Plus, it is large enough to accommodate the SD pistol with light or laser attachment and a spare magazine as well as assorted small valuables or documents.

Many new shooters may experience something of a learning curve when they first start target practice. Of course, if you add darkness, surprise, and the stress of unexpected attack, accuracy may be an issue for more than just beginners. Those interested in personal protection inside the home are going to want to be 100 percent sure of their target identification, and a good quality light source is a necessity in any defense kit. To ensure this, Smith & Wesson's Home Defense Kit comes with the company's own Micro90 mountable weapon light. This compact LED flashlight weighs only 1.4 oz. and features a blindingly bright output of 90 lumens, a lot at typical household distances and more than enough to differentiate friend from foe (and temporarily blind

The S&W SD40 is chambered in the popular .40 S&W caliber with a 14+1 capacity.

The S&W SD9 is a well-established, recoil operated, striker-fired, semi-auto ideal for concealed carry and home defense. The 9mm pistol boasts a 16+1 capacity. *Photo: Smith & Wesson*

and disorient an intruder or assailant). This light will fit most any accessory rail-equipped pistol or standard Picatinny rail, and it even includes the CR2 lithium battery you need, which provides for a full two hours of constant working time. The Micro90 features tough polymer construction with an aluminum bezel and ambidextrous on/off switches with momentary and constant on functions. The well-designed light is easily attached or removed, if you want to alternate between holstered concealed carry and home protection, and the battery can be replaced without removing the light.

Of course, the most important part of the kit is the gun, and the SD9 and SD40, in 9mm and .40 S&W caliber, are already well-established. These recoil operated, striker-fired, semi-automatic polymer pistols are proven and you can have one in two of the most popular and widely available cartridges.

They're considered double-action pistols, as the action of the slide partially charges the striker mechanism. Squeezing the trigger fully charges the striker and then releases it to fire the gun. The main advantage with striker-fired guns is that they provide a consistent trigger squeeze for every shot (between 7 and 8 lbs. in the case of the SD), which makes mastering trigger control for new shooters easier.

They both feature many standard enhancements that shooters want, including a front sight with an insert of tritium, a radioactive hydrogen isotope that emits a bright green glow and has a half-life of over 12 years. This allows for fast target acquisition in low light environments, while the steel rear sight includes two white dots. Both pistols have the same dimensions and weight, featuring a stainless steel, 4-inch barrel and slide with a black Melonite finish. Melonite is a nickel-based metallic mineral that provides extreme durability, hardness, and corrosion resistance.

The SD does not have an external mechanical safety, but it does feature many internal and passive safeties, including a trigger safety bar that prevents the trigger from being retracted unless it is fully engaged. Additionally, it has a striker block/drop safety, which prevents the firing pin from going forward and striking the primer on a live round (such as from inertia as a result of dropping the handgun) unless the trigger is squeezed.

You can visually confirm if there is a cartridge case in the chamber through a loaded chamber window located at the top of the pistol, just where the back of the chamber meets the slide. There is no magazine disconnect safety, and the gun will fire without a magazine inserted. This pistol is designed to fall in between the entry level Sigma series and the high end M&P, but many will consider it an improvement over both. In addition to its standard accessory rail, the SD features a slim and ergonomically designed grip with front and rear checkering and textured side panels as well as an 18-degree angle for natural pointability. It is smaller than the M&P grip and lacks the interchangeable grip panels, but its narrower dimensions will more comfortably accommodate shooters with smaller hands.

The frame of the SD has left and right memory pads just above the trigger guard to help remind new shooters of the importance of finger off the trigger until ready to shoot. All SD pistols come standard with two standard-capacity magazines (where allowed by law), which hold 16 rounds in the 9mm version and 14 in .40 S&W. The pistol is not compact but small enough for certain types of concealed carry for those wishing to do so, and it will fit in standard holsters designed for the Smith &Wesson M&P.

Another valuable consideration for new shooters is Smith & Wesson's lifetime warranty. A friend once asked me if these sorts of "lifetime" warranties were for the life of the pistol or of the original owner. Neither, I told him. Warranties are only

SPECIFICATIONS
SMITH & WESSON HOME DEFENSE KIT SD9 AND SD40 PISTOL

CALIBER: 9mm and .40 S&W
BARREL: 4 in. stainless steel
OA LENGTH: 7.2 in.
WIDTH: 1.29 in.
WEIGHT: 22.7 oz. (unloaded)
SIGHTS: Front Tritium, rear white dot
GRIPS: Textured polymer
ACTION: Double-action striker fired
FINISH: Melonite black
CAPACITY: 16 rounds 9mm,
   14 rounds .40 S&W
ACCESSORIES: NanoVault 200, S&W
   Micro90 compact pistol light,
   two magazines
PRICE: $499
800-331-0852
WWW.SMITH-WESSON.COM

good for the lifetime of the company that issues them, and with a company that has been in business since 1852, that is a serious guarantee.

There are many choices facing the new gun owner, and having a single kit from a name brand company like Smith & Wesson (and at reasonable cost) is a great benefit. The SD9 and SD40 Home Defense Kits provide an excellent solution for gun owners seeking a one stop source for their self-defense needs. The only thing missing from the kit is the ammunition and in that regard, there are many good options.

SPRINGFIELD ARMORY XD, XD(M) AND XD-S

The popularity of polymer-framed, striker-fired pistols has really taken off in the last several years, and few such guns are more popular than the Springfield Armory XD line, with good reason. These solid, reliable, and accurate pistols offer American shooters a high degree of value, quality, and out of the box performance, and they are available with a wide array of options.

The choices continue to expand as Springfield has in recent years introduced the outstanding XD(M) line and the brand new compact XD-S pistol. The original XD pistol is of course based on the HS2000, designed and manufactured in Croatia and now the standard issue handgun for that nation's military and police forces. Springfield Armory, recognizing the gun's potential, licensed it for sale in the U.S. and renamed it the XD, or "X-treme Duty," in 2002. Since then, it has received multiple industry awards, and XD pistols continue to be made in Croatia to Springfield's demanding standards.

The most distinctive safety feature on all XD pistols is their grip safety, which prevents it from firing unless fully depressed. Other safety features include a striker block/drop safety, which prevents the firing pin from going forward and striking the primer unless the trigger is squeezed, and a trigger safety, which blocks the trigger from any rearward movement unless the lever on the front of the trigger is depressed.

A loaded chamber indicator is located on the slide, at the top

The original Springfield XD pistol comes in many calibers and sizes. Shown here is the 9mm sub-compact OD. *Photo: Springfield Armory*

The Springfield XD Tactical offers a longer barrel for improved bullet performance and accuracy. *Photo: Springfield Armory*

of the pistol, just where the back of the chamber meets the slide. A striker status indicator is located at the rear of the slide facing the shooter and is easily seen and felt to ensure that the gun is in battery and ready to fire. There is no thumb safety, although some models have this available as an option.

All XD pistols include a very simple takedown with a lever that makes maintenance easy for all users, and they are renowned for their ergonomics and natural pointability. Hammer forged barrels improve accuracy and durability, and all metal parts feature a Melonite coating, which is a nickel-based metallic mineral that provides extreme durability, hardness, and corrosion resistance. Internally, the XD shines with a dual spring, captive guide rod recoil system and has all its critical parts solidly forged or machined from billet, including the steel inserts in the polymer frame.

Of course, all Springfield XD variants come standard with an excellent XD Gear Package, which includes a well-designed polymer belt holster, double magazine pouch, and magazine-loading tool. Both the magazine pouch and holster feature accessory rails to store flashlights, lasers, and even the magazine-loading tool. Also included are two magazines with a polished stainless steel finish, polymer base pads, and a lockable and padded plastic carrying case with cable lock.

XD SERVICE

The Service model offers the widest array of options and caliber choices including 9mm, .357 Sig, .40 S&W and .45 ACP. With a full-sized grip and 4-inch barrel, this has become the pistol by which all others are measured. It is also the only pistol in the XD line to feature

SPECIFICATIONS
SPRINGFIELD ARMORY XD SERVICE

CALIBER: 9mm, .357 Sig, .40 S&W, and .45 ACP
BARREL: 4 in.
OA LENGTH: 7.3 in.
WEIGHT: 28-30 oz. (unloaded)
SIGHTS: Dovetailed front and rear steel three-dot
GRIPS: Polymer
ACTION: Semi-auto
FINISH: Various
CAPACITY: 16 (9mm), 12 (.40 S&W and .357 Sig), 13 (.45 ACP)
PRICE: $549-$680
800-680-6866
WWW.SPRINGFIELD-ARMORY.COM

The latest version of this Croatian-made gun with several improvements is the Springfield XD(M), shown here with a 4.5-inch barrel in 9mm.

The Springfield XDS .45 ACP is designed with a single-stack magazine and very thin grip for maximum concealability.
Photos: Springfield Armory

V-10 barrel porting as an option (.40 S&W and 9mm only), which significantly helps control muzzle rise for faster follow-up shots. Interestingly, the .45 ACP model adds .25 inches in height but also has higher capacity than the .40 S&W and .357 Sig models.

SPRINGFIELD XD(M)

Springfield Armory upped the ante with their XD(M) line, which features many significant improvements over the standard XD pistol. Most notably, the XD(M) line offers all match-grade barrels and a significantly higher magazine capacity, up to 19 rounds in 9mm and 16 rounds in .40 S&W. It's available in these calibers plus .45 ACP (but not .357 Sig). A special competition model of this pistol was introduced with a longer slide than was previously available. In terms of its design, the XD(M) features a more aggressive checkering pattern and replaceable backstraps as well as improved slide serrations. These pistols are available in a wide array of finish options but do not yet include dark earth color frames. Ported barrels are also not currently an option, but night sights are. Fiber optic sights will soon be available for the full XD(M) line, not just the competition models.

XD(M)-5.25 COMPETITION SERIES

The XD(M)-5.25 Competition Series, previously available in 9mm, now comes in .45 ACP and .40 S&W. Like the original XD, this pistol is a polymer-framed, recoil-operated, double-action only, striker-fired semi-auto. The Competition Series sports a 5.25-inch long barrel, and with that comes a huge 7.25-inch sight radius. A longer sight radius allows the shooter's eye to better visually track front sight movement that can throw off your shots, thereby allowing for enhanced sight correction, hold, and accuracy. The longer barrel contributes to increased muzzle velocity and accuracy.

The steel hammer-forged match-grade barrel is factory select fit and is capable of outstanding accuracy. In .45 ACP, it is possibly the most accurate pistol I have ever tested. In fact, according to

Springfield, each barrel is hand selected and matched to an individual pistol to achieve the best fit. The gun's accuracy potential is aided greatly by the competition-ready sights.

The fully windage- and elevation-adjustable rear sight extends completely to the rear of the pistol to make maximum use of the sight radius. It is serrated to prevent any glare and blacked out to better allow your eye to focus on the front sight for much faster and clearer sight acquisition. The factory installed rear sight also sits very low on the slide, which is machined with cutouts to allow for what Springfield refers to as a "melted" look, with the rear sight sitting partially in the slide itself, not on top of it.

The excellent rear sight is paired off with a super bright interchangeable fiber optic front sight that shines like a beacon to the eye and greatly enhances the sight picture. Red is the standard color, but orange and green are included to accommodate user preference. The brightness of the front sight has to be seen to be fully appreciated and shines even in low light or overcast conditions. The sights are set to point of aim, placing the front sight directly on top of the bullseye at 25 yards.

The steel slide on the XD(M) features a smoother transition from the frame to the top of the slide than the standard XD as it narrows. It has much more aggressive slide serrations on the front and rear that are more numerous, deeper, and longer for better grasping and easier manipulation during speed drills or in adverse conditions. The slide is black Melonite coated, and the same finish is applied to all of the major metal parts for extreme durability, hardness, and corrosion resistance.

The top of the slide features a 2-inch long lightening cut that keeps the large pistol's weight at 32 ounces empty. Indeed, the gun feels

SPECIFICATIONS
SPRINGFIELD XD(M)-5.25 COMPETITION SERIES

CALIBER: .45 ACP
BARREL: 5.25 in.
OA LENGTH: 8.3 in.
WEIGHT: 32 oz. empty
GRIPS: Polymer
SIGHTS: Adjustable black rear and fiber optic front
ACTION: Semi-auto
FINISH: Black Melonite
CAPACITY: 13+1
PRICE: $795
800-680-6866
WWW.SPRINGFIELD-ARMORY.COM

much lighter than it looks, but this isn't done for comfort. Reducing the mass of the slide allows it to function quicker for faster lockup times and cycling. Moreover, reduced mass allows it to function more reliably with a wider range of ammunition. This is exactly the edge that speed shooters look for. The weight difference actually brings the Competition Series with its 5.25-inch barrel and long slide to the same weight as a 4.5-inch XD(M).

Safety features abound on the XD(M). They include a grip safety, which prevents the pistol from firing unless it is fully depressed. It prevents the slide from moving back unless it is depressed, something to keep in mind when trying to lock the action open or otherwise work the slide. Other safety features include a striker block/drop safety, which prevents the firing pin from going forward and striking the primer on a live round from inertia as a result of dropping the pistol, unless the trigger is squeezed. A standard trigger safety blocks the trigger from any rearward movement unless the lever on the front of the trigger is depressed. The trigger has a very short reset, allowing for faster follow-up shots, a darn good thing in a survival gun.

The loaded chamber indicator is located on the slide at the top of the pistol just behind the chamber. This indicator pops up if there is a cartridge case in battery, providing immediate visible and tactile confirmation. This can be especially handy in low light situations. A striker status indicator, located at the rear of the slide, is a silver colored pin that is easily seen and felt to ensure that the gun is in battery and ready to fire.

The XD's frame is already well-known for its excellent ergonomics and natural pointability, which uses the shooter's natural hand position to more easily get the gun on target. This can be especially important under stress, when you're much more likely to revert to the natural wrist angle that is ingrained in muscle memory. The XD(M) improves on this design with a modified and narrower contour that allows you to more easily reach and engage the ambidextrous magazine release with significantly less need to adjust your hand position.

The snow tire-like tread pattern that makes up the grip's serrations not only adds to its look and feel but has been specifically

The Steyr Arms C9-A1 is a synthetic polymer-framed, striker-fired semi-automatic in 9mm with 15+1 capacity. *Photo: Steyr-AUG*

The Steyr C9-A1 comfortably fits the needs for a full-size home defense pistol and a comfortable concealed carry gun. *Photo: Steyr-AUG*

designed to provide maximum multi-directional grip and control. Greater fit is achieved with the three included interchangeable backstraps to accommodate different hand sizes, shapes, and user preferences. The three-grooved Picatinny accessory rail on the frame's dust cover provides even greater versatility for installing lights or lasers.

Both the .45 ACP and .40 S&W versions of this gun are truly full-sized and, with 13+1 capacity in the former and 16+1 in the latter, the grip does indeed fill one's hand. However, compared to other high-capacity .45 ACP polymer-framed pistols, the XD(M) feels surprisingly smaller thanks to the outstanding engineering of the frame. Perhaps not ideal for the small handed, but most others should find this an easy grip to acquire.

Taking the gun off the bench for some offhand drills only made it more comfortable to shoot, and the fiber optic front sight aided greatly in speed shooting and staying on target. It should come as no surprise that the features that make this an excellent gun for competition are also extremely well suited for the needs for personal protection and home defense, although perhaps not ideally suited for concealed carry.

STEYR C9-A1

Known best for its now classic bullpup rifle, Steyr-AUG was an early developer of innovative auto-loading semi-automatic pistols. So, it is only fitting that Steyr continues to introduce new improvements in pistol design for American shooters. The newly improved Steyr Arms C9-A1 is a synthetic polymer-framed, striker-fired 9mm with 15+1 capacity. It is based on the original M9 pistol, introduced in 1999.

I teach a lot of beginners, and they all want the same thing: a gun that is good for personal protection in the home but could also fit their needs for concealed carry. Most of these first time buyers want one gun that everyone in the family can comfortably use. In this regard, the Steyr really stands out, thanks to its ergonomics and other thoughtful touches.

The most significant new feature is the dramatically improved

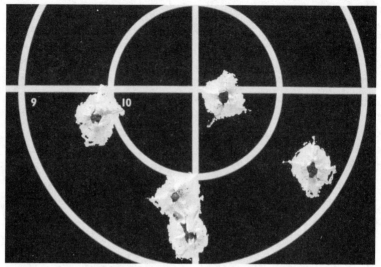

The Steyr C9-A1's 3.6-inch barrel is cold hammer forged for accuracy and features a fully supported chamber for reliable use of +P or +P+ ammunition. *Photo: Steyr-AUG*

trigger system, available only for the 9mm pistol. The redesigned Reset Action mechanism results in an incredibly smooth two-stage trigger with an extremely light first stage, allowing for prepping of the trigger, and a very crisp second stage with just the slightest amount of take-up. The trigger exhibited no over-travel and a very short reset, with a 5-lb. trigger pull that actually feels significantly lighter.

Steyr achieved this improvement over their already good trigger by using a small roller on a cross-pin that can be seen on the frame below the rear sight. This roller intersects the striker firing pin and greatly smoothes its travel, resulting in the super clean break of the trigger. However, this change does eliminate the loaded chamber indicator available in previous models, since it relied on the same pin. This may be a feature that is missed by some, but no amount of indicators could ever replace proper safe gun handling and actual inspection of the chamber.

It should also be noted that the old system prevented you from replacing the rear sights if so desired, since the bottom of the rear sight base was in contact with the old loaded chamber indicator. The new system does allow you to swap sights if night sights or a different option is desired. The sights themselves are drift-adjustable and come in the traditional three-dot patterns that American shooters are used to — two white dots in the rear and one bright red dot on the front sight. This replaces Steyr's standard triangle/trapezoid sights, which were originally designed for rapid target acquisition. However, a more recognizable sight picture will likely make for easier training and comfort.

The other significant improvement is in the grip design, and this is one area that will please a great number of shooters who have had to simply accommodate themselves to pistols that didn't quite fit their hands. Steyr has altered the grip angle for improved ergonomics and natural pointability, so that aiming follows the natural line of one's index finger to the target. A high grip angle places the web of your hand more in line with the axis of the bore, decreasing perceived recoil, maintaining better control of the gun, and reducing muzzle rise.

The grip and frame material itself is a reinforced polymer that feels stronger and harder than that found on many polymer-framed pistols. The grip shape provides a very narrow profile with a width of only 1.2 inches and will comfortably fit in a wide array of hand sizes. The grip features a deep finger groove with horizontal cuts along the front and back and effective stippling on the sides, while the frame has an enlarged trigger guard for use with gloves. The trigger guard is not straight, however, as it angles upward in the back to provide a higher grip angle. The grip narrows toward the back slightly, which further helps those with small hands to achieve a secure grip.

SPECIFICATIONS
STEYR ARMS C9-A1 PISTOL

CALIBER: 9mm
BARREL: 4-in. cold hammer forged
OA LENGTH: 7.2 in.
WEIGHT: 27.2 oz. empty
GRIPS: Reinforced polymer
SIGHTS: Three-dot
ACTION: Semi-Auto
FINISH: Black Mannox
CAPACITY: 15+1
PRICE: $649
205-655-8299
STEYRARMS.COM

Steyr is apparently not following the ambidextrous control fad, and left-handed shooters are out of luck here. All of the operational controls on the C9-A1 are set up for right-handed shooters, as is standard for most manufacturers, but they are easily accessed and activated. The slide lock is easy to use and is protected by a small frame extension to avoid unintentional engagement during firing. The frame has memory pads on both sides for the index finger of the firing hand that serve as finger-off-the-trigger reminders. A now requisite Picatinny rail graces the dust cover at the front of the frame, allowing for any of the common lights and/or lasers to be easily attached. Disassembly is simple with a push button that allows the rotation of the right-side takedown lever.

There is a noticeable opening at the back of the grip well, into which a rail is cut. This is for attaching a stock to the pistol, which is unavailable to civilians but offered for law enforcement and government agencies. Also, the pistols are currently shipping with a steel 15-round mag that features witness holes on both sides to check the number of rounds remaining. Steyr does produce a 17-round mag available for LE use and may eventually be included for civilian sales as a standard item.

The new C9-A1 comfortably fits the needs for a full-size home defense pistol and a comfortable concealed carry gun by combining elements of two very successful designs — adding to the gun's versatility. Steyr has used the frame from their full-sized duty pistol with its larger magazine capacity and improved grip and paired it with the slide and barrel from their compact model. The shorter slide makes the pistol handier, lighter, easier to conceal under clothing, and faster to draw from a holster if needed.

The slide on the C9-A1 is shorter than those found on most comparable pistols, and this aids in weight reduction, as does the slight angling at the top. However, the slide still maintains a very boxy profile. The 3.6-inch barrel is cold hammer forged for accuracy using standard rifling and features a fully supported chamber for reliable use of +P or +P+ ammunition, which is preferred by some for law enforcement and self-defense use. All metal parts have what Steyr calls its "Mannox" finish, providing an attractive and non-reflective even black finish and complete corrosion resistance to the elements. It is extremely wear and abrasion resistant for holster use. This gun is designed with several safety features, including a positive trigger safety that appears as a lever on the front of the trigger, as well as a drop safety and firing pin catch. Together, these features ensure that the pistol will not fire unless the trigger is intentionally depressed. There is a limited access lock that secures the gun so that the trigger cannot be squeezed and the pistol cannot be disassembled. The lock is the same as the disassembly button next to the takedown latch and is easy to activate. Even with the access lock engaged, the slide will still retract to allow you to check the chamber. Conveniently, Steyr ships each gun with two of the small keys.

The Steyr C9-A1 won't fill every need a gun owner may have, but it does stand out as a high-quality pistol that reliably and comfortably accommodates male and female, large-handed and small-handed shooters alike. It provides a powerful package that easily fits the role of home protection and concealed carry.

TAURUS PT92 9MM

The Brazilian firm Taurus first began producing firearms in 1941, and while it is certainly not the oldest firearms company around, it is definitely one of the best known to American shooters. One big reason for their success is the PT92 pistol, first imported to the U.S. in 1984.

Outwardly, this recoil-operated, steel-framed handgun, with its 9mm 17+1 round capacity and traditional single-/double-action hammer-fired system very much resembles the modern Beretta M9. While the PT92 is undeniably an offspring of the Beretta, Taurus has made this pistol their own. Indeed, internally it is very different.

As the story goes, in 1980, Beretta sold its Sao Paulo factory with all the machinery and equipment to Taurus, having concluded a government contract to manufacture firearms for Brazil's military. Taurus immediately began producing their own Beretta-style pistols, dubbing them the PT92 and PT99 (with adjustable sights). In doing so, Taurus kept what they felt was best about

The Brazilian-made Taurus PT92 is based on the original Beretta 92 and is made on Beretta machinery.
Photo: Taurus

the original design and improved every other aspect of it. The end result is the current Taurus 92B-17.

Like the original pistol, the 92 keeps the safety securely mounted on the frame instead of on the slide. This allows you to engage it more easily. The new version has an ambidextrous and elongated safety, making it all the easier to use with a firm click up for safe and down for fire.

The Taurus has a decocker as part of the safety, so when it is pressed all the way down the hammer safely drops from full to half cock and from single- to double-action mode. By retaining and improving the frame-mounted safety, you can select cocked-and-locked carry if so desired. The Taurus PT92 comes with steel fixed three-dot sights; the front sight is machined into the slide itself, while the rear is dovetailed into the slide and thus is drift adjustable for windage.

The large cocking serrations on the slide make slide manipulation a lot easier, especially under inclement conditions or when exposed to dirt or liquids. The open slide covers a 5-inch steel barrel with a 1:9.8 twist rate and six right-hand grooves. In order to reduce the weight of this mostly steel pistol, Taurus uses an ordnance grade aluminum alloy frame. The frame and slide have been specially designed for added safety and to help prevent any chance of cracking or failure from using overcharged ammunition.

The Taurus PT92 steel-framed pistol in 9mm features 17+1 round capacity and a traditional single-action/double-action hammer-fired system. *Photo: Taurus*

However, Taurus specifically cautions against the use of +P or +P+ ammunition.

The frame has a very familiar squared off trigger guard at the front. This feature is so common that many shooters may think it was always so, but the original Beretta had a more traditional rounded trigger guard, and it was Taurus who first changed this design feature. Another upgrade over the original Taurus PT92 is the addition of a built-in accessory rail on the dust cover that is large enough to accommodate most any tactical light or light/laser combo unit.

The front and back of the frame feature vertical slide serrations that do a good job of providing a firm hold without biting your hand with an overly aggressive checkering pattern. The rear of the frame has a well-contoured beavertail that helps properly align your shooting hand with the trigger and adds greatly to the comfortable feel of the handgun. It helps prevent hammer bite, which can happen when too high of a hold causes the hammer to "bite" the web of your hand.

The 5-inch steel barrel of the Taurus PT92 produces solid accuracy; however, Taurus specifically cautions against the use of +P or +P+ ammunition. *Photo: Taurus*

My original Taurus 92 carried checkered wood grips with a gold Taurus medallion. The current version carries a more practical and durable black rubber grip that, while perhaps not as attractive, gives the pistol an all-black, all-business demeanor. The grips feature good checkering and carry Taurus' distinct charging bull logo.

In addition to the frame-mounted safety, the PT92 has a loaded chamber indicator, which is actually the external extractor itself. With a case in the chamber, the extractor will protrude slightly and has a bright red marking on top. This provides both a visual and sensory indication (in the case of a low light situation) of a chambered round. There is no magazine disconnect safety however, and the pistol will fire with a round in the chamber and no magazine.

Taurus has added another safety feature not available on the original 92: the Taurus Security System. This can be seen as an inconspicuous round tab at the rear of the frame. With the provided special key, you can lock the action of the pistol so that the slide will not retract and the trigger cannot be depressed or the hammer cocked. Of course, the pistol should be unloaded and the chamber cleared before placing the handgun in the locked condition.

The Taurus sports a hammer drop safety in the form of a firing pin block. This bar blocks the firing pin from going forward unless the trigger is fully depressed, preventing the gun from firing from inertia (i.e. being dropped). As the trigger is depressed, a firing pin block lever raises the firing pin block so that when the hammer strikes the firing pin, it can go fully forward to fire the pistol.

The PT92 shares its progenitors' distinct action locking mechanism, which uses a separate locking block very similar to what was found in the World War II-era Walther P38. Most recoil-operated semi-auto pistols employ a block integral with the barrel that operates by causing the barrel to tip up when the slide moves rearward. With the Taurus PT92, the locking block shifts down to unlock the slide — allowing it to move rearward while the barrel remains parallel to the frame.

Other than the safety, the pistol does not have any ambidextrous controls. The steel magazine release is located in the familiar place for American shooters, right at the back of the trigger guard on the left side of the frame. The original Beretta 92 had the magazine release at the bottom rear of the frame on the left side. The steel slide release is very easy to engage with the thumb for right-handed shooters.

One of my favorite features of the Taurus 92 has always been its ease of disassembly and maintenance. Simply remove the magazine, lock the slide to the rear, rotate the takedown lever down by depressing the corresponding button on the right side of the frame, and release the slide to go forward, maintaining a firm hold. The solid steel guide rod and guide rod spring can then be removed with caution, as they are not captive.

SPECIFICATIONS
TAURUS 92B-17

CALIBER: 9mm
BARREL: 5 in.
LENGTH: 8.5 in.
HEIGHT: 5.5 in.
WIDTH: 1.6 in.
WEIGHT: 34 oz.
SIGHTS: 3-dot fixed
GRIPS: Checkered polymer
ACTION: Double action/single action
FINISH: Black
CAPACITY: 17+1 rounds
PRICE: $641
305-624-1115
WWW.TAURUSUSA.COM

You can then remove the barrel.

At 34 ounces and with an overall length of 8.5 inches, the PT92 is not going to be mistaken for a pocket pistol. This is a full-sized gun and handles like one. The grip will fill the hand of the average shooter, and those with smaller hands may have some difficulty. The attractive matte black finish has an almost satin texture and look to it, and it is evenly applied to all the metal surfaces, leaving the gun with a durable and protective coating to help prevent corrosion.

The main advantage to a full-sized gun like this one can be felt on the range. Recoil with self-defense ammunition was extremely comfortable, and using target ammunition, it was negligible. Any shooter could comfortably fire the PT92 all day and not have to worry about flinching or anticipation. The pistol functioned flawlessly right out of the box with no cleaning, maintenance, or break-in period required. I fired it over two days using a mix of ammunition, including full metal jacket and hollowpoints.

The well-rounded trigger, which has a smooth surface, was very comfortable in both double and single action with an 11-pound double-action pull and a 5-pound single-action pull. In double action, the pull remains smooth and consistent throughout its travel, and there is no stacking or over-travel. In single action, it works as a two-stage trigger with a slight amount of travel before the sear engages, and then you get a clean, crisp break.

The Taurus 92 is eminently well-suited for home defense, as well as for comfortable and fun shooting on the range. The time-proven design lends itself to outstanding reliability and good accuracy. Taurus further improved the new version of the PT92 with a 17-round magazine, replacing the old 15-round ones that were originally issued with the gun. A limited 10-round magazine version is available for those states and localities where it is required. With a variety of options (including .40 S&W, as well as a stainless steel model), there is something to satisfy most any shooter.

The Walther PPQ (Police Pistol Quick Defense) — a single-action-only polymer handgun with a double-stack magazine that's available in 9mm and .40 S&W.

WALTHER PPQ M2

The Walther PPQ (Police Pistol Quick Defense) is a single-action-only polymer striker-fired handgun with a double-stack magazine available in 9mm and .40 S&W. The original PPQ has a distinct paddle-style ambidextrous magazine release. This lever system extends along the bottom of the trigger guard from the grip and is very easy to use. However, for American shooters, Walther introduced the PPQ M2 — eliminating the paddle magazine release and replacing it with a push button release, which is not ambidextrous but is reversible.

With an eye toward police duty as well as the growing competition market, the latest iteration of the PPQ M2 sports a 5-inch barrel and 15-round capacity magazine, although a slightly extended 17-round mag is available, too. The black polymer frame features an extremely comfortable and well-fitting grip with an aggressively textured design all around that helps keep the gun firmly in hand without chafing. The pistol comes standard with three different sized backstraps to adjust the fit to your hand, and one of these includes a distinct beavertail. In addition, there is a lanyard loop for military or police use (or just for the butter fingered).

There is no manual safety and, as such, the exterior controls are

The 5-inch barrel of the PPQ M2 is an inch longer than the standard PPQ and offers you higher bullet velocities and improved accuracy.

reduced to the button magazine release and the 2-inch long slide release/catch, which is ambidextrous. There are three internal safeties designed to prevent the gun from being fired unless the trigger is depressed. This includes a firing pin block drop safety. The polymer trigger face features a release tab similar to other striker-fired pistols, providing additional safety. The front of the large trigger guard is squared off and serrated, while the front of the frame has a Picatinny accessory rail system for easy installation of tactical lights or laser units.

The steel slide and barrel are Tenifer coated. This process, technically called salt bath ferritic nitrocarburizing, provides a permanent finish that has greater resistance against friction and almost twice the corrosion resistance of stainless steel or chrome. The slide features large serrations at the rear and front for improved control when manually cycling the action, as well as an enlarged ejection port for improved extraction and reliability. The low profile, three-dot white sights are adjustable. The rear sight is windage

SPECIFICATIONS
WALTHER PPQ M2 5 INCH

CALIBER: 9mm
BARREL: 5 in.
OA LENGTH: 8.1 in.
WEIGHT: 26 oz. empty
GRIPS: Reinforced polymer
SIGHTS: Three-dot
ACTION: Semi-auto
FINISH: Black Tenifer
CAPACITY: 15+1
PRICE: $749
479-242-8500
WWW.WALTHERARMS.COM

In 9mm, recoil from the Walther PPQ M2 was negligible and the author found it was easy to stay on target during rapid-fire drills.

adjustable while the front can be adjusted for elevation by removing it and replacing it with different height posts. The top of the slide is ridged to prevent any glare from obstructing the sight picture. The PPQ M2 was designed with a loaded chamber indicator located on the right side of the slide; it appears as a bright red marking visible on the slide itself under the rear of the extractor.

The 5-inch barrel on the PPQ M2 is an inch longer than on the standard PPQ and offers you some distinct advantages. A longer barrel produces higher bullet velocities and thus more energy on target. The slide is an inch longer than standard, providing a longer sight picture and improved accuracy. To compensate for the added length, Walther put six ports on the top of the slide. These do not serve as gas ports, but rather help to reduce the pistol's weight and serve to air cool the barrel. The front of the slide under the barrel has been skeletonized to reduce weight, and the recoil spring remains the same length as that of the standard PPQ. One of the more distinct features of the pistol is its extremely well-designed trigger. As the action completely pre-charges the striker, the trigger has a very smooth and light operation. This is what Walther describes as their "quick defense" trigger. It is a two-stage trigger, although on the range it felt almost like a single stage thanks to its incredibly smooth operation. There is 0.4 inch of travel for the trigger to break at a very crisp 5.6 pounds, and a super short 0.1 inch of forward travel to achieve reset. This pistol has no second-strike capability.

Disassembly of the PPQ M2 is a bit distinct from some other pistols, but not altogether dissimilar. Simply remove the magazine, ensuring that the pistol is unloaded by visually and manually checking the chamber. Next, let the slide go forward, and keeping the pistol pointed in a safe direction, squeeze the trigger to release the striker. Release the trigger, and pull down on the frame tabs located just ahead and above the trigger. The slide and barrel assembly will immediately release and can be pushed the rest of the way forward off of the frame.

On the range, the Walther PPQ M2 performed phenomenally well. Despite the pistol's unquestionably large size, it has surprisingly thin grips a little over an inch wide. The shape and contour of the grips, as well as the texturing, fit my hand very comfortably. The longer slide and barrel are designed in such a way that the gun weighs the same as the 4-inch PPQ. In 9mm, recoil was barely noticeable, and it was easy to stay on target during rapid-fire drills. Given the weight, recoil, and grip design, this is one full-sized pistol that can be easily handled by any shooter. Even the 15-round steel magazines were easy to top off without much effort.

The PPQ M2 is being marketed for the concealed carry market in addition to police use, although I suspect that most shooters selecting this pistol for CCW will prefer the standard 4-inch barrel version rather than the 5-inch model. Still, the Walther PPQ M2 5 inch would serve extremely well for both home defense and steel competition, as the added barrel length does significantly improve bullet performance and keeps the handgun extremely controllable.

REVOLVERS

One of the earliest single-barrel repeating handguns was the revolver, so named because the cartridges were stored in a cylinder that revolved to line each cartridge up with the barrel in turn. The oldest self-contained cartridge-firing revolvers operated in single-action mode, meaning you had to manually cock the hammer for each shot in order to fire the gun. These types of single-action revolvers are still being made, but are relegated to use by collectors, history buffs, and cowboy action shooters. While they can certainly be used for self-defense (and many were used that way in the past), they are not ideal for the modern handgun user.

The modern revolver was developed more than 100 years ago and fires either in single action/double action or double-action only (if it has an internal hammer). Double action means that pulling the trigger both cocks and releases the hammer to fire the gun. This one motion does everything you need to shoot a modern

Small compact revolvers like the Taurus model 85 are very convenient for concealed carry and reliable. *Photo: Taurus*

revolver. The result is that, in operation, double-action revolvers are very simple to use. They don't have a safety latch you need to disengage before you can fire or other extraneous controls.

Simplicity is the hallmark and main advantage of the revolver for defensive use. Pushing or pulling a simple latch swings the cylinder of the revolver open, revealing the separate chambers that each hold one cartridge. To unload, tip the barrel up and press the extractor rod in the front. To load, tip the barrel down and insert the cartridges and close the cylinder. The revolver is now ready to fire. Even those with weak hands or other ailments can easily accomplish this simple operation. Since there are no other buttons or mechanisms, the revolver, now loaded, is always ready to be fired, and you don't have to worry about doing anything other than aiming the gun and squeezing the trigger. If a cartridge malfunctions in an emergency, you can just squeeze the trigger again, and the cylinder will rotate to the next cartridge and fire that one. (On the range, if a cartridge fails to fire, keep the gun pointed downrange and wait 30 seconds before proceeding.)

Revolvers can be more versatile in terms of the ammunition they can use. Since the chambers are individual, the bullet shape can be more varied. Also, each chamber is sized primarily for diameter, so it is easy to use smaller-sized cartridges that are the same caliber. The most common revolvers seen for defensive use are chambered in .357 Magnum and .38 Special. Both of these cartridges have the same diameter, but the Magnum is longer and more powerful.

If you buy a revolver chambered in .357 Magnum, you have the option of loading it with .38 Special ammunition, which is cheaper and has a lot less recoil. A revolver chambered in the more powerful cartridge will have a slightly longer cylinder and will generally be larger and heavier than one built only for .38 Special ammunition. However, the ammunition versatility enables you to switch cartridges if ammunition of one type is harder to find. The other advantage is that different people with varying sensitivities to recoil can change the ammunition used in the same gun. Be aware that, while you can load the shorter .38 Special cartridges in a revolver chambered for .357 Magnum, the inverse is not true and should never be attempted.

The Ruger GP100 is a full-size double-action/single-action revolver available in .357 Magnum/.38 Special and .44 Special. *Photo: Michael E. Cumpston*

With a revolver, you have much more versatility in grip selection. Under the grips of most revolvers is a small metal frame. The grips simply fit around this, and you can choose between a small grip, which is easier to conceal, or a larger one, which can make the gun much more comfortable (depending on your hand size) and easier to shoot.

Revolvers are much less prone to getting jammed or malfunctioning, and they can be fired through clothing (such as from inside a pocket) if necessary with much less risk of the clothing interfering with the operation of the gun. They are easier to clean, since there is no disassembly — you just open the cylinder, unload it, and clean it. Finally, in a worst-case scenario where there is a struggle and you have to fire at contact distance (meaning that the barrel of the gun is pressed against an assailant), this pressure will not stop the revolver from functioning as it will an autoloader.

Large-frame revolvers like the Smith & Wesson Model 686 are suitable for a wide range of uses, including hunting.

One of the main disadvantages to a revolver for personal protection is in its limited round capacity. Revolvers typically accommodate six rounds in the cylinder, but smaller pocket-sized revolvers may only have a capacity of five. There are larger revolvers that will fit as many as eight rounds. The other disadvantage is that revolvers are slower to reload; however, a speed strip or speed loader can expedite the process given enough practice.

One consideration that applies to concealed carry in particular involves revolvers that have an exposed hammer. An exposed hammer gives you the option of firing the gun in the standard double-action mode or in single action by manually cocking the hammer. In single-action mode, the trigger becomes much lighter to fire and has less distance to travel. This makes it easier to shoot with greater accuracy, but it is very seldom needed in a self-defense type situation. The disadvantage is that the exposed hammer can get caught on clothing if you are trying to draw it from a holster quickly when carrying concealed.

While revolvers are generally very reliable, they are not jam proof (contrary to popular perception). Jams or malfunctions can occur as a result of an ammunition issue that can lock up the cylinder and prevent it from turning. Likewise, if dirt or debris gets stuck under the cylinder extractor, the cylinder won't turn and the gun will not fire. Clearing these malfunctions requires opening the cylinder (if you can), dumping the entire contents, clearing the debris, and reloading. If you have no spare ammunition, you will need to salvage the dumped rounds that are still good. This will be time consuming. When it comes to revolvers for survival, there are many good choices today. Here are some of the best.

RUGER GP100

Ruger makes tough guns. And in a survival situation, tough is what you want. Their full-size standard double-/single-action revolver is the GP100, available in .357 Magnum/.38 Special and .44 Special with a standard capacity of six or five rounds, respectively. They can be had in different barrel lengths and in alloy or stainless steel. For survival, I would go with the model 1705 all stainless steel, chambered in .357 Magnum/.38 Special and with a 4.2-inch barrel.

SPECIFICATIONS
RUGER GP100 MODEL 1705

CALIBER: .357 Magnum/.38 Special
BARREL: 4.2 in.
OA LENGTH: 9.5 in.
WEIGHT: 40 oz. empty
GRIPS: Hogue Monogrip
SIGHTS: Adjustable
ACTION: Single action/double action
FINISH: Stainless steel
CAPACITY: 6
PRICE: $829
336-949-5200
WWW.RUGER-FIREARMS.COM

SMITH & WESSON MODEL 686 PLUS

If you look on the side of any Smith & Wesson revolver, you can see the Spanish term "Marcas Registradas," or registered trademark. The reason for this is that S&W guns were so incredibly popular in Latin America that some unscrupulous manufacturers blatantly copied and distributed them. This compliment-of-sorts was a testament to the reputation, high quality, and reliability of the company's products. This tradition for quality started in 1852, when Horace Smith and Daniel B. Wesson founded the company that bears their names, and it continues to this day in their complete line of pistols and revolvers. Smith & Wesson is, in

An excellent choice for a survival situation is the S&W Model 686 Plus, with its seven-shot cylinder. That gives you one more, "just in case." *Photos: Smith & Wesson*

fact, America's largest handgun maker and offers one of the widest selections with many outstanding features.

It is impossible in the scope of this book to cover every S&W revolver, but one excellent choice for darn near any survival situation is the Model 686 Plus. Unlike the standard six-shot 686, the Plus has a seven-shot cylinder. This revolver has among the highest build quality of any revolver, and S&W is always my first choice. It is chambered in .357 Magnum/.38 Special +P and features all stainless steel construction and adjustable sights. It has a fully supported 4.125-inch barrel and is built on the L-Frame, which is a good size for a tough, powerful revolver.

SPECIFICATIONS
S&W MODEL 686 PLUS

CALIBER: .357 Magnum/.38 Special
BARREL: 4.125 in.
OA LENGTH: 9.6 in.
WEIGHT: 39 oz. empty
GRIPS: Rubber
SIGHTS: Adjustable
ACTION: Single action/double action
FINISH: Stainless steel
CAPACITY: 7
PRICE: $849
WWW.SMITH-WESSON.COM

SMITH & WESSON J FRAME

Small frame Smith & Wesson revolvers (J-Frame) are perhaps the single most popular concealed carry revolver you can buy. While there are several styles, for pocket carry I find that the ones with a shrouded hammer work best, as there is nothing to get caught on clothing when you draw from concealment. Stick with .38 Special or (if you feel the need) .357 Magnum.

SMITH & WESSON MODEL 442

The Smith & Wesson Model 442 is a good basic five-shot small-frame revolver chambered for .38 Special and rated for +P ammunition for defensive use. With a fully enclosed internal hammer, an aluminum alloy frame for weight reduction, and a steel cylinder, it weighs only 15 ounces empty and measures just a bit over 6 inches in length. The 442 features double-action only operation for reliability and convenience, and it comes with very compact rubber boot grips that offer a firm hold and superior concealability.

SPECIFICATIONS
SMITH & WESSON MODEL 442

CALIBER: .38 Special +P
BARREL: 1.875 in.
OA LENGTH: 6.31 in.
WEIGHT: 15 oz. empty
GRIPS: Synthetic
SIGHTS: Fixed
ACTION: Double-action only
FINISH: Black
CAPACITY: 5
PRICE: $459
WWW.SMITH-WESSON.COM

SMITH & WESSON MODEL 340PD

Smith & Wesson's Model 340PD uses a unique scandium alloy frame to achieve an incredible combination of strength and weight reduction. This material is not inexpensive, but the result is the lightest weight revolver you can get that is capable of handling the .357 Magnum cartridge. Further weight reduction comes from the use of a titanium alloy cylinder and all together this five-shot compact revolver weighs a scant 11.4 ounces. I own one of these, and my wife prefers to use it as her every day carry piece because of its weight. It is indeed easy to forget you have it with you. The fully enclosed internal hammer makes drawing

The Smith & Wesson 340PD is an extremely lightweight revolver that will handle .357 Magnums but not comfortably. *Photo: Smith & Wesson*

SPECIFICATIONS
SMITH & WESSON MODEL 340PD

CALIBER: .38 Special +P/ .357 Magnum
BARREL: 1.875 in.
OA LENGTH: 6.31 in.
WEIGHT: 11.4 oz. empty
GRIPS: Synthetic
SIGHTS: HI-VIZ fiber optic green
ACTION: Double-action only
FINISH: Scandium and Titanium alloy
CAPACITY: 5
PRICE: $1,019
WWW.SMITH-WESSON.COM

it from a purse holster a very easy and snag-free affair. The front sight is a bright fiber optic that makes fast target acquisition much easier, especially under stress. Because of its light weight, firing full power .357 loads from this revolver can be brutal, and I far prefer to use .38 Special +P loads here.

TAURUS JUDGE MODEL 4510

Brazil-based Taurus is the largest revolver manufacturer in the world second only to Smith & Wesson, and they offer a wide selection ranging from super lightweight and compact revolvers to mega hunting revolvers. They are very similar in design to

The Taurus 4510, known as The Judge, shoots both .45 Colt and .410 shotshells. New defensive loads have been developed for this platform. *Photo: Taurus*

Smith & Wesson revolvers but offer a unique take as well. One gun that Taurus pioneered that has been extremely popular is The Judge, or Model 4510 — a five-shot revolver chambered in the .410 shotgun round.

The .410 provides you the advantage of multiple projectiles in one charge, as well as the ability to select the type, form, and number of projectiles. It has the added advantage that its dimensions are similar enough to the venerable .45 Long Colt that it can be chambered to fire both. This provides the versatility to fire and load multiple types of ammunition for use close up or at longer ranges as needed.

Taurus's Judge is available in various models and finishes, with both a 2.5- or 3-inch barrel and cylinders that can accept either 2.5- or 3-inch .410 shotshells. Other options include fiber optic front sights, Crimson Trace laser grips, ported barrels to help control muzzle rise, and even a length of Picatinny rail under the barrel for accessories like lights and lasers. All Judges come with Taurus' soft, recoil absorbing "ribber" grips.

It should be noted that when you fire multiple projectiles, they divide the force of the shot between them. Each one hits with only a proportional percentage of the total force. This produces less penetration than would a single projectile. The disadvantage is that there may not be enough force to penetrate sufficiently to damage vital organs. The benefit is that, at close range, you get multiple hits with one shot and avoid over-penetration, which can be of particular concern in a home defense situation.

The other issue to be aware of is that these guns feature very light rifling. Rifling gives the bullet spin, which makes a single projectile more accurate. However, the effect on a shot shell with multiple projectiles is that is causes the pattern to spin and spread wider than it would out of a smoothbore barrel, thus increasing the likelihood that some of the projectiles will miss the target altogether.

According to Taurus, the average spread of .410 shot from the short-barreled Judge is about a 2-foot circle at just 10 feet, and at 15 feet that spreads to an almost 3-foot circle. The lesson here is that with most any .410 load, the closer the better. Clearly, this round has serious limitations. Despite its versatility, it is an odd-ball round, and I never understood why The Judge was so popular. For survival, I would stick with one of their more standard revolvers in .357 Magnum.

MEGA PISTOLS

Technically, a handgun is a firearm that has no stock and is designed to be fired using one hand. This definition can accommodate a lot of things that most people would not describe as handguns, thus the mega pistol. The mega pistol is basically a rifle that has the stock removed and has a much shorter barrel. They are, generally speaking, far too large to carry discreetly or to conceal, but make for excellent home defense or vehicle guns. These pistols deliver higher-powered ammunition, greater velocity, larger magazine capacity, improved accuracy, long-range effectiveness, and ready accessorizing (sometimes all of the above).

Note: some of these pistols come with what is called an "arm brace," which looks like a stock and could be used as a stock, but it is not. The Feds have said that you can have the arm brace on your pistol and that you can shoulder it, then they changed their minds and said shouldering the arm brace was a felony, then they changed their minds again and, as of this writing, it is legal to shoulder. As an arm brace, it offers greater balance and stability to these front-heavy guns.

AMERICAN SPIRIT ARMS

A new and innovative company producing mega pistols is American Spirit Arms out of Scottsdale, Arizona. This company manufactures plenty of standard high-quality parts and accessories for your AR as well as complete rifles, and is best known for their non-reciprocating, side-charging handle designs. ASA rifles and carbines are available in multiple calibers, from the ubiquitous 5.56/.223 to the increasingly popular .308 and even 9mm. These rifles, carbines, and pistols all come with a lifetime warranty, and select models offer an accuracy guarantee as well, something you don't often see.

The ASA 7.5 Side-Charging Pistol chambered in 5.56mm NATO is based on a standard AR design but has no stock — just a buffer tube covered by a foam sleeve that can be used as a cheek rest and a short 7.5-inch barrel with a 1 in 7-inch twist rate. Its Samson Rail handguard free-floats on the barrel and is readily adaptable for installing accessory rails where you need them. There is a full-length, uninterrupted Mil-Std 1913 Picatinny rail on top for optics. ASA offers a 9mm version of this pistol with all the same features, except the included box magazine has a 25-round capacity. The 7.5-inch chromoly barrel has a 1 in 10-inch twist rate and is likewise free floating.

SPECIFICATIONS
ASA 7.5 SIDE-CHARGING PISTOL

CALIBER: 5.56x45mm
BARREL: 7.5 in. 1:7 twist
OA LENGTH: 24.5 in.
ACTION: Semi-auto
SIGHTS: Rail
FINISH: Black
CAPACITY: 30-round magazine
PRICE: $1,399.99
WWW.AMERICANSPIRITARMS.COM

The ASA 7.5 Side-Charging Pistol chambered in 5.56mm NATO is based on a standard AR design, but has no stock — just a foam sleeve-covered buffer tube. *Photo: American Spirit Arms*

Perhaps the smallest AR pistol commercially available is the Armalite M-15 6-Inch Pistol.
Photo: Armalite

ARMALITE M-15 6-INCH

Armalite is the original name in ARs. In fact, AR stands for Armalite Rifle. It is hardly a surprise that this company should continue to innovate with what is perhaps the smallest AR handgun commercially available, the M-15 6-Inch Pistol. This pistol gives up nothing in firepower or functionality to its full-sized brethren, although you will see a larger muzzle flash, even with the custom designed flash hider/compensator, and reduced velocities as a result of the short 6-inch barrel. Still, with the added folding receiver extension and included arm brace, this pistol is well balanced and folds to an extremely portable 17 inches. Note that the pistol should not be fired with the receiver extension folded. You also get a Key-Mod handguard for adding accessories, an ambidextrous charging handle and safety selector, and a crisp two-stage trigger.

SPECIFICATIONS
ARMALITE M-15 PISTOL 6 INCH

CALIBER: 5.56mm NATO
BARREL: 6 in. 1 in 7-in. twist
OA LENGTH: 17 in. folded
WEIGHT: 6 lbs.
SIGHTS: Folding
FINISH: Black
CAPACITY: 30-round magazine
PRICE: $1,999
WWW.ARMALITE.COM

ARSENAL SAM7K

Arsenal, Inc. is the exclusive U.S. distributor/manufacturer of Bulgarian Arsenal AK rifles and pistols and has a well-deserved reputation for excellent quality. A standout among their selection of AK pistols is the SAM7K Pistol. This thing features all of the usual high-quality functionality of other Arsenal AKs and comes with a high output tactical flashlight built into the polymer lower handguard for ease of use in low light conditions. (The flashlight uses two easily replaceable 3 Volt lithium CR 123 batteries.) The semi-auto pistol is chambered in the traditional 7.62x39mm and will accept any standard AK mag. Its receiver is milled from hammer-forged steel for extra strength and durability and features a 10.5-inch, chrome-lined, hammer-forged barrel, an ambidextrous safety, and a rear peep sight, as well as a rear sling swivel and side optics mount.

Arsenal, Inc. has a well-deserved reputation for excellent quality. A standout among their selection of AK pistols is the SAM7K. *Photo: Arsenal, Inc.*

SPECIFICATIONS
ARSENAL SAM7K-02

CALIBER: 7.62x39mm
BARREL: 10.5 in.
OA LENGTH: 20 in.
WEIGHT: 8 lbs.
SIGHTS: Post and peep
FINISH: Black
CAPACITY: 30-round magazine
PRICE: $1,499
WWW.ARSENALINC.COM

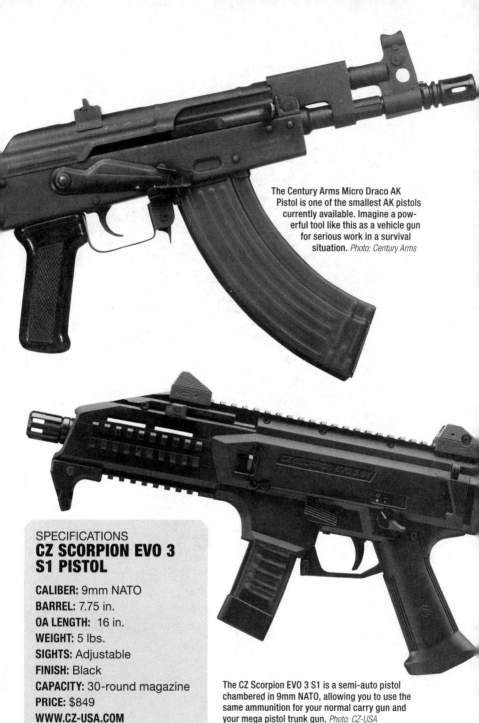

The Century Arms Micro Draco AK Pistol is one of the smallest AK pistols currently available. Imagine a powerful tool like this as a vehicle gun for serious work in a survival situation. *Photo: Century Arms*

SPECIFICATIONS
CZ SCORPION EVO 3 S1 PISTOL

CALIBER: 9mm NATO
BARREL: 7.75 in.
OA LENGTH: 16 in.
WEIGHT: 5 lbs.
SIGHTS: Adjustable
FINISH: Black
CAPACITY: 30-round magazine
PRICE: $849
WWW.CZ-USA.COM

The CZ Scorpion EVO 3 S1 is a semi-auto pistol chambered in 9mm NATO, allowing you to use the same ammunition for your normal carry gun and your mega pistol trunk gun. *Photo: CZ-USA*

172

CENTURY MICRO DRACO AK

Century Arms has a lot of experience in importing and manufacturing AK rifles and pistols. They have also displayed a great deal of innovation with some new models, including the Micro Draco AK Pistol. As the name implies, this is one of the smallest AK pistols currently available. This milled receiver semi-auto pistol is chambered in 7.62x39mm, has fixed iron sights, standard AK controls, and will accept all standard AK mags. Its short 6.25-inch barrel is topped off with an A2-style flash hider to tame muzzle blast, and due to its short length, there is no handguard, so use caution on long strings of fire. Incredibly, this pistol is only 14.5 inches in length overall and weighs less than 5 pounds.

SPECIFICATIONS
CENTURY MICRO DRACO

CALIBER: 7.62x39mm
BARREL: 6.25 in.
OA LENGTH: 14.5 in.
WEIGHT: 4.85 lbs.
SIGHTS: Fixed
FINISH: Black
CAPACITY: 30-round magazine
PRICE: $800
WWW.CENTURYARMS.COM

CZ SCORPION EVO 3 S1

The CZ Scorpion EVO 3 S1 Pistol is a semi-auto powerhouse chambered in 9mm NATO. This is one mega pistol that keeps things simple by allowing you to use the same ammunition for your normal carry gun and your mega pistol trunk gun, plus its longer 7.75-inch barrel adds extra velocity to the standard 9mm cartridge. Along the top of the receiver, there are 11 inches of Picatinny rail for installing optical magnified or red-dot sights. Standard and fully adjustable low profile diopter sights are included but can easily be removed. All of the controls are constructed from polymer and are almost entirely ambidextrous, including the magazine release, safety selector, and a reversible changing handle. The design makes this an easy gun to shoot accurately at much longer distances. The Scorpion ships with two translucent 20-round magazines, but 30-round ones are available.

INTER ORDNANCE M214 NANO

Inter Ordnance, also known as I.O. Inc., recently relocated to a new factory in Florida with a full line of U.S.-made AKs, ARs, and other products. They have possibly the smallest quad rail AK pistol available, the M214 Nano. The Nano is chambered in 7.62x39mm and will accept all standard AK magazines. The Nano's stubby, 7-inch barrel is topped off with an aggressive muzzle break, and the quad rail allows for easy optics installation to improve your chances over the standard AK sights. The stamped receiver keeps the weight down, and all the controls are standard for an AK, but the safety has an added bolt hold open device. They also make AR pistols.

SPECIFICATIONS
I.O. INC. M214 NANO

CALIBER: 7.62x39mm
BARREL: 7 in.
OA LENGTH: 17 in.
WEIGHT: 5.5 lbs.
SIGHTS: Adjustable
FINISH: Parkerized
CAPACITY: 30-round magazine
PRICE: $604.95
WWW.IOINC.US

POF P415-634 AND P308-636 AR PISTOLS

Patriot Ordnance Factory, Inc. (POF-USA) AR pistols feature a regulated short-stroke gas piston system instead of the traditional direct impingement operation. Instead of gas and carbon fouling traveling back into the receiver to actuate the bolt and bolt carrier, gas is relegated to the front portion of the gas block, and vents there after actuating an operating rod that works the action. This keeps the receiver and chamber much cleaner and operating at a lower temperature. This gas system is adjustable to compensate for extreme fouling and suppressor use while ensuring reliable operation.

POF offers two AR pistols: the P415-634 chambered in 5.56mm NATO with a 7-inch barrel, and the P308-636 chambered in 7.62 mm NATO with a 12.5-inch barrel (a real mega pistol). Both feature deeply fluted free-floating barrels, as well as an ambidextrous magazine release, safety selector, bolt catch, and safety selectors. Additional extras include drop-in single-stage triggers, KNS anti-walk pins, extended integrated trigger guards, anti-tilt buffer tubes, dual extraction chambers, and Magpul pistol grips and magazines. The upper and lower receivers are NP3 coated for added durability.

SPECIFICATIONS
POF P415-634

CALIBER: 5.56mm NATO
BARREL: 7 in.
OA LENGTH: NA
WEIGHT: NA
SIGHTS: Three-dot adjustable rail
FINISH: Black
CAPACITY: 30 rounds
PRICE: $2,129.99
WWW.POF-USA.COM

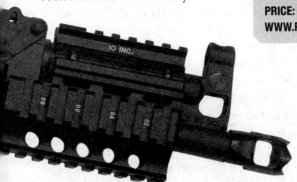

The M214 Nano from Inter Ordnance, also known as I.O. Inc., is based on the AK and chambered in 7.62x39mm. This mega pistol will accept all standard AK magazines. *Photo: I.O. Inc.*

The SIG Sauer MPX-P is a fully ambidextrous short-stroke piston system pistol in 9mm that mimics an AR in its controls and operation.
Photo: SIG Sauer

SPECIFICATIONS
SIG SAUER MPX-P

CALIBER: 9mm NATO
BARREL: 8 in.
OA LENGTH: 16.85 in.
WEIGHT: 5 lbs.
SIGHTS: Folding AR-type
FINISH: Black anodized
CAPACITY: 10/20/30
PRICE: $1,576
WWW.SIGSAUER.COMW

SIG SAUER MPX-P

SIG Sauer has been in the firearms business for over 150 years, and most of that time has been focused on producing military arms. Their pistols are a favorite among law enforcement and, in recent years, they have expanded to offer a complete line of true mega pistols as well. In the 9mm category, there is the excellent SIG Sauer MPX-P. This fully ambidextrous, semi-automatic, gas-operated, short-stroke piston system pistol with a rotating bolt is designed to mimic an AR in its controls and operation.

The pistol's upper and lower receivers are made from forged aluminum, so despite its size, it is surprisingly lightweight. The MPX is incredibly modular. With nothing but an Allen wrench, the handguard can be removed and replaced. That same Allen wrench can be used to easily and quickly remove the barrel/gas piston assembly, giving you a choice of installing a 4.5-, 6.5-, or 8-inch barrel. With the 8-inch barrel and handguard, only the A1-style flash suppressor is exposed, and there is a full 14 inches of uninterrupted Picatinny rail space on top for optics. The threaded barrel is suppressor ready.

SIG556XI RUSSIAN WITH SB15

Traditional SIG rifles combine AK-type reliability with AR-style ergonomics, and the most interesting example in the mega pistol category is the SIG556xi Russian chambered in 7.62x39 with SB15 stabilizing arm brace. This is a truly modular gas piston-operated pistol with quick change barrels, handguard, and lower receivers. The controls are completely ambidextrous, and the gas system is adjustable to compensate for fouling or suppressor use. The pistol accepts all standard AK magazines for greater versatility.

SPECIFICATIONS
SIG556XI RUSSIAN WITH SB15

CALIBER: 7.62x39mm
BARREL: 10 in.
OA LENGTH: 26.7 in.
WEIGHT: 6.3 lbs.
SIGHTS: Folding
FINISH: Black
CAPACITY: 30-round magazine
PRICE: $1,599
WWW.SIGSAUER.COM

SIG P516 PISTOL

The SIG P516 pistol is designed for those who prefer the standard AR system, but with the added improvement of a four-position adjustable short-stroke gas piston method of operation. The semi-auto pistol is chambered in 5.56mm NATO and features a 7.5-inch free-floated, nitride-treated barrel and standard controls. Also included is the SIG arm brace, which distributes the balance of the rifle and offers greater stability for one-handed shooting.

SPECIFICATIONS
SIG P516 WITH SB15

CALIBER: 5.56mm NATO
BARREL: 7.5 in.
OA LENGTH: 24 in.
WEIGHT: 6 lbs.
SIGHTS: Folding
FINISH: Black
CAPACITY: 30-round magazine
PRICE: $1,754
WWW.SIGSAUER.COM

SIG P716 PISTOL

The SIG 716P is another of a growing collection of true big-bore mega pistols. Chambered in 7.62mm NATO, this semi-automatic pistol carries a 12.5-inch free-floated barrel, adjustable short-stroke gas piston operation, and familiar AR controls. It will accept Magpul P-Mags, and the quad rail handguard and full-length Picatinny rail on top make adding optics and accessories a snap. It includes flip-up sights and the SIG Arm Brace.

SPECIFICATIONS
SIG 716P WITH SB15

CALIBER: 7.62mm NATO
BARREL: 12.5 in.
OA LENGTH: 30.2 in.
WEIGHT: 8.6 lbs.
SIGHTS: Folding
FINISH: Black
CAPACITY: 10-round magazine
PRICE: $2,252
WWW.SIGSAUER.COM

WMD BEAST

The Beast Pistol from WMD is just the thing if you're tired of all-black mega pistols. This semi-auto AR pistol has a barrel, upper and lower receiver and bolt carrier group all treated in NiB-X Nickel Boron. NiB-X Nickel Boron is a compound that is harder than chrome and has less friction, while providing extreme corrosion resistance. It can be left matte or polished smooth, and has a distinct slippery feel with no lubrication needed. This natural lubricity means it can run dry and is much easier to clean. The Beast features a Diamondhead free-floated rail handguard and an aggressive muzzle break. Its Melonite-treated barrels are available in lengths of 7, 8.5, and 10.5 inches.

SPECIFICATIONS
WMD BEAST

CALIBER: 5.56mm NATO
BARREL: 10.5 in.
OA LENGTH: 26.5 in.
WEIGHT: 5.5 lbs.
SIGHTS: Folding
FINISH: NiB-X Nickel Boron
CAPACITY: 30-round magazine
PRICE: $1,450
WWW.WMDGUNS.COM

The SIG 716P is chambered in 7.62 mm NATO with a 12.5-inch free-floated barrel, adjustable short-stroke gas piston operation, and familiar AR controls. *Photo: SIG Sauer*

RIFLES

*W*hen it comes to survival guns, the rifle is man's best friend. If you need to reach out and make contact, there is no better choice. It is accurate and powerful like no other weapon. At close ranges, it allows you to make a precision shot. At long distances, it can keep bad guys away or take down game animals. The rifle allows you to handle more powerful cartridges with comfort and ease. If I could only own one gun, it would be a rifle.

AR-15: THE ULTIMATE SURVIVAL GUN?

When it comes to survival, the best choice is a rifle that combines power, speed, accuracy, capacity and reliability, ease of use, versatility, accessories, and light weight. To me, there is only one choice: the AR rifle. Its popularity ensures the availability of plenty of spare parts for repairs. Its modularity makes it easy to repair and work on. This modularity allows the versatility to change barrels and cartridges within a certain range.

The AR is the single most versatile rifle available. It can be adapted to fire over a dozen different rifle and pistol calibers. The design makes it easy to install optics and scopes; the collapsible stock allows the length to be adjusted so different-stature shooters can comfortably use the same rifle. All of these features help explain why it is so popular.

The AR serves primarily for self-defense, used to quickly and accurately engage multiple assailants should the need arise. You could certainly use other rifles for such tasks, and I will recommend many, but the AR stands above them all. It is true that the AR may not be the best firearm to use in all defensive situations. Sometimes a shotgun or a pistol will be better suited for specific jobs. The AR is traditionally chambered in the 5.56x45mm NATO (interchangeable with the .223 Remington caliber) cartridge. Some have questioned the effectiveness of this cartridge, but the U.S. Military has been using this round as their primary rifle caliber for 60 years, through many wars and other interventions. If it were not effective, we would not still have it. As with any firearm, the weight and type of bullet can be easily changed to deliver better performance, and while not all loadings may be ideal for hunting, many are used effectively on deer, feral hogs, coyote, and other game animals.

Some have argued that a 5.56mm AR is bad for home defense because the round will over penetrate and pass through walls, endangering other occupants or neighbors. Yet Police SWAT teams are increasingly switching from 9mm submachine guns to 5.56mm ARs exactly because they penetrate less than the 9mm, especially with proper ammunition selection.

The AR is extremely weather resistant and was designed that way

The author believes the AR is the single most versatile and practical survival rifle there is, and there are many excellent models like the BCM HSP Jack Carbine here.

from the start for military use. The receiver is aluminum, the stock polymer, the barrel and bolt carrier chrome lined and phosphate finished. The rifle is not completely rust or corrosion resistant, but it is almost as close as it gets. It was designed to be lightweight at about 6.5 lbs. The carbine version is very compact and can be easily broken down into two parts for ease of transport.

When it comes to parts and accessories, manufacturers are busy producing almost anything you can imagine. It is very easy to take a 6.5-lb. AR carbine and turn it into a futuristic 11-lb. powerhouse. There are many AR manufacturers, and most of their guns are built to Mil-Spec, meaning that they have complete parts interchangeability. I will include a few full reviews below, but first I'll give a round-up of some of the popular AR manufacturers.

Note: When it comes to survival, don't try to get fancy. Many ARs are sold specifically for competition, varmint hunting, in odd calibers, or with non-standard features to appeal to select shooters. That is not what you want. You want the standard Mil-Spec AR carbine. Keep it simple. When it comes to accessories, add only what you think you really need and will actually use. Special coatings or treatments are fine and even the use of custom drop-in trigger kits is OK, as these can be easily replaced with Mil-Spec trigger kits.

AR MAKERS: A LOOK AT THE BIG PLAYERS

REMINGTON

Eliphalet Remington founded the Remington Arms Company, LLC, in Ilion, New York in 1816. It is the oldest American firearms company still in operation, and it makes both guns and ammunition. While Big Green, as they are sometimes called, is best known for producing hunting shotguns and bolt-action rifles, they are now a full participant in the AR market. This was largely a result of their joint ownership of longtime AR makers Bushmaster and DPMS. The Remington Autoloading Model R-15 was primarily intended to capture the hunting market for ARs, and their offerings in this regard change the traditional black rifle into camouflage.

Several versions of the R-15 are offered with a variety of camo patterns, collapsible or fixed stocks, 18- and 22-inch barrel configurations, and upgraded furniture from Magpul. An AAC muzzle device is an option on many models, offering flash suppression and muzzle rise compensation, plus it's ready for a quick-detach suppressor as well. Two-stage target triggers are standard, and the R-15 is available in .223, .30 Remington AR, .450 Bushmaster, and .204 Ruger. Prices range from $1,276 to $1,327 MSRP.

For big-bore hunting, Remington offers the R-25 chambered in a choice of .243 Win., 7mm-08 Remington, and .308 Winchester. It comes with a free-floated 20-inch barrel, and like all of Remington's AR offerings, no sights are included. All of their rifles are set up for use with optics. MSRP on the R-25 is $1631.

New AR models are increasingly being designed specifically for hunting, such as this new AR from Remington.

DPMS

DPMS stands for Defense Procurement Manufacturing Services, which was founded by Randy Luth in St. Cloud, Minnesota in 1985. The company originally manufactured military contract parts for the M-16 and other weapons systems. They expanded into the civilian market with parts for the AR-15 rifle, growing to make their own lower receivers and barrels. Eventually, DPMS began offering complete rifles and carbines for military, law enforcement, competitive shooters, hunters, and the commercial market, and they continue to do so today. In addition to selling complete rifles, the company manufactures a full line of parts and parts kits, upper and lower receivers, and barrel combinations for the AR enthusiast.

As one of the largest manufacturers of AR-style rifles in the U.S., DPMS is a leader in innovation and produces a very wide variety of ARs. Their tactical rifles go from restricted NFA short-barreled and full-auto weapons to Mil-Spec guns for military and police teams. Specialized ARs include a series of Tactical Precision rifles for use by dedicated marksmen and snipers.

Some AR-15 models are very economically priced and come with name brand quality like the Bushmaster Carbon 15 carbine.

On the civilian side, semi-automatic tactical rifles are offered in a variety of configurations, as well as competition rifles, precision rifles, and a full line of hunting and varmint guns. Caliber choices run the gamut and include .223 Rem/5.56mm NATO, .300 Blackout, .308 Win./7.62mm NATO, .204 Ruger, .243 Win., .260 Rem., .338 Federal, 6.5 Creedmoor, and 6.8 SPC. DPMS is well known for offering shooters solid value, and their prices range from $719 to $2,589.

BUSHMASTER

Founded in 1973 in Windham, Maine by Richard Dyke, Bushmaster Firearms quickly rose to fame (or infamy) as one of the top AR rifle makers in the world. Indeed, it seems that their reputation in this regard is second only to Colt. Both company names are inexorably tied to the AR, with the exception that Bushmaster pretty much only makes ARs. Today, the company shares its ownership with Remington and DPMS, among other firearms companies.

Bushmaster ARs have become extremely popular among law enforcement and have a reputation for durability and reliability. While government sales continue as a priority for Bushmaster, they also have a very active civilian market. Its designs include AR pistols, rifles, and carbines, as well as carbon fiber models. The company sells a complete line of parts and accessories for home rifle builders, including complete lower and upper receiver assemblies.

Bushmaster's most common offering is their XM-15 carbine, a standard Mil-Spec rifle built with quality and value in mind. Recognizing that many buyers customize their rifles, Bushmaster offers an MOE series of carbines with the most popular Magpul furniture installed. Various Cerakote models are available. Their Carbon fiber rifles with carbon upper and lower receivers are super lightweight and very economical. A line of long-range competition and precision rifles can be had, as well as big-bore hunting rifles with a variety of specialized features. Popular caliber options include 5.56mm NATO/.223 Rem, .22 LR, .308 Win/7.62mm NATO, 6.8mm Rem SPC, 7.62x39mm, and .300 AAC Blackout. Prices range from $949 to $1,508.

The Del-Ton FDE-TRX carbine is an example of a ready-to-go survival gun that comes from the factory loaded with many extra features. *Photo: Del-Ton*

DEL-TON

Del-Ton started in Elizabethtown, North Carolina as an AR parts and accessories business that has since expanded to include a full line of complete rifles. Focusing on assembling high-quality parts and materials, Del-Ton offers excellent customer service, outstanding carbines and rifles, and great value. Del-Ton has a very handy website that allows you to select the specific rifle that fits your needs, and includes a huge quantity of parts and accessories. There are complete build kits available if you want the pleasure of building your own rifle and already have a stripped lower receiver.

With excellent access to the best suppliers and parts, and with great attention to detail in their rifle builds, Del-Ton provides the option of customer-selected upgrades and parts for a truly custom rifle. All of their rifles — from the lightweight DT Sport to the DTI Evolution — share many Mil-Spec features and parts. The company offers 20 different models of carbines and full-sized rifles with standard or Magpul furniture chambered in 5.56mm and with prices ranging from $699 to $1,300.

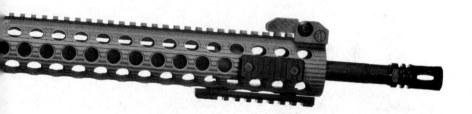

ARMALITE

Contrary to popular belief, AR does not stand for "assault rifle;" it stands for Armalite Rifle, and it is indeed this company that invented the AR. Originally incorporated in 1954, it was part of Fairchild Engine and Airplane Corporation, and used the engineering knowledge acquired from high-tech airplane construction to build the first rifle made from aluminum and composite reinforced fiberglass: the AR-10 chambered in 7.62mm NATO. This was not the final AR, but the synthesis of what would become designer Eugene Stoner's AR-15 — his magnum opus.

Armalite sold off the rights to the AR-15 to Colt, but the patents eventually ran out and now anyone can make an AR (Colt still owns the name, however). Over the years, Armalite has changed hands and locations, but today it is based in Geneseo, Illinois. Incidentally, Armalite was the first to develop a true 7.62mm NATO-chambered AR, a scaled up AR-15 renamed the AR-10B to avoid confusion with the original AR-10. The full line of AR-10B and AR-10A rifles can be had in a variety of configurations with standard or Magpul furniture and in a military sniper

Even rifles designed more for competition, like this Armalite M-15 3-Gun, are well suited for survival use.

version. These carbines and rifles are available in 7.62mm NATO, .338 Federal, .243 Win. and .260 Rem.

Moreover, the company makes a standard AR called the M-15, as well as parts and accessories and .22 LR conversion kits. The M-15s are available in a variety of configurations as rifles and carbines and chambered in 6.8 SPC, 7.62x39mm, and 5.56mm/.223 Rem. Prices range from $989 to $3,100.

STAG ARMS

The Stag Arms Company is best known for their development of left-handed ARs. In these models, the upper receiver has been mirrored so that the forward assist and ejection port are on the left side. The dust cover rotates upward, while the bolt and bolt carrier have been adjusted for left-hand ejection. When combined with an ambidextrous safety, bolt and magazine release, and charging handle, the rifle becomes fully left-handed.

I don't recommend buying a non-Mil-Spec AR for survival. Parts interchangeability could be an issue during times of scarcity. If you are left-handed, you just have to get used to a right-handed rifle. However, Stag Arms sells complete rifles and carbines in standard right-hand versions, as well as complete right- and left-hand upper receivers, standard lower receivers, parts, and accessories. The company states that they manufacture 80 percent of their parts in house with an infinite shot guarantee on their barrels. Among their available options are carbines and rifles as well as tactical and 3-Gun competition models. A varmint hunting model can be had, too, as well as a piston-operated version. Caliber choices are limited to 5.56mm NATO/.223 Rem. and 6.8 SPC. Stag Arms ARs are well made and innovative while still offering good value. Prices range from $940 to $1,500.

Stag Arms produces an emergency survival kit with emergency tools, food, first aid, and flashlight and, of course, rifle and ammo. *Photo: Stag Arms*

SMITH & WESSON

Smith & Wesson is certainly a known entity with shooters world-wide. Their real success, of course, first came with revolvers and later pistols. In 2006, though, the company took a decidedly bold step by introducing their own line of AR-style rifles, the M&P15 series. The M&P name, which stands for Military and Police, has its own provenance in Smith and Wesson lore, as it is the name of one of their most popular revolver lines.

The M&P15 rifles and carbines are available in a variety of con-figurations, including many state compliant models that account for the restrictions on certain features that some states impose. In addition to standard carbines that have gained popularity among law enforcement, the storied firm offers camouflage versions for hunting, and models with upgraded Magpul furniture. A varmint rifle is available, too. Many of the models offered feature distinct 1 in 8-inch twist rate barrels with 5R rifling. Caliber choices are limited to 5.56 NATO/.223 Rem. and .300 Whisper/.300 AAC Blackout, but in 2009, the company introduced the M&P15-22 chambered in .22 LR. In addition to complete rifles and carbines, they sell upper receivers and a full line of accessories. Prices start at $499 for the M&P15-22 and at $839 for the standard M&P15 and can rise to $1,949 for special signature models.

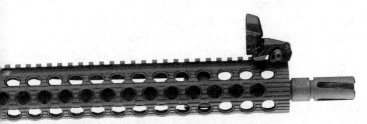

Even venerable arms companies like Smith & Wesson are now producing AR rifles like this M&P15. *Photo: Smith & Wesson*

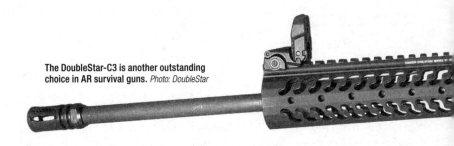

The DoubleStar-C3 is another outstanding choice in AR survival guns. *Photo: DoubleStar*

DOUBLESTAR CORP.

Based in Winchester, Kentucky, DoubleStar started as J&T Distributing, named after Jesse and Teresa Starnes who started the business, initially selling AR parts and accessories. After more than two decades, they decided to start producing their own line of complete AR rifles based on their experience in dealing with high-quality parts. Now, they have expanded by adding Ace Limited (maker of distinctive and very popular AR stocks) and the DoubleStar Training Academy to their list of companies.

DoubleStar manufactures an extensive list of AR rifles and carbines as well as their own 1911 pistol. Short-barreled rifles for law enforcement and civilian use (with the NFA paperwork) are available in 7.5-, 10.5-, 11.5- and 14.5-inch barrel lengths. Carbine ARs include a variety of color furniture options, a patrolman's carbine, and even a zombie model complete with bayonet. A super lightweight model is available.

For 3-Gun competition, DoubleStar offers a specialized 18-inch barreled rifle with top features. Full-sized rifles with 20- and 24-inch barrels are offered in camo patterns for hunting, as well as specialized precision guns. Caliber choices include 5.56mm NATO/.223 Rem., .300 Blackout, 6.5 Grendel, 6.8 SPC, and 9mm. Prices range from $979 to 1,799 at the top end.

KNIGHT'S ARMAMENT

C. Reed Knight in Titusville, Florida founded Knight's Armament Company in 1982, a firm specializing in production of the highest quality AR rifles for select military units. The company is best known for its innovative weapon systems and accessory designs, including a handguard rail interface system that simplifies the process of adding accessories and mission critical equipment to the rifle.

Most notably, Eugene Stoner, the inventor of the AR, joined the company in 1990, and he further improved and refined his original design. Stoner led the development of a new 7.62mm NATO AR named the SR-25 that was later adopted as a standard sniper rifle by the U.S. Navy SEALs. Stoner then turned his attention to improving the AR-15 and developed the SR-15, which many consider the finest of all AR variants. An improved bolt design delivers increased reliability and durability over standard ARs. Stoner stayed at Knights Armament working on rifle development until his death in 1997.

The company continues to produce accessories, parts, complete rifles, and upper receivers for the military and civilian markets. Their rifle categories include the original SR-25 in 7.62mm NATO/.308 Win. as well as the SR-15 chambered in 5.56mm NATO/.223 Rem. The only other option is the SR-30, which is chambered in the increasingly popular .300 Blackout cartridge. Prices for base rifles range between $2,200 and 2,750.

LEWIS MACHINE & TOOL COMPANY

In 1980, Karl Lewis started Lewis Machine & Tool Company, or LMT, which is now headquartered in Milan, Illinois. The company manufactures complete weapon systems and parts for the military and government agencies, including the M-16 and M203. It is best known, however, for its development of the monolithic rail platform — a one-piece upper receiver combining the usually

separate handguard and upper receiver into one unit for added strength and durability. It also includes a quick barrel change system and a free-floating barrel.

LMT incorporated this system into their LM308MWS rifle chambered in 7.62mm NATO/.308 Win. The inherent durability and versatility of the rifle as well as its outstanding accuracy led to its adoption as a standard issue designated marksman rifle

Lewis Machine & Tool Company's (LMT) LM308MWS rifle chambered in 7.62mm NATO/.308 Win. is a standard-issue designated marksman rifle for the British Army. *Photo: LMT*

by the British army. The version of this rifle available in the U.S. varies slightly from the UK one. You can purchase traditional gas impingement rifles and carbines or piston-operated ones with or without the monolithic rail platform and quick change barrel system. Different barrel lengths are available in blackened stainless or chrome-moly, as well as a complete sharpshooters weapon system. Caliber choices include 7.62mm NATO/.308 Win, 5.56mm NATO/.223 Rem, 6.8 SPC, and .300 Whisper, and prices range from $1,371 for a base rifle to $5,197 for a complete rifle system.

MOSSBERG

O.F. Mossberg & Sons is another company that surprised many when it entered the AR market. It was founded in 1919 in North Haven, Connecticut by Oscar Frederick Mossberg, a native of Sweden, and his sons. The company made a name for itself producing sporting rifles and shotguns, as well as a wide variety of outdoor equipment and sporting goods. It remains a family owned and operated business to this day; indeed, it is the longest continually run family firearms company in the U.S.

Mossberg is probably best known for manufacturing the fastest selling shotgun in history, the Mossberg 500, with over 10 million produced since its introduction in 1961. With a variety of models available, there is a version adopted for official duty use by the U.S. Military. Today, Mossberg continues to make rifles and shotguns with a well-earned reputation for quality and value.

Only very recently has Mossberg started producing an AR-type rifle called the MMR (Mossberg Modern Rifle). Two versions are currently available. The first is the MR Hunter, which comes optics-ready with no sights and a smooth aluminum handguard that leaves the 20-inch rifle barrel free floating for improved accuracy. This rifle is available in black or two different Mossy Oak camouflage patterns. The MMR Tactical carbine is available only

in black and includes a collapsible stock and a free-floated barrel with a quad rail handguard. The 16-inch barrel includes a flash hider. Both rifles have the distinct Stark SE-1 pistol grip with an internal battery compartment and extended trigger guard. Caliber choice is limited to 5.56mm NATO/.223 Rem., and the standard MSRP is $978.

ROCK RIVER ARMS

As is often the case, experience and knowledge gained in the course of career can lead the entrepreneurial to go it alone. Rock River Arms is no exception. Founded in 1996 in Colona, Illinois by brothers Mark and Chuck Larson after stints with various other firearms manufacturers, the company started out making 1911 pistols. Production of AR-type rifles and carbines soon followed, and the brothers quickly gained a reputation for quality, innovation, and value. Indeed, Rock River Arms is one of a very few AR manufacturers making left-handed models where the ejection and controls on the upper receiver are reversed.

Most notably, the Rock River Arms LAR-15 rifle was selected in 2003 after an extensive trial as the issue carbine for the Drug Enforcement Administration. Today, the company makes a full

Mossberg's MMR Hunter 5.56 Tree Stand is a factory camouflaged hunting AR. *Photo: Mossberg*

line of complete AR pistols, rifles, and carbines and is re-entering the 1911 market with a polymer-framed pistol. They sell an extensive line of parts and accessories, too, including complete upper and lower receivers. In addition to making most of their ARs in right- and left-handed versions, you can select standard direct gas impingement operation or gas piston operation.

Among the offerings, you have a wide choice of calibers, including 5.56mm NATO/.223 Rem., 7.62mm NATO/.308 Win., 6.8 SPC, .458 SOCOM, and carbines in 9mm and .40 S&W. Most recently, Rock River Arms has introduced an AR chambered for the Russian 7.62x39mm cartridge and modified to accept most standard AK magazines. Prices range from $1,010 to $1,740.

STURM, RUGER & COMPANY

It seems that no firearms company can avoid competing in the exponentially popular AR market, and Sturm, Ruger & Company is certainly no exception. Originally founded in 1949 by William B. Ruger and Alexander McCormick Sturm in Southport, Connecticut, the company's heraldic eagle logo was designed by Sturm and remained after his untimely passing. Sturm Ruger (or just plain Ruger as it is most commonly known) made a name for itself with Bill Ruger's .22-caliber pistol, which copied the looks of a German Luger.

The company's next great success was also in the rimfire market with the Ruger 10/22 rifle. Like the Mark I pistol, the 10/22 became one of the most successful rimfire guns ever made. Ruger's first modern tactical rifle was the popular Mini-14, a version of the military M-14 chambered in 5.56mm NATO/.223 Rem. Ruger has introduced and continues to produce a wide array of bolt-action, single-shot, and autoloading rifles, as well as centerfire and rimfire pistols and revolvers for hunting, target shooting, and law-enforcement use. Today, it is one of the largest firearms manufacturers in the United States.

The Ruger SR-556FB uses a short-stroke gas piston system of operation, which many feel is more reliable. *Photo: Ruger*

When Ruger decided to enter the AR market, making the same rifle as everyone else was not an option. Instead, they introduced their take on the AR, the SR-556. These rifles and carbines are available only with a two-stage gas piston system of operation, and they carry on the company's reputation for extreme durability. Variations include a standard carbine with quad rail handguards and a more economical version with a modified handguard. A varmint hunting long-barreled version is available. Caliber selection is limited to 5.56mm NATO/.223 Rem., but a separate upper receiver assembly can be had in 6.8 SPC. Prices range from $1,375 to $1,995.

SPIKES TACTICAL

Founded in 2001 in Apopka, Florida, Spike's Tactical has a reputation for building very high-quality ARs as well as innovative parts and accessories. This includes their own line of polymer 30-round magazines and the extensive use of nickel boron coating on their bolt carrier groups and other parts. NiB-X Nickel Boron is a compound that is harder than chrome (Rc70 hardness) and has less friction (similar to Teflon) while providing extreme corrosion resistance and natural lubricity.

Spike's Tactical manufactures a ST-T1 buffer that is CNC machined from solid billet aluminum bar stock and filled with tungsten powder. This eliminates the rattle of traditional metal disks used as buffer weights and provides for smooth cycling and less buffer noise. In addition, they manufacture top end quad rail handguards in different lengths and weights. The rifles that they currently offer are limited to 16-inch carbines and short-barreled rifles, including one with an integral suppressor. However, in the past the company has offered a wider variety of options with longer barrels and more custom work, which is still available on demand.

The current offerings focus on the needs of personal defense, law enforcement, and competition, and caliber choice is limited to 5.56mm NATO/.223 Rem. and .300 Blackout. Given their reputation for quality and Mil-Spec features, pricing is very competitive and ranges from $950 to $2,750.

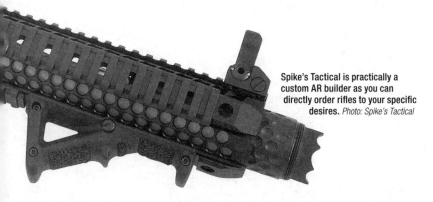

Spike's Tactical is practically a custom AR builder as you can directly order rifles to your specific desires. *Photo: Spike's Tactical*

BARRETT FIREARMS MANUFACTURING

In 1982, when Ronnie Barrett started his company in Murfreesboro, Tennessee, he had one goal in mind: build a semiautomatic rifle capable of handling the massive .50 BMG round. It is this large 10-round rifle, the M-82, for which Barrett is best known. Its adoption by the U.S. Military for long-range sniping and its appearance in feature films didn't hurt, either. Since then, Barrett has developed other rifles chambered for this heavy machine gun round.

It was only in 2007 that Barrett entered the AR market with their version of this classic gun: the REC7 (Reliability-Enhanced Carbine). This is the only AR-type rifle that the company manufactures, and it is built with the same durability and attention to detail as their .50-caliber rifles. The REC7 is a carbine-length AR with an easy front access adjustable gas piston operating system. The bolt carrier and carrier key are all one piece to prevent bolt tilt. This rifle is available complete or just as an upper receiver ready for installation in your own lower receiver. Caliber selection is limited to 5.56mm NATO/.223 Rem. or 6.8 SPC. It's a premium rifle, as is to be expected from Barrett, and the MSRP is $2,520.

AR-15 REVIEWS: A LOOK AT THE BEST SURVIVAL GUN MODELS

DPMS TAC2 AR CARBINE

With the huge and growing interest in AR rifles among competitors, hunters, and recreational shooters — yes, even survival — DPMS offers an incredibly varied catalog of options to satisfy most every AR-related desire. In the competition/tactical/recreation category, they recently introduced the TAC2 carbine, which offers many unique and welcome features.

The DPMS TAC2 is a semi-automatic AR carbine chambered for 5.56 NATO with a traditional direct gas impingement system. And it is this gas system that represents its most distinct feature. Unlike most carbines, the TAC2 has a rifle-length gas system that places the front of the gas tube only about three inches from the muzzle on the 16-inch barrel.

As the bullet passes the gas hole, excess gas is diverted back down the gas tube to put pressure on the gas key and operate the bolt, thus cycling the action. Too little gas and the action will not cycle properly, resulting in short stroking and misfeeds — or failures to eject. Too much gas and the recoil signature is increased, and you end up with more fouling and heat in the receiver, plus more wear and tear on the internal parts. The longer that the bullet is in the barrel after it passes the gas hole, the more gas is pushed back through the gas tube and back into the gas key. This is called dwell time. By lengthening the gas system and shortening the barrel, the dwell time is greatly reduced. While it is still properly timed and sufficient to reliably operate the TAC2, it is shortened to the point that the recoil signature is a much softer push. Of course, less recoil means it is easier to keep the rifle on target for faster follow-up shots, which can be very important in survival situations.

This rifle-length gas system is surrounded by the DPMS M111

1The DPMS TAC2 is a semi-automatic AR carbine chambered for 5.56 NATO with a traditional direct gas impingement system. What's unique is its rifle-length gas system.

modular handguard system. This one-piece aluminum handguard is free floated, so there is no contact with the barrel, and it features a full length of Picatinny rail on top that meets up with the flattop upper receiver for more than 18 inches of uninterrupted rail. This much rail space makes for the easy installation of more advanced optics, including night vision and thermal extenders as well as top-mounted laser units.

The modular handguard has a rounded and fairly smooth profile for comfort, and it provides multiple rail attachment locations at 45-degree angles all around, making it a simple matter to add rail extensions where you need them while leaving the rest of the handguard bare. Plus, it comes standard with one 4-inch rail section under and two shorter rails at the 6 and 9 o'clock positions for mounting lights, lasers, or a bipod.

A free-floated handguard avoids contact with the barrel and improves accuracy since it prevents the application of uneven stress. The barrel itself is made from 4140 steel, which has slightly less carbon content than Mil-Spec, but retains significant durability and corrosion resistance. The carbine's 16-inch barrel is chrome-lined and has a lightweight contour throughout, which is still significantly heavier than a pencil barrel and somewhat smaller than an AR bull barrel. The TAC2 barrel has a 1 in 9-inch twist rate, allowing it to stabilize a wider range of bullet weights, including very low weight expanding ammunition. This twist rate adequately stabilizes heavier bullet weights, too, although for the heaviest .223 ammunition, you may prefer a faster twist rate, such as 1:8 or 1:7.

The barrel is topped off with a very distinctive Panther flash suppressor that significantly reduces muzzle flash to preserve night vision. This steel muzzle device has a Mil-Spec phosphate finish and features four long ports and an aggressively scalloped front with some sharp edges. These can be effective as a glass breaker or standoff device in close quarter survival situations.

Internally, the rear of the barrel extension features M4 feed ramps that are cut wider and lower than those found on a standard AR rifle and are designed to improve reliable feeding of rounds from the magazine into the chamber. This can be especially important in carbines under less than ideal conditions where dirt, grime, and moisture can be introduced.

The bolt and bolt carrier are phosphate finished and chrome-lined, and the bolt carrier has a standard commercial contour. The gas carrier key has been properly staked, which helps to ensure that the gas key does not become loose under fire. All manufacturers will stake their gas keys in some way, but a sure sign of quality is a properly staked one that shows that a hammer and punch has been used with enough force to move sufficient metal into the carrier key screws.

Both the upper and lower receiver are manufactured from forged 7075 T6 aluminum and feature a well-applied hardcoat black anodized finish. The controls on both upper and lower receivers, dust cover, forward assist, bolt release, magazine release, charging

The TAC2 barrel has a 1 in 9-inch twist rate, which allows the barrel to stabilize a wider range of bullet weights including very low weight expanding ammunition.

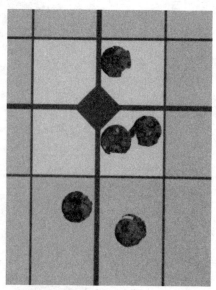

On the range the DPMS rifle performed well with not a single malfunction over several days of shooting. And that's with no maintenance performed between sessions.

handle, and safety selector are all located in the familiar places with nothing ambidextrous. The finish is excellent and has a smooth, almost satin texture. The lower receiver features very nice, deep engraving, and the fire and safe setting are marked on both sides of the receiver. The safety selector has a distinct tab on the right side of the rifle so you can visually ensure the rifle is in the fire or safe position.

DPMS has significantly upgraded the usual Mil-Spec furniture by adding the Magpul MOE polymer grip. This grip is wider than the standard one and includes a palm swell for the web of your hand, and that places your hand lower on the receiver and directly in line with the trigger. Moreover, it has internal storage space for extra batteries or spare parts and is covered in an aggressive texturing for a more ergonomic grip in inclement conditions. The buttstock has been upgraded with a six-position collapsible Magpul ACS stock. This unit allows for easy length of pull adjustments for use by differently statured individuals or when wearing heavy clothing or body armor. Its frame design and position lock prevent unintentional adjustments of your preferred length setting, and it has a significant amount of internal storage space. The ACS has a reversible quick-detach sling attachment point and a rubber buttpad for a non-slip, much more secure shoulder engagement. There is a standard sling attachment point, and the stock has extended check welds on both sides that provide internal storage space and increase comfort.

Other Magpul upgrades on the TAC2 include the polymer extended trigger guard, which is significantly more comfortable than a standard one and enlarges the area for easier use with gloves. The rear sight is the Magpul MBUIS folding sight, which is windage adjustable, deploys very quickly when needed, and folds away when not. It provides a good sight picture, although I personally prefer a larger aperture. The front sight is of the standard AR variety, adjustable for elevation. Another advantage of using a rifle-length gas system as found on the TAC2 is that it maximizes the distance between the rear and front sight, providing you a longer sight radius and making accurate shooting easier.

The TAC2 has a standard Mil-Spec single-stage trigger that broke at just over 6 lbs. with a fair amount of creep, but this is actually better than most AR triggers. Creep is the distance that the trigger moves under tension before it breaks and the gun fires. Too much creep can make it difficult to tell when the shot will break and affects precision shooting. My own preference is for a lighter and crisper trigger, like the many drop-in models available from aftermarket manufacturers like Timney or Geissele.

On the range, the rifle performed well with not a single malfunction over several days of shooting and with no maintenance performed between sessions. The rifle is a bit longer than the most compact carbine because of the Panther flash hider and ACS stock. It is a tad on the heavy side for a carbine at 8.5 lbs. empty. This is likely due to the full-length gas system and handguard. Still, it felt very well balanced and handled easily.

The extra weight and shorter dwell time noticeably reduced the perceived recoil. The 5.56mm cartridge does not have a lot of recoil normally, but with the further reduced recoil, staying on target was easier, and the rifle was a joy to shoot. For accuracy testing,

SPECIFICATIONS
DPMS TAC2 AR

CALIBER: 5.56mm NATO
BARREL: 16 in. chrome-lined 1:9 twist
OA LENGTH: 38 in. stock extended, 34.25 in. collapsed
WEIGHT: 8.5 lbs. empty
STOCK: M111 modular handguard with Magpul grip and stock
SIGHTS: Magpul MBUIS
ACTION: Semi-auto
FINISH: Black hardcoat anodized
CAPACITY: 30-round magazine
PRICE: $1,299
320-345-9223
WWW.DPMSINC.COM

I used a bench rest at 100 yards. The final results were between 1 and 2 MOA (Minute of Angle, or about 1 inch at 100 yards), which is quite good for this type of rifle. My best group, using Black Hills 60-grain V-Max, measured 1.24 inches.

I have had the opportunity to shoot many DPMS rifles over the years, and I am continually impressed with their consistent quality, innovation, and commitment to the shooter. The TAC2 is sure to please and delivers all that it promises.

WINDHAM WEAPONRY MPC AR CARBINE

Windham Weaponry, named after the town of Windham, Maine where the guns are made, may be an unfamiliar name, but it is far from a new manufacturer. The factory, machinery, owner, and most all the employees were formerly under the Bushmaster name. Now, that same experience and attention to detail are being devoted wholeheartedly to this endeavor.

I was quite eager to see how the new Windham Weaponry MPC 16 would look and perform, and I was not disappointed. The rifle is an M4-style carbine with a direct gas impingement system chambered for 5.56 NATO. The rifle's solid, proven design and features — without a lot of extra bells and whistles — lend themselves ideally for use as a survival rifle.

Both the upper and lower receiver are manufactured from forged 7075 T6 aluminum and have a hardcoat black anodized finish. The upper receiver has a flattop design with a removable carry handle and A4 dual aperture sights that are elevation and windage adjustable. There are no indexing marks on the top Picatinny rail; so, you would need to take care when removing and replacing optics in order to maintain proper zero.

The 16-inch chrome-lined barrel has an M4 profile and is made from Mil-Spec 4150 chrome-moly vanadium steel. Chrome-moly results in increased carbon content in the steel and adds significant strength and durability, both very desirable features in a duty rifle. The barrel has a fairly standard 1 in 9-inch twist rate, which does a good job of stabilizing a wide range of bullet weights, including very low weight projectiles.

Another Mil-Spec feature is the addition of M4 feed ramps at the back of the chamber. The standard threaded muzzle is topped off with a removable A2 flash hider, and the front sight base is elevation adjustable. Some folks are sticklers for properly F-marked bases on carbines; the Windham Weaponry AR is not so marked, but this is a distinction with very little real world application. Because of the difference in sight radius of a carbine over a rifle, an F-marked sight base is infinitesimally lower than a standard base. This is only an issue when using iron sights at distances past 200 yards, and it can easily be corrected by installing a taller front sight post.

The CAR black plastic handguards have double aluminum heat shields and were extremely effective at protecting the carbine-length gas tube (as well as my hand) from a hot barrel during a full day of range testing. The bolt and bolt carrier are phosphate finished and chrome-lined. The bolt carrier has a Mil-Spec M16 contour (as opposed to a cheaper commercial bolt), which is stronger and heavier to ensure longer and more reliable operation — and it's paired off with a standard carbine buffer. It should be

The Windham Weaponry MPC 16 doesn't have a lot of extra bells and whistles, which makes it a top pick of the author for a survival gun.
Photo: Windham Weaponry

SPECIFICATIONS
WINDHAM WEAPONRY MPC 16

CALIBER: 5.56mm/.223 Rem.
BARREL: 16-inch chrome-lined 1:9 twist
OA LENGTH: 36.25 in. stock extended,
  32.5 in. collapsed
WEIGHT: 6.9 lbs. empty
STOCK: M4 double heat shield
  handguards/6-position telescoping
  buttstock
SIGHTS: Removable A4 adjustable rear
  sight and A2 standard base front
ACTION: Semi-auto
FINISH: Black hardcoat anodized
CAPACITY: 30-round magazine
PRICE: $1,086
855-808-1888
WWW.WINDHAMWEAPONRY.COM

noted that Mil-Spec M-16 bolt carriers are legal to install in semi-auto rifles.

The controls on both upper and lower receivers, dust cover, forward assist, bolt release, magazine release, charging handle, and safety selector are all located in the familiar places with nothing ambidextrous. The trigger guard is the fold down aluminum type for use with gloves.

The M4-type collapsible buttstock has six positions for length of pull to adjust for shooters of varying stature or with use while wearing body armor, and it features the Windham Weaponry logo. The stock was well installed and exhibited excellent fit with very little play. Also, the fit between the upper and lower receiver was excellent with only the slightest amount of play between the two. The lower receiver comes with a standard military-type plastic pistol grip with finger grooves and a slightly flared magazine well.

The trigger is of the standard, single-stage AR variety with the

The 16-inch chrome-lined barrel on the Windham AR has an M4 profile and is made from Mil-Spec 4150 chrome-moly vanadium steel.
Photo: Windham Weaponry

typical utilitarian feel I have come to expect. Unfortunately, that means it's not great, and the trigger exhibited a fair amount of noticeable creep that felt quite gritty, but mercifully avoided any stacking or over-travel. It did break consistently at 7.5 lbs., and it should be noted that this was not developed as a sniper-grade rifle but rather as a utility survival gun. And in that regard, it should serve well.

At 6.9 pounds, this isn't the lightest AR carbine one can purchase, but it is lighter than some of the feature-laden alternatives out there, and its short overall length and excellent balance make it easy to handle and pleasant to shoot. During my entire range session, I never

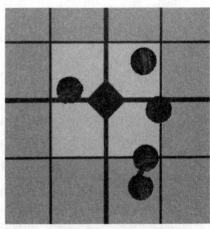

During his range sessions, the author did not experience a single malfunction of any sort from the Windham, and it performed admirably, certainly capable of 1 MOA accuracy.

experienced a single malfunction of any sort, and the rifle performed admirably. Accuracy from a bench rest at 100 yards was about what one should expect from a Mil-Spec rifle, with groups measuring from the best of the day at 1 MOA to the worst at 4 MOA and averaging in between. With the right ammunition and a better trigger, this rifle is certainly capable of pinpoint accuracy.

Windham Weaponry ships their rifles in a black hard plastic case with one 30-round magazine, a sling, and a well-illustrated operators manual. Currently, the company's offerings include state-compliant models.

THE DEL-TON .308 AR HEAVY HITTER

I have had the good fortune of testing and reviewing several AR rifles from Del-Ton over the years, and they have all had several things in common: impeccable build quality, solid accuracy, and absolute reliability. They have been traditionally chambered in 5.56mm/.223 Rem. That is, until the company decided to produce one in .308 Win/7.62x51mm.

The new Del-Ton DTI .308 rifle is the company's first big-bore AR, clearly designed for hunters. It is a fact that the latest trend in AR rifles is toward ones chambered in the powerful .308 Win. (or 7.62 NATO) round. However, the .308 AR has not been embraced by the military, and as a result, there is no such thing as a Mil-Spec .308 AR like there is for the .223 variety. The result can be a mishmash of different designs with non-interchangeable parts, but the industry does seem at least to have settled on some basics. Del-Ton's DTI .308 thankfully fits firmly within these unofficial standards. With a few exceptions, the vast majority of ARs chambered in .308 Win. will accept a standard magazine, with the most popular being produced by Magpul and Lancer.

Parts interchangeability is also a priority, and the DTI .308 will accept many parts that fit the standard and plentiful .223 ARs, such as the buffer tube, stock, grips, trigger, and safety. This rifle follows the "common" pattern of the Gen I DPMS .308 ARs for which several manufacturers now produce aftermarket parts such as handguards.

The Del-Ton DTI .308 rifle is the company's first foray into the big-bore AR market. It's a heavy hitter that appeals to hunters, but has obvious survival gun application.

Like most AR owners, I like to try to use my rifle as much as possible, including for hunting. ARs, despite the way they are portrayed in the media, are gaining more and more popularity as hunting guns thanks to their versatility and ease of use, as well as their accuracy. This just happens to make them ideal all-around survival guns. Unfortunately, in some states such as Virginia where I live, a larger caliber than .223 is required for big game hunting, which includes deer. Del-Ton fielded enough calls for a .308 AR specifically for hunting deer, hogs, and bear that they decided to follow through. The new rifle maintains clean lines and a basic design with features to appeal to hunters, such as a short overall length and low weight for its class, making it easy to lug to your stand.

The DTI .308 is a carbine-length AR with a direct gas impingement system. The 16-inch chrome-moly vanadium barrel features a heavy profile and a 1 in 10-inch twist rate, preferred for the widest variety of bullet weights. It has a carbine-length gas system. The muzzle is threaded and topped with an A2-style

Parts interchangeability is a priority and the DTI .308 will accept many parts that fit the standard and plentiful .223 ARs, such as the buffer tube, stocks, grips, triggers and safety. *Photo: DTI*

flash hider that can be removed and replaced with a different style muzzle device or a direct thread suppressor (which are also gaining popularity among hunters).

The barrel features a durable and weather resistant manganese phosphate finish, including under the front sight base/gas block (which sometimes gets overlooked on less professional builds). The elevation-adjustable A-frame front sight is standard for an AR and includes a sling swivel and a bayonet lug (just in case). At the rear of the barrel, Del-Ton made sure to include M4 feed ramps to improve reliability and feeding.

Del-Ton has done a smart thing with this rifle's handguards: instead of a heavy and unnecessary tactical quad rail, they have plain circular aluminum handguards with an aggressively knurled texture. These allow the barrel to remain free floating, which improves accuracy, while the basic design keeps the rifle's weight down to a minimum. The texture helps keep the rifle firmly in the hand even under inclement conditions. Frankly, you don't want to add a bunch of unnecessary accessories to a hunting rifle regardless, although the DTI .308 is amenable to customizing for a more tactical use.

The gun's forged 7075 T6 aluminum upper receiver is of a flat-top design with Picatinny rail. As .308 upper receivers are longer than those on the .223 you get almost a full 7 inches of rail to comfortably mount an optic. The rifle does not include backup rear sights, but these can easily be installed. The charging handle is robust and easy to operate even with an optic mounted, and the upper receiver includes a fully functional forward assist (which some hunters prefer for a quieter chambering), as well as a steel dust cover to keep dirt and debris out of the action when in the field. Both the upper and lower receivers are hardcoat anodized in a smooth and consistent black.

The lower receiver, likewise forged from Mil-Spec aluminum, has an enlarged integral trigger guard that makes gloved use (especially on those cold mornings) much easier. The beveled magazine well makes for easy magazine changes if needed, and the rifle features all the standard right-handed controls common to all ARs, including the magazine release, bolt catch, and safety selector. Incidentally, the safety selector is not ambidextrous (although one could be easily installed) but it does have "safe" and "fire" markings on both sides for easy status identification.

The furniture on the DTI .308 is very much Mil-Spec with an A2 grip and M4 buttstock. These are functional, but with so many high quality and frankly more comfortable aftermarket grips and stocks available, it is one of the few upgrades that I would make. Fortunately, the buffer tube is standard Mil-Spec diameter for a .223 rifle and will readily accept any stock designed for an AR-15. It comes with a heavy H buffer to compensate for the heavier recoil and bolt carrier needed.

The bolt carrier itself is made from durable, phosphate-finished 8620 steel with a 9310 steel bolt. Both have been heat-treated and plated, and the carrier interior is chrome lined for durability and corrosion resistance. The carrier key is chrome lined, too, and secured with grade 8 screws that have been staked and sealed.

The Mil-Spec single-stage trigger is not bad as far as such triggers go, and it broke at 6 pounds with quite a bit of travel. This is fine for a survival rifle, but for hunting and more precision shooting, I prefer a crisper and lighter trigger. Fortunately, the rifle's design allows for the use of any of a number of drop-in trigger assemblies that offer a lighter trigger and/or a two-stage design preferred by many hunters — one upgrade that is well worth the investment in terms of more comfortable shooting and improved accuracy.

On the range, the Del-Ton DTI .308 was light, short, and easy to handle. At only 8 pounds empty, it's an impressively lightweight .308 AR. You certainly notice the difference in recoil between this and a standard .223 AR, and the rifle requires a more aggressive forward leaning stance in order to keep your balance during rapid fire drills. The recoil is not at all uncomfortable, however, or difficult to manage.

I tested the Del-Ton .308 right out of the box with no maintenance performed over two days of shooting. I did experience two failures to eject during this process, but that is typical and acceptable within any break-in period and while running a rifle dry. Most direct gas impingement ARs far prefer to run with a good supply of lubricant on the bolt and bolt carrier. This is especially the case with ARs chambered in .308, in my experience.

SPECIFICATIONS
DEL-TON DTI 308

CALIBER: .308 Win.
BARREL: 16-inch chrome-moly vanadium. 1:10 twist
OA LENGTH: 37.25 in. stock extended, 34 in. collapsed
WEIGHT: 8 lbs. empty
STOCK: M4 stock and free-float handguard
SIGHTS: A2 front and rail
ACTION: Semi-auto
FINISH: Black hardcoat anodized
CAPACITY: 20-round magazine
PRICE: $947.62
910-645-2172
WWW.DEL-TON.COM

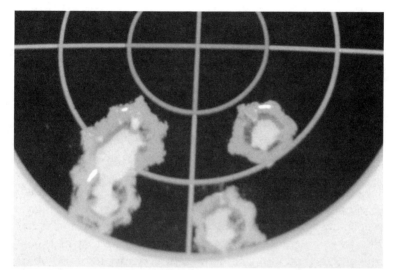

The average five-shot group size across all types of ammunition tested in the DTI .308 was sub 2 MOA — very good for a .308 carbine of this type.

For accuracy testing, I fired the DTI .308 from a sturdy bench rest. The average five-shot group size across all types of ammunition was sub 2-MOA, which is very good for a .308 carbine of this type. The rifle did exhibit a slight preference for the lighter 155-grain ammunition with my best group measuring 1.16 inches. Match-grade ammunition is typically not recommended for hunting, and my preferred hunting load, the Federal Fusion 180-grain soft point, still averaged just over 2 MOA. Given that most of my deer hunting in the heavy woods of the Shenandoah Valley takes place between 50 and 75 yards, the group sizes would be more than adequate. It should be noted that the heavier bullets produce lower velocities overall, but the difference is less than 200 fps — not enough to make a terminal difference.

As a dedicated hunting rifle, the DTI .308 has much to recommend it, not least of which is that Del-Ton has succeeded in keeping the retail price below $1,000, which is not an easy thing to do for a .308-chambered AR. The rifle comes ready for use with a Magpul 20-round magazine. The only thing you need to change is a preferred optic and any upgrades such as trigger and stock, which are minimal and easy to install. The Del-Ton DTI .308 is an outstanding American made rifle with a lifetime warranty for the original purchaser.

AK RIFLES

The AK and all of its variants have the distinction of being the most prolific firearm ever produced. Worldwide, it is estimated that more than 100 million AK rifles have been made. The AK-47 and the AKM (Modernized) remain the most popular and well-recognized rifles in world history for good reason. The design is simple and robust. It can be mass-produced quickly and at low cost. Its ergonomics may be lacking, but the simplicity of its controls and method of operation make it very easy to quickly train new shooters in its use. It is compact, lightweight, powerful, and incredibly reliable even in the worst conditions. News photos of combat zones routinely show AKs with broken or missing stocks, missing dust covers, taped-together parts, rusted and filthy, yet still functional. In other words, it's already proven itself as a very good survival gun.

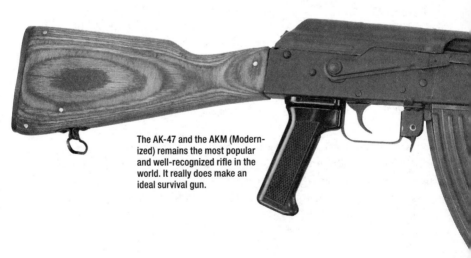

The AK-47 and the AKM (Modernized) remains the most popular and well-recognized rifle in the world. It really does make an ideal survival gun.

AKs have become very popular in the U.S., so there are plenty of aftermarket accessories here that can improve the rifle's ergonomics, transportability, accuracy, and comfort. Be aware that there are many AK variants and that parts interchangeability will be very high but not necessarily 100 percent. The two biggest differences are between rifles with a stamped steel receiver and those with a milled receiver. However, the parts most important to keeping the rifle running (bolts, firing pins, and trigger groups) are interchangeable or can be readily adapted to be interchangeable.

AKs are typically found in their original 7.62x39mm chambering, but starting in the 1970s, the Russians adopted the 5.45×39mm round, so these can be found in the U.S. as well. In addition, after some Eastern European countries joined NATO, they switched their AKs to fire the 5.56mm NATO round, so these are now mixed in domestically. The problem is that the AK was never designed to fire a straight-walled case like 5.56mm, so malfunctions are possible. The advantage to having a 5.56 AK is that you get the AK toughness in a much more common cartridge that will be easier to find in a survival situation. My personal preference is to stick with the rifle's original caliber and simply stock enough ammunition.

I.O. INC. AK SPORTER RIFLE

Increasingly, domestic manufacturers are making AKs wholly out of U.S.-made parts. Thanks to I.O. Inc. (also known as Inter Ordnance), you can now own an American-made variant of this famed rifle, the AK Sporter. This long-stroke piston system rifle is chambered in the traditional 7.62x39mm, and its construction and design are based directly on Polish AKM blueprints, complete with a stamped steel receiver.

I.O. Inc.'s AK Sporter carries a 16.25-inch barrel with a chrome-lined bore and chamber. The gas cylinder and bolt support rod are chrome-lined, too, for long-term durability and corrosion resistance. The barrel is topped off with a removable slanted muzzle brake, a simple design that forces some of the escaping gas from the barrel up and to the right to counter the effect of recoil. This was originally intended to aid full-auto fire, and in a semi-auto rifle, most shooters will not notice any difference. The muzzle brake provides no flash suppression, however, and if preferred, it

I.O. Inc.'s AK Sporter features a 16.25-inch barrel with a chrome-lined bore and chamber. Shown here is the M214 AK.
Photo: I.O. Inc.

can be easily replaced with one of several aftermarket products. Under the barrel is the removable cleaning rod, which conveniently locks into place.

The Sporter comes with several upgrades over the traditional AK, including a tough polymer handguard with a built-in accessory rail at the bottom. This Picatinny rail provides 4 inches of space for mounting vertical foregrips, lights, lasers, or a bipod if so desired. It avoids sharp edges, so it remains comfortable in your support hand. On either side of the handguard toward the front there are small mounting holes where you can attach one or both of the included 1.75-inch lengths of accessory rails. The polymer pistol grip has been enlarged over the standard cold war era design and includes a finger groove to help fill your hand for better control of the rifle and to improve ergonomics and comfort. They've redesigned the buttstock with a distinct taper and a soft rubber buttpad — reminiscent of a sniper stock. The stock remains compact with a 13.5-inch length of pull that will comfortably accommodate most

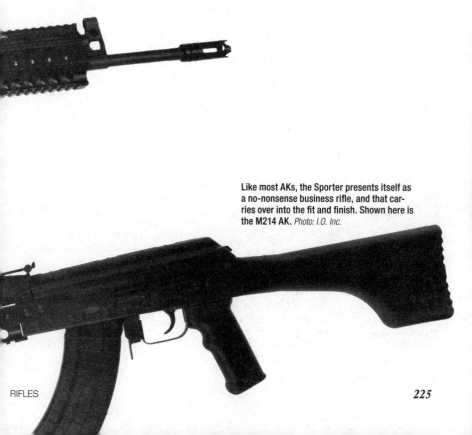

Like most AKs, the Sporter presents itself as a no-nonsense business rifle, and that carries over into the fit and finish. Shown here is the M214 AK. *Photo: I.O. Inc.*

shooters and features a left-side sling attachment point.

The iron sights on the Sporter are like those found on most AK variants: utilitarian and of the notch and post variety. Offering about 13 inches of sight radius, the front sight is adjustable slightly for windage and elevation, while the rear leaf sight has elevation adjustments out to an optimistic 1,000 meters. The sights are on the small side but are easily acquired. Mounting optics or accessories on AK-type guns has always been an issue that various aftermarket manufacturers have sought to ameliorate with a variety of rail-equipped forends and upper handguards. The Sporter has a left-side steel CNC machined scope mount, and I.O. Inc. produces a suitable aluminum scope mount that is sold separately. I received this mount on the sample rifle provided, and it proved sturdy and dependable during a full shooting session. It provided 4.5 inches of usable Picatinny rail on top for mounting optics such as red-dot and holographic weapon sights, but it was too high to make use of the irons for co-witnessing. However, the I.O. Inc. side rail mount does have a quick detach feature, should the iron sights be needed.

For accuracy testing the I.O. Inc. Sporter, the author fired at 100 yards from a bench using a sandbag rest. His best group measured just over 2 inches.

Like most AKs, the Sporter presents itself as a no-nonsense business rifle, and that carries over into its fit and finish. The entire rifle has a tough, flat black Parkerized finish that is evenly applied with a slightly textured feel to it. I found it attractive, and it matched up well with the black polymer furniture. Like most AK variants, the Sporter boasts somewhat loose tolerances in its fit, and there is a small amount of play, especially in the receiver cover and upper handguard/gas tube. Loose tolerances are one of the AK's benefits, which allow it to function reliably in all types of conditions and with little or no maintenance. I.O. Inc, includes one of their own high-quality magazines that will fit in all 7.62x39mm AK variants. These are made in the style of the Bulgarian waffle pattern mags from a high strength polymer like that found on the receivers of various handgun manufacturers. The waffle pattern affords a firm, slip-resistant grip, and the all-polymer construction is not only strong, but also corrosion, scratch, and weather resistant (far more so than steel magazines). These 30-round mags use a steel spring for reliable feeding and are available in flat black, desert brown, and clear. The clear polymer mags offer the added benefit of providing a constant round count, letting you know when it's time to replace magazines before running dry. On the range, they rocked into place easily and provided reliable functioning for a full day of shooting.

In handling, the Sporter is similarly sized to a carbine AR and handles well, albeit a bit front heavy in its balance. The recoil of the 7.62x39mm round is not much more than that of the 5.56 NATO to which many are accustomed. Ballistically, the 7.62x39mm round is similar to a .30-30 Winchester and is deemed effective for hunting deer. Reportedly, its effective combat range extends to 300 meters. In firing offhand as well as from a bench rest it was easy to stay on target shot after shot.

A full day of range testing produced no failures to feed or eject; however, there was a slight sear disconnect issue when firing from the bench rest only. Off the bench the rifle had a tendency to double fire, making my accuracy testing impossible. I contacted I.O. Inc., and they immediately sent a replacement rifle that did not have these issues. The trigger was of the standard AK variety, with a single-stage 3.5-lb. pull and slightly less than half an inch of travel. That is

SPECIFICATIONS
I.O. INC. AK SPORTER RIFLE

CALIBER: 7.62x39mm
BARREL: 16.25 in. 1:10 RH twist
OA LENGTH: 36 in.
WEIGHT: 6.5 lbs. empty
STOCK: Black polymer
SIGHTS: Iron adjustable
ACTION: Semi-auto
FINISH: Black Parkerized
CAPACITY: 30+1
PRICE: $575.95
866-882-1479
WWW.IOINC.US

a lot of travel for a single-stage trigger, and it was difficult to tell when the trigger would break, making the shooting fundamentals of breath control and follow through all that more important. In addition, there was a slight amount of trigger slap — where the trigger bounces forward suddenly after firing, hitting your trigger finger as a result of the hammer interaction with the disconnector. A brief break-in period largely resolved this issue however, and it did not affect the function of the rifle in any way.

For accuracy testing, I fired at 100 yards from a bench using a sandbag rest and an I.O. Inc.-supplied 3-9x40 Rubber Armored Scope. I shot several different types of U.S. commercial ammunition, and the end result in terms of accuracy was on par with Warsaw Pact expectations. My best group measured just over 2 inches with the average group overall closer to 3 MOA. This is acceptable combat accuracy, especially at closer ranges.

CENTURY ARMS YUGO M70AB2 FOLDING STOCK RIFLE

Century Arms probably makes and imports more AK rifles and handguns than anyone else in the market today. Pick up an AK at a gun shop or range, and chances are it was made by Century. The M70AB2 rifle, produced by Century International Arms with original and U.S. parts, is a faithful reproduction of the AK variant made in the former Yugoslavia.

Century's M70AB2 is chambered in 7.62x39mm with a rotating bolt, and it fires from a detachable 30-round box magazine. This particular model comes standard with an under-folding metal stock and a synthetic pistol grip and handguard. Several other variants of this rifle are available.

As the M70 was designed to be able to fire rifle grenades (using blank ammunition), it had to be able to withstand a great deal of increased pressure. The stamped steel receiver on the rifle is actually based on an RPK receiver. At 1.5mm, it is thicker than the standard AK receiver and includes a distinctly bulged front trunnion. The RPK is the designated squad automatic weapon for many nations and is basically a long-barreled AK with a bipod

Century Arms' M70AB2 rifle is a long-stroke gas piston AK chambered in 7.62x39mm. This particular model comes standard with an under-folding metal stock.

and larger magazine capacity.

In order to achieve maximum pressure from blank cartridges and increase range for the rifle grenades, there is a gas cutoff device. That device, which looks like a lever, is located at the front of the gas system and above the handguard. It rotates upward to prevent gas from entering the piston area. It directs all gas pressure forward out of the barrel. Conveniently, it also doubles as a sighting device, in combination with the front sight, for the rifle grenades (not included) and is graded from 50 to 240 meters. Plus, a grenade launcher attachment is included and attaches to the threaded barrel by simply replacing the slanted muzzle brake. It is certainly possible to fire standard ammunition with the gas shutoff in place, but don't expect the action to cycle. Needless to say, firing rifle grenades produces a lot of additional pressure inside the receiver — enough to blow off the steel receiver dust cover on top of the rifle. To prevent this, the engineers at Zastava added another thoughtful feature: a plunger at the rear of the receiver that locks the takedown tab on the rear recoil spring assembly in place. This tab holds the receiver cover in place, too. In order to remove the cover and disassemble the rifle, the plunger must be depressed. This applies to reassembly of the rifle.

Another distinct feature on the M70 is its elongated handguard with three cooling slots instead of the usual two. This addresses one of the drawbacks of the AK design, which is that the standard short handguards don't do a very good job of protecting your support hand from barrel heat under sustained fire. A longer handguard offers you greater purchase area and better protection.

The Yugoslavians seemed to be ahead of the curve in considering the needs of troops in low light combat situations. The steel front and rear sights have a secondary flip-up option that features phosphorous or tritium inserts to aid in aiming. These inserts are long gone, but enterprising individuals should have little trouble painting new phosphorous into the sight indentations if so desired. Like most AKs, the rear sight is adjustable for elevation from zero to an optimistic 1,000 meters.

Note that unlike many other AK rifles, the M70AB2 does not have an optics rail interface mounted on the left side of the receiver. Likely, this is because it would interfere with the metal under-folding stock. If you wish to mount an optic on this rifle, consider one of the many aftermarket rail mounts available that replace the top handguard or the rear sight. Using a rail adapter that replaces the receiver cover may require some fitting, as there is a slight cutout for the plunger that secures it at the rear.

The typical AK, like many modern military rifles, has a chrome-lined barrel to prevent corrosion and fouling. The Yugoslavians (for unknown reasons possibly related to lowering production costs) decided not to chrome line the barrels on their AKs.

In testing, the author appreciated the M70's original under-folding metal stock, which reduced the rifle's overall length to less than 26 inches.

Likewise, the Century M70 does not have a chrome-lined barrel. With modern ammunition and proper maintenance, though, this is not an issue, and the Yugoslavians certainly did not seem to have any trouble using M70 rifles on each other during their civil war. Moreover, while the AK is not known for its accuracy, the chromeless barrel on the M70 should in theory produce better results downrange. The bolt and bolt carrier are chrome-lined, as these are the key moving parts most susceptible to fouling that could affect function.

Many will also appreciate the original under-folding metal stock, since it reduced the rifle's overall length to less than 26 inches. For transportation and vehicle ingress and egress, this makes the gun very handy, and it can be fired with the stock folded (which is very welcome in tight confines). There is a large button on the left side of the stock where it joins the receiver,

SPECIFICATIONS

CENTURY ARMS YUGO M70AB2

CALIBER: 7.62x39mm
BARREL: 16.5-inch 1:10 twist
OA LENGTH: 25.75 in. folded, 35.25 in. extended
WEIGHT: 8 lbs. empty
STOCK: Synthetic handguard/ metal folding stock
SIGHTS: Iron sights
ACTION: Semi-auto
FINISH: Parkerized
CAPACITY: 30-round magazine
PRICE: $ 619.95
800-527-1252
WWW.CENTURYARMS.COM

which serves to lock and release it. The shoulder section folds easily out of the way when not needed and deploys quickly for shoulder firing. What the stock has in convenience, it lacks in comfort, and securing a good cheek weld can be a challenge. The stock has a sling attachment point on the release button that allows for the use of a single-point sling. For two-point sling carry, there is a corresponding sling attachment point at the front of the gas system. This is farther forward than the front of the handguard (where it is found on most AKs). The ergonomic synthetic pistol grip is very comfortable and provides a firm hold. It matches the synthetic handguards very well.

As mentioned, the threaded barrel has a removable slanted muzzle brake, which helps direct gas up and to the right, countering muzzle climb. It does not, however, reduce muzzle flash, and you may prefer to install an aftermarket flash hider. The barrel does have a bayonet lug and comes standard with an under barrel cleaning rod.

The remaining controls on the M70AB2 are all standard for an AK and are simple to use and master. The right-side safety selector is easily pushed up for safe and down for fire. The one-piece bolt carrier and handle are very smooth and easy to operate, and double as a forward assist. The ambidextrous magazine paddle release is slightly larger than those on most AKs, making it easier to use. I have to say that the Tapco trigger group functioned well, with only a slight amount of travel and a relatively clean break at 4 pounds.

I found the fit and finish of the M70AB2 to be outstanding. Its matte black Parkerized finish was evenly applied and smooth. The stock, handguard, grip, and bolt are all well-made and fit tightly

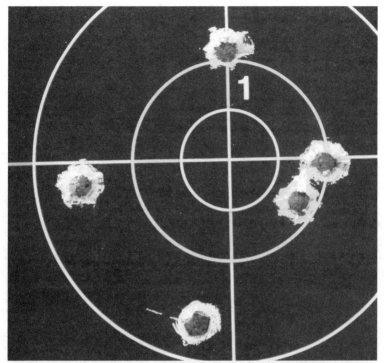

The author tested the M70AB2 at 100 yards from a bench rest using three different types of ammunition, including Russian ammo, and iron sights. Accuracy was about 3 MOA, standard for AK rifles.

together. Tight tolerances were the rule on the magazine well, and held the mags in place with no rattle. On the range, the M70 handled superbly. The handguards did a good job of keeping my hand cool during some rapid-fire strings, and the rifle functioned flawlessly with only one minor hiccup. One fired steel case round of Russian ammo failed to extract and got stuck in the chamber, requiring a sharp hit on the charging handle to pop it out.

For accuracy, I tested the M70AB2 at 100 yards from a bench rest using three different types of ammunition, including Russian ammo, and iron sights. While I believe that a scope would have produced better results, I was not disappointed, and the average group measured 3 inches at that distance, which is fairly standard for most AK rifles.

The HK33 rifle is still in standard use today by the Malaysian and Thai militaries, and surplus 40-round aluminum magazines are plentiful. *Photo: Public Domain*

The M70AB2 from Century Arms represents an excellent value for anyone interested in an AK rifle, while at the same time offering some distinct and unique features that set it apart from other AKs. With easy to find magazines and the many available aftermarket accessories, this can prove to be a truly handy and powerful survival gun that is there when you need it and easily stores away when you don't.

HECKLER & KOCH 5.56MM RIFLES

The name of Heckler & Koch has long been associated with high-quality German engineered guns and with good reason. Founded after World War II by two former Mauser engineers, H&K quickly rose to the forefront in German military small arms production. The firm's submachine guns, pistols, and battle rifles have found widespread use and acclaim with armies and law enforcement agencies worldwide.

The most common HK rifle is the G3, chambered in 7.62mm NATO. In addition is the HK33, chambered in 5.56mm NATO. Both of these rifles have semi-auto civilian versions available and are made to very high-quality standards. However, quality doesn't come cheap. That, plus U.S. laws that have added scarcity to the mix, results in original HK rifles that have been priced out of the range of many shooters. Although non-sporting arms cannot be imported, they can be "made in the USA" from a mix of foreign and U.S. parts or all U.S. parts. Currently, PTR Industries and Century Arms offer U.S.-made variants of these rifles.

Century Arms offers the 5.56x45mm C93 rifle, the firm's U.S.-made semi-auto version of the Heckler & Koch 33 assault rifle, complete with military 40-round magazine. HK made a semi-auto version of the HK33 for import to the U.S. known as the HK93, which was supplied with now very hard to find 25-round magazines. A shortened select-fire version, the HK53, was sold to American law enforcement agencies and was equipped with a collapsible stock.

Thanks to Century, a 5.56 roller-locked HK-type rifle is available at reasonable cost. The C93 compliments Century's G3 HK

The Century Arms C93 is based on the original Heckler & Koch HK33A2 assault rifle.
Photo: Mika Järvinen

clone, which is offered in 7.62 NATO and is in line with the firm's many offerings, including several AK variants. The HK33 rifle is still in standard use by the Malaysian and Thai militaries, and surplus 40-round aluminum magazines are plentiful. The C93 matches the original's dimensions and weight and proves itself a compact, lightweight, reliable, and handy rifle.

The C93, true to its HK heritage, uses a distinct method of operation. No need to argue between different gas or piston systems here; the C93 has no gas system or piston. Instead, it uses a delayed blowback roller lock system. Normally, a blowback-operated semi-auto requires a heavy bolt to keep the action closed until chamber pressure lowers to a safe level. The HK roller lock system uses two rollers on either side of the bolt head to do the same thing, obviating the need for a heavy bolt. When the rifle fires, the force of the case moving rearward under recoil acts as a piston, pushing back on the bolt head and forcing the rollers on either side into channels. This allows the bolt carrier to move fully rearward where the recoil spring then pushes the bolt carrier and bolt head forward back into battery.

Since the entire system relies on the full force of the cartridge case retracting under recoil, and since cases naturally expand when fired, a novel solution was developed to ensure reliable operation under various conditions. The rifle's chamber is fully fluted so that some of the escaping gas can come back around the case and separate it from the chamber to aid in extraction. This eliminates the need to use lubricated cases and ensures proper functioning even with dry or dirty ammunition.

Rifle operation is fairly straightforward. Place a loaded magazine in the mag well, retract the forward left-side cocking lever completely to the rear and release. The rifle requires the full force of the recoil spring to properly load a round and close the chamber. The cocking lever does not serve as a forward assist if a round is not fully chambered. There is no forward assist, although some rifles may include serrations on the bolt that can be pushed forward with the thumb and act as a forward assist. Disassembly is a very simple affair once the rifle has been cleared and the magazine removed. Start by removing the locking pin, which secures the buttstock to the receiver. The buttstock slides straight off from the receiver, while the bolt head, carrier, recoil spring, and guide rod all slide out as a single unit. The pistol grip assembly can then be rotated downward and removed.

Looking at the bolt assembly from the front, turn the bolt head counterclockwise until it can be separated from the bolt head carrier. Then rotate the bolt-locking piece until it comes loose as well, but with caution as it is under spring pressure. Reassemble the bolt assembly in the reverse order, making sure to depress the bolt head retaining lever in order to rotate the bolt head back into its locked position. To remove the trigger assembly from the grip housing, simply rotate the selector lever until it is pointing straight up and then pull the selector out from the grip assembly. This allows the trigger assembly to lift straight up and out of the grip housing.

As a delayed blowback rifle, the C93 tends to foul quite a bit (although no worse than the many AR rifles I have had to clean over the years). With fewer small parts than the AR and no gas tube, it is noticeably easier and faster to clean. The operating system keeps the gun shooting and reliable even with significant fouling. The C93 is assembled by Century in its Vermont plant from military surplus parts, with the barrel and receiver made in the U.S. The 16.25-inch barrel is turned from bar stock and features a 1:9 twist rate (same as a standard AR rifle). The receiver is stamped, welded, and machined.

All parts exhibit a tight (but not too tight) fit, and the welding is extremely well done. The black Parkerized finish is evenly applied and attractive. Plastic furniture was quite nice, and had a black, pebbled finish. The all-plastic grip assembly comes with aggressive checkering on both sides and finger grooves.

Anyone familiar with the HK G3 rifle will be immediately struck by the light weight and smaller dimensions of the C93. It is very similar in size, weight, and handling to a fully extended M4-style AR rifle. The C93's forward-mounted, left-side charging handle is easy to reach and operate, and it allows you to keep a firm hold on the pistol grip. The grip assembly has a large opening for ease of use with gloves, and the largish, stamped metal, two-stage trigger has a slight takeup and breaks at 9 pounds. The right-side push-button magazine release can be operated with the trigger finger (as on an AR) and easily allows the magazines to drop free. Seating a new mag in place may require rocking it into place. The iron sights are well designed and have a fixed front post and rotating rear drum, mechanically adjustable for windage and elevation. The rear drum sights have an open square notch set for 100 yards and three apertures set for 200, 300, and 400 yards.

One reminder of the rifle's

SPECIFICATIONS:
CENTURY ARMS C93 SEMI-AUTO RIFLE

CALIBER: 5.56x45mm
BARREL: 16.25 in. with 1:9 twist rate
OA LENGTH: 36.5 in.
WEIGHT: 8.2 lbs. (without magazine)
SIGHTS: Iron with fixed front post and adjustable aperture rear
SIGHT RADIUS: 18.9 in.
GRIPS: Plastic
ACTION: Semi-automatic
FINISH: Parkerized
CAPACITY: 40+1 rounds
PRICE: $649.95
800-527-1252
WWW.CENTURYARMS.COM

military heritage is the folding carrying handle, a feature for which most shooters won't have much use (and it actually gets in the way of all but the shortest optics and optic mounts). The C93 comes standard with two 40-round military-issue aluminum magazines and an original bayonet and scabbard. Additional surplus 40-round magazines are easily had, and HK has recently been importing 30-round, German-made, tough as nails steel magazines that are not inexpensive.

Foreign and U.S.-made steel bipods for the C93 and HK rifles are available and add some military styling to the rifle as well as weight. The handguard includes a slot that allows the bipod to slide into place, although some fitting may be required. The shorter magazines work better with the bipod, however.

For the range, I installed an aftermarket claw scope mount and the compact Vortex SPARC red-dot sight. Function was flawless with this pleasant, light-kicking little rifle, and the cases were briskly ejected forward. Allowing the bolt to go forward with the full force of the recoil spring is very important, however, and on two occasions, it did not fully close. In this case, a forward assist would have come in handy. The C93 rifle proved accurate enough, and my best group was 1.5 inches at 50 yards.

FN FAL

The FN FAL (Fusil Automatique Léger) is as iconic a rifle as the AR or the AK, or at least it should be. I would describe it as the AK of the West. It was used by more than 90 countries throughout the Cold War and fielded by every NATO country except the United States. It was so widely used by Western nations that it earned the moniker of the "Right Arm of the Free World."

The FN-FAL is a semi-automatic rifle using a short-stroke gas piston system and is almost always chambered in 7.62mm NATO/.308 Win. It's a robust and reliable battle-proven rifle that employs a standard 20-round magazine with a non-reciprocating left-side charging handle. Civilian versions are available in the U.S. and are manufactured by Century Arms as well as by DSA Arms, the latter of which makes several tactical and survival variants.

More than 90 countries throughout the Cold War used the FN FAL. It earned the moniker of the "Right Arm of the Free World." *Photo: SSGT J.R. Ruark*

The original rifle was designed for select fire, so it can be found with light or heavy barrels, and it has its own proprietary bipod. Most models come with a top mounted folding carry handle. This seems unnecessary except when using the rifle in full auto. A downside of the carry handle is that it cannot be used with longer optics. As the rifle is all steel and very sturdy, it is on the large and heavy side. This helps tame the recoil significantly, but it can be burdensome to carry for long periods and difficult for smaller shooters to handle.

As the FAL was produced in so many different countries, there is a difference between inch- and metric-patterned rifles. Not all parts will inter-

SPECIFICATIONS:
DSA SA58 PARA CONGO

CALIBER: 7.62x51mm NATO
BARREL: 18 in.
OA LENGTH: 37.5 in./folded 28.5 in.
WEIGHT: 8.76 lbs. (without magazine)
SIGHTS: Iron with rail
SIGHT RADIUS: 22 in.
GRIPS: Plastic
ACTION: Semi-automatic
FINISH: Parkerized
CAPACITY: 20+1 rounds
PRICE: $1,975
DSARMS.COM

change between the two, including the magazines. Metric-pattern rifles are the most commonly seen in the States. Standard FAL have a bolt with a recoil spring assembly that extends into the stock, but other models have been redesigned with folding stocks. Most notable, however, is the gas adjustment system that allows you to adjust for a specific load or in case of fouling. The Century Arms version is fairly standard and economical, while DSA Arms offers more variants.

FN-SCAR

FN, or Fabrique Nationale, has been the main supplier of small arms to the U.S. military for some time now. They manufacture the M-16 and M4 rifles as well as the M240 and M249 general purpose machine gun and squad automatic weapon, or SAW. They also produce the SCAR 16 in 5.56mm and SCAR 17 in 7.62mm for the U.S. Special Forces.

The SCAR 16 and 17 are available as semi-automatic only civilian rifles and use a short-stroke gas piston system of operation that is adjustable for use with or without a suppressor. The free-floated barrel improves accuracy, and all controls are fully ambidextrous with a reversible reciprocating forward charging handle. Note that the charging handle can be used as a forward assist. The polymer stock is both adjustable for length of pull and folding (to the right) and can be fired in the folded position. There is a very handy adjustable cheek riser for use with optics. The rifle comes with an integrated standard top rail for optics and additional accessory rails. The rifle's receiver is made of aluminum to reduce weight, while the lower unit is polymer.

The folding sights are fully adjustable, and the controls, with the exception of the charging

SPECIFICATIONS:
FN SCAR-16

CALIBER: 5.56x45mm
BARREL: 16.25 in.
OA LENGTH: 27.5 to 37.5 in.
WEIGHT: 7.25 lbs. (without magazine)
SIGHTS: Iron with rail
GRIPS: Plastic
ACTION: Semi-automatic
FINISH: Black or dark earth
CAPACITY: 30+1 rounds
PRICE: $2,995
FNAMERICA.COM

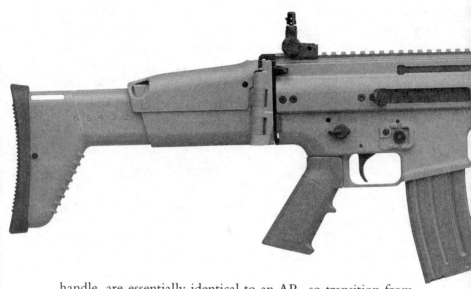

handle, are essentially identical to an AR, so transition from one system to the other is easy. The SCAR 16 is lightweight, extremely reliable, and available in black or flat dark earth color. It uses standard AR magazines, so compatibility is not an issue.

SIG556XI TACTICAL MODULAR RIFLE

The SIG556xi rifle from SIG Sauer has a strong military pedigree and offers many modular features that make it a great survival rifle. The SIG556xi is based on the SG550, the standard issue rifle for the Swiss military, and it keeps the modular abilities of its predecessor but adds touches that will be more appreciated by an American audience. In particular, the new rifle uses standard AR magazines instead of the expensive and hard to find proprietary translucent SIG mags.

Unlike the standard AR to which it will undoubtedly be compared, the SIG556xi is a gas piston-operated semi-automatic rifle, although select fire models are available for sale to government agencies. A rotating bolt ensures proper lock up and very much resembles the bolt found on an AK. The basic principle and accompanying reliability is the same. Its gas system has three

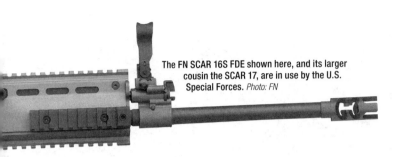

The FN SCAR 16S FDE shown here, and its larger cousin the SCAR 17, are in use by the U.S. Special Forces. *Photo: FN*

settings to control the amount of gas that is fed into the gas tube and piston.

If the rifle becomes extremely fouled to the point that reliability suffers, the second setting directs more gas into the system to increase reliable cycling. This is only a temporary measure, and the system should be returned to the normal first setting as soon as it is convenient. The extra gas from position two places more wear and tear on the rifle and increases recoil. The third position provides the proper amount of gas force for proper cycling with suppressor use.

The SIG556xi's 16-inch steel barrel is not chrome lined; instead, it is nitride treated. The result is an extremely corrosion resistant barrel with improved wear and fatigue resistance and lubricity. This dispenses with the need for a chrome lining and can actually improve accuracy, as chrome lining can be unevenly applied. One of the modular features of the SIG is that the barrel can be removed without tools in the field and replaced with different length barrels that are available in 10-, 14.5-, and 16-inch lengths. Switching calibers is also very easy, and using either 5.56 NATO or .300 Blackout requires only a barrel change. Plus, the 556xi allows for the use of 7.62x39 ammunition. This requires changing the barrel, bolt, and lower receiver to accommodate AK magazines. You can very easily accomplish all of these changes in the field, and since only the upper receiver is serialized, you can have as many unrestricted lower receivers as you like.

The ability to switch between 5.56 NATO and 7.62x39mm is a great boon to anyone in the field, since you should always be able to find one of these two cartridges in abundant supply

The SIG556xi rifle from SIG Sauer has a strong military pedigree and offers many modular features that make it a great survival rifle.

(along with AR and AK magazines). SIG tested several varieties of AK magazines to check for reliable functioning and reportedly encountered no issues. The 16-inch 5.56 model tested here had a 1 in 7-inch twist rate and was topped off with a removable three pronged flash hider. The rifle in 7.62x39 has a 1 in 9.5-inch twist.

The handguards are replaceable to fit survival needs. The sample rifle tested was equipped with smooth, lightweight polymer ones. These will readily accept Magpul rail kits and accessories for adding additional mission critical equipment, such as IR lasers or lights. The optional aluminum or carbon fiber handguards are readily adaptable to different length rails.

The side-folding stock makes transport much easier and brings the size of the rifle down to very compact dimensions. A removable polymer cheek rest is attached in order to raise the eye elevation up to optics more comfortably. However, I found that with the stock folded, this cheek rest interfered with the operation of the charging handle. You could switch the ambidextrous

Switching calibers in the SIG556xi is very easy. And changing to either 5.56 NATO or .300 Black-out requires only a barrel change. The 556xi allows for the use of 7.62x39 ammunition, too. This requires changing the barrel, bolt and lower receiver to accommodate AK magazines.

charging handle to the left side of the rifle or remove the cheek rest. By the way, the standard folding stock does not have any length of pull adjustments, a feature to which AR users have become accustomed. However, there are optional receiver end plates that allow for the use of standard AR extension tubes and your choice of the vast array of AR stocks.

The upper receiver is steel and made from a stamping, like the AKM. It is the serialized part. The nearly 16 inches of Picatinny rail on top are actually one piece and part of the top handguard, which is made from aluminum. There is plenty of room for extended optics, night vision devices, and laser units. Steel and aluminum flip up diopter sights are standard, with windage adjustments on the rear sight and elevation on the front. The sights flip

SIG SAUER 556XI

CALIBER: 5.56mm
BARREL: 16 in. Nitride 1:7 twist
OA LENGTH: 35.8 in. extended,
26 in. folded
WEIGHT: 7.1 lbs. empty
STOCK: Folding polymer
SIGHTS: Folding adjustable
ACTION: Semi-auto
FINISH: Black
CAPACITY: 30-round magazine
PRICE: $1,466 - $1,599
603-772-2302
WWW.SIGSAUER.COM

up easily and lock into place with a push button retention system.

The charging handle can be reversed from the standard right side to the left; however, cases will continue to eject to the right regardless. At the rear of the charging handle port there are rubber gaskets on both sides of the receiver that allow for the operation of the handle while doing an excellent job of keeping out dust and debris from the action. The lower receiver is made from aluminum and features ambidextrous safety selector and magazine releases. The safety selector has a short 45-degree downward rotation for the fire mode, at least in the semi-automatic model tested. The left-side bolt release is a lever that operates in the opposite fashion from those found on pistols. To lock the bolt to the rear, the bolt hold/release tab must be pushed down. To release it, you must push up on the bolt release or use the charging handle.

The receiver has an integral extended trigger guard for use with gloves, and the polymer pistol grip has built-in internal storage space for spare batteries or parts and a very aggressive texture on the sides for a firm grip. The SIG556xi weighs and handles very similar to an AR. It is light and handy, and the reliability over two days of testing was impeccable. The rifle features a two-stage trigger, which may seem odd at first if you're used to the Mil-Spec single-stage AR or AK trigger. According to SIG, the trigger pull should be a standard 7.5 pounds combined.

Reloading spent brass is a concern here for the survivalist, as the SIG556xi has a distinct tendency to leave ejected cases with dents to the case mouth.

For accuracy testing, I used a 3-9x Trijicon scope from a stable bench rest position at 100 yards, firing five-shot groups. The results were good, especially with the heavier HPR ammunition that the

1 in 7-inch twist rate barrels generally prefer; this 75-grain round produced sub-MOA results. Standard Mil-Spec 62-grain ammunition should be capable of respectable accuracy from the SIG556xi.

SIG Sauer has produced an excellent, completely modular and versatile battle rifle for the modern warrior. The ability to quickly and easily adapt the rifle to meet various needs and conditions in the field, including the use of both 5.56 NATO and 7.62x39 ammunition and magazines, is impressive.

STATE-COMPLIANT RIFLES

So far, I have included what I believe to be the best survival rifles you can own. However, in a handful of states, there are gun control restrictions that can range from the merely inconvenient to outright prohibition on the ownership of certain styles of semiautomatic rifles. Obviously, state laws vary widely and can change on a fairly routine basis, so the information presented here should only be used as a guide and not by any means as legal advice.

Generally speaking, the restrictions or conditions for ownership of semi-automatic rifles by some states and localities are based on so-called "assault weapon" laws. Currently, the states that have restrictions include California, Connecticut, Hawaii, Maryland, Massachusetts, New Jersey, and New York. Some cities and localities impose their own restrictions, such as Washington D.C. If you live in any of these places, make sure to check with a local dealer or manufacturer to stay on the right side of the law.

CALIFORNIA

California bans guns specifically by name as well as by certain features. The most notable and common restriction is magazine capacity limits. Magazines over 10 rounds are outlawed altogether. It gets worse. In California, any centerfire semi-automatic rifle with a pistol grip and a detachable magazine is considered an "assault rifle" and is restricted. So, you either eliminate the pistol grip or you eliminate the detachable magazine (or move!). To get around this, manufacturers have developed a magazine

release block for ARs and AKs that require the use of a tool to operate. These devices are being challenged and may well be illegal already.

CONNECTICUT

Connecticut bans guns by name as well as by feature and, of course, magazine capacity limit is 10 rounds. Semi-auto centerfire rifles with a detachable magazine are restricted if they have any of the following: a folding or collapsible stock, pistol grip, forward grip, flash hider, or a grenade launcher. Some state complaint rifles are available.

MARYLAND

All AK rifles in any format are banned in Maryland, and magazine capacity for all guns is limited to 10 rounds. Magazines and rifles owned before the ban are grandfathered and may be retained. Oddly enough, some AR rifles are allowed.

MASSACHUSETTS AND NEW JERSEY

Massachusetts has a 10-round magazine capacity limit and bans semi-auto centerfire rifles based on certain features. To get

Several manufacturers like Black Rain Ordnance make state-compliant rifles for those states that have banned certain types of semi-automatic rifles based on their appearance. *Photo: Black Rain Ordnance*

around this, manufacturers produce state compliant rifles with no bayonet lugs, threaded barrels, folding or collapsible stocks, or flash hiders.

NEW YORK

New York's law on "assault rifles" is among the most absurd. Basically, any semi-automatic centerfire rifle with a pistol grip is restricted, as is magazine capacity to 10 rounds (although it is illegal to load more than 7 rounds in the magazine!). The solution is some rather strange looking rifles with no pistol grip, fixed stocks, bayonet lug, threaded barrel, or flash hiders.

ALTERNATIVE RIFLES

No state, however, restricts non-semi-automatic rifles. This includes bolt-, pump-, and lever-action rifles. While these may not be ideal for a survival situation, they are certainly effective for hunting and self-defense. Several manufacturers have recognized this and produced rifles that are very effective survival guns. Here's a look at a few of the best ones.

MOSSBERG

The Mossberg MVP (Varmint and Predator) rifle is a standard bolt-action rifle that uses AR magazines. It's available in both .308 and .223 and will accommodate high-capacity mags. It can be had in several configurations. This offers the versatility of using common

AR magazines in an unrestricted bolt action. You will not be able to shoot as fast, but you will have better reliability (thanks to fewer moving parts) and accuracy.

The MVP FLEX features a polymer stock with a pistol grip and an AR-style collapsible stock. It has Mossberg's quick-detach system that allows the stock to be removed for easy and compact transport. The MVP Scout has a full polymer stock and features a threaded barrel with an A2-style flash hider (which makes it easier to install a suppressor), fiber optic sights, and a Picatinny rail for optics. You also get a tactical oversized bolt handle and forward-mounted side rails for extra accessories. To learn more, visit mossberg.com.

REMINGTON

The Remington Model 7615P is a pump-action rifle that uses standard AR mags, and is designed for law enforcement. Although Remington only sells it to police and government agencies, there

The Mossberg MVP (Varmint and Predator) is a standard bolt-action rifle that uses AR magazines. *Photo: Mossberg*

is no restriction on private ownership, and they are available on the used market. This rifle is lightweight with a polymer stock and is fast shooting. Not as fast as semi-auto, mind you, but as fast as any bolt action. It's available in several configurations, including versions with pistol grips and collapsing stocks. It has a 16.5-inch barrel with a Parkerized finish. Visit remingtonle.com for more info.

RUGER MINI-14 AND MINI-30

Ruger does make two semi-automatic magazine-fed rifles that are very well suited for survival and may fly under the radar of some "assault weapons" laws. The Ruger Mini-14 and Mini-30 Ranch Rifles have no pistol grip and sport plain muzzles without flash hiders or threads. The Mini-14 is chambered in 5.56mm, while the Mini-30 is chambered in the 7.62x39mm AK round. Both, however, use proprietary magazines with either a 5-round capacity or, where allowed, a 20-round capacity.

The Mini-14 is chambered in 5.56mm, the Mini-30 in 7.62x39mm AK. Both, however, use proprietary magazines.
Photo: Jan Hrdonka

SPECIFICATIONS
RUGER MINI-14
MODEL 5820

CALIBER: 5.56mm
BARREL: 16.12 in.
OA LENGTH: 34.75 in.
WEIGHT: 6.6 lbs. empty
STOCK: Polymer
SIGHTS: Ghost ring
ACTION: Semi-auto
FINISH: Stainless
CAPACITY: 5- or 20-round
magazine
PRICE: $1,139
WWW.RUGER.COM

These are light and handy rifles.

Ruger's Minis are available in a standard wood stock and blued barrel or what I would recommend — synthetic stock and stainless steel. They are also available in different barrel lengths, and I would opt for the shorter 16-inch barrel models. The Ruger Ranch Rifle is based on the extremely tough and reliable military M1 Garand-style action. It uses a self-cleaning gas piston system of operation that keeps on working even in the worst conditions. Both rifles come optics ready and include a Picatinny rail and scope rings.

The World War II-era M1 Garand, chambered in .30-06 caliber, is legal to own in any state. The Garand was the first semi-auto issued to American fighting men. *Photo: Public Domain*

M1 GARAND: AMERICA'S ORIGINAL BATTLE RIFLE

There are, of course, semi-automatic rifles that do not have a pistol grip, collapsible stock or a detachable magazine, and the granddaddy of them all is the World War II-era M1 Garand. Garands are legal to own in any state and hopefully that doesn't change. The M1 Garand was the first semi-auto issued to American fighting men when our enemies and allies were still carrying bolt-action rifles little different from those of World War I. This revolutionary design was adopted by the U.S. Military in 1936 after more than a decade of development and even then saw some key changes before ending up as the rifle carried to victory in WWII and Korea.

In fact, the M1 Garand was so successful that it continued to see use in Vietnam and with reserve troops into the early 1970s, although it had been officially replaced in 1957 from front line service. Even then, the Garand was still in use with the militaries of a dozen friendly nations that we equipped, including the Greek Army well into the 1980s.

Designed by Canadian-born John C. Garand, a long-time Springfield Armory engineer, the rifle that bears his name is a long stroke, gas piston-operated, eight-shot clip-fed semi-automatic rifle chambered in the same .30-06 cartridge as its predecessors, the 1903 Springfield and the M1917 Enfield.

The long-stroke piston on the M1 is similar to that found on the AK-47 and constitutes a long steel operating rod that is one piece with the charging handle and joins the rotating bolt, which features two locking lugs on its face. When firing, the operating rod, handle, and unlocked bolt move back as one unit, improving the rifle's reliability in field conditions but also negatively affect precision accuracy. In addition, the bolt handle can serve as a forward assist to properly seat a round. Nevertheless, the M1 was considered very accurate and was used in the sniper role with scoped variants as well as in modern competition.

It is possible that Mr. Garand may have come up with different features on his rifle if left to his own devices, but the terms that the military contract called for set the stage. The most off-putting feature to our modern eyes is undoubtedly the clip mechanism,

The Garand has a fixed internal magazine, which is fed from the top with a spring metal clip holding eight rounds. Without the clip, the M1 becomes a single-shot weapon with the shooter only being able to load one round at a time. *Photo: JO1 Brian Brannon, USN*

which was demanded instead of a removable magazine. Although many people use the terms interchangeably, a clip and a magazine are not at all the same. A magazine holds the ammunition to feed into the gun; a clip holds the ammunition to be loaded into the magazine. The M1 has a fixed internal magazine, which is fed from the top by a spring metal clip holding eight rounds. Without the clip, the M1 becomes a single-shot weapon with the shooter only being able to load one round at a time. The eight rounds are staggered in the clip, and there is no top or bottom, so it doesn't matter on which side the top round is located (which is handy for a battle rifle). On the last round fired, the clip automatically ejects, and the bolt locks to the rear.

Retracting the bolt and depressing the clip latch located on the left side of the receiver manually ejects a full or partially full clip. Magazines can be topped off, but this is not easy or recommended, and it is far better to eject a partially expended clip and replace it with a fresh one. Both 2- and 5-round clips are commercially available.

Operating the M1 is simple, but takes a bit of practice at first. Once the bolt is locked to the rear, a full clip is inserted through the top of the receiver and pressed down. The bolt then automatically releases to go forward and load the first round. It is best to do this with the thumb of the right hand while using the palm to hold back the bolt handle, otherwise the bolt could slam

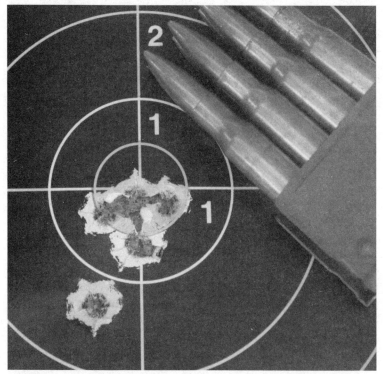

Even using iron sights the Garand is capable of outstanding accuracy and continues to be popular for competition.

onto your thumb with some force, causing the infamous "Garand thumb." Moreover, the safety catch is somewhat novel and reminds me of those found on SKS rifles. To engage the safety on the M1, depress the metal catch in front of the trigger guard toward the trigger. This moves the steel tab into the trigger guard, partially blocking access to the trigger. When you are ready to fire, simply place your finger on the trigger and push the safety bar forward and out of the trigger guard area.

The final gas system adopted for the M1 uses a hole in the bottom of the barrel toward the front of the rifle to divert gas against the front of the operating rod. The short gas tube located underneath the barrel at the front was made from stainless steel to prevent corrosion; it was then painted black since the stainless steel would not be easily Parkerized. This accounts for the difference in finish of this part from the rest of the rifle. It should also be noted that a lot of military .30-06 ammunition is corrosive because it has sodium in the primer and requires the use of water to clean properly and prevent rust.

The M1 can weigh between 9.5 and more than 10 lbs. empty, depending on the type of wood used. Add a sling and butt stock cleaning kit, and the scale tips up. Of course, this much weight soaks up a lot of recoil, which helps with weapon fatigue and faster follow-up shots.

During World War II, Springfield Armory (the government armory not the Springfield Armory we know of today) and Winchester Repeating Arms produced approximately five million Garands. After the war, another nearly 1.5 million were produced by Springfield Armory, Harrington & Richardson Arms, and International Harvester Corporation. Almost every M1 has undergone some sort of arsenal repair or rebuilding, which often included new barrels and replacement parts from different manufacturers. Even Beretta produced Garands using Winchester machinery after the war, and Beretta parts can be found on M1s imported from service with European armies.

I have owned several, all purchased through the Civilian Marksmanship Program or CMP. These differ significantly from M1s that may have found their way back to the U.S. from commercial importers. That's because CMP guns are all genuine U.S. Government surplus that have been inspected, repaired and test fired by CMP armorers and are free of those annoying import marks.

Maintenance and disassembly of the M1 Garand is straightforward, although at first glance it does seem like there are a lot of parts to keep track of; of course, they must be reassembled in the correct order, too. Also, it is best to assume that any ammunition you use, with the exception of modern commercial stuff, is corrosive — requiring you to clean accordingly.

On the range, the old warhorse I tested performed well with no malfunctions using a mix of Greek military surplus ammunition (also purchased from CMP) and modern commercial hunting ammo. The front blade sight is fixed, but the rear peep is outstanding with elevation adjustments in 25-yard increments out to 1,200 yards with easy windage adjustments. Mounting a scope on a Garand is no easy task and in order to keep the rifle as close to original as possible I stuck with iron sights.

This is a large, heavy rifle, and I can't say that I would have relished having to carry it in combat. It is easy to understand why a lot of American soldiers preferred the M1 Carbine. Still, the rifle is very well balanced, shoulders easily, and the recoil — even with the full-sized .30-06 battle round — very manageable.

Accuracy on the range firing at 100 yards from a bench rest and using the standard iron sights was very good — as good as most of the scoped ARs I shoot. My best group was a pretty impressive 1.4 inches using Remington ammo, but the Greek 1980s vintage surplus stuff also produced a 1.4-inch group. Keep in mind that this is out of a WWII vintage, semi-auto, beat up, rebuilt, Greek loaner rifle using ammo that was made in Greece when Jimmy Carter was president.

SPECIFICATIONS
U.S. M1 GARAND
.30 CALIBER

CALIBER: .30-06 Springfield
BARREL: 24 in.
OA LENGTH: 43.5 in.
WEIGHT: 10.5 lbs. empty
STOCK: Walnut
SIGHTS: Fixed blade front, adjustable peep rear
ACTION: Semi-auto
FINISH: Parkerized
CAPACITY: 8-round clip
PRICE: $525
256-835-8455
WWW.ODCMP.COM

Many variants of the M1 Garand were created during and after the war, including a never issued tanker and paratrooper model as well as select fire versions and ones with detachable magazines. Some were also chambered and issued in 7.62x51mm NATO, especially once the .30–06 round was phased out. The best place to get a real American M1 Garand is still through the CMP, and they have various grades available, although supplies are dwindling. Rack Grade guns are the cheapest and have the most replacement parts and wear. Criteria for purchase is easy to meet, and CMP ships the rifle directly to your door.

M1 CARBINE

The M1 Carbine was introduced just in time for World War II to arm specialized and rear echelon troops with a lightweight semi-auto rifle that filled the gap between the 1911 pistol and a full-sized battle rifle. At less than 6 pounds and just over 35 inches in length, the M1 Carbine filled that role perfectly. Too, it found popularity among frontline troops who appreciated its increased capacity and lighter weight.

A folding stock version was produced for airborne units, making the little carbine even more compact. Its popularity is evidenced by the numbers produced — over 6.5 million — and by its length of service, which stretched from WWII to Vietnam. Despite the high numbers produced, many of these remain in the hands of foreign armies and governments, still used for police departments and reserve units.

This is a detachable magazine semi-automatic, and mags are standard at 15 rounds, although 30-rounders are quite plentiful. The standard model does not have a

SPECIFICATIONS
AUTO ORDNANCE M1 CARBINE

CALIBER: .30 Caliber
BARREL: 18 in.
WEIGHT: 5.4 lbs.
LENGTH: 35 ¾ in. overall, 25 ¾ in (folded)
STOCK: Wood
FINISH: Parkerized
SIGHTS: Blade front sight, flip-style rear sight
MAGAZINE: 15 or 30 Rounds
MSRP: $816 to $903
508-795-3919
WWW.AUTO-ORDNANCE.COM

Surplus M1 Carbines with 15- and 30-round magazines are still available, but Auto Ordnance also makes a very accurate replica.
Photo: Auto Ordnance

pistol grip, but many do have a bayonet lug so they may be restricted in some states. Also note that it fires a cartridge that has become uncommon. The .30 Carbine cartridge is adequate for most survival uses, but many consider it to be underpowered by today's warfighter standards. It may not be easy to find when you need it, either. Even so, you can still find surplus carbines for sale, but the prices keep rising. You won't find an original WWII rifle for cheap, since the vast majority were rebuilt after the war by adding a bayonet lug and improved sights. Even the Iwo Jima memorial got this one wrong when the sculptor armed one of the Marines with a bayonet lugged M1 instead of the plain barrel original.

But if you want an original configuration M1 Carbine that you can shoot and that won't cost you a small fortune, Auto-Ordnance (part of Kahr Arms) offers new M1s in both full- and folding-stock configuration. These faithful reproductions are chambered

The World War II-era M1 Carbine uses a .30-caliber pistol round. 6.5 million carbines were produced. *Photo: Auto Ordnance*

in the original .30 caliber, pistol-sized round. Each features walnut wood stocks, a Parkerized finish, plain 18-inch barrel, and the original simple flip-style sights.

The carbine does have the improved flip safety that was changed early in the war since troops sometimes got confused between the push button magazine release and the original push button safety (located very close to each other). It comes with an original-style 15-round magazine and will accommodate later 30-round mags as well.

SKS RIFLE

Before there was the AK, there was the SKS (Samozaryadnyi Karabin Sistemi Simonova). This semi-automatic rifle features a full wood stock and is chambered in the 7.62x39mm cartridge, same as the AK. In fact, the AK was introduced into service less than a year after the SKS, making the SKS instantly obsolete. Despite this, the SKS was produced in huge quantities in many

countries, being especially popular in China.

Their mistake can be your gain, as SKS rifles in their standard configuration are not considered to be an evil "assault rifle" and are not regulated as such, yet they make great survival guns. As military surplus, they are relatively inexpensive and fire the easy to find 7.62x39mm round. The SKS has a fixed 10-round magazine that is loaded from the top, either singly or by using very convenient and fast 10-round stripper clips. The bolt locks open on an empty magazine and reloading is very easy. The magazine does have a release that hinges the magazine down and allows you to dump any rounds left in it.

SPECIFICATIONS
SKS CARBINE

CALIBER: 7.62x39mm
BARREL: 20.34 in.
WEIGHT: 8.8 lbs.
LENGTH: 40.16 in.
STOCK: Wood
FINISH: Blued
SIGHTS: Iron adjustable
MAGAZINE: 10 rounds fixed
MSRP: $200 to $500

Before there was the AK there was the SKS, a semi-automatic rifle chambered in the 7.62x39mm cartridge with a fixed 10-round magazine. *Photo: Public Domain*

The SKS employs a very reliable and robust short-stroke gas piston system of operation that keeps fouling to a minimum. This versatile gun features an integral folding bayonet, which could be used as a defense against animals in a survival situation. Even if you ran out of ammunition, you would still have a formidable weapon. The controls are very simple. You get a reciprocating charging handle and a simple safety lever located on the right side of the trigger guard. The SKS is a military rifle and built tough to last. They are not routinely imported, so you will have to look to the surplus market for one.

PISTOL-CALIBER RIFLES

Having a handgun and a rifle in the same caliber is nothing new. There are plenty of examples of gunfighters carrying lever-action rifles and single-action revolvers in the same chambering. When you think about it, there is a distinct advantage in this for survival. You are limiting your need to stockpile or carry different types of ammunition, and you are simplifying your needs. By shooting a pistol caliber out of a rifle, you achieve several things: you improve your accuracy exponentially, reduce the recoil significantly, increase the velocity and power of your ammunition, and finally, dramatically improve your range.

The bottom line is that when you shoot a pistol caliber out of a rifle, you are maximizing the effectiveness of the caliber and getting all you can out of it. Still, it is a pistol caliber, and it will never measure up to a centerfire rifle cartridge of similar caliber, but for many it is an acceptable compromise. My advice on carbines and rifles chambered in pistol rounds is first: stick with commonly found cartridges, second: look for a semi-automatic carbine, and third: choose one that uses the same magazines as your handgun.

HI POINT CARBINE 995TS 9MM

Hi Point makes cheap guns, I am sorry to say; they look cheap and they feel cheap. However, we are not all named Rockefeller, and one thing that Hi Point guns do is work and work surprisingly

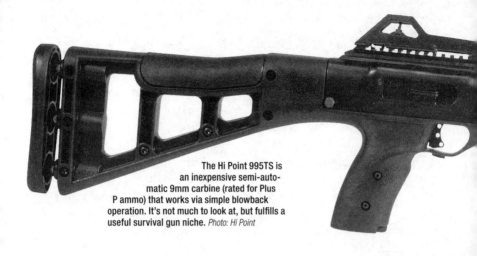

The Hi Point 995TS is an inexpensive semi-automatic 9mm carbine (rated for Plus P ammo) that works via simple blowback operation. It's not much to look at, but fulfills a useful survival gun niche. *Photo: Hi Point*

well. The 995TS is a semi-automatic 9mm carbine (rated for Plus P ammo) that works on the simplest of all principles: blowback operation. That means it uses a very heavy bolt. The carbine is limited to 10-round single-stack magazines, but there are extensions that will give you a couple of extra rounds, and there are 20-round mags as well. The main advantage here is that the carbine and the Hi Point 9mm pistol use the same magazine.

The receiver is made from stamped steel, and the plastic stock is available in a variety of colors. The sights are rudimentary but effective and adjustable. This carbine does have lots of accessory rails and simple controls that I always found a bit clunky to use. There is a left side safety lever and a button magazine release on the same side of the pistol grip. The charging handle is on the left side

SPECIFICATIONS
HI POINT 995TS

CALIBER: 9mm
BARREL: 16.5 in.
WEIGHT: 6.25 lbs.
LENGTH: 31 in.
STOCK: Polymer
FINISH: Blued
SIGHTS: Iron adjustable
MAGAZINE: 10 Rounds
MSRP: $315
HI-POINTFIREARMS.COM

The Beretta CX4 Storm is available in 9mm and .40 S&W and is capable of accepting Beretta pistol magazines. *Photo: Rama*

and reciprocates when firing. The bolt locks open on an empty magazine for convenience. This carbine is available in other calibers that match up to the company's other pistols. It won't win any beauty contests, but its simple design makes it extremely reliable.

BERETTA CX4 STORM

The CX4 is available in 9mm and .40 S&W and is capable of accepting Beretta pistol magazines from any full-size Beretta PX4, 90-series and 8000 series (with an adapter). That means that this carbine can accept the Beretta 92 (the military M9 pistol) mags, too. In a survival situation, I would go with the M9 magazines for the CX4, as ammo and magazines are plentiful. This semi-automatic carbine is, like

SPECIFICATIONS
BERETTA CX4 STORM

CALIBER: 9mm
BARREL: 16.6 in.
WEIGHT: 5.67 lbs.
LENGTH: 31.5 in.
STOCK: Polymer
FINISH: Blued
SIGHTS: Iron adjustable
MAGAZINE: 10-15-20 Rounds
MSRP: $800
WWW.BERETTA.COM

the M9 pistol, very attractive with race car looks and outstanding ergonomics.

You get a cold hammer forged chrome-lined barrel for improved accuracy and extended barrel life. The simple blowback operation ensures superior reliability, and the polymer stock features plenty of accessory rails and a length of top rail for optics. The controls are simple and ambidextrous, or reversible, including the reversible safety, magazine release, and charging handle. Empty cases can be made to eject either left or right to accommodate everyone. The sights are easily user adjustable, and the length of pull can be altered with the use of spacers to accommodate different-sized shooters.

KEL-TEC SUB 2000

Kel-Tec is not a household name, but makes some of the most innovative firearm designs I have ever seen, and they are constantly building a better mousetrap. The area of pistol carbines

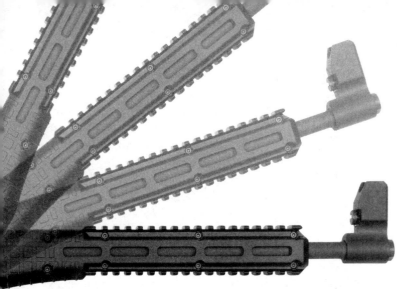

The Kel-Tec SUB 2000 is a very unconventional carbine capable of folding in half for easy transport and quick deployment. *Photo: Kel-Tec*

SPECIFICATIONS
KEL-TEC SUB 2000

CALIBER: 9mm
BARREL: 16.1 in.
WEIGHT: 4 lbs.
LENGTH: 16 to 29.5 in.
STOCK: Polymer
FINISH: Blued
SIGHTS: Iron adjustable
MAGAZINE: 10-15-20 Rounds
MSRP: $500
WWW.KELTECWEAPONS.COM

is no exception. The SUB 2000 is a very unconventional carbine that is capable of literally folding in half for easy transport and quick deployment when needed. The front of the rifle folds upward and locks into place over the top of the rear of the rifle.

This semi-automatic blowback-operated carbine is available in 9mm and 40 S&W. Its receiver and stock are polymer, and the controls extremely simple with a cross-bolt safety at the top of the grip and a left-side push button magazine release on the grip. The charging handle is actually located below the shoulder stock and is thus fully ambidextrous and out of the way. The SUB 2000 is available in variants to accept several different standard pistol magazines, including Beretta 90 series, Glock 19, SIG, and Smith & Wesson.

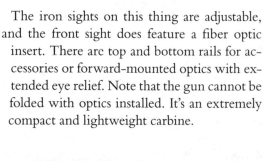

The iron sights on this thing are adjustable, and the front sight does feature a fiber optic insert. There arc top and bottom rails for accessories or forward-mounted optics with extended eye relief. Note that the gun cannot be folded with optics installed. It's an extremely compact and lightweight carbine.

JUST RIGHT CARBINES

While the Just Right Carbine looks like an AR, it is very distinct while keeping many of the ergonomics and controls of the AR for familiarity and convenience. The carbine uses Glock magazines and a blowback semi-automatic system of operation. It features an ambidextrous charging handle and ejection. Barrel and bolt assemblies can be swapped out to change calibers. This is extremely handy in a survival situation because with one rifle and a couple of barrels and bolts, you can make use of whatever ammunition you find available.

The Just Right Carbine uses Glock magazines and a blowback semi-automatic system of operation.
Photo: Just Right Carbines

The standard AR furniture and trigger controls mean that you can make upgrades and repairs with easy to find AR parts. There is plenty of rail space for optics and accessories, and the AR stock is fully adjustable for length of pull. The magazine

SPECIFICATIONS
JR CARBINE

CALIBER: 9mm
BARREL: 16.25 in.
WEIGHT: 6.5 lbs.
LENGTH: 30.25 to 33.5 in.
STOCK: Polymer
FINISH: Blued
SIGHTS: Rail
MAGAZINE: 10-15-20 Rounds
MSRP: $774
JUSTRIGHTCARBINES.COM.

release is located on the left side of the magazine well. It functions well once you get used to it. The magazine well is interchangeable for use with 9mm, .40 S&W, and .45 ACP Glock mags. Just Right Carbines sells complete conversion kits for all of these calibers.

SPECIFICATIONS
ATI MILSPORT AR

CALIBER: 9mm
BARREL: 16 in.
WEIGHT: 6.4 lbs.
LENGTH: 32.5 to 35.5 in.
STOCK: Polymer
FINISH: Black
SIGHTS: Rail
MAGAZINE: 10-15-20 Rounds
MSRP: $899
AMERICANTACTICAL.US

ATI MILSPORT 9MM CARBINE

There are 9mm AR carbines that use steel box magazines, but there is no reason someone couldn't make an AR that used the more common and easier to find (and afford) Glock magazines, and now there is. ATI, or American Tactical Imports, offers its Milsport AR Carbine that just happens to match this description. It's as complete an AR as you can have minus the gas system. Instead, the ATI Milsport uses a blowback system of operation, as is common in pistol-caliber semi-automatic carbines.

The magazine well is smaller than on a standard AR to accommodate the Glock magazine and the mag release button, while located in the traditional location, has an extender that allows it to operate properly. Otherwise, all the controls are standard for an AR. You can install standard AR backup sights, and the top features a full-length of Picatinny rail for optics. The shell deflector and dust cover are functional, but the forward assist is not. Instead, you can manually push the bolt forward if need be.

MARLIN CLASSIC MODEL 1894C LEVER ACTION

Pick up any lever-action rifle and images of the Wild West immediately come to mind. My mind conjures up Chuck Connors in The Rifleman TV show firing his lever action in lightning fast succession from the hip. Yul Brynner paid tribute to this move in the sci-fi western classic, Westworld, where he plays the original Terminator, a murderous android cowboy. It was a better movie than it sounds.

The Marlin Model 1894C is chambered in .357 Mag./.38 Special and readily accepts and fires both cartridges. It is extremely well paired with a .357 Mag. single- or double-action revolver.

Lever-action rifles became incredibly popular because of their high capacity and high rate of fire, the AR of its day. Manufacturers like Marlin developed them in several calibers to fit a variety of needs and one of the most popular variants were those that fired pistol cartridges. Just like today, when we have various semi-auto carbines that fire pistol ammunition and many that use the same magazine as popular pistols, back in the day folks recognized the convenience and economy of being able to use one type of ammunition in multiple platforms.

Lever actions did see some limited military use but, as the function of the lever made it difficult to fire from the prone position, they never gained much widespread popularity in this role. Marlin has been known as a lever-action rifle company since about the 1880s onward, and for good reason. The company has been an innovator and leader in the industry developing many new technologies and improvements for this classic design and manufacturing them in a wide variety of rifle and pistol cartridges.

The current Model 1894C reviewed here is chambered in .357 Mag./.38 Spl. and readily accepts and fires both cartridges. It is extremely well paired off with a .357 Mag. single- or double-action revolver. This is a truly compact, lightweight, accurate and hard-hitting rifle with a nine-shot capacity tubular magazine. In recent years, Marlin has moved production from North Haven, Connecticut, to Ilion, New York, and as an old Marlin fan I was eager to test out the change.

The Model 1894C's steel barrel is a compact 18.5 inches long. The original Model 1894 had a 24-inch barrel but the C, or compact model is excellent for transportation or fielding in heavy brush. The barrel features six-groove deep-cut Ballard-type rifling. Such rifling has significantly fewer lands and grooves than the micro groove Marlin originally pioneered that had shallower grooves to provide less bullet distortion and improved accuracy in small bore calibers. However, the Ballard rifling used here is better suited for higher caliber bullets.

The rifle's sights are of a very traditional style with an elevation adjustable semi-buckhorn folding rear sight and a ramp front blade with brass bead and Wide-Scan hood. The rear sight is attached to a spring steel sight base that is dovetailed onto the top of the barrel. It folds down to stay out of the way for scopes and has a softly sloping 'U" shape with a center notch. To adjust for elevation simply use your fingertips to lift the rear sight slightly and move the sight elevator forward or back to alternately lower or raise it.

To adjust for windage, the rear sight base must be tapped slightly right or left for proper adjustment. The front sight is of the post and dot variety with a bright brass bead that offers good contact against the rear sight. It is protected with a spring steel hood in what Marlin calls a Wide-Scan-style, which is almost oval in shape to offer a wider field of view on target.

This was one of the first lever-action rifles to feature a flat solid top receiver and side ejection making it extremely well suited for mounting a scope with the included hardware. The top of the receiver is pre-drilled and tapped and will accommodate several aftermarket scope bases and mounts. Marlin ships each rifle with an offset hammer spur that is reversible for left- or right-hand use. This spur provides you with sufficient access to operate the hammer with a scope mounted.

The Model 1894C was one of the first lever-action rifles to feature a flat, solid-top receiver and side ejection making it extremely well suited for mounting a scope with the included hardware.

The entire rifle, minus the stock, is made with five machined solid steel forgings and carries a deep blue finish with Marlin's "Mar-Shield," a tough and corrosion resistant outer layer. The receiver encompasses the single-stage lever action, which sports a squared and flat finger lever. On the right side of the receiver is the loading gate that allows you to load a round singly or to top off the magazine. To unload the rifle, simply cycle the action until the rifle is empty.

The tubular spring loaded magazine resides under the barrel and can accommodate up to nine rounds of .357 Mag. or .38 Special ammunition. To load, simply press the front of the bullet into the loading gate and then forward with your thumb until it is seated and the loading gate closes. This can be a bit of a thumb buster — especially if you aren't paying attention and attempt to reload quickly or after a full day on the range.

The sliding bolt ejects the cartridges to the right side and the firmer the lever is operated the better they eject. Failure to aggressively work the lever can result in failures to eject as well as difficulty loading, so don't be afraid to put some juice into it. The

Marlin 39A abounds with safety features. The bottom of the receiver at the grip has a safety tab preventing the rifle from firing unless the lever is closed completely. The exposed hammer has a built-in hammer drop safety when it is placed in the half-cock position. The cross-bolt safety can only be applied when the hammer is either in half cock or full cock to the rear. The cross-bolt safety is a round button located at the rear of receiver toward the top just in front of the hammer and acts as a hammer block. To activate, simply push it in from left to right and a button that reads "safe" pops up on the right side of the receiver. To deactivate, push the button in from right

On the range the Marlin handled very easily with its short overall length and light weight, not unlike an AR. Firing .38 Special ammunition offered very little recoil and the .357 Magnum loadings were still very pleasant to shoot. It's a less than obvious, yet very effective survival gun.

to left and it pops up with a red circle on the left side of the receiver.

For the rifle to fire, the hammer must be cocked manually or via the cycling of the action. The hammer can be safely lowered on a live round by placing the safety on and depressing the trigger while manually holding the hammer and slowly lowering it to the half-cock position. When ready to fire again simply cock the hammer and place the cross-bolt safety in the fire position. If you lower the hammer with the safety on, you cannot deactivate the safety until the hammer is cocked fully again; however, the safety can go on and off if the hammer was already in the half-cock position before you engaged the safety.

One interesting safety issue with all tubular magazine firearms is that each round sits behind the next, the tip of the bullet making contact with the primer of the one in front. With pointed ammunition, inertia from firing the rifle or from dropping it could

SPECIFICATIONS
MARLIN MODEL 1894C

CALIBER: .357 Mag./.38 Spl.
BARREL: 18.5 in.
OA LENGTH: 36 in.
WEIGHT: 6 lbs. empty
STOCK: American black walnut
SIGHTS: Adjustable iron sights
ACTION: Lever action
FINISH: Blued
CAPACITY: 9
PRICE: $707.95
WWW.MARLINFIREARMS.COM

cause a primer detonation with catastrophic results. This is not a concern, however, with the 1894C when using pistol ammunition that is not pointed.

The all-wood straight grip stock is made from a very nice grade of American black walnut and has a deep matte finish and is well fitted to the rifle. The fore-end and pistol grip are finely cut checkered with a traditional diamond pattern. The comb is fluted and raised for an improved grip and better cheek weld. Steel swivel studs fore and aft make it easy to attach a sling for field carry and the rear of the stock comes with a comfortable brown rubber buttpad with the company's distinctive Marlin man on horseback logo.

In firing the Marlin 1894C I found the action to be a bit stiff and require a fair amount of aggressive handling. This reminded me a bit of a pump-action shotgun in that if you soft-pedal it, it just won't work properly. After a day of working the flat square steel lever I also began to think that maybe gloves would have been a good idea, as the rifle has some sharp angles that started to feel rough after a while. Fortunately, the trigger guard itself is very good sized and using some leather gloves when operating this rifle would be no problem and certainly increase user comfort. When using the lever quickly and aggressively there is a chance of pinching the palm between the lever and the receiver slightly.

The gun's single-action trigger did not have any creep or over-travel and broke consistently at 7 pounds, which I felt was a bit high for a single-action trigger, but did not significantly affect accuracy or function. On the range, the rifle handled very easily with its short overall length and light weight, making it feel like an AR. Firing .38 Special ammunition offered very little recoil while the stout .357 Magnum loadings were still very pleasant to shoot. Handgun hunters have been using the .357 Magnum for deer for many years and having a hot cartridge in a rifle like this — with a longer barrel that produces significantly higher velocities — could be very effective on deer at intermediate distance.

I experienced no malfunctions on the range other than those associated with insufficiently aggressive operation of the action. Once I got the hang of it I was able to put shots on target consistently and quickly (but not as quickly as Chuck Connors). Using the iron sights, I tested for accuracy at 50 yards from a sand bag rest and a sturdy bench. The results were very consistent across all choices, averaging between 2 and 3 inches. I expect better results could easily be had with a mounted scope or red-dot optic.

THE SCOUT RIFLE

The concept of the scout rifle was developed by recognized gun expert, the late Lt. Col Jeff Cooper. The idea was to have an all-purpose rifle that was short, lightweight, handy and could be had most anywhere in the world with little hassle. The rifle needed to be accurate with iron sights to 500 yards and powerful enough to take down large game animals for hunting or self-defense. For this, Cooper selected a bolt-action rifle (as these are far less restricted than semi-auto rifles) less than 40 inches long and weighing under 6.5 pounds. He also chose the .308/7.62 caliber as an ideal all-purpose round and, as it is common with many militaries around the globe, easy to find.

There are many rifles that fit Cooper's criteria but then he added one very distinctive feature — a forward-mounted magnified optic with extended eye relief. Extended eye relief scopes are more commonly seen on handguns but there was method to Cooper's madness. Speed and reliability were two of his concerns (another reason to opt for a bolt action) and he wanted to keep the area above the action free of any obstruction (like a scope). This allowed for the rifle to be reloaded faster with stripper clips and ensured that ejection of empty cases was not engendered in any way. Lastly, Cooper felt that having an extended eye relief scope prevented the development of tunnel vision and allowed the operator full peripheral vision and situational awareness. One drawback of extended eye relief scopes is that they lack the full magnification

The Steyr Scout gives you the option of mounting an extended eye relief scope, and even has a built-in bipod that tucks up into the stock.

of larger rearward-mounted optics. Cooper felt that 2-3x magnification was sufficient.

There were some other less distinct features that Cooper insisted on but they are not necessary to the core concept of the scout rifle. After all, he was building the rifle in his mind from scratch so anything is possible. Only one company actually built Cooper his scout rifle while he was alive, the Steyr Scout. Since then, several more companies have come forward with their own Cooper-inspired scout rifles.

STEYR SCOUT

The original Scout Rifle, it has all the features Cooper wanted. It's a lightweight rifle with backup ghost ring iron sights mounted on the receiver and not the barrel, a magazine cutoff device to be able to fire one shot only or with a 5-round detachable magazine. The polymer stock has a backup 5-round magazine in the

The Steyr Scout, developed for Lt. Col. Jeff Cooper, was a short, fast, bolt-action rifle designed as the ultimate do-anything survival gun.

SPECIFICATIONS:
STEYR SCOUT

CALIBER: .308 Win.
BARREL: 19 in.
OA LENGTH: 38.6 in.
WEIGHT: 6.6 lbs.
  (without magazine)
SIGHTS: Iron with rail
STOCK: Plastic
ACTION: Bolt
FINISH: Black, gray or green
CAPACITY: 5+1 rounds
PRICE: $1,699

buttstock. The fore-end of the stock sports an integral bipod that folds up completely into the stock, an accessory rail and five sling attachment points, another Cooper notion.

The Steyr Scout has a three-position safety with a fire option and two levels of safety, one locks the bolt and one does not. Of course, the rifle is available in different colors and calibers, as Cooper recognized that in some countries civilians are not allowed to own firearms that can function using military calibers. Extended capacity magazines (up to 20 rounds) are also available.

RUGER GUNSITE SCOUT RIFLE

Ruger developed their own scout concept and dubbed it appropriately the "Gunsite Scout Rifle." Gunsite is, of course, the training facility established by Jeff Cooper. The rifle features a forward-mounted Picatinny rail for optics, ghost ring backup iron sights,

The Ruger "Gunsite Scout Rifle" was developed in conjunction with the staff at the world famous shooting facility.

SPECIFICATIONS:
RUGER GUNSITE SCOUT

CALIBER: .308 Win.
BARREL: 16.1 in.
OA LENGTH: 38.5 in.
WEIGHT: 7.1 lbs.
  (without magazine)
SIGHTS: Iron with rail
STOCK: Laminate
ACTION: Bolt
FINISH: Black, gray or black
CAPACITY: 10+1 rounds
PRICE: $1,139

a detachable 10-round box magazine (5 rounders are available), and a traditional scope mounting option. It is available in several different calibers.

The rifle was developed in conjunction with the Gunsite Academy and features their name engraved on the receiver. Interestingly, this rifle features a grey laminated wood stock that is weather resistant and includes rubber spacers that can be used to adjust the length of pull at the buttpad. A synthetic stock model is also available, and

The Savage Scout rifle is built on Savage's legendary action and has the company's excellent AccuTrigger.

in both stock types the barrel remains free floated. The barrel, available in two different lengths and in either stainless steel or blued, is cold hammer forged for improved accuracy and longer life. The barrel is topped off with a choice of different muzzle devices, a flash hider being the most common.

SAVAGE SCOUT

Savage is known for making very accurate rifles at reasonable prices. The Model 11 Scout is no exception. They key to any modern Savage rifle is the AccuTrigger, which allows you to adjust the trigger pull for increased comfort and accuracy. The Savage AccuStock provides a rigid interface between stock, action and barrel, and supports parts along the entire length rather than at just two points. This diminishes pressure on the barrel and improves accuracy.

SPECIFICATIONS:
SAVAGE 11 SCOUT

CALIBER: .308 Win.
BARREL: 18 in.
OA LENGTH: 40.5 in.
WEIGHT: 7.8 lbs.
  (without magazine)
SIGHTS: Iron with rail
STOCK: Synthetic
ACTION: Bolt
FINISH: Flat dark earth
CAPACITY: 10+1 rounds
PRICE: $818

The handy little Mossberg MVP Scout can accept both M1A and AR-10 mags.

Like other scout rifles, the Savage 11 Scout is a bolt action with a forward-mounted optics rail, backup iron ghost ring sights, and a synthetic stock. Savage adds a cheek riser to the stock for improved comfort, a detachable box magazine with 10-round capacity, and a muzzle brake, along with three sling swivel points. It is only available in one size and one caliber.

SPECIFICATIONS:
MOSSBERG MVP SCOUT

CALIBER: .308 Win.
BARREL: 16.25 in.
OA LENGTH: 37.5 in.
WEIGHT: 6.75 lbs.
  (without magazine)
SIGHTS: Iron with rail
STOCK: Synthetic
ACTION: Bolt
FINISH: Black
CAPACITY: 10+1 rounds
PRICE: $761

MOSSBERG SCOUT

Mossberg seems to be mostly known for their Model 500 shotgun, but the company makes plenty of popular rifles as well including the Mossberg MVP Scout. One thing that sets the MVP Scout apart is that it can accept both M1A and AR-10 magazines. The longer length top Picatinny rail allows for more expansive options for optics while the backup iron ghost ring sights include a front fiber optic for improved visibility.

The short barrel is threaded so it can accept standard AR muzzle devices (Standard A2 flash hider is included) as well as a suppressor if so desired. The trigger pull is user adjustable from 3 to 7 pounds, the bolt handle is oversized for

The Springfield Armory Scout Squad is a hard-hitting .308 semi-auto that accepts a forward-mounted optic.

easier use, and the synthetic stock includes side rails for mounting accessories. The rifle can be purchased with a Vortex scope and comes with a sling as well. It is only available in one size and caliber.

SPECIFICATIONS:
SPRINGFIELD M1A SCOUT SQUAD

CALIBER: .308 Win.
BARREL: 18 in.
OA LENGTH: 40.33 in.
WEIGHT: 8.8 lbs.
  (without magazine)
SIGHTS: Iron with rail
STOCK: Synthetic
ACTION: Semi-auto
FINISH: Black, tan
CAPACITY: 10+1 rounds
PRICE: $1,849

SPRINGFIELD M1A SCOUT SQUAD

Jeff Cooper was asked about the scout rifle concept using semi-autos and he was certainly not opposed but insisted on reliability. There is hardly a more battle proven and reliable semi-auto rifle than the M1 Garand and the M1A. Springfield Armory has been churning out M1A rifles for some time and has developed a scout version as well.

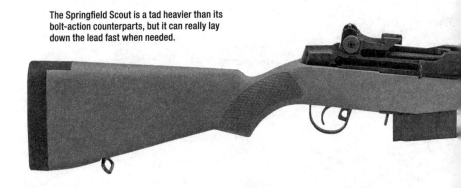

The Springfield Scout is a tad heavier than its bolt-action counterparts, but it can really lay down the lead fast when needed.

The Springfield Armory M1A-A1 Scout Squad takes the standard M1A concept and turns it into a much smaller and handier rifle with forward-mounted Picatinny rail, synthetic stock, and a recoil-reducing muzzle brake. The rifle sports an 18-inch barrel, two-stage trigger, aperture adjustable iron sights, a standard box magazine, and gas piston-operated reliability in 7.62 NATO.

CLEANING KITS

In any survival situation, maintaining your equipment is essential. If you fail your gear, your gear will fail you. This especially applies to firearms, which must be kept clean whenever possible to stay in good working order. Fortunately, there are innumerable CLP, or "Clean, Lubricate and Protect" kits that can help you do this at home or in the field.

TACTICAL ATLAS CLEANING MAT

There are a lot of folks buying ARs, many for the first time. Reading the manual and taking a class is a good idea if you don't have much experience with the platform, but one item that can help you keep your rifle clean and running properly is the Tactical Atlas, or TACAT, firearm parts cleaning mat. It's available for several different guns, but the AR mat shows you in full-color photographic detail all the parts of the AR and how to clean them.

Made from two layers of military grade vinyl, this mat will last and keep your furniture or workspace clean from solvents or scratches. The vinyl has an anti-slick surface on top and bottom to keep small parts from sliding off and getting lost (a big reason why I always have a supply of spare parts) and will keep the mat on your work surface. The material is resistant to oil and solvent and wipes clean easily when you are done. The gun mat is large enough to accommodate a full-size AR and will protect the finish on your rifle.

When you are cleaning your AR (or any gun for that matter), there are few feelings worse than putting it back together and finding you have parts left over. The TACAT mat will help you make sure that all the parts go back into the right places, and you should always perform a function check on any gun that you have cleaned and reassembled. Indeed, the mat makes for a great teaching and learning tool for all of the small parts of your rifle, as well as easy disassembly and reassembly.

MS CLEAN KIT

Anyone who has spent time in the military will be familiar with the soft nylon cleaning pouch issued with the M-16. This pouch was designed for the old Alice Clip system and is dated to say the least. The new MS Clean Kit was designed by a veteran to modernize the cleaning system for the M-16/AR-15 rifle. Instead of a

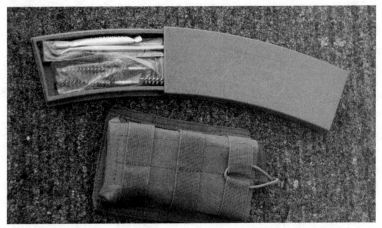

The MS Clean Kit for the M-16/AR-15 rifle uses a hard polymer case that is the same size and shape as a standard 30-round magazine.

soft pouch, this innovative kit uses a hard polymer case that is the same size and shape as a standard 30-round magazine. This makes it easy to store in issued mag pouches, while at the same time it will not fit in the magazine eliminating any chance of confusion.

The hard case is built tough and tested by being run over with military vehicles. Inside the hard case is a full cleaning kit with steel sectioned rods and all the most popular accessories. Steel rods are far more valuable in the field than pull-through cleaners because they can be used to dislodge bore obstructions. In my time in the National Guard, the armorer would not accept rifles back until they were spotless. This involved Q-tips, pipe cleaners, and dental picks. Dental picks, cleaning brush, and bore/chamber brushes in several calibers are included with the MS Clean Kit, as well as patches and your choice of Froglube, FIREClean or slip2000 cleaning solvents and oils.

MS Clean Kits are available in several colors to help identify them and distinguish them from your actual magazines, including black, red, orange, O.D. green, and flat dark earth. There is extra room in each kit for additional small items. Different colored and empty kits are available to make your own kit or to use for spare parts or first aid supplies.

OTIS GUN CLEANING KITS

If you are out on the range or in the field and need a quick bore clean on the spot, there is nothing better or easier than a pull-through cleaning cord. Otis has been specializing in cleaning kits that use this system for some time, and they sell a lot to military and law enforcement. These kits are very compact and easy to use, but the new Ripcord is even simpler.

The Ripcord is a flexible rod made from a steel cable for strength, and the outside of the cord is wrapped in soft cloth like Nomex, designed to withstand temperatures up to 700 degrees. This material acts as both a brush and a patch, removing fouling in the barrel with no solvents required as you pull the cord from the breech end through the bore and out of the muzzle. One end of the steel cable has a thicker helix-shaped rubberized core, which firmly presses the Nomex material into the lands and grooves for a complete cleaning. The ends of the cord are threaded to install other Otis cleaning accessories. The Ripcord easily rolls up into a small, flat coil, so you can store it anywhere and have it with you when you need it. In extreme cases, the coil is stiff enough to help you push out most bore obstructions as well. It is available in the four most popular calibers: 5.56mm, 7.62mm, 9mm, and .45 cal.

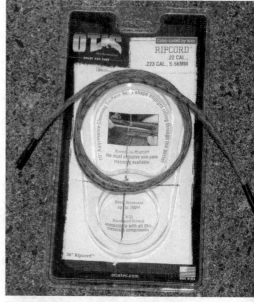

The Otis Ripcord is a flexible rod that acts as both a brush and patch to remove fouling in the barrel with no solvents required. You simply pull the cord from the breech end through the bore and out of the muzzle.

RAND CLP is an all-in-one eco-friendly cleaner, lubricant and protectant. It reminded the author of the old CLP (Cleaning, Lubricant, Protectant) used in the military.

TAC-SHIELD CLEANING KIT

Compact and portable cleaning kits are extremely valuable when you are out on the range or traveling. The Tac-Shield Cleaning Kit, available in .45, 9mm, and .223 calibers, certainly fits the bill with a lot of added features that can make it indispensable. The kit includes a standard brass push-through segmented cleaning rod (the .223 kit has a pull-through cable instead), 25 cleaning patches, bronze bore brush, bronze cleaning jag, slotted polymer cleaning tip, cotton mop, and a very comfortable and convenient rod handle. Pretty standard fare for most cleaning kits, however, the Tac-Shield also includes a six-piece set of bits for repairs and adjustments that fit onto the cleaning rod handle. The whole system comes in a tough, compact plastic carrying case with a clear lid and secure latch to keep it closed.

OILS AND SOLVENTS

RAND CLP

In the old days of corrosive black powder, soldiers used water and bear fat to keep their guns clean and oiled. Today, there is a plethora of options, each promising incredible results. For the most part, I have found that one cleaning solvent is pretty much equal to the next. However, a few products do stand out.

Rand CLP is an all-in-one eco-friendly cleaner, lubricant, and protectant. Indeed, it reminds me a bit of the old CLP we used in the military. Instead of having to mess with one solvent to remove carbon, lead, and copper fouling and another oil/lubricant to protect the metal, the Rand CLP does it all with one application. It is odorless and completely non-toxic as well. I used it on my 1,000-round-plus gun training trip to keep my firearm running, and it made cleaning a lot easier and faster. Another nice aspect of the Rand CLP is that it will not attract dust or lint, and it improves operation of the action as well. Once you use this solvent, it also makes subsequent cleanings easier.

LYMAN BUTCH'S BORE SHINE

Some ARs are used for tactical training, others for competition, and yet more for long-range varmint shooting and precision. Each type of use requires a specific type of AR, and each type of specialized AR functions best with a lubricant dedicated for its intended use. Precision shooters know that heavy fouling can affect accuracy, chamber pressure, and muzzle velocity.

Designed by a competitive benchrest shooter, Butch's Bore Shine from Lyman Products Corp. is a non-abrasive chemical solvent that easily and quickly removes carbon, copper, lead, wax, and plastic buildup from rifles, pistols, and shotgun bores. The best way to use this product is to pre-treat your bore before you shoot. This helps keep the copper fouling from building up in the first place and makes cleaning much easier and faster.

FROGLUBE

FrogLube was developed by Navy SEALs for extreme tough duty in the harshest environments and is very popular. I like it because it is completely biodegradable and made from a food-grade substance. The stuff is odorless, although a faint wintergreen smell is added. The CLP bonds with the metal on your firearm to create a protective barrier that keeps out moisture and prevents fouling. The company recommends application of the lube into the barrel when the weapon is still hot so that it is more readily absorbed into the pores of the metal surface. It will preserve and protect plastic, wood, and rubber parts.

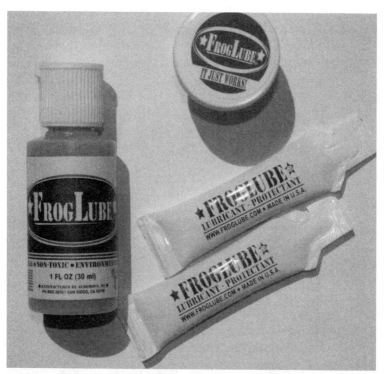

Possibly one of the best known and most well-received CLPs on the market today, FrogLube was developed by Navy SEALs for extreme tough duty in the harshest environments.

SHOTGUNS

T he shotgun has been the go-to big stick for everyone from stagecoach operators and farmers with attractive daughters to soldiers and patrol officers. The modern day 12-gauge shotgun is arguably the single most versatile weapon you can own. Just by changing the ammunition type, you can hunt any animal in North America from fowl to bear. Plus, interchangeable barrels and choke tubes expand the versatility to an even greater extent. Barrels can be had in different lengths with interchangeable chokes and some even with rifling to improve slug accuracy. The shotgun could be the ideal, do-anything survival gun.

In the realm of personal protection, standard 00 buckshot

Survival shotguns don't have to be high capacity or tactical. A basic over/under like this Ruger Red Label can keep you fed and safe.

load carries a payload of nine .33-caliber lead pellets traveling at 1,300 fps. To put it another way that is 484 grains of lead hitting a target with over 1,800 foot pounds of fight-stopping force, assuming all the pellets hit the target.

What about effective range? With standard 12-gauge 2.75-inch 00 buckshot out of a cylinder bore 18-inch barrel, my average is a 10-inch spread at 15 yards. Using some of the new loads that are designed to tighten patterns, I average less than half that spread, doubling the effective range. Personally, a 20-inch spread of buckshot for self-defense would be my maximum; keeping in mind that velocity drops off significantly at distance. Basically, you can expect 30 to 50 yards maximum effective range, depending on your load. Any farther than that, switch to slugs. Outdoors and in more built-up environments, this is a good distance and provides extremely effective results. A solid hit will disable an assailant very quickly, and you can avoid the problem of over-penetration. This can be a particular concern when operating in suburban or urban environments where innocents may be present. Pellets that go astray and miss the target lose energy quickly at distance.

eowners prefer the shotgun for home defense
e reasons, but unless you are someone of serious
robably don't have a lot of 30- and 50-yard interior
ore likely, 10 yards will be the maximum distance
you may have to defend from inside your home (probably closer
than that). At that distance, the pellets in a shotgun pattern don't
have much time to spread, and the shot pattern can act more like
one solid mass.

In fact, at close distances there is a danger of buckshot or other
heavy loads over-penetrating — easily punching through walls
and light barriers and retaining enough energy to harm family
members on the other side. At typical inside-the-home distances,
lighter loads are preferable, and many opt for birdshot, which is
among the lightest you can get (at least in terms of pellet size, not
payload). You are still dealing with close to 500 grains of lead
traveling at 1,200 fps in one very tight pattern. That is over 400
lead pellets each less than .10 caliber and individually they lose
force very quickly with no danger of over-penetration. Against
a soft target at close range, birdshot can be extremely effective,
while still protecting family members who are hiding out or
sleeping in adjacent rooms.

The downside of the shotgun is the size of the ammunition.
This limits both magazine capacity and how much you can carry.
On the plus side, 12-gauge ammunition has never been in short

supply and is readily available everywhere. Even during the great ammunition shortage of a few years ago, the shelves always had plenty of 12 gauge.

PUMP-ACTION SHOTGUNS

For most people using a shotgun, especially when it comes to survival situations, the pump action has been the way to go for over a century. Pump-action shotguns were issued to troops in WWI and are still being issued today. Most every police car has a pump locked in place and readily accessible to an officer needing a bit more firepower.

Indeed, pump actions have a lot to offer, the biggest benefit being rock-solid reliability as long as you do your part. That means aggressively working the pump (no short stroking) to get the gun into action and keep it reliably ejecting spent cases and feeding live rounds. However, to many modern shooters who are accustomed to semi-automatics, a manually operated firearm seems antiquated and slow. Fortunately, there are also plenty of very effective and reliable semi-automatic shotguns now being produced that offer every bit of versatility and reliability that pump guns provide. But first, here is a look at the best pump-action shotguns to pull you through any survival scenario.

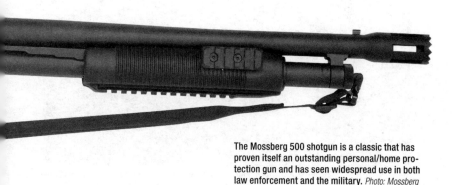

The Mossberg 500 shotgun is a classic that has proven itself an outstanding personal/home protection gun and has seen widespread use in both law enforcement and the military. *Photo: Mossberg*

MOSSBERG 500

To say that the Mossberg 500 shotgun is a classic would be a bit of an understatement. It is one of the most popular shotguns ever made and has been in continuous production since the early 1960s with millions manufactured. A 12-gauge model 500 was the second gun I ever owned and the first one I bought for myself. I learned to shoot trap and skeet with it. O.F. Mossberg & Sons, Inc. is, in fact, the largest manufacturer of pump-action shotguns worldwide and the oldest family-owned gun maker in America, having been founded in 1919.

But the 500 is good for far more than busting clay birds. It has proven itself an outstanding personal/home protection gun and has seen widespread use in both law enforcement and the military in various configurations. The model 590A1 Mossberg can be found in current use with various branches of the U.S. Military and is reportedly the only pump-action shotgun to satisfy the Mil-Spec 3443 requirements, which include an endurance test of

The standard home defense Mossberg shotgun is a 5+1 capacity 12-gauge pump-action shotgun with a tough synthetic stock, 18.5-inch barrel with a cylinder bore and a short 13 inches of pull.

3,000 rounds of buckshot. This alone makes it a good choice for a survival shotgun, plus it comes in 7- and 9-round versions.

The standard home defense Mossberg shotgun is a 5+1 capacity 12-gauge pump action with a tough synthetic stock, 18.5-inch barrel with a cylinder bore, and a short 13 inches of pull (the distance from the trigger to the buttstock) for greater maneuverability in tight quarters. Changing the stock to add a pistol grip or to make it longer is a fairly easy proposition, and there are many customization options for this ubiquitous scattergun.

SPECIFICATIONS
MOSSBERG 500
GAUGE: 12 ga.
BARREL: 18.5 in.
OA LENGTH: 37.25 in.
WEIGHT: 6.88 lbs.
SIGHTS: Bead front
STOCK: Polymer
ACTION: Pump
FINISH: Matte black
CAPACITY: 5+1 rounds
PRICE: $484
WWW.MOSSBERG.COM

The aluminum receiver on the 500 has a matte black, non-reflective finish and features dual action bars for improved reliability and action strength, as well as Mossberg's tang-mounted thumb safety, a design preferred by many. This safety can be easier to engage, and its top-mounted design makes it simple to check the condition of the shotgun. The trigger housing assembly and trigger guard are black polymer and house the steel trigger parts. It can be easily removed for cleaning. The steel slide release is located at the rear of the trigger guard on the left side of the receiver.

Shells eject to the right using dual extractors, and the shell elevator has an anti-jam design to prevent double feeds — or misfeeds in case of user error — such as short stroking the slide. There are typically no real sights provided (just a bead at the top front of the barrel) but the top of the receiver is drilled and tapped for easy installation of ghost ring rear sights or a rail system for mounting various types of optics.

Action lockup is achieved through a solid steel-to-steel connection that locks the bolt to the barrel extension through a lug. The steel magazine tube, which is screwed into the receiver and located under the barrel, holds five rounds of 2 ¾- or 3-inch shells. As expected in a defensive shotgun, there is no removable magazine plug restricting its full capacity, as may be found on many sporting shotguns. The standard polymer fore-end is ribbed for a firm hold. There are many aftermarket fore-ends available with integral tactical lights or rails.

The Model 500's 18.5-inch steel barrel has a matte black, non-reflective finish to match the receiver and magazine tube. It has a definitively substantial feel, heavier than a standard barrel and will accept both 2 ¾- and 3-inch shells. All Model 500 Mossbergs feature an easily removed and changed barrel for added versatility. A longer barrel with interchangeable tubes as well as a rifled barrel add the versatility to use this shotgun for hunting as well as personal defense.

Recoil is very manageable, and the overall short length and short length of pull make this a very handy shotgun that is both light and easy to handle. Training for survival situations is key, and with any pump-action shotgun, especially under stress, lack of practice can be extremely detrimental to your long-term health. Under stress, there is a tendency for inexperienced shooters to short stroke shotguns; that is, to fail to bring the fore-end completely to the rear and completely to the front in an aggressive manner.

One variant in particular that I recommend is the Mossberg 500 Thunder Ranch model. It has an excellent fit and finish, lots of tactical accessories and features available, and a reasonable price point.

REMINGTON 870

The Model 870 is one of the most popular guns Remington makes, and it sits at the top spot for the most manufactured shotgun in the world. On April 10th, 2009, the 870 reached the milestone of ten million sold. And it's no wonder that it's so darn popular. Introduced as the fourth shotgun in the Remington series, it planned to fix the flaws of the previous models to outsell the Winchester Model 12. It was designed to be rugged, reliable, streamlined, and economical.

The Remington 870 is so popular in part because of how versatile it is. It is the shotgun most often used by law enforcement, and it has also seen military use. It has a major presence among civilians as a home defense weapon, as well as a hunting shotgun. It is so widespread that there are many different versions, such as the MCS (Modular Combat Shotgun), which was designed to be quickly modified with different barrels, magazine tubes, and stocks for different purposes, from urban combat to door breaching. Or the 12-gauge Police model that chambers 3-inch magnum shells and has a shortened fore-end and sling mounts.

The Remington 870 is the most-produced pump-action shotgun in the world and is available in many configurations, including this 200th Anniversary model. *Photo: Remington*

SPECIFICATIONS
REMINGTON 870 TACTICAL

GAUGE: 12 ga.
BARREL: 18.5 in.
OA LENGTH: 38.5 in.
WEIGHT: 7.5 lbs.
SIGHTS: Bead front
STOCK: Polymer
ACTION: Pump
FINISH: Matte black
CAPACITY: 6+1 rounds
PRICE: $443
WWW.REMINGTON.COM

The standard Remington 870 is chambered in 12 gauge and can fit 2.75- and 3-inch shells. It comes with a wood stock, 28-inch vent rib barrel, and the Rem Choke standard interchangeable choke system. A Modified choke is included. The magazine tube can hold up to four shells but comes plugged to comply with waterfowl hunting regs, which limit it to 2+1 capacity. Of course, the plug is easily removed to convert the gun for serious work. The standard stock has a 14-inch length of pull, including a thick recoil pad that will accommodate most adults.

The Remington 870 Tactical may be a better survival gun choice, however, with a 6-round magazine tube and an 18.5-inch fixed cylinder choke barrel . As with all 870s, the push button safety is located at the rear of the trigger guard with the action release tab at the front. Dual action bars ensure reliable operation, and the receiver is made from steel. Given the popularity of the 870, it should come as no surprise that accessory options are nearly limitless. Indeed, if all you had for survival guns was one model 870, you'd be doing pretty well.

KEL-TEC KSG

Kel-Tec has taken the pump shotgun and completely reengineered it from the ground up into something so much better than before, so much so that it can hardly be recognized as a … shotgun. Kel-Tec is best known for their significant use of polymer injection molding in the manufacture of various firearms, most significantly the P-3AT .380 ACP pocket pistol. They also make innovative semi-auto rifles that use AR magazines and, more recently, a bullpup .308 Win. semi-auto rifle, the RFB.

The Kel-Tec KSG is a bullpup, pump-action, downward ejecting, dual extended magazine tube 12-gauge shotgun with 14+1 capacity using 2.75-inch shells or 12+1 with 3-inchers. Bullpup in a long gun simply means that the action has been moved back to occupy the space where the stock is located, shortening the overall length of the rifle or shotgun while maintaining a full-length stock and barrel. The most common examples of this design can be found in the Steyr AUG, French FAMAS, and the British L85A2 rifles. Of course, Kel-Tec was not the first company to come up with a bullpup shotgun, nor even the first to make one with dual magazine tubes (that was the South African Neostead shotgun), but they may have perfected the concept and are certainly the only American-made option.

At only 26 inches in overall length, the gun feels miniscule and unlike any other shotgun I have handled. With its Parkerized 18.5-inch cylinder bore barrel, it meets the legal minimum length and requirements to be purchased in all 50 states, just like any other pump-action shotgun.

The dual magazine tubes ride under the barrel and are flush with the muzzle at the front for a distinctive triangular look. They are made from hardened steel and are welded in place for strength

The Kel-Tec KSG is a bullpup pump action, downward ejecting, dual extended magazine tube 12-gauge shotgun with 14+1 capacity using 2.75-inch shells. *Photo: Kel-Tec*

At only 26 inches in overall length the KSG bullpup feels miniscule and unlike any other shotgun the author has ever handled.

and durability. Overall, I got the feeling that the KSG designers thought of everything. There are even witness holes at the top of both magazine tubes to let you know how many rounds remain in each (although I would have engraved numbers next to the holes). I haven't seen witness holes on any other tactical shotgun, but the KSG's bullpup design lends itself to a more convenient use of them, since the magazine tubes are easily visible without having to readjust your grip.

You can select which magazine tube to feed from with a simple ambidextrous throw lever located behind the pistol grip just forward of the ejection port. Push the selector all the way to the right, and the action feeds from the right magazine tube; push it completely to the left, and rounds are fed from the left tube. The middle position blocks both magazine tubes and allows for the operator to clear the chamber without having to completely empty either tube. It is also the position used for disassembly. The action on all pump shotguns will lock up and must be either fired or you must toggle a release to open. The KSG rather ingeniously places the pump release in front of the trigger guard and takes the shape of an elongated ambidextrous lever that can easily be activated with the trigger finger simply by pushing it down. There is a simple ambidextrous cross-bolt safety located at the top of the pistol grip and, while a bit stiff, it can be pushed to the right to deactivate or to the left to activate.

The KSG's receiver is made from hardened steel and is Parkerized black. The portion of the barrel directly above the pistol grip has a polymer cover and very little of the barrel is exposed overall. The stock, grip, and even the trigger are made from matte black glass fiber reinforced nylon and feature square block texturing. The grip itself is hollow and could offer a lot of space for keeping accessories such as extra batteries for lights, lasers, or optics, but Kel-Tec isn't (yet) offering a cover to turn this into usable storage. The grip does have two holes located behind the trigger that are used to hold the takedown pins during disassembly. The rear of the stock is covered by a soft rubber buttpad that helps soak up recoil and keeps the gun firmly on the shoulder.

The top of the KSG has a steel Picatinny rail that provides 12 inches of real estate for backup iron sights and optics. The pump features six inches of Picatinny rail molded into the polymer material and is ideal for a forward pistol grip and light/laser combo. There are steel sling loops at the front on either side of the barrel and a rear sling loop built into the stock, which makes for very convenient carry with the included nylon sling.

Maintenance and disassembly are well thought out and simple for the user. By removing the two receiver-mounted cross pins, the grip assembly can be lifted out and the stock pulled out rearward. Then the bolt can be removed for cleaning. To remove the barrel from the receiver assembly, just loosen the nuts at the front of each magazine tube and slide the barrel forward.

Loading the KSG is a simple matter but requires a bit more reach than on a traditional shotgun. Also, loading a single round into the chamber must be done from underneath through the ejection port. To load each magazine tube, place the selector lever toward the tube you want to load first, which blocks the other tube. Then reverse the selector to load the opposite magazine.

I found that the pump is fairly long and, if gripped too far back, your hand hits the trigger guard before the pump comes all the way rearward, resulting in short stroking and malfunctions. This problem is completely eliminated with the use of a vertical fore grip, however, and as with any pump-action shotgun, you still have to aggressively and completely work the action to avoid short stroking or double feeds. However, with the action located so far back the KSG seems extremely well balanced and feels much lighter than the nearly 7 lbs. would indicate. The position of the action significantly affects the recoil signature, placing it much farther back against the shoulder, pushing straight back and almost completely eliminating muzzle rise. The recoil feels significantly lighter than on a standard shotgun and is actually comfortable even with slug and buckshot loads, all with a fairly smooth

One advantage of the Kel-Tec KSG: You can select which magazine tube to feed from with a simple ambidextrous throw lever located behind the pistol grip just forward of the ejection port.

7.5-lb. trigger pull. With a full load of 15 rounds, the extra weight soaks up even more recoil but still handles extremely well, and the gun will fire as fast as you can work the pump. I did not test out any 3-inch loads, however.

Switching between one magazine tube and the other was easy with very little practice by using my hand on the pistol grip and without having to release the grip. The shells from the KSG eject downward instead of forward and quite aggressively at that (similar to the Ithaca Model 37), leaving a nice pile of empties on the ground at your feet. This could prove quite a benefit for left-handed shooters who too often have to deal with empty cases ejecting across their noses.

While the shotgun in general is king of home defense, I have never been a fan of using it for this purpose. My concerns always included heavy recoil, which dissuades practice especially for smaller-stature shooters, long and unwieldy handling especially in tight home defense environments, and limited magazine capacity. However, the Kel-Tec KSG has made me a convert and true believer and resolves pretty much all of my objections. The bullpup design provides a stock with more accuracy and control, and it effectively reduces recoil to very comfortable levels, all in an extremely compact package. The dual extended magazine tubes give it the firepower of most high-capacity pistols.

SPECIFICATIONS
KEL-TEC KSG

GAUGE: 12 ga.
CHAMBER: 2.75 and 3 in.
BARREL: 18.5 in. cylinder bore
OA LENGTH: 26.1 in.
HEIGHT: 7 in.
WEIGHT: 6.9 lbs.
SIGHTS: Picatinny rail
STOCK: Polymer
ACTION: Pump
FINISH: Matte black
CAPACITY: 7+7+1 or 6+6+1 rounds
PRICE: $880
KELTECWEAPONS.COM

UTS-15 BULLPUP TACTICAL SHOTGUN

Another dual magazine pump-action shotgun is the UTS-15 Bullpup (which stands for Urban Tactical Shotgun 15-rounds) from UTAS, a Turkish company that has produced shotguns for some of the major names in the American firearms industry. Turkey, a NATO member, has long been a major player in the firearms business with a highly skilled workforce and the latest technology and equipment.

The bullpup design places the action inside the stock at the very rear of the gun. As a result, the overall length is made much shorter without having to sacrifice barrel length or effectiveness. Indeed, I measured the overall length with the short choke tube installed at 29.5 inches, while barrel length measured 20.5 inches.

This stout little 12-gauge pump action boasts dual magazine tubes that ride side-by-side above the barrel with each holding seven rounds of 2 ¾-inch shells or six rounds of 3-inch magnum shells. With a round in the chamber, this provides you with a total capacity of up to 15 rounds with no reloading. You can blast away, firing as fast as you can pump the action.

The UTS-15 Bullpup Tactical Shotgun is another 12-gauge dual magazine pump-action shotgun with 14+1 capacity. It's not hard to envision this short powerhouse concealed in one's survival backpack or bug-out bag.

While the UTS-15 is very short in overall length, it does seem a bit overly tall and stout. However, it is in fact very lightweight, coming in at less than 7 lbs. empty. This is thanks to its unique construction. According to UTAS, it's the first shotgun ever produced with a receiver made completely from fiber reinforced injection molded polymer. More than 80 percent of the gun is this material, which significantly increases corrosion and wear resistance while reducing weight and providing very strong and durable construction. In addition, the receiver has dual lengths of cooling holes along each side which, when combined with the bullpup mechanism, give it a very futuristic look. Above the top row of holes, there are white numbers from zero to seven on both sides to provide a round count. These holes match up with corresponding holes along the steel magazine tubes, and the white tip at the front of the magazine follower shows very clearly the number of

At the rear of each magazine tube is a dust cover that must be opened to load, and closed for the shotgun to operate. The top of the receiver has nearly 19 inches of continuous Picatinny rail. *Photo: Luk*

rounds remaining. You do have to view the side of the shotgun to see the round count, however.

At the rear of each magazine tube is a dust cover that must be opened to load shells. It must be closed for the shotgun to operate. Opening them reveals the follower tube. The top of the receiver has nearly 19 inches of continuous Picatinny rail, which makes it very easy to install the included iron sights or any preferred MBUIS or optic. The included sights are aluminum and very solid with an elevation-adjustable front sight and windage-adjustable rear. That rear sight can be flipped from a standard large peep aperture to a V-notch.

On the left side of the receiver are front and rear removable sling attachment points. These are steel and solidly built. All the steel and aluminum parts on the UTS-15 have a matte black chrome, anodized, or black oxide finish that matches well with the matte black non-glare textured finish on all the polymer parts.

At the rear of the Picatinny rail, protruding prominently through an opening in the top of the cheek rest/action cover, is the magazine tube selector switch. Leaving the selector in the middle position causes the action to feed from the magazine tubes in an alternating fashion until the gun runs empty. There is no need to flip the switch between tubes unless a specific tube is desired — in which case, orient the selector away from the tube you want to use. If only one tube is loaded, you can shut the other off, preventing it from being used. If set to auto select, the action will not alternate between the tubes but will only draw from the loaded magazine tube.

The polymer cheek rest is actually the action cover and can be easily rotated upward from the front in order to inspect the rear of the magazine tube, action, and chamber area. This really will only need to be done to clear a jam or malfunction and for disassembly. The chamber can be more easily checked with the action open from the right side of the gun. At the rear of the stock, an effective rubber energy-absorbing recoil pad is a cushy 1-inch thick.

The polymer pistol grip looks and feels just like a standard grip, and the safety selector lever is located in the same place on the left side of the receiver as on an AR, so it will be familiar to many.

The Federal Flite Control 00 Buckshot load patterns very tightly even at long distances and delivers nine .33-caliber pellets to the target — that's a lot of firepower.

The trigger is very reminiscent of an AR trigger, too, and the aluminum trigger guard is well enlarged for gloved use. The slide release button is located at the bottom of the stock approximately half way between the buttstock and the pistol grip. This is an added safety mechanism, as it keeps your hands away from the trigger when operating the slide or unloading a live round. I did find it slightly inconvenient, however.

When the action is closed, you can shut the steel dust cover, which is retained with a magnet. This dust cover keeps debris out of the action when the gun is not in use and opens automatically when the action is cycled. The pump itself is made from polymer and is comfortably long with two serrated handholds. As it does

SPECIFICATIONS
UTAS UTS-15

GAUGE: 12 ga.
CHAMBER: 2.75 and 3 in.
BARREL: 20.5 in. cylinder bore
OA LENGTH: 29.5 in.
WEIGHT: 6.9 lbs.
SIGHTS: Picatinny rail
STOCK: Polymer
ACTION: Pump
FINISH: Matte black
CAPACITY: 7+7+1 or 6+6+1 rounds
PRICE: $1,249
UTAS-USA.COM

not contain a magazine tube like a traditional shotgun, UTAS decided to make the most of the available space.

The 4140 steel barrel is chrome lined and threaded to accept any standard Beretta choke tube. Two knurled choke tubes were included: a short cylinder tube, which only extends about .75 inch, and a tactical door breaching/flash suppressor one with a standoff spiked end cap and alternating ports. This tube adds 2 inches to the barrel. A steel tube to extend the barrel an additional 8 inches is included for those who want to use the UTS-15 for hunting. The bolt body and head are precision machined and heat treated from 4140 steel, and the bolt head features three locking lugs.

Operating the UTS-15 was actually very easy and straightforward. First, open the dust cover for the magazine tube you want to load and push the exposed follower forward until it locks. Then load six rounds forward into the tube. To load the seventh round, simply drop it in the tube. When you close the dust cover, the follower releases and applies proper tension to the rounds in the tube. With the action open, you can load a round into the chamber. I found the loading process to be easy and quick, and it kept the shotgun oriented in the right position for fast use.

To fire, switch the safety selector to the proper position, pull the trigger, and work the slide action to cycle and continue firing. As is the case with any pump-action shotgun, the pump must be operated aggressively. I found this to be especially true with the UTS-15. There is little room for error here, and none for people who short stroke the pump. The empty cases eject to the right, so left-handed shooters will end up getting hit on the chin with empties. Still, my left-handed friend who shot the UTS-15 did not consider this to be a deal breaker for him.

The shell loading and feeding system is very reliable. A spring-loaded carriage guides and pushes the shells from the magazine tube to the chamber for positive feeding, even if holding the shotgun upside down. Recoil was extremely manageable and, with the low bore axis of the barrel, there was negligible muzzle rise even when using heavy-hitting slugs and buckshot loads.

SEMI-AUTO SHOTGUNS

AMERICAN TACTICAL IMPORTS TACSX2 12 GAUGE

ATI is currently importing high quality yet very economically priced pump action and semi-automatic tactical self-defense shotguns from Turkey. Made by Ottoman Guns, both models come with many standard features and are ready to be used right out of the box. The ATI TACSX2 shotgun in 12 gauge is a five-round semi-automatic with an 18.5-inch steel barrel and flat black polymer furniture.

The barrel will accommodate 2.75- and 3-inch shells and has a smooth bore fixed cylinder choke. A standard post front sight is included and appears to be permanently affixed. The receiver is

The ATI TACSX2 shotgun in 12 gauge is a 5-round semi-automatic with an 18.5-inch steel barrel and flat black polymer furniture.

Turkish shotguns have a well-deserved reputation for quality, reliability and value and the TACSX2 shotgun from ATI is no exception.

aluminum with a flat black hard-coat anodized finish that is well applied and matches the finish on the barrel. On top of the CNC-machined aluminum receiver are serrations to eliminate any glare. There is no rear sight; but the receiver does have machined cuts to accept a dovetailed or claw mount for an optic. Having the receiver drilled and tapped to add a ghost ring sight is another option. Inside the receiver, the steel bolt features an extended tactical charging handle for ease of use even with gloved hands. The bolt release is located on the right side of the receiver toward the front and below the ejection port. The bolt and charging handle as well as the shell lifter are all finished in a tactical matte black.

Behind the polymer trigger guard is a cross-bolt safety. At the front of the trigger guard on the left side of the receiver is the magazine lock lever. The magazine lock auto engages when the trigger is depressed. On the last round fired, the bolt locks to the rear. With rounds in the magazine, retracting the bolt handle can clear the round in the chamber. This ejects the live round from the chamber and allows the bolt to close while leaving the live shells in the mag. To make ready, manually reload a round into the chamber. To completely unload, retract the slide to eject a shell and then depress the magazine lock lever to release a fresh round from the magazine into the action; cycling the action manually ejects the round. This will need to be done for each shell in the magazine until it is emptied.

The magazine tube is steel and has a capacity of four rounds, plus one in the chamber. The forearm is made from a black polymer and extends the entire length of the magazine tube, providing plenty of space for a comfortable hold. It is aggressively checkered on the sides. The stock has a comfortable 14-inch length of pull and is made from a matching black polymer with aggressive checkering on the pistol grip. There is an accommodation for a sling swivel near the toe of the stock and a generous rubber recoil pad. There is, however, no provision for a sling swivel at the front of the shotgun or on the forearm. This gas piston–operated shotgun features dual action bars for strength and reliability.

Handling for this shotgun was extremely easy with an overall length of only 39 inches. At an unloaded weight of 6.5 pounds, it was a pleasure to carry. Shooting birdshot was very easy and comfortable, but moving to buckshot, especially given the gun's low weight, was a bit stouter. Slugs, on the other hand, were completely uncomfortable to shoot, but not unmanageable. All types of ammunition functioned reliably with no malfunctions, and the gun fired as fast as I could pull the trigger.

Speaking of the trigger, it was very crisp and light at about 5.5 pounds. Shotguns are not generally admired for their triggers, but this one was notably easy to use, which helped with accuracy results when using slugs.

Turkish shotguns have a well-deserved reputation for quality,

SPECIFICATIONS
ATI TACSX2 SHOTGUN

GAUGE: 12 ga. 3-in. chamber
BARREL: 18.5-in. cylinder
OA LENGTH: 39 in.
WEIGHT: 6.5 lbs.
SIGHTS: Fixed post front, dovetail rear
STOCK: Polymer
ACTION: Semi-auto
FINISH: Matte black
CAPACITY: 4+1 rounds
PRICE: $399
AMERICANTACTICAL.US

reliability, and value, and this one from ATI is no exception. It retails for just over $300, which is good even for a pump gun, and here you get so much more. If you prefer ATI's Turkish-made pump action, it has many of the same features and retails for even less, leaving plenty of dough left over for ammo and practice.

BERETTA 1301 TACTICAL

The Beretta 1301 Tactical shotgun is a gas operated, semi-automatic 12-gauge chambered for 2.75- and 3-inch shells. It has a tubular magazine with a 5+1 round capacity using 2.75-inch shells (4+1 round capacity with 3 inch). The cold hammer forged HP (High Pressure) 18.5-inch steel barrel has a fixed cylinder bore choke (or what Beretta calls their "Optima-Bore"), and it is rated to fire standard and steel shot ammunition.

At the heart of the 1301 Tactical is its distinct gas system, which is specifically designed to function across different loads and to cycle faster than any other shotgun. Indeed, Beretta promises that their "BLINK" gas system will cycle and fire 36 percent faster

The Beretta 1301 Tactical Shotgun is a gas-operated, semi-auto 12 gauge chambered for 2.75- and 3-inch shells. Its distinct gas system is arguably the fastest one available.

than any other semi-automatic shotgun on the market. One of the main challenges to semi-auto shotgun reliability has always been gas carbon fouling. The 1301 Tactical uses a cross tube gas piston with an elastic scraper that works like a gasket. This makes the gas system self-cleaning for continued smooth operation shot after shot (you still should clean the shotgun when you are done shooting for the day).

The controls on the 1301 Tactical are very well designed and thought out. The push button safety located at the front of the large polymer trigger guard is oversized with a distinct red circle to indicate that the shotgun is in the Fire condition. The safety will only function when the internal hammer is in the cocked position, and it is reversible for left-handed shooters. The right-side charging handle is oversized and easy to operate with gloves. To lock the charging handle to the rear for loading, the carrier stop push button (located at the bottom rear of the cartridge loading gate) must be fully depressed. The right-side bolt release is oversized, too, and textured for fast and easy operation.

The author added Mesa Tactical's Urbino Pistol Grip Stock and the +2 round magazine extension from Nordic Components for a total of 8-round capacity on the beefed up Beretta 1301 Tactical.

Mesa Tactical's SureShell Aluminum Carrier and Rail holds an extra six rounds at the ready with Picatinny rail on top. It was a superb addition to the Beretta 1301 Tactical.

The 1301's ghost ring tactical sights are very robust and well protected with a large white dot at the front sight and two white dots at the fully windage and elevation adjustable rear. The sights can be removed and replaced if you prefer a different sight picture or tritium insert sights for low-light conditions. A short 3-inch Picatinny rail system comes factory installed in front of the rear sight over the receiver. This is well suited for a small red-dot sight.

The standard factory stock is very comfortable and well designed. The long polymer fore-end allows the barrel to sit low for a better hand grip and is adorned with aggressive checkering while remaining thin and comfortable. The polymer stock matches the aggressive checkering pattern for a firm grip and is adjustable for length of pull. It comes with a very short 13.5-inch length of pull as standard to keep the shotgun very compact. Indeed, the overall length is nearly 1.5 inches less than my Remington 870, which has an 18-inch barrel.

The 1301 is a very easy to handle and lightweight (6.5 lbs.) gun but, thanks to the gas system, recoil is extremely comfortable and manageable even with slugs. As there are plenty of aftermarket manufacturers making parts for the 1301 I added a few improvements. Mesa Tactical's SureShell Aluminum Carrier and Rail keeps extra ammunition at the ready. This all milled 6061-T6 aluminum hard-coat anodized to a matte black unit features rock steady durable construction made to take abuse. The left-side shell holder carries six spare shells, although 4- and 8-round versions are also available. This one-piece unit includes a top Picatinny rail section for mounting optics and is easily installed and secured using the drilled and tapped holes on top of the shotgun's receiver.

Mesa Tactical's Urbino Pistol Grip Stock offers several distinct advantages as well. The flat black injection molded nylon stock is extremely durable with a short length of pull at 12.5 inches. This allows for comfortable use with body armor or heavy clothing. The pistol grip features a very soft rubber grip over-mold that affords a very secure purchase and helps tame recoil. However, it is the optional Limbsaver buttpad that really absorbs even the heaviest recoil while keeping the stock firmly on your shoulder. The stock has an optional cheek riser for higher optics and several different sling attachment options.

The 5-round magazine capacity was still an issue for a true survival shotgun so I installed the +2 round magazine extension from Nordic Components. The all metal MXT Extension Kit increased my magazine capacity to a full seven rounds and the magazine extension was flush with the front of the barrel. The kit includes a barrel clamp for increased sturdiness that features a Picatinny rail on one side for forward-mounted accessories such as lights and lasers on one side and a QD, or quick-detach sling swivel point on the other.

There is no question that the tactical shotgun has reached a new zenith in the Beretta 1310, especially when combined with upgrades from Mesa Tactical and Nordic Components. The way in which this shotgun absorbs recoil and allows for even smaller shooters to easily shoulder the gun (thanks to the short length of

pull stock from Mesa Tactical) and fire full-power defensive loads pain (and flinch) free makes it ideal for home defense by most any family member. The reliable semi-automatic action removes any user error from short stroking a pump-action shotgun (which can occur under stress) and provides for lightning fast shooting against multiple targets.

The Remington Versamax is another very well made semi-auto 12-gauge. The Versamax Tactical model features an 8-round capacity magazine. *Photo: Remington*

REMINGTON VERSAMAX TACTICAL

The Remington Versamax is another very well made semi-auto 12-gauge shotgun. The tactical model features an 8-round capacity magazine, but to do this Remington had to make the shotgun a bit longer with a 22-inch barrel. This makes the Versamax Tactical less wieldy in tight quarters.

SPECIFICATIONS
REMINGTON VERSA MAX TACTICAL

GAUGE: 12 ga.
BARREL: 22 in.
OA LENGTH: 44 in.
WEIGHT: 7.75 lbs.
SIGHTS: Fiber optic/rail
STOCK: Polymer
ACTION: Semi-auto
FINISH: Matte black
CAPACITY: 8+1 rounds
PRICE: $1,456
WWW.REMINGTON.COM

However, the real strength in the design is its supreme reliability using the Versaport system. Inside the barrel and chamber there are several ports that increase or decrease recoil energy based on the length of shotshell used. The Tactical model is designed to only accept 2.75- and 3-inch shells, unlike the standard Versamax that will take the big 3.5-inch shells. The dual piston system is self-cleaning when the action is cycled. This has allowed stress testing where one thousands rounds were fired without cleaning.

Further improving the gun's durability and reliability is the fact that the barrel and internal components are nickel plated, providing corrosion resistance. The controls are improved with an oversized push button safety at the rear of the trigger guard, which is oversized for use with gloves. The bolt release button and charging handle are significantly enlarged and extended for fast and easy use.

The sights on the Versamax Tactical comprise a bead dot located in the middle of the vent rib over the barrel and a high visibility and interchangeable fiber optic front sight. You have a choice of three colors: green, red, or white. The gun also comes with an optics rail that can be easily installed at the top of the receiver for use with a red-dot or holographic optic. In addition, a front rail can be added for tactical lights or lasers. One welcome aspect is that the Versamax includes interchangeable chokes for more options in a survival situation. The Tactical model includes an improved cylinder choke and an extended tactical choke that make the shotgun almost two inches longer and adds front serrations that can be used as a standoff device.

The polymer stock is very comfortable, and this shotg
duces significantly reduced recoil. The length of pull on t
can be adjusted with the included spacers by as much as one inch
to accommodate the shotgun to the user.

NON-NFA SHORT-BARRELED SHOTGUNS

Having a shorter barrel on a shotgun makes it more compact and easier to wield in smaller confines, also easier to transport. Traditionally speaking, obtaining a short-barreled shotgun has always been a headache since they are regulated by the Federal National Firearms Act, which requires a lot of paperwork to obtain. But there is a catch. When you regulate something, you have to define it very specifically. Under the Gun Control Act something can be labeled as a firearm but under the National Firearms Act (NFA) not labeled as a firearm.

A firearm that is over 26 inches in length and has never had a stock (so it cannot be fired from the shoulder) is considered neither a handgun nor a long gun, but is still a firearm. Moreover, it is not included in the NFA. So, you can have a short-barreled rifle or shotgun as long as it is over 26 inches long and has no stock. These may be regulated by state law but under federal law are just treated as a firearm or "Any Other Weapon." Both Mossberg and Remington have taken advantage of this to offer short-barreled shotguns without the regulatory hassle.

It should be stated that both of these guns are being marketed for home defense and they are indeed very compact and well suited for that task. However, early reports suggest recoil can be severe, especially with full power loads. Remington has developed a self-defense low recoil buckshot load that may be better suited. Inside a home with short distances, birdshot may also be very effective, especially a heavier No. 4 or No. 6 shot.

MOSSBERG 590 SHOCKWAVE

The Mossberg 590 Shockwave 12-gauge pump-action shotgun features the same tough as nails construction as the military-grade Mossberg 590. It features a polymer birdshead grip, which I find significantly more comfortable than a pistol grip at taming recoil, and a 14-inch cylinder bore heavy walled barrel. The total length is just over 26 inches, with a top-mounted ambidextrous safety, and reliable dual extractors and twin action bars. The pump of the gun has a hand strap to ensure that the support hand stays rear of the muzzle during operation and it aids significantly in maintaining a firm grip. There is a front bead sight and the magazine end cap has a sling swivel. The capacity is a full 5+1 rounds of 2.75-inch shells, impressive for its small size.

SPECIFICATIONS
MOSSBERG 590 SHOCKWAVE

GAUGE: 12 ga.
BARREL: 14 in.
OA LENGTH: 26.37 in.
WEIGHT: 5.25 lbs.
SIGHTS: Bead front
STOCK: Polymer
ACTION: Pump
FINISH: Matte black
CAPACITY: 5+1 rounds
PRICE: $455

Mossberg's new 590 Shockwave is short and carries a lot of punch, but is not considered an NFA weapon, thus avoids much of the regulatory hassle.

REMINGTON MODEL 870 TAC-14

The other option in this category is the Remington Model 870 TAC-14, which is based on the standard Remington 870 with an extremely smooth and reliable action. Like the Mossberg, this survival gun is a 12-guage pump-action shotgun with a cylinder bore 14-inch barrel and a bead sight. The entire thing is just over 26 inches in length. It has a very similar polymer birdshead grip for comfort and features a Magpul M-Loc forend, which features a forward and rearward "lip" to keep the hand on the pump. The M-Loc forend allows you to easily install accessories like a light or laser, add-ons that can help greatly in target identification and aiming, especially if firing from the hip. Unlike the Mossberg, however, the Remington TAC-14 only has a 4+1 capacity and a right-handed safety button located at the rear of the trigger guard.

SPECIFICATIONS
REMINGTON MODEL 870 TAC-14
GAUGE: 12 ga.
BARREL: 14 in.
OA LENGTH: 26.3 in.
WEIGHT: 5.6 lbs.
SIGHTS: Bead front
STOCK: Polymer
ACTION: Pump
FINISH: Matte black
CAPACITY: 4+1 rounds
PRICE: $443

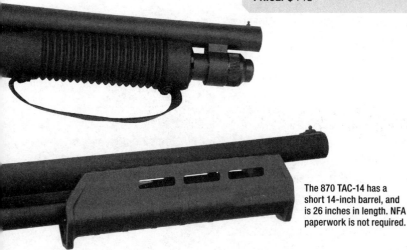

The 870 TAC-14 has a short 14-inch barrel, and is 26 inches in length. NFA paperwork is not required.

AMMUNITION & RELOADING

*W*hen it comes to ammunition specific to survival, simpler is better. There are a lot of different calibers and cartridges out there, and everyone has their favorites. It may be that you have to rely on whatever ammunition you can find and having many guns in many different calibers is to your advantage. There is also the approach that you should stick with the most common and popular cartridges and avoid the outliers, no matter how popular they may seem. This is the viewpoint expressed in this book.

When it comes to cartridge selection as it applies to survival, my policy is that if I can't

find it in plentiful supply at the local hardware store, I am not interested. This excludes a lot of very effective and trending cartridges.

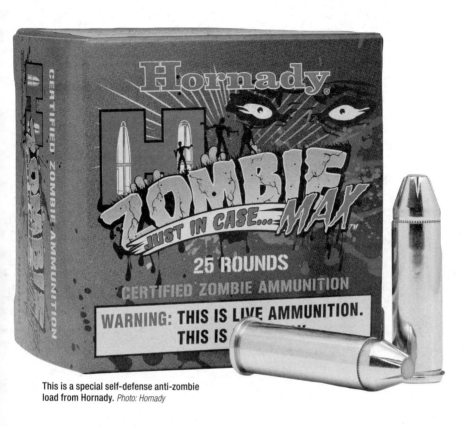

This is a special self-defense anti-zombie load from Hornady. *Photo: Hornady*

My preference is for cartridges that have withstood the test of time, retaining their popularity. This includes ammunition in common use with militaries and police departments as standard issue (not specialty ammo for Special Forces, SWAT, or snipers). You should also understand the difference between training or range ammunition and actual defensive or hunting ammunition.

FMJ RANGE AMMUNITION

Standard, cheap full metal jacket (FMJ) ammunition, whether U.S. or foreign made, is perfectly suitable for range use and training. In fact, I prefer it. It's cheaper, which allows you to train and shoot more. It will typically kick less, increasing your comfort on

Full metal jacket ammunition in military packaging. *Photo: LCPL Kamran Sadaghini*

the range and extending your range training sessions by avoiding fatigue. The FMJ's bullet shape is a solid conical form with nothing to get caught up and stop the gun from cycling. However, the stuff is loaded faster and with less special attention than defensive ammunition. If you get a malfunction, you want it to happen on the range, not in a defensive encounter. The occasional range malfunction can actually help you train for clearing jams quickly. It helps you identify a problem by feel and sight, and if one occurs during an actual incident, you will be better prepared to handle it.

It should be noted that FMJ ammunition is standard issue for militaries the world over, not just because of international agreements against using expanding ammunition but also because an FMJ bullet will normally penetrate deeper than an expanding bullet. On the battlefield, this is an advantage, especially when trying to shoot through barriers. Depending on the type of survival situation you are experiencing, FMJ ammunition may be the best option for you. Also, if you are stockpiling ammo, FMJ is more affordable and is often available on the surplus market.

DEFENSIVE AMMUNITION

Ammunition specifically designed for personal protection or hunting is far different from the ammo that you will find for normal range use. This ammo is significantly more expensive than FMJ and (depending on your budget) harder to stockpile. It is loaded with a much higher degree of precision. It typically uses an expanding bullet and comes in smaller boxes with fewer rounds. Expanding ammunition is designed to … expand once it hits a soft target. You will find that its bullets tend to have a lead core (although some of it can be solid copper instead) surrounded by a copper or other material jacket and topped off with a deep cavity. In any survival situation, it is vitally important to understand what your ammo can and can't do.

In the spring of 1986 in Miami, eight FBI agents cornered two bank robbers, and the shootout that ensued sparked an intense debate and adjustment of how law enforcement officers were armed and trained nationwide. Early in the gun battle, one suspect was shot with a 9mm round that went through his arm and into his chest. That wound (the first of several) proved fatal, but not before he was able to kill two FBI agents and wound several more. The entire gun battle lasted less than five minutes with almost 150 rounds fired.

Following this tragic incident, the FBI spent considerable effort in studying wound ballistics and ammunition. How was it that, despite numerous wounds, the two suspects were able to continue fighting? The key is in understanding what types of wounds can stop a person. It turns out that only damage caused by blood loss or immediate central nervous system trauma can drop an attacker in his tracks. The most important factors in this regard are shot placement, size of the wound cavity, and penetration. The FBI determined in their testing that, at a minimum, a bullet must be able to penetrate at least 12 inches in ballistic gelatin (and up to 18

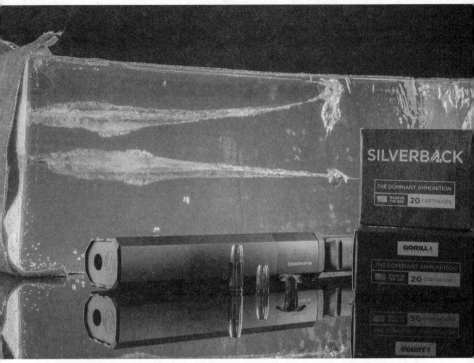

Defensive ammunition is tested using ballistic gelatin. You want a minimum of 12-14 inches of penetration, maximum bullet expansion and weight retention through various barriers.
Photo: Gorilla Ammunition

inches is preferable) in order to hit and damage vital organs and blood vessels.

It is important to understand that ammunition is not just sold by caliber and bullet style; it is also sold by bullet weight. On any box of ammunition will be listed the weight of each bullet in grains. One ounce of lead weighs 437.5 grains. When you buy .45 ACP ammunition, and it says on the box that it is 230-grains for example, that means each bullet is more than half an ounce of lead and copper.

Bullet weight is important because different weight bullets perform differently based on the twist rate of the barrel. The bigger the bullet, the more mass it has and, assuming you are launching it at the same velocity, the more force it produces. There is a reduction in velocity with heavier bullets. Generally, velocity is more important than bullet weight.

A heavier bullet will produce more force forward and back, which you will feel as increased recoil. The biggest issue with bullet weight, however, is in reliability with a semi-automatic firearm. If you select ammunition that is too light, it may not produce sufficient force to reliably cycle the action. I have seen this before with 9mm pistols firing ammunition that is less than 115 grains. Different bullet designs may not function consistently in some firearms. Make sure to test your preferred load with your gun to find a good match.

+P AMMO

Some defensive handgun ammunition will be marked +P or sometimes even +P+. All ammunition is supposed to be loaded to a standard pressure for each caliber according to the Sporting Arms and Ammunition Manufacturers' Institute (SAAMI). It is their job to set "industry standards for safety, interchangeability, reliability and quality" for all ammunition. In 9mm for example, the standard pressure is 35,000 PSI, and for +P 9mm ammunition, it is 38,500 PSI. Your gun may not be rated to handle the higher pressures of +P ammunition, and the owner's manual should be consulted. Using high pressure ammunition may damage your gun and cause injury to you. Ammunition that is rated +P+ is even more critical, since there is no standard pressure for it.

Ammunition that is rated +P will produce higher velocities and more force but will not necessarily penetrate or perform better. Modern defensive ammunition is designed to account for the bullet's velocity to maximize performance. It will expand reliably at the standard pressure for which it was designed. There is no advantage in sending the bullet flying faster, and for some of these bullets it may actually hinder their performance. From a practical standpoint, the only real reason for using +P ammunition is in firearm performance and reliability. Some guns may just prefer the high pressure rounds and perform more reliably with them.

Military surplus ammunition can occasionally be found at very low prices, but poor storage can lead to deterioration and unsafe condition. *Photo: Todd Huffman*

MILITARY SURPLUS AMMUNITION

Old ammunition is a special concern because, depending on its age, manufacture, purpose, and how it was stored, it can have serious repercussions for you and your gun. The first issue is that you should assume all military surplus ammunition is corrosive. Without proper cleaning using a water-based solvent your bore can turn into a rusty mess.

Some surplus ammo was made for machine guns, with primers harder than diamonds, so they may not function properly in semi-automatic or commercial guns. If the ammunition was exposed to moisture, humidity, or temperature extremes, it can have problems as well. Typical malfunctions include misfires (where the cartridge simply refuses to go off), hang fires (where there is a delay in the cartridge detonating by as much as 8 seconds), and squib loads (where the cartridge develops insufficient pressure and a bullet gets stuck in the barrel). Be extra careful of that last one, since you do not want to make the mistake of firing a second round with a bullet still stuck in the barrel. If you fire your gun and the sound or recoil seem "off" to you, stop shooting and check the barrel for obstructions. Surplus ammunition should be inspected for damage or corrosion. If it does not look good, don't shoot it no matter how cheap it is.

Yet another concern is that military surplus ammunition was made for combat — not for hunting or civilian ranges. A fair amount of it has a steel core in the bullet, designed to pierce armor. The easiest way to check is to use a magnet. If the magnet sticks to the bullet, you have steel core ammunition. At an outdoor range, especially if shooting into a dirt berm, this is not an issue. At indoor ranges, this type of ammunition is strictly prohibited as it causes damage to the range and backstop. Even when shooting outside, caution should be exercised. If there is a lot of dry brush or leaves or anything else that can catch fire you should be aware that steel core ammunition can cause a spark if it happens to hit something hard like metal or a rock.

PISTOL AMMUNITION

Keeping things simple, I only recommend the following calibers for survival situations.

.22 LR

When it comes to self-defense, the venerable .22 LR, or Long Rifle, is of limited use to say the least (it is still lethal, however), but when it comes to survival, it can be a Godsend. This cartridge is chambered in rifles and handguns, and it can be used to hunt small game for food or to eliminate pests within a range of 150 yards. It is very useful for training, as it is much less expensive than centerfire ammunition. It is also much smaller than most centerfire ammo, so it can be stockpiled more easily. Finally, it is ubiquitous and easy to find. The recent shortage of availability was due to people hoarding it, not for lack of production. In essence, .22 LR became a victim of its own popularity. However, at the date of this writing, the stuff is back and is filling up gun store shelves by the crate, so go get some.

Another advantage of the .22 LR, besides your ability to carry and store a lot of it, is its use with a suppressor. A suppressed .22 pistol or rifle, especially when sub-sonic ammunition is used, is incredibly quiet — barely louder than an air gun. If you are in a situation where you need to hunt but don't want to be detected or raise alarm, it's an ideal choice.

Like all ammo, .22 LR comes in a variety of types with different velocities, bullet weights, and shapes. Sub-sonic .22 LR is designed to travel below the speed of sound, but you can also opt for high-velocity rimfire and pick between hollowpoint and solid bullets. The most common weight for .22 LR is 40 grains, but heavier as well as much lighter bullets can be found, though light bullets may not cycle the action on some semi-automatics. Semi-auto firearms can be finicky with the type of .22 LR that is used and will function better with some brands over others. Finally, .22 LR tends to foul a lot, so you will need to maintain your firearm with regular cleanings after use.

Tip: Lead will oxidize over time, so if you are stockpiling .22 ammunition for long term storage, get copper-plated bullets rather than solid lead.

9MM

With all of these caveats, my personal recommendation for the best all-around handgun survival cartridge is the 9mm. Any well-designed modern defensive round in 9mm will give you all the expansion and penetration you are likely to need. It is among the easiest cartridges to find on store shelves because it is so popular, so you are unlikely to find yourself out of ammo. It is probably the cheapest (or close to it) non-rimfire handgun ammo you will find, especially if you buy in bulk. It has very moderate recoil in all but the smallest handguns. It lets you accommodate more rounds in the same size gun, giving you greater firepower. And it's available in just about every type of handgun, including some revolvers. All of these reasons make it easy to train frequently and very shootable for different members of your family.

Make sure to stock up on plenty of 9mm ammunition, it is the most common and popular handgun caliber in the world. *Photo: HPR*

First introduced in 1902, the standard 9mm cartridge — which goes by many different names, including 9mm Luger, 9x19mm, 9mm NATO, and 9mm Parabellum — has remained unchanged (except for dramatic improvements in bullet design and powders), and it is the most popular and common pistol caliber in the world. No wonder it is used by a majority of law enforcement in the U.S. It is the standard pistol round for all NATO militaries, too. In a survival situation, especially in a pistol-caliber carbine, it can be used for hunting small- and mid-sized game. The 9mm is available in a variety of bullet weights from 115 to 147 grains and styles from FMJ to hollowpoint. When buying for defensive applications use hollowpoint ammunition, and look for either a bonded or a solid copper bullet.

.45 ACP

The .45 ACP is a near contemporary of the 9mm Luger cartridge. The .45 ACP was first produced in 1905 and officially adopted for use by the U.S. military in 1911. The foremost concern in developing this round was to have a semi-automatic firearm with sufficient stopping power. Its large, 230-grain, nearly half-inch in diameter FMJ bullet traveling at over 800 fps did the trick. For more than 70 years, it was the standard pistol round of the U.S. and performed reliably in every major encounter.

While there is no question that the .45 ACP is an extremely effective survival round and very popular and easy to find, there are a few drawbacks. First: with modern defensive ammunition, the difference in terminal performance between

The venerable .45 ACP now has modern defensive loads from many manufacturers. The round hits hard, but is more expensive than 9mm to shoot.

the .45 ACP and the 9mm is almost essentially non-existent. Second: the .45 ACP is significantly larger and heavier, and it costs more. That fact makes stockpiling, storage, and transportation an issue. The larger round means lower capacity, as fewer can fit in the same sized magazine. And the round produces greater recoil, which can affect shooter comfort and speed.

.357 MAGNUM/.38 SPECIAL

Revolvers are not ideal for survival situations; however, if you select one for this application, the most popular and versatile combination is to have one chambered in .357 Magnum. A revolver chambered in this hot caliber will also accept .38 Special, so you have the option of using two different kinds of ammunition, depending on what you can scrounge up.

The original .38 Special round was introduced in 1898 as a military cartridge, and it went on to serve well into the 1960s. It found a lot of popularity with law enforcement, and until the 9mm replaced it in the 1980s it was still one of the most popular police cartridges in use. It's a dependable, soft shooting, if slightly underpowered, cartridge. The lack of punch is what eventually led to the creation of the .357 Magnum in 1934.

While .38 Special ammunition is fairly inexpensive, .357 Magnum, with its longer case and higher pressure loading, is even pricier. The magnum round was primarily developed for hunting and self-defense, especially when dealing with barriers. It has historically yielded the best results of any defensive handgun cartridge in terms of terminal effectiveness, and it remains an outstanding survival gun choice. In a carbine (typically a lever action), the .357 magnum is even more effective as both a survival and hunting round. This cartridge has nearly twice the power of a .38 Special with a lot more noise, muzzle blast and recoil.

RIFLE AMMUNITION

5.56MM NATO/.223 REM.

The .223 Remington cartridge was originally developed for the military to be used in a lightweight rifle. This eventually became the M16, which was adopted as the standard U.S. military rifle in the early 1960s, and the military version of the .223 Rem. became the 5.56mm. Firing a lightweight bullet at very high velocity was found to be accurate and effective against light armor and enemy targets, and it allowed the individual soldier to carry more ammunition. As the cartridge came to be adopted by all NATO countries, it was redesigned in 1980 as the 5.56×45mm NATO.

While on the outside the .223 and 5.56 NATO are identical and considered interchangeable, there is a difference in that the 5.56 NATO generates more pressure and uses slightly thicker brass. It is safe to use both .223 and 5.56 NATO in a rifle that is chambered in 5.56 NATO, but using 5.56 NATO in a rifle that is truly chambered for .223 may generate excessive pressures and should be avoided. Many rifles say they are chambered for .223, but are in fact chambered for 5.56 NATO. It is best to check with the manufacturer.

As this is the standard military round and as the AR-15 has found such immense popularity with U.S. civilians and law enforcement, supply is generally very plentiful. There is a significant military surplus market that can keep costs down when buying in bulk. Manufacturers have developed a lot of different loadings designed for hunting and long-range shooting, with excellent results. This leads to the issue of selecting bullet weight.

Very lightweight bullets travel at higher velocity with a flatter trajectory and are popular for varmint hunting. However, I do not recommend anything lighter than 55 grains in a survival rifle. Grain weights of 55 and 62 have been the military standard. You may want to keep a supply of higher weight (up to 72 grain) hollowpoint bullets for use in hunting, as these can be effective on deer. Match ammunition is also handy for more accurate shooting as well.

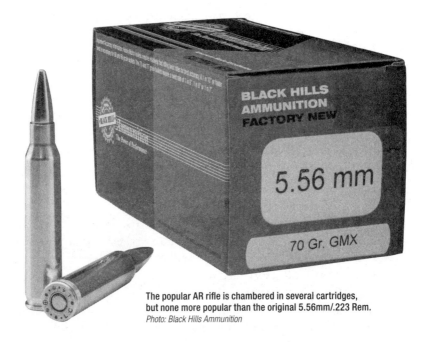

The popular AR rifle is chambered in several cartridges, but none more popular than the original 5.56mm/.223 Rem.
Photo: Black Hills Ammunition

In an AR, barrels come in different twist rates. The original M16 had a 1 in 12-inch twist rate, which destabilized the bullet and caused it to yaw, causing a more severe injury. Later, a 1 in 9-inch twist rate was found to still allow for a yaw with lighter bullets and improved accuracy. You can get custom 1 in 8-inch twist rates, but the new military standard is a 1 in 7-inch twist, which stabilizes the greatest range of bullet weights. If you can, try to stick with this higher twist rate.

The original M16 and full-sized AR-15s had barrels that were 20 inches long. This was found to be the optimal length to maximize bullet velocity. However, the M4 carbine is now the most popular choice in the military. Both it and the civilian AR carbine have a barrel length of 16 inches. On average, you lose 50 fps of velocity per inch of barrel in an AR, so a carbine reduces bullet velocity by 200 fps versus the 20-inch rifle.

Some have complained that the .223/5.56 is underpowered and underperforms in combat, yet it has remained in service for over 50 years. Given the weight, cost, popularity, low recoil, and accuracy, it remains my top recommendation for a survival rifle cartridge.

7.62MM NATO/.308 WIN.

The 7.62mm NATO cartridge, which is interchangeable with the civilian .308 Winchester, was first adopted as a NATO standard in 1953. It remains in military service today, so ammunition is plentiful and readily available virtually worldwide. As the cartridge is manufactured in many countries, there is a significant supply of inexpensive military surplus ammo, too.

Originally, the .308 was intended for use in issue service rifles, but it was determined to be more powerful than necessary so the 5.56mm NATO round supplanted it. In recent years, the round has found resurgence when mission requirements called for a more powerful service rifle. However, its most popular use in the military is for general purpose machine guns, so some surplus ammunition may come in links (which are easily removed).

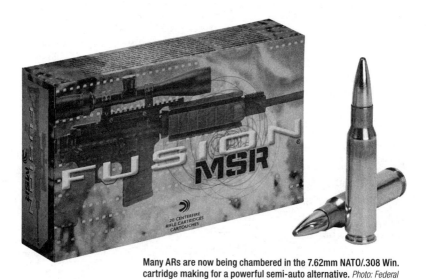

Many ARs are now being chambered in the 7.62mm NATO/.308 Win. cartridge making for a powerful semi-auto alternative. *Photo: Federal*

It should be noted that the 7.62mm NATO and .308 Win. are not entirely identical, and the .308 is loaded to a higher pressure, although I have never found any issues using either cartridge in either type of rifle. That said it's a fairly powerful round capable of taking any North American game animal and is much more effective at longer ranges, serving well in sniper rifles. In fact, for law enforcement, the .308 is largely relegated to sniper use.

Many ARs are now being chambered in .308 and these present a powerful semi-automatic alternative to ARs in the more traditional 5.56mm NATO. You do get a heavier rifle with less capacity and more recoil, and there is no Mil-Spec standard .308 AR.

There are many commercial manufacturers for the .308 that produce excellent hunting and target ammunition. Such stuff is premium and will come at a premium price. For a survival situation, I would stock up on the military surplus ammo, though, which often comes in weatherproof "battle packs" of 150 rounds.

7.62X39MM RUSSIAN

The 7.62×39mm round dates from World War II. It was the standard Russian rifle and machine gun round until the 1970s and remains in service both in Russia and its various satellite and client states. As it was the standard cartridge of the AK rifle and, as the AK is the most popular rifle ever made (over 100 million and counting), it should come as no surprise that the 7.62x39mm is possibly the most produced cartridge on Earth. Surplus ammunition is plentiful and inexpensive, and the growing popularity of

As it was the standard round of the AK rifle it should come as no surprise that the 7.62x39mm is possibly the most produced cartridge on Earth.
Photo: Century Arms

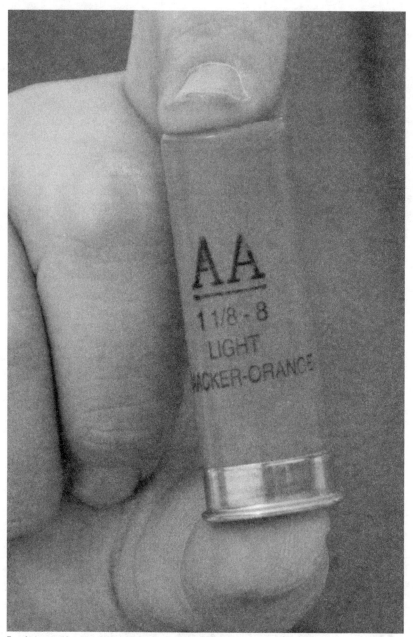

For shotguns, 12-gauge 2.75-inch shells are the most common and easiest to find.

the Kalashnikov has U.S. manufacturers producing this cartridge, which now includes hunting ammunition.

Like the AK, the 7.62x39 is made tough, often using steel cases that have been lacquered for corrosion resistance and reliability. There is a growing number of rifles being chambered in the cartridge, including ARs. Ballistically, it's considered a medium-range round with low recoil and is very effective on game animals. Caution should be taken when using surplus or foreign made ammunition, though, as it may have a steel core inside the bullet.

SHOTGUN AMMUNITION

12-GAUGE SHOTGUN

There is no question that the shotgun is a versatile tool, but using it and getting the most out of it require a thorough understanding of all its features. Different length barrels and the use of interchangeable chokes, which are constrictions at the end of the barrel, allow shotguns to be used for a range of situations and purposes. The shotgun's single most versatile aspect, however, is its ability to shoot an incredibly wide variety of ammunition. You can shoot slugs (one solid projectile) from a shotgun, but most of us will stick with shot, which are different-sized pellets made of lead or steel.

The basic rule of thumb is that the larger the shot size (denoted by smaller numbers), the farther it will travel and the more it will penetrate. Thus, the smaller the game you are hunting, the smaller the shot size needed. With this handy chart of the most common ammunition, you can determine what you need and when.

In terms of size, 12 gauge is the most common and easiest to find, so I would stick with that. Larger or smaller shotgun shells may produce more or less recoil, but what really counts is what is inside the hull. Shotgun shells come in different lengths, but the most common is 2.75 inches in length. Longer shells will give you more power and more recoil but reduce the magazine capacity. Still, most shotguns will accommodate the longer, or "magnum" shells, so if that is all you can find in a survival situation, you can

COMMON SHOT SIZE	SHOT DIAMETER (INCHES)	NO. OF SHOT IN AN OUNCE	BEST USED FOR
Slug	Depends on gauge and ammunition design	--	Effective on larger game such as deer or hogs, especially over short ranges. Even with a rifled barrel, shots should be limited to 100 yards or less.
00 Buck	.33	8	Can be used for whitetail deer, but only at ranges of 50 yards or less and where legal. It is a good choice for heavy brush. It is most used for self-defense applications.
No. 2	.15	90	Excellent for geese and ducks and, with a full choke, for turkeys or fox.
No. 4	.13	135	A fine choice for longer range turkey shooting, using a full choke.
No. 5	.12	170	A great load for small game like rabbits and squirrels, as well as pheasants, grouse, and partridge.
No. 7½	.095	350	Typical choice for trap shooting and ideal for smaller birds such as quail, dove, pigeon, woodcock, and rail.
No. 8	.09	410	A light load that can be used for the small birds mentioned above but is also common for skeet shooting.
No. 9	.08	585	The high number of pellets per ounce makes this load the preferred choice for skeet shooting, which occurs at shorter ranges than trap.

still use them. In addition, there are specialty shorter, or "low recoil" offerings, but these may not cycle properly in all shotguns, particularly semi-autos.

Another very good idea is to purchase a gauge adapter or subcaliber device. This may not work in all types of shotguns, but it basically allows you to use a smaller-sized shell — such as 16-, 20- or .410-gauge — in your 12 gauge. Again, in a survival situation, you may have to make do with whatever ammunition you can find, and 20 gauge is the next most popular size you'll likely encounter. Such adapters or chamber inserts are about the same size as the shells themselves, so they can be easily transported for use when needed.

By far the most common type of 12-gauge ammunition is the smaller shot sizes, usually No. 7.5 or No. 8. You can find this stuff anyplace that sells ammunition in boxes of 25 or packs of 100 at very economical prices. Even during the ammunition shortage (due to mass buying and hoarding), you could always find this ammo in plentiful supply. Following an economic collapse, or mass terrorist strike in which services are disrupted, it can be used for hunting small game and birds, but in self-defense, it is only effective at short distances of no more than 7 yards.

I recommend stockpiling 12-gauge 00 Buckshot as the preferred survival shotgun ammunition. This is not inexpensive, however. You should also keep a small supply of slugs and birdshot.

AMMO STORAGE

All ammunition should be stored in a cool, dry place away from moisture and humidity. Modern ammunition is made with sealants to protect against the elements, but nothing lasts forever. If properly stored, it will remain effective almost indefinitely, but if not stored properly, its lifespan can be significantly reduced. Ammunition you carry with you on a daily basis, either on your body or in a vehicle, is subject to being knocked about, exposed to dust, debris, lint, and sweat, as well as temperature changes, etc. My recommendation is to replace this ammunition at least annually.

Generally speaking, if ammunition looks old or corroded, it should not be used. However, in a survival situation, you may

Store ammunition in its original packaging or well-marked waterproof military cans in a cool, dry place.

not have this luxury. Exercise care as old or corroded ammunition has the possibility of malfunctioning and even causing damage to your firearm or you. If you try to clean your ammo, do not use any solvents or oil, as it's much more likely to damage it. Even if you can't see it, solvents and lubricants can get into your ammunition and compromise the chemicals that make up the powder and primer.

RELOADING

Many people stock up on reloading supplies as a long-term survival strategy. Reloading ammunition is a multistep process that can be made easier and faster with a more advanced loading press. The basic process involves recycling spent cartridge cases. Generally, you only reload brass cases and plastic shotgun shells. You cannot reload steel cases or cases that are too damaged.

Start by sorting and cleaning your brass using a tumbler. You should only reload one type of ammunition at a time. You need the right size and type of primers, bullets, and gunpowder. There are many different types of gunpowder, and how much you use depends on the type. There are entire manuals that detail the correct powder measurements. You want to make sure to get it right.

You will need to resize the case and remove the old primer. For rifle ammunition, you will also need to trim the case. The cases will need to be deburred, the case mouth expanded, a new primer inserted, the powder measured and loaded, and finally, a new bullet seated. With a simple press, you do this one cartridge at a time. With a complex or "progressive" press, you can conduct multiple steps on a number of cartridges at a time. A case that stays in good condition can usually be reloaded as many as five times before the brass becomes too weak. There are also some commercial ammunition reloaders who sell ammo at a discount.

In a survival situation, are you really going to have time to pick up your fired brass? If you are going to all the trouble of stockpiling reloading supplies, why not just stockpile actual ammunition instead? That is my recommendation. The only reason to reload ammunition is to build up a stockpile of loaded ammunition at

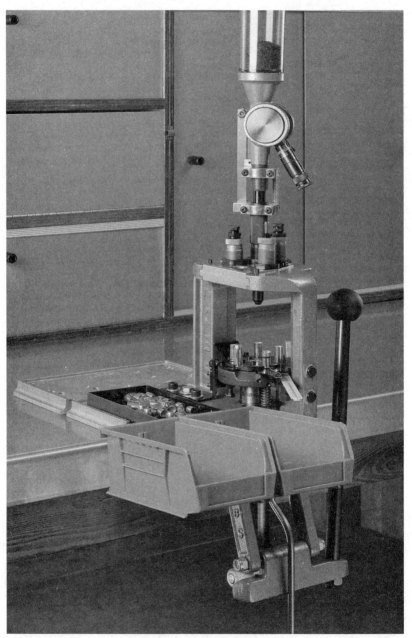

A progressive reloading press like this one can make reloading fired brass cases much faster. *Photo: RCBS*

a discount. Reloading your own can save up to 60 or 70 percent off the cost of factory new. If you have the time, then this may be a good way to build up a stockpile. Keep in mind, though, that under the duress of a disaster scenario you are unlikely to have much time to spend reloading.

NOTE: Some manufacturers warn against using reloaded ammunition, but there is nothing inherently wrong with it. Many people save a lot of money reloading their own empty cases. The danger is in buying ammunition from individuals who reloaded the ammo themselves. You have no idea how many times the brass has been loaded before or what precautions have been taken. For an individual reloader, it is easy to get distracted and load a double charge of powder in a cartridge, or no powder at all. This can create a very dangerous situation, and it is vitally important to avoid all distractions when reloading.

I would also avoid solid lead, uncoated, or unjacketed ammunition or bullets, at least in semi-automatic handguns. Lead ball ammunition can work well, but it requires extra care in cleaning, as the soft lead can build up in the barrel's rifling. With some types of barrels, the manufacturer will warn specifically against using solid lead ammunition with no jacket. Solid lead bullets are cheaper because they don't have a copper jacket, but saving every last penny should not be the priority here.

RECOMMENDED RELOADING RESOURCES

Reloading Manuals by the Ammo and Powder Manufacturers

Cartridges of the World, 15th Edition

Handloader's Digest, 19th Edition

The ABCs of Reloading, 9th Edition

Available at GunDigestStore.com

SAFE & SECURE LONG-TERM GUN STORAGE

GUN SAFES

As gun owners, we are each responsible for gun safety, and a large part of that includes safe storage. Of course, what constitutes safe storage can vary from person to person and from one situation to the next. Someone with a large firearm collection and small children at home will have far different needs than an adult living on their own who owns one gun. The amount of space in your home and financial considerations are another factor. There are, however, plenty of choices to meet anyone's safe storage needs, from basic lockable cases to giant fireproof safes.

Safety isn't the only storage consideration. During times of civil unrest or societal breakdown, keeping your valuable firearms and ammo from falling into the wrong hands could bear on the outcome of your own survival.

Many people prefer a long gun for home defense over a handgun. Certainly, a shotgun or rifle is a more effective fight stopper than any handgun. In some states and localities, it is easier to own a long gun than a handgun. A long gun isn't going to fit neatly in your nightstand, but it will fit under your bed or in a nearby closet, and there are many options that offer safe long gun storage with fast access for these accommodations.

American Security Products makes a nice, flat, back-lit electronic combination safe with a front opening door that fits neatly under most beds. The AMSEC Defense Vault is large enough to fit several long guns on its slide-out foam-lined tray and allows for quick access. The safe can be anchored to the floor for additional security.

The TacVault from GunVault allows owners of ARs or other long guns to safely and securely store two fully loaded rifles or shotguns in a compact standing safe that can easily be concealed in a closet or behind a door. The safe includes a shelf for storing extra ammunition or magazines as well as other accessories, like a tactical light. The TacVault runs "off the grid" on a single 9V battery and gives you the choice between a user-selectable access

SURVIVAL SNAPSHOT: GUN STORAGE

PROS: A good quality safe prevents unauthorized use, theft or damage.

CONS: Limited and more difficult access (opt for a fast open safe for personal handgun).

AUTHOR'S TOP PICK: For security choose a steel long gun combination safe and bolt it down. For speed the GunVault finger-tip combination fast open pistol safe.

AUTHOR'S TIP: Hidden may not be secure and secure may not be hidden. There are safes that can do both.

REQUIRED ACCESSORIES: Safe organizers to maximize space, dehumidifier to protect guns.

OPTIONAL ACCESSORIES: Internal lights and outlets, fireproofing.

code and a biometric lock that can store up to 10 fingerprints to provide access to multiple family members. The biometric lock opens instantly with a scan of your finger for lightning fast access, an especially convenient feature under high stress conditions or in the dark when codes may be hard to remember and buttons tough to see.

The whole unit is 48 inches tall and only 10 inches wide, and the steel construction is pry proof. It can even be bolted to a wall for added security, an option which you should avail yourself. It uses 14-gauge steel for the body and 12-gauge for the door and features padded foam lining to protect the finish on your firearms.

Cannon Safes offers fireproof vaults in several sizes, including the 48-gun Commander Series, which features a nearly 6-inch thick steel and composite door with 1.5-inch locking lugs all around. If you are worried about someone stealing the entire 1,700-lb. safe, it can also be bolted to the ground (just in case). The Commander provides 90 minutes of 1,200-degree Fahrenheit fire protection to the contents and has internal light systems, power outlets, and USB and Ethernet connections to protect essential computer equipment. The interior is fully shelved and upholstered to accommodate rifles, shotguns, and a lot of pistols, and the door is secured by a backlit electronic combination lock with three layers of hardened steel plate.

Your bed presents another storage option. The box spring on your bed is really just a lot of wasted space — space you could use to store more guns, thanks to the BedBunker. This solid 10-gauge steel-walled horizontal safe lets you keep guns secure and hidden under your mattress. In fact, each

The TacVault allows owners of ARs or other long guns to safely and securely store two fully loaded rifles or shotguns in a compact standing safe that can easily be concealed in a closet or behind a door. *Photo: GunVault*

The BedBunker safe turns empty space beneath your mattress into a just-in-case gun vault.
Photo: BedBunker

section will hold as many as 35 rifles or shotguns and 70 handguns on two internal shelves, and you can double the storage space by using two units side by side.

I have standing safes, and they take up a lot of space in a closet, basement, or other room. They are neither subtle in appearance nor very convenient to access. The BedBunker, by contrast, gives you pretty quick access at nighttime: just push the mattress to one side. The ¼-inch, 140-lb. steel door has a gas piston system with which it opens, and an internal security bar prevents access if the hinges have been compromised. Plus, you can internally bolt two units together under a king- or queen-sized bed.

This is a serious, no nonsense safe, fire rated for up to two hours to protect your guns, valuables, and important documents, and it features a thick felt lining to prevent scratches or damage on the finish of your guns. Each section weighs 650 lbs. empty, so make sure your floors can handle it.

Another concealment option is the Sleepsafe Securevault, which looks like a standard night stand or office file drawer but provides three large drawers of fast access security. It's a complete 2mm-thick steel safe encased in a custom solid wood frame to match your décor. It has a built-in battery-powered biometric scanner discreetly located on one side that can store up to 10 fingerprints and pops open instantly for fast access to a firearm. There is no need to worry about power outages with the internal battery, and there is a programmable code that can be used to gain access.

Each of the three drawers is built sturdy and locks securely into the steel vault so that even if the wooden cabinet exterior is destroyed, the integrity of the safe remains solid. The internal storage space is 27 inches wide by 19 inches deep and 26 inches tall, evenly divided between the three drawers, each of which can hold up to 100 lbs. To further secure the safe, it can be bolted to a wall behind the cabinet, making it immovable. Think looters, smash-and-grabs, and other nastiness that can occur in a disaster scenario.

Liberty Safes produces a full line of large and small high-quality safes for firearms storage. But they also make safe accessories, and one invaluable tool is the SafElert Portable Alarm. This security tool is housed in a polycarbonate body (which looks like a restaurant pager) and connects to your Wi-Fi network to send you an alert whenever the object that you have placed it on/in is tampered with.

You can protect your car, guns, and other valuables from any jostling, prying, moving, opening, hitting, or even overheating. The device will even alert you if the humidity in your safe gets too high and when the batteries run low. You can opt to receive the text alerts on your smart phone or via e-mail. The annual service fee through Elertus Cloud Services is very low, less than the cost of a box of ammo, and you can program up to five devices to receive the alerts so that other family members can be made aware.

SafElert won't replace a traditional safe but does offer additional peace of mind when you are away from home. And it's versatile enough to protect almost anything. In addition, you can identify and select what specific concerns you want to monitor, including ambient heat, humidity, and/or movement. The unit runs off two easy-to-find AA batteries.

KEEP ORGANIZED

Keeping a gun safe well-organized helps to maximize the amount of storage space. It also ensures that your survival tools — guns, ammo, knives, etc. — are where you need them when you ... need them. One company offering great solutions for organization is Gun Storage Solutions. Their Handgun Hangers product line (as the name implies) is an organizer designed specifically for all types of handguns, and the different models make use of every inch of available space in your safe. The heavy, rubber coated steel cable wires hold handguns in place through the barrel and either hang down from the front or rear of a shelf. One unit, the Over-Under Handgun Hanger, allows you to store one gun above and one below a shelf simultaneously.

Previously, I just had all my handguns in soft cases stacked one on top of the other, which made it impossible to find what I needed without essentially emptying the safe. Now, each pistol can hang in plain view under the shelf (in previously wasted space), and each is kept away from its neighbor, avoiding scratches. This makes it far easier and faster to find what I need, saving time and making the safe look a lot more organized and less cluttered.

In addition, Gun Storage Solutions has a convenient system for increasing long gun storage space with their Rifle Rods product. The Rifle Rods attach to the inside top of your carpeted safe with hook and loop tape and have a long plastic rod that goes inside the barrel to keep long guns upright, instead of leaning against each other or the side of the safe. Oftentimes, scoped rifles can present a big problem fitting into standard safes, since the extra height can prevent them from fitting into the preset holders included inside the walls.

If you don't have a carpeted safe, Gun Storage Solutions has a special industrial grade fabric that works perfectly with their hook and loop Rifle Rods. It can be applied with glue, a staple gun, or upholstery tacks and adds another layer of protection for your firearms. A special foam floor covering is available, too, that provides extra cushioning if needed.

The company produces other storage solutions such as their Mag-Mounts, a powerful magnetic strip that adheres to any metal surface and allows for the easy storage of magazines or even spare

Gun Storage Solutions offers various systems for maximizing the space in your safe to store more guns securely. Photo: Gun Storage Solutions

parts. You can put this anywhere inside your safe or even on the outside for maximum storage and organization.

Another gun storage maker, Battenfeld Technologies, Inc., has a comprehensive line of storage gear including the very handy Lockdown vault line of accessories. For handguns, Lockdown makes four- and six-gun vinyl-coated racks that can sit in your safe or on a shelf and keep each gun visible, separate from its neighbors, and secure. The larger six-gun rack can accommodate just about any size revolver or pistol, plus it lets you keep more guns in the same amount of space.

Another consideration is all the wasted space on the walls and door of your safe, both inside and out, as well as on the walls of your closet. Lockdown turns all of that into usable storage area. Their hanging organizers feature multiple attachment systems, including magnets for your safe and hooks for carpeted interiors. You can hang them on walls with standard nails as well.

The most versatile of these (to my mind) are the various universal hanging organizers, which come in large and small sizes and for single handguns. The large organizer features six pockets of different sizes with mesh lining (so you can see what is in them) and elastic closures at the tops (to keep your stuff secure). All of my various small items from knives to jewelry and even guns can be easily stored, and the largest pockets feature zipper closures. The organizer has a rigid back that keeps the unit steady even with heavier items and makes it easier to hang.

The small hanging organizer is ideal for electronics, cell phones, or smaller documents like passports, etc. A stand-alone universal handgun hanger will accommodate most pistols or revolvers with a mesh lining and elastic bands at top and bottom for a variety of barrel lengths, the wedge shape keeping them secure. Other hanging accessories include hard plastic document holders for small and large papers, notes, and record books. A fireproof safe can be especially useful for storing hard to replace personal papers like birth certificates, wills, insurance, and other legal documents. Both document holders include a divider, and the large holder can hold up to 500 sheets.

For inside your vault or for a shelf on a bookcase, check out

Lockdown's Vault Drawer, which attaches to the bottom of a shelf, maximizing every inch of usable space. It is large enough to store additional documents and strong enough to hold pistols. It installs easily without tools.

The Lockdown Magnetic Key Rack attaches to your safe either inside or out and includes nine labeled key rings to make sure you don't forget what each key is for. They also offer magnetic barrel rests to secure long guns in the upright position inside or outside a vault. This can be especially handy when moving guns around so they don't end up falling over and getting damaged. Each barrel rest will hold up to three rifles or shotguns and has a rubber overmolding to protect the gun's finish.

Lockdown really does offer a comprehensive basket of products for anyone's storage needs. The list goes on and includes an innovative lighting kit that employs a long strip of LED lights that can be easily run throughout the interior of a safe or vault and makes seeing and finding items much easier. Another area of concern is that no matter how heavy your safe may be, thieves may still try to take the whole thing, contents and all, to open later at their convenience. They may also tip the safe over in an attempt to break into it at a weaker point. All of this will undoubtedly damage the contents, even if the thieves are unsuccessful. For this reason, it's important to anchor all safes to a wall or floor. Lockdown offers an anchor kit that allows you to safely attach your safes to wooden support beams or floors, as well as to concrete.

Finally, after organizing, cleaning, storing, and securing your valuable firearms, make sure not to forget the worst enemy of all: rust. Even in a climate-controlled environment, there can be varying degrees of temperature, moisture, and humidity, all of which can severely affect and corrode metal parts. Lockdown sells dehumidifier rods, silica gel, and a hygrometer, all good ideas to measure and control the temperature and amount of moisture in the air inside your gun locker.

HIDDEN STORAGE

There are many reasons why you may want to conceal your valuables or firearms in your home, but most often it is to thwart would-be thieves. We have all heard the saying "out of sight, out of mind," and are often reminded not to leave desirable items in plain view inside our vehicles.

Any thief, whether they break into your home or vehicle, will want to maximize their take in the shortest amount of time. They will look first in the most obvious places. For cars, that may be in the glove box, under the seat, and inside the console, whereas in a home, it may be inside dresser drawers, night stands, closets, or under the bed. In addition, anything of value that may be sitting out in plain view (such as small safes that can be easily removed and opened later) are prime targets.

When it comes to firearms, keeping them easily accessible is a priority for many. Of course, a gun in the bedroom doesn't do much good if you are in your basement when you need it. The best solution is to have your gun on your person at all times, but if that is not an option, there are alternatives. For anyone with a small amount of ability, many objects and places around the home can be readily converted to secret storage spots without going to the extreme of building secret rooms, false walls, trap doors, etc.

Small electronic combination safes can be kept in a bedside drawer and opened very quickly when needed. *Photo: Sentry*

Air vents are a simple, if obvious choice, but so are TV stands, bookshelves, and cabinets that can be adapted. By making the kick plate at the bottom of the front of the shelf removable, items can be hidden underneath.

Several companies manufacture inconspicuous-looking household items that have been adapted to conceal firearms or other valuables. However, the items listed here offer only concealment — not security; that is, they do not lock or prevent anyone who finds them from gaining access to the items inside. Extreme caution should be exercised especially around children (who tend to be curious by nature), and I cannot advise anyone to store loaded guns in this manner without taking additional safety precautions if little ones are around.

EVERY DAY ITEMS

Concealment Books from Personal Protection Products (PSP) are sold as a set and are actually boxes disguised to look like leather bound hardcover books. Felt-lined, they can hold most small- to full-size pistols or revolvers in complete anonymity. The boxes feature a magnet "lock" that keeps them closed until intentionally opened. For additional secrecy, the removable cover from a real book could be attached to the outside of the Concealment Book — just don't forget which book hides your guns.

Also from PSP is a very nice wooden Concealment Mantle Clock that opens from the top to reveal sufficient space for most large auto pistols or revolvers. The dual-purpose timepiece is felt-lined and secured with two magnets to prevent it from

Personal Protection Products (PSP) makes several concealment items for guns, including fake books and a hollow globe. *Photo: PSP*

Tactical Walls makes several types of gun concealment products from mirrors to wall shelves. The only drawback to this "hidden in plain sight" approach is lack of locking device. It is primarily a concealment product. *Photo: Tactical Walls*

opening unintentionally. And, for ultimate versatility, PSP offers a Quick Draw Gun Magnet, a polymer-coated, screw mountable, round magnet that can securely hold up to 10 lbs. This magnet can be mounted under a desk or shelf, inside a car, underneath furniture, or anywhere else one could imagine and securely holds a gun in place.

For long gun hides, Tactical Walls offers inside-your-wall hidden storage with a tough ABS plastic molded compartment in different sizes that are designed to fit between the studs of a 16-inch on center standard 2×4 wall. All you have to do is find the studs, cut a hole in the drywall, and install the Tactical insert. To keep it hidden, you can cover it with clothing (in a closet) or with a painting, mirror, or other piece of wall art. In addition, they sell complete units with sliding mirror covers that can include a magnetic lock as well. And the company offers a renter's version that does not require any permanent modifications to your walls.

Another very ingenious Tactical Walls product is known as Concealment Shelves. These mount directly on a wall and offer an attractive decorative touch while securing a hidden gun. The bottom of the shelf hinges down for fast access, and the shelves have magnetic locks for added security. (These are easily opened with the included magnet.) The shelves are made of wood in various finishes and include a customizable foam lining for a perfect fit. Optional accessories include interior LED lights that come on when you open the hidden shelf.

BEDSIDE SECURITY

A pistol in a bedside table is an old cliché for a good reason: it can provide quick access when needed most. The BackUp Bedside Shotgun Rack turns your bed and mattress into a storage device to keep a firearm, shotgun, or other long gun at the ready. Made entirely of high strength polymer, the BackUp features two large adjustable hooks to accommodate a variety of shotgun models without marring the finish and fits securely between the mattress and box spring. The shotgun mounts close to flush with the bed and is easily concealed with the sheets or comforter. All you have to do is reach down and grab your scattergun when trouble shows up.

For handguns, the Pillow-Pal Bedside Holster Holder is a convenient high-impact ABS polymer device that mounts between the mattress and box spring. It can accommodate any belt holster to hold your pistol or other safety device (such as pepper spray or flashlight) in place. With its low profile, it is convenient to transport and use while traveling. Several other manufacturers make bedside holsters in a variety of styles.

CAR AND TRUCK SAFE STORAGE

Leaving a firearm unattended at home or in your vehicle is a recipe for disaster, which is why secure vehicle storage should be a priority. This not only protects your valuable guns from theft but also helps prevent unauthorized use. Fortunately, there are many options specifically designed for keeping guns safe and out of sight while on the road.

One simple storage unit from DU-HA takes advantage of the unused space under the rear seat in many trucks. This tough polymer under seat storage unit keeps guns and survival needs neatly organized in one place. It's even available in colors to match your vehicle's interior, plus it's lightweight, and installs easily. It does not lock, however, so additional security for firearms is necessary.

CaseCruzer offers a tough-as-nails lockable polymer emergency footlocker that can fit in the trunk of must vehicles and provides for most all of your emergency needs. It is easily removable with convenient handles to transport between vehicles or between home and car. The airtight padded interior compartment protects your guns — as well as food supplies — from moisture or corrosion.

For real heavy duty secure storage, however, TruckVault makes steel drawer vaults with steel dead bolt locking systems to fit just about any car or truck. These are very strong, provide a lot of storage space for multiple handguns and long guns, and offer not just secure storage but protection from moisture, condensation, and even fire. They're a great solution for the well-stocked bug-out vehicle.

LONG-TERM STORAGE

Militaries the world over are used to having to deal with the long-term storage of firearms, usually older guns that are no longer in service. When one weapon system is retired for a new one, the old guns are stored just in case they should be needed again. Anyone who buys or collects old surplus guns will be familiar with the thick, greasy Cosmoline in which they were originally smothered to prevent rust.

There are any number of reasons why you might want to store extra firearms in a separate location long-term. It may be a second or vacation home, a hunting cabin, or with a friend or family member. Some people may even choose to bury a few guns (just

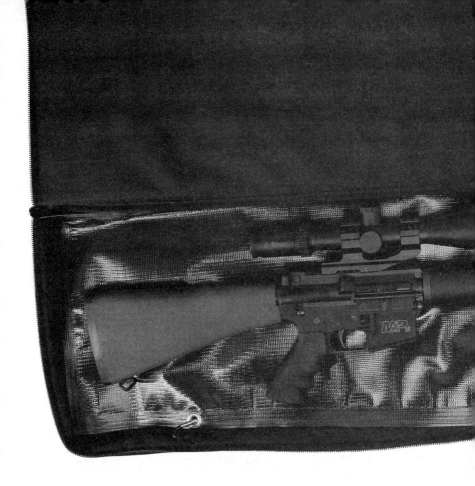

don't forget where). The biggest enemy to long-term firearms storage is corrosion and, thankfully, you don't have to use vats of bear grease any longer.

Today's solution for long-term storage and corrosion protection is ZCORR Vacuum Storage and Preservation bags. These heavy foil-based bags are currently in use by the U.S. military and provide complete protection against moisture and corrosion. ZCORR has expanded their line of products with new soft cases, complete with the same level of rust protection but built with an even tougher internal liner. The liner is what really makes the bags rust, water, and corrosion proof. Each liner is coated with a vapor phase corrosion inhibitor that bonds to metal surfaces and protects them. The liners are removable from the bag if they need replacement, which ZCORR says you may need after five years

For long-term storage and corrosion protection ZCORR Vacuum Storage and Preservation bags are the ultimate solution. The foil-based bags provide complete protection against moisture and corrosion.
Photo: ZCORR

of heavy use. The liners are tear resistant, feature a high-grade zipper closure to easily keep a firearm in the bag, and a one way vacuum valve to remove all air. And you can put two of them in one soft case.

The soft case itself is made from 1000D Cordura and measures 14×42 inches to accommodate most any size rifle or shotgun. An outside compartment measures 11x3 inches and can easily accommodate ammo, handguns, accessories, and other gear with two smaller internal pockets. ZCORR also makes a full line of ammo and parts storage bags with the same anti-corrosion properties. These are re-sealable, reusable, and feature a clear plastic side so you can easily see what you stored away and find it when you need it. These bags are available as military ammo can liners and will not harm primers.

DISCREET CARRY

*A*s the saying goes: If you expect trouble, then don't go there. Don't walk down a dark alley alone. Don't travel into dangerous neighborhoods at night. Don't try to grab a snake that you found in the woods. These are obvious (or they should be), but sadly we don't always know when something is dangerous or might become so.

Survival means being prepared. In nature, survival often depends on remaining unseen. Shakespeare's wisdom in this case was accurate when he wrote, "the better part of valor is discretion." (This often gets misquoted as "discretion is the better part of valor" but Falstaff's sentiment in Shakespeare's Henry the Fourth is

The Liberator AR carbine case from Renegade Ridge Tactical, a division of Crooked Horn Outfitters, is extremely discreet and offers significant tactical features for very rapid deployment.

correct.) He was referring to feigning death on the battlefield to survive (whether to fight another day or to play possum, I do not know).

If survival is your priority, then discretion is indeed a virtue. It is impossible to have all of your contingency emergency supplies with you at all times, but typically when most people are away from home, they are still close to their vehicle. If you already treat your vehicle like a moving purse, it is time to get organized.

I carry the bare minimum on my person: handgun, spare magazine, cell phone, and a knife. I also try to carry a flashlight as often as I can, even if it is just a key ring light; when you need it you need it, and it may just save your life. You can also carry a portable tourniquet kit and pepper spray. In your vehicle, you can of course carry much more, like a three-day emergency pack and a long gun. Here are some of the discreet carry tools and gear to get you organized now, while you still have time to do so.

DISCREET CARRY BAGS

Regardless of how or what you pack to stay prepared away from home, there is no need to advertise it. There are a lot of ways to keep survival supplies accessible and out of sight. Generally speaking, most people prefer to go about their daily business undisturbed by others, seeking neither to raise alarm nor have anyone question their whereabouts or intentions. For gun owners, this can be particularly important, as the repercussions of a misunderstanding can be severe. Most gun cases that are intended for transport to and from a range, home, activity, or place of business do a very good job of protecting the contents — but also tend to identify them. Indeed, almost all of my gun cases practically scream "tactical" and "gun inside."

I am fortunate to live in a neighborhood where gun cases do not raise alarm, but they certainly could if someone fearful of firearms saw them in my trunk at the local shopping center, for example. Some resourceful individuals have taken it upon themselves to convert much more innocuous-looking items into firearms conveyances. Colorful backpacks, gym bags, and tennis racket cases have all been used as impromptu (albeit somewhat deficient) gun cases, just to avoid being hassled.

Luckily for the rest of us, several manufacturers have seen the consumer need for discretion and responded with dedicated gun cases with proper sizing, padding, and internal straps. These new lines of discreet carry cases may appear to be designed for skateboards, sporting equipment, or musical instruments, but they conceal and protect your guns.

While I have seen several of these types of cases for long guns, there have not been as many produced for handguns. I assume that given their smaller size, it was thought that there was less of a need. But that is not so, especially when it comes to different modes of concealed carry. Carrying a defensive firearm on your

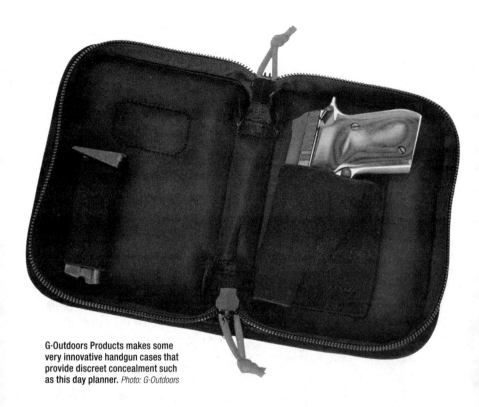

G·Outdoors Products makes some very innovative handgun cases that provide discreet concealment such as this day planner. *Photo: G·Outdoors*

person is always best, but for some, it is simply not convenient or comfortable. For these gun owners, off body carry is preferred and that requires a discreet handgun case.

I know ladies who prefer to carry in a purse with a special quick access compartment for their handgun. This, however, requires that they maintain control of their purse at all times and keep constant awareness of where it is. It will not do to simply put it down and walk away forgetting it.

G·Outdoors Products is one such company that offers very innovative and convenient handgun cases that go beyond being simply discreet by offering actual concealment. Many people keep jumper cables or emergency road kits in the trunk of their vehicles; it is all part of being well prepared. G·Outdoors produces a bright red case marked "jumper cables" on the outside, as well as a bright red triangular-shaped case with a reflective strip marked "Roadway Hazard Markers." Inside these legitimate-looking highway safety cases is a well-padded lining with hook and loop pockets for a full-sized handgun and two spare magazines. These may be kept in a vehicle full time as a very discreet trunk gun for emergencies. (Just make sure to also have actual jumper cables and vehicle emergency equipment!)

Walking around all day carrying a case of road flares or jumper cables is not very discreet, however, and for these instances where off body carry is desired, the company makes a line of concealed carry day planners. These are available in two sizes with a nylon fabric covering and dual zipper closure that provides fast and easy access. Inside the smaller of the two cases there is room for a compact handgun and a spare magazine with the sewn-in pouches. The larger case will hold a full-sized handgun and two spare magazines in interior pouches.

Both cases are well padded to protect the contents but don't leave much room for actual day planner objects like a pad of paper, pen, or calendar. Just don't open your "planner" during any meeting. Both plainly say "Day Planner" right on the front, so no one will ever suspect there is anything else inside. All of the cases have double zipper opening for fast access and are lockable for added security.

G·Outdoors Products makes other discreet concealment cases as well, one which looks like a tissue box — with actual tissues! — and the other as different-sized first aid kits of the sort one would typically find in the trunk of a vehicle.

Tablet computers have become so ubiquitous that it makes perfect sense that a tablet computer bag could/should be combined with a covert off body carry holster for CCW use. The new iPAC Pistol Case from TUFF Products does exactly this with its attractive and discreet shoulder bag.

The main compartment will fit any tablet up to 8 by 10 inches, which includes the iPad 2, 3, 4, and Air with case. A front accessory pocket holds all of your extra notepads, pens, business cards, etc. At the back of the case is a dedicated holster pocket with quick access zipper system and internal universal holster that will accommodate a full-size pistol (with or without accessory light/laser) and a spare magazine. The case is made from durable nylon and comes in a tan color. An adjustable shoulder strap is also included.

Off body carry can be a very convenient and comfortable way to have a concealed pistol with you regardless of the weather or your clothing. The only caveat is that you have to make sure to keep constant control of it at all times. Do not leave the bag unattended or put it down and forget it someplace. This is a hard lesson that anyone who carries concealed off body needs to remember. Of course, knowing it is holding both your gun and an expensive tablet computer should incentivize the average person to keep an eye on the iPAC Pistol Case.

Discreet cases for long guns are also very popular. The Liberator AR carbine case from Renegade Ridge Tactical, a division of Crooked Horn Outfitters, is extremely discreet and offers significant tactical features for very rapid deployment. Externally, the Liberator is made from 400 Denier Mil-Spec Cordura nylon and has a large tennis racket or small guitar shape 11 inches wide and 36 inches tall, making it both tough and very unobtrusive. It has reinforced handles at the side and top and five D-ring loops for maximum carry versatility, including shoulder strap, back pack carry, and can even be mounted on a vehicle headrest and lay across the back of the front seat.

The top of the bag features a Hypalon Quick-Draw deployment strap that allows the top third of the case to open instantly and hinge down with one quick pull, exposing the stock and pistol grip of your AR Carbine for instant deployment. The interior of the bag is well padded, sturdy, and easily accommodates a carbine with a full 30-round magazine and optics. There are no internal or external pockets; however, there is a removable 6x9-inch Molle pouch that attaches to one side and is designed for a backup pistol or spare AR magazines. This pouch features a quick opening system and can be used separately for concealed carry.

Another very convenient diversion case is the COVRT M4 rifle case from 5.11 Tactical. This bag has the advantage of closely resembling a rather generic-looking civilian backpack. Its longer than normal length could be easily seen by the casual observer as a gym bag or simply containing a musical instrument or diving gear and fins. As is true with all 5.11 Tactical products, the case is built to a very high standard and has a plethora of additional features. Available in two subtle color patterns, the bag sports tough water resistant nylon construction with a smooth lining to protect your rifle and high-grade YKK zippers should provide long-lasting service. It is large enough to easily fit a collapsed M4 carbine with up to a 16-inch barrel and has a well-padded ambidextrous single cross body shoulder strap with accessory attachment points. The mesh padding appears on the back of the bag to protect you and increase comfort.

The front of the COVRT M4 bag includes two compartments for additional gear, magazines, or ammunition. The smaller top compartment can roll down and has a hook and loop panel area for ID with additional MOLLE webbing. The main rifle compartment comes with an internal barrel catch/muzzle trap to protect the bottom of the bag, and a top and side carry handle are also included.

In testing this product, I was able to store and transport AR carbine rifles with collapsible stocks from different manufacturers with little difficulty, although some with larger muzzle devices barely fit. The bag fit well with the adjustable shoulder strap and felt very comfortable as advertised, plus all my range gear easily fit in the accessory pockets.

DISCREET ON-BODY CARRY

Keeping a firearm secured and concealed on your person requires some degree of versatility, as the weather can often dictate apparel choices. During cooler months, I have the luxury of carrying a larger gun, which I can more easily cover up with a coat or jacket. Woolrich manufactures a full line of tactical clothing to complement this fast growing segment of the outdoor market. Among the many options in the Elite Tactical line is the Discreet Carry Jacket with a heavy boulder-washed cotton twill outer layer and a warm polyester Sherpa liner. Discretion is certainly the key here, and this casual jacket does not announce "gun guy" to the world when you wear it.

It does, however, include many valuable features that concealed carriers and off-duty law enforcement officers will appreciate.

Woolrich's Elite Tactical Discreet Carry Jacket features heavy duty construction and several hidden pockets for concealed carry.
Photo: Woolrich

The girth adjustable hip-length jacket is long enough to cover up a high ride outside the waistband holster or any inside the waistband, or IWB carry. The large pockets will fit most mid-sized handguns and are reinforced for security, plus they feature accessory loops to lock down your gear. The back of the jacket has a hidden accessory tunnel where one could store plastic restraints or run com wires.

With insulated sleeves, the Woolrich Discreet Carry Jacket keeps you warm without restricting your movements and looks perfectly casual in all situations while providing you quick access to your firearm and other gear.

When shorts and t-shirt weather hits, the choices for methods of carry as well as type of gun to carry may need to change. The priority at all times is to keep your firearm concealed and avoid unwanted attention. Most of us already carry something less than a full-sized handgun to help achieve this goal. Smaller handguns are not only easier to conceal but weigh less and make carry a bit more comfortable.

Ankle holsters can offer very deep concealment of small handguns but require training for a fast draw. *Photo: Uncle Mike's*

If you are wearing less clothing, you may want to downsize your carry gun even more. Pocket pistols offer the maximum amount of concealability, especially the pocket .380s paired off with a suitable pocket holster. DeSantis and Uncle Mike's make some good, solid pocket holsters in different sizes. The advantage here is that you can grip your gun and prepare for a very fast draw if trouble seems likely without arousing any suspicion, since it just looks like you have your hands in your pocket.

Pocket holsters are not limited to semi-autos and there are several that will fit small frame revolvers. Some are designed to accommodate guns with lasers attached. The squared-off design of pocket holsters prevents the gun shape from printing through your pants material and, even if it does, it just looks like you have

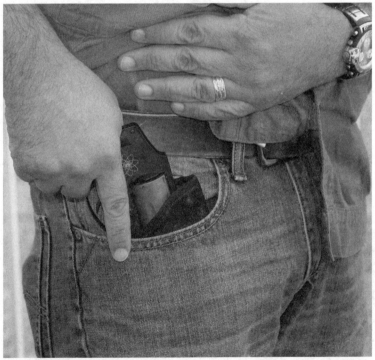

Pocket holsters allow for deep concealment of small revolvers and pistols, which can be carried very comfortably.

A very popular option for concealed carry is the inside the waistband (IWB) holster. With the gun and holster riding inside the pants only the grip of the gun is exposed. *Photo: Galco Gunleather*

your wallet in your front pocket. All of the good pocket holsters feature some type of tacky polymer or rubber material on the outside so when you draw your gun, the holster stays in your pocket, and you don't end up standing there holding a holster-covered gun.

You can keep using your standard waistband holster if you prefer, just make sure you have a light covering garment to keep it concealed, which may be difficult or too hot in the summer. One option I like for waistband carry that provides total concealment with no covering garment is the Sneaky Pete Holsters "Cell Phone" case. This clever little thing just looks like a leather cell phone case but provides instant access to a small-sized pistol.

Another very popular option is to use an IWB holster. With the gun and holster riding inside your pants, only the grip of the gun is exposed, keeping it mostly concealed. The gun rides much closer to the body in this fashion, preventing printing against clothing, which can reveal the gun. Still, it is advisable to wear a loose covering over top that is long enough to keep the gun concealed when you raise your arms, or when you bend over.

Inside the waistband carry requires consideration for wearing clothing a bit larger than normal. It is a good idea to purchase pants that have a slightly looser fit to accommodate the room the gun takes up, as well as looser covering garments such as button shirts or t-shirts one size larger. Several manufacturers sell short sleeve button shirts with extra room and access flaps to provide for quick access.

The next decision is between tucked and untucked. For many of us, walking around with an untucked shirt is just not gentlemanly or simply not appropriate in professional settings. Fortunately, many holster manufacturers, including Blackhawk, have developed tuckable IWB holsters. These feature extended clips that leave a deep gap between the top of the clip that goes outside the belt and the bottom of the clip that attaches to the holster — you simply tuck your shirt over the gun and into the clip. From the outside, all that is visible is the belt clip itself. Of course, manufacturers have devised clips that fit between your pants and your gun belt (you do use an actual gun belt, don't you?) which almost

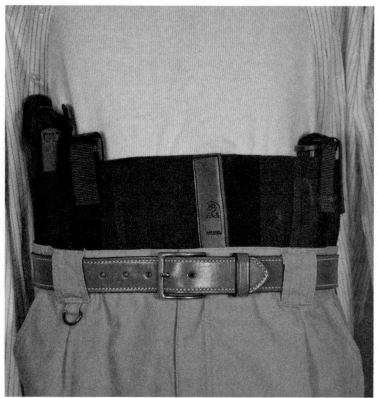

Belly Band Holsters offer excellent concealment and comfort with room for spare magazines or other gear. *Photo: DeSantis*

completely hides the clips so only a small portion that hooks onto the belt is visible.

Keep in mind that this is going to slow down your draw, as you will need to pull your shirt out of your pants to access your gun. Re-holstering won't be any easier either, since to get properly accommodated you will need to find a discreet place to tuck your shirt back into your pants.

A belly band holster (basically just an elastic band with a pocket) is another option for deep concealment with cross draw carry. You only have to undo a few buttons on your shirt to gain access — or rip them if in a hurry. It may also be a good idea to wear an undershirt with waistband or IWB carry, as this will keep sweat off your gun and prevent chafing, little tips that will improve comfort. Some IWB holsters, such as those from Crossbreed, have extended backings that protect the gun from you and you from the gun, so you don't have to wear an undershirt. With most small concealed carry guns, you do end up sacrificing ammunition capacity for size and weight. This makes it all the more important to carry a spare magazine (for a semi-auto) or speed strip (for a revolver). Spare magazines and speed strips can be carried loose but preferably in a separate pocket from keys, change, and other junk. I prefer speed strips over speed loaders because they lay flat in my pocket and still provide a fast revolver reload. Several manufacturers produce small single-stack magazine holders for waistband carry. Since these are fairly innocuous, it is less necessary to keep them concealed.

DISCREET CARRY FOR WOMEN

Carrying a gun, whether openly or concealed, is not always comfortable for women. The heavy piece can pull on your clothing or poke into your ribs whenever you sit down. And women's fashions are quite unforgiving when it comes to attaching or concealing a firearm. Luckily, things are starting to change, as companies develop products that allow women to finally carry in comfort and style. Some even take advantage of hiding places that are uniquely available to women, like bras and purses. Here we present a rundown of some of the options available. While not every carry system will appeal to every woman, with so many choices, you're sure to find at least one holster that works for you.

INSIDE-THE-WAISTBAND

Flashbang Holsters is a company devoted entirely to holsters specially designed for women. Their inside the waistband holster model, called the Ava, features a molded holster attached to a leather back piece. The inner surface is lined with soft purple suede for comfort and to allow the holster to conform to your body's shape. This back piece is smaller than those on most men's holsters, so it's comfortable on a woman's shorter torso. Two very strong metal clips hook on to the waist of your pants, making it sturdy and stable. Unlike many waistband holsters, it does not require that a belt be worn, giving its user more clothing options. The holster and clips are adjustable and can be worn at the front, side, or back of the hips. There are left- and right-hand versions that can be ordered to fit a wide range of handguns.

Flashbang makes another clip-on holster model, called the Betty. Smaller than the Ava, but also much more versatile, the Betty is simply a molded holster with a single clip. Its small size means that it can be worn in a variety of ways to suit anyone's taste: strong side, cross draw, small of the back, appendix, or inside a pocket or purse. Its combination of a strong clip and light retention on the gun mean that you will not have to worry about the holster coming out with the gun when you draw. It is available for a wide variety of handguns in right- or left-handed versions.

OUTSIDE-THE-WAISTBAND

Safariland makes many excellent holsters, but the Model 5195 Low Ride is specifically recommended as a hip holster for women. The holster is offset from the belt loop by about 25 degrees, so while the belt loop follows your natural curve, the gun is still held vertically. This angle, combined with the gun's low ride position on the hip, means that the grips won't dig into your ribs. It simply makes it easier for someone with a short torso to draw, and is approved for use in the International Defensive Pistol Association, or IDPA. It can be concealed under a jacket, but in general, outside the waistband holsters are not easy to hide. The model 5195 can be ordered to fit a wide variety of pistols. It's available in right- and left-handed versions and comes with a waterproof and scratch-resistant finish. The holster is compatible with the other belt loops, clips, and paddles from Safariland, so you can customize it to suit your taste.

Flashbang's belt holster is an all-leather design called the Sophia. Designed to slide onto the belt rather than clip on, it can fit any belt up to 1 ¾-inches wide. Eschewing the forward cant used in most belt holsters, it holds the gun vertically and close to the body, minimizing bulkiness, visibility, and pressure on the wearer's ribs. It can be ordered in right and left hand and to fit a wide range of small handguns.

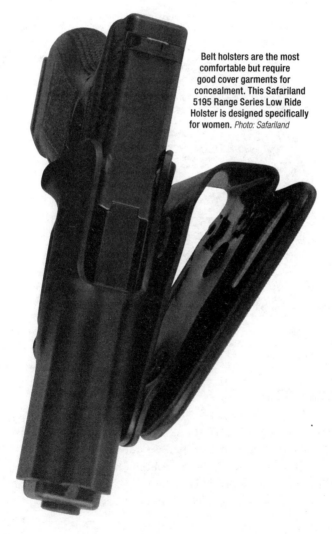

Belt holsters are the most comfortable but require good cover garments for concealment. This Safariland 5195 Range Series Low Ride Holster is designed specifically for women. *Photo: Safariland*

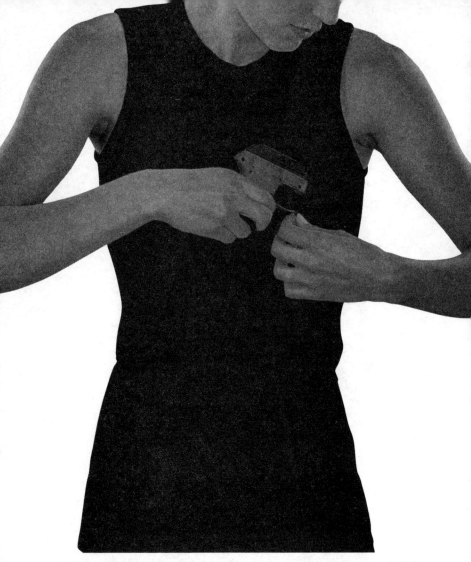

Activewear holster shirts like this one from 5.11 make for a convenient and secure method of concealed carry during workouts. *Photo: 5.11*

ANKLE CARRY

Ankle holsters are a very comfortable option for concealed carry if you find carrying a gun at your torso to be restrictive. The Galco Ankle Lite is a simplified version of the company's popular Ankle Glove model. A wide neoprene band holds it on your calf with Velcro and is padded on the inside with sheepskin for comfort. The leather holster has a retention strap for added security. It'll fit a range of pistols and revolvers and is available in right- or left-handed versions. One nice option is that it comes in black or khaki to match the most popular pant colors, just in case it should happen to peep out at the cuff.

ACTIVEWEAR

Jogging and exercising present a unique challenge for concealed carry, since most holsters cannot attach to athletic wear and would not feel comfortable during strenuous activity. PistolWear has developed a line of athletic holsters to fill this gap. The firearm goes into a pouch attached to a bellyband that is concealed under your shirt. The band is comfortable and won't bounce or shift when you move. The material is lightweight and breathable, and the gun is completely enclosed so it won't poke into your skin. In fact, the holster is so comfortable that you may decide to use it for everyday carry, as long as you don't need to tuck your shirt in. This line includes two sizes: the PT-One and the PT-Two. The PT-One can hold a compact- or full-size gun, and has a separate little pouch for a spare magazine. It comes in left- and right-handed versions. The PT-Two is designed for a compact gun and lacks the extra magazine pouch. This style is ambidextrous. Both models are available in white, black, or nude for least visibility.

In addition, 5.11 has produced one of the most comfortable and discreet options for women's concealed carry in their sleeveless holster shirt. A tank top with underarm holster pockets on both the left and right sides, the shirt distributes the weight of the gun evenly across the fabric so it is less noticeable to the carrier. There are no itchy straps or belts involved. The shirt is available in black or white and can easily be incorporated into your casual or business wardrobe. The holster pockets are lined to prevent the gun from printing through to the outside of your clothes.

BRA HOLSTERS

Many women dislike the added bulk and weight that comes with carrying a gun on the hip. A better concealment option may be a bra holster. Your natural curves create an easy and convenient space to fit a firearm. The Flashbang is a molded plastic holster with a leather strap that attaches around the center bridge in the front of your bra. The strap can be adjusted for angle and so that it either hangs down below the bra or is held right up under the band. The gun is drawn by reaching up under your shirt. The Flashbang can be ordered to fit a wide range of handguns and in right- and left-handed versions.

Flashbang also makes another bra holster model called the Marilyn. Instead of attaching to the center of your bra, its strap goes around the bra band under your armpit. The holster then clips into the cup so that the gun rests partly inside the cup. You may need to adjust your bra fit to accommodate it, but once settled, it's quite comfortable. This is one of a very few holsters that can be worn with a slim-fitted dress and still be concealed. Drawing the gun requires that you reach right down into the front of your shirt, which may seem odd, but this won't matter in an emergency situation. The Marilyn comes in left- and right-hand versions to fit a long list of handgun models.

CONCEALED CARRY PURSES

When it's too difficult to carry your firearm on your body, a holster purse may fit the bill. Be advised that guns in purses are much more easily lost or stolen than ones you carry on your person, and you should take a personal defense class that covers gun retention in this situation. Nonetheless, holster purses remain extremely popular. Once limited to nondescript black bags, concealed carry purses are now blossoming into a bonanza of colors and styles. Gun Tote'n Mamas sells a line ranging from tote bags to evening bags and every style in between.

These are available in several colors, including floral tooled leather and zebra and leopard print. For dressier events, there are now several models of small evening bags with holsters that

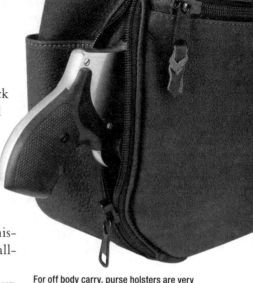

fit subcompact handguns. Check out Everyday Tactical's Cocktail model, an evening purse that comes in black leather, patent, and faux crocodile. Even smaller is their Wrist Bag, designed to be carried as a clutch or wristlet and available in several colors. Despite its sophisticated look, it can still hold a small- or mid-sized handgun inside.

For women who cannot give up their favorite handbag or who have several different bags that they love,

For off body carry, purse holsters are very convenient but make sure to retain control of your purse. *Photo: Galco Gunleather*

concealed carry is still possible. Famed for their luxurious and high-quality holster bags, Galco has now come out with the removable Carry Safe Holster System. This nylon holster Velcro attaches onto a patch that can be clipped anywhere in your bag. The Velcro allows you to easily adjust the position and angle of the holster any way you like so that the gun is readily accessible regardless of your bag's shape. The entire holster mount can be moved from bag to bag very simply, allowing you to convert any purse, briefcase, or handbag into a concealment case. At only $30, this is a bargain compared to the cost of buying multiple carry bags. The holster is available in four sizes to fit most carry guns.

There are holster options available to you whether you're dressed up for an evening out or dressed down to go for a jog. Regardless of a woman's size, clothing, or activity level, she should always feel that a firearm can be easily incorporated and carried with her. With so many options out there, a lady should never have to suffer through an ill-fitting or uncomfortable holster when she can so easily go armed in style.

OPTICS & SURVEILLANCE

Optics and surveillance are two very different priorities, but both involve seeing before being seen. This has obvious survival benefits. It can help you avoid troublesome situations and people. You can scout areas at a distance for supplies. It can serve as an early warning and identification system. And when needed, it can help you place accurate, precision shots where they are needed for hunting or self-defense.

OPTICS

When we think about optics, we tend to focus on things like riflescopes and binoculars. You may not have the luxury of having both available, and if you have to pick, go with the rifle scope. Of course, no one likes to be surveilled through a scope on a rifle, so exercise caution and discretion. If you are routinely using your rifle scope for surveillance work, you may want to remove it from the rifle. There are quick-detach scope mounts that will retain zero as long as you reattach them consistently. Retaining zero just means that a scope that is jostled or removed and re-attached will still shoot to the same spot where it was sighted in originally. Quality modern scope mounts will allow you to retain zero more effectively.

RETICLES: MIL-DOT VS. MOA

Variable power optics allow you to zoom in for a closer and more detailed look. At the lower setting, these optics provide a much wider field of view for scanning a larger area. In the old days, riflescopes were much simpler affairs with fixed magnification and a plain crosshair. Modern scopes, on the other hand, are much more complicated but have features that make consistent long-range shooting possible. To start, you must grasp the difference between MOA (Minute of Angle) and Mil-Dot reticles and adjustments.

Minute of Angle refers to the degrees in a circle (360) and each degree has 60 Minutes. As you move farther away from the point of origin, the angle gets larger. Think of it like a slice of pie: as you go from the center to the crust, the slice gets wider. At 100 yards, one MOA measures 1.047 inches. The turrets on your scope that you use to sight in your rifle are almost always measured in ¼ MOA, so that means one click of turning moves the reticle about .25 inch right or left, up or down at 100 yards. If you are shooting at a target that is 200 yards away, one click moves the reticle .5 inch, and if you are shooting at a target 50 yards away, one click moves it .125 (or 1/8) inch.

Some scopes have both an MOA reticle with internal hash marks and MOA turret adjustment. A good example is the BURRIS C4 3-9x40 Rifle Scope, C4 Wind MOA Reticle. This keeps things simple as the hash marks and the turret adjustments match. Incidentally, MOA is the standard American measuring system.

A Mil-Dot is based on radians, of which there are 6.28 in a

Mil-Dot reticles are standard use in modern Western militaries and offer good range finding estimations. *Photo: Lance Cpl. Reece E. Lodder*

circle. There are 1,000 Milliradians, or Mils, in one radian. If you convert one Mil-Dot to our American inch-based system, one Mil measures 3.6 inches at 100 yards and 3.6 feet at 1,000 yards. There are 3.44 Mils in one MOA. This system was designed specifically for range estimation for artillery and long-distance rifle use. Inside your Mil-Dot reticle, there will be hash marks set at one Mil distance (as found in the Weaver Tactical 3-15x50 SF Rifle Scope, Mil Dot Reticle, as just one example). Others will include intermediate hash marks at the half Mil-Dot points. You can measure the size of the dots in mils and end-to-end for greater precision.

yards	drop	clicks	Wind 10
100	1.6	+6	0.2
200	0	0	2.5
250	-2.8	4	4.0
300	-7.1	9	5.9
350	-13.0	14	8.2
400	-20.6	20	10.8
450	-29.9	25	14.0
500	-41.2	31	17.5
550	-54.7	38	21.6

243 105 Amax

yards	drop	clicks	Wind 10
600	-70.3	45	26.2
650	-88.5	52	31.3
700	-109.2	60	37.0
750	-132.9	68	43.3
800	-159.6	76	50.2
850	-189.7	85	57.7
900	-223.4	95	66.0
950	-261.1	105	75.0
1000	-303.0	116	84.7

243 105 AMax

If you have already used a ballistic calculator to measure your specific bullet and rifle combination's bullet drop at different distances, you can make yourself a cheat sheet or "dope card."
Photo: AliveFreeHappy

Most optics that have Mil-Dot reticles have MOA turret adjustment. This necessitates some math to make adjustments, but there are handy formulas to help.

To determine distance to the target (assuming you have an idea of the size of the target), use this formula:

American System:
(Distance in yards) = 1000/36 (or 27.7) x (Object size in inches)/Mils

Metric System:
Distance in kilometers = Size in meters/Mils

For example, a 6-foot tall man that measured 3 Mil-Dots would be almost 665 yards away. You will almost never know the exact size of the target in inches; you will be guessing. However, this is where the Mil-Dots help. If you can see where your shot hit, you can measure the distance from the hit to the target in Mils and adjust accordingly. You can also use the Mil-Dot reticle to adjust for windage and bullet drop. So, to hit your target, you can hold over in Mil-Dots or adjust your reticle. You also need to calculate your bullet drop, which depends on your ammunition and rifle. If you shoot and see that the bullet hit 2 Mils low, for example, you have to convert the Mils to MOA in order to make the adjustments on your scope (remember one MOA is 3.44 Mills). Unless you need to know exactly, I suggest rounding and simply multiplying 3.5 by the Mils you need to get the MOA. In this case, it is 3.5 x 2 = 7 MOA. Since one MOA is four clicks of your turret, that equals 28 clicks to reach 7 MOA of adjustment. You could also just hold over the proper distance with no math.

The best approach is to spend the money and get a Mil-Dot scope where both the reticle and the adjustments are in Mils. The adjustments will be in 1/10 Mil which is about 0.36 inches per click.

UNDERSTANDING FOCAL PLANE

Riflescopes come in first (front) and second (rear) focal planes. If you have a fixed-power scope, it makes no difference. If you have a variable magnification scope, it matters a lot. Most scopes use the rear focal plane. This means that the size of the reticle changes relative to the target as you increase or decrease magnification. The reticle size is actually staying the same, but as the target gets larger or smaller because of the magnification changes the crosshairs and any hash marks appear wider (at low magnification) or narrower (at high magnification).

Obviously, since the size of the reticle relative to the target changes, you can't use it for measuring distance. To compensate, manufacturers set the hash marks on the reticle to be accurate for measuring distance at the highest magnification only. Since you typically only need to measure distance accurately for long range, this isn't much of an issue, but it does need to be kept in mind.

Some tactical scopes instead place the reticle at the first or front focal plane. In this case, the size of the reticle changes with the magnification so that no matter how much you zoom into the

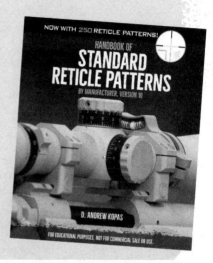
target, it takes up the same number of Mils. In this way, you can measure the distance at any point in the magnification range.

People who shoot long range make themselves a cheat sheet, or "dope card," with known sizes and distances. This allows them to make rough estimates in the field quickly. Of course, you can also download calculators to your smartphone that will do this for you or you could buy a range finder.

.223 AND .308 BULLET DROP AND SIGHTING IN

The second a bullet exits the barrel, gravity takes hold and starts to pull it down toward the ground. The longer the bullet is in the air traveling, the farther down it will drop. This is why, when you are shooting at various distances, it is important to know the distance and how far your bullet will drop so that you can compensate.

Gravity is not the only thing acting on your bullet, however; there is also the air. How long your bullet stays in the air depends on its shape. Various shaped bullets have different levels of drag, and some will fly longer and straighter than others. The weight of

The bullet drop for the .308 cartridge is somewhat different than the .223 — especially at longer distances as seen on this Remington R-25 GII.

the bullet is another factor. Gravity exerts more force on a heavier bullet and pulls it down faster. Ironically, heavier bullets also have more energy and, at longer distances, can actually drop less. Finally, you have to consider the initial velocity of the bullet. The faster it starts, the longer it stays airborne.

If you are a tactical shooter and just looking to hit a man-sized silhouette at intermediate range (out to 300 yards), your worries are minimal. Past that, it starts to matter. It also matters a lot if you are a hunter or otherwise need to make a precision shot. Knowing your distance and bullet performance for your specific load will allow you to make the needed changes on your scope or simply to hold over.

COMPENSATING FOR THE .223

To keep things simple, let's stick with standard 55- and 62-grain FMJ military loads in .223. On any rifle, the sights are some distance above the bore line, another factor to consider. At short distances, the bullet will impact below your point of aim, then travel upward and intersect the point of aim at the distance where you sighted in, then start to drop. It's not that your bullet is actually rising as it leaves the barrel — it starts falling immediately — it's that the bore line of your barrel is tipped upward. What your bullet actually crosses is your line of sight.

Barrel length is another factor that affects velocity. The shorter the barrel, the less velocity you get. On a .223 AR, you lose about 50 fps for every inch of barrel you take off. The typical test length for barrels can be 24 inches, so if you are using a 16-inch carbine, you need to deduct about 400 fps.

The popular advice is to sight your .223 AR at 50 yards, and you will be zeroed in at 200 yards. As the urban myth goes, because of the arc of travel of the bullet, you will hit dead center at 50 and 200 yards with a 50-yard zero. This is actually not correct. Using a 16-inch barrel and a 55-grain bullet at 500 yards, you lose almost the entire height of a person, and even at 200 yards, the bullet is 3.2 inches below the point of aim. The situation is worse for a 62-grain .223 FMJ bullet, since the higher weight reduces muzzle velocity to around 2,700 fps. If you zero in at 50 yards, it will hit 4.2 inches low at 200 yards. At 500 yards, you hit 72.2 inches (6 feet) low, and at 1,000 yards, it is 549.3 inches low — or more than 45 feet! Add to all of this any crosswind, temperature, humidity, elevation, barometric pressure, etc. and you can see just how complex long-range shooting can be.

COMPENSATING FOR THE .308

It turns out that zeroing a .308 AR at 50 yards works just as well (not very well, obviously). Using standard military FMJ 150-grain ammo from a 20-inch barrel rifle, you only drop 4.3 inches at 200 yards. In fact, the bullet drop and performance is about the same as for the .223 round fired from a carbine — though the .308 has a lot more energy. This energy has the advantage at longer distances, and the .308 doesn't drop as far as the .223 past 500 yards. This load at 1,000 yards drops 480.2 inches (5 feet less than the .223 above).

The lesson here is that if you need precision at medium distances or want to come anywhere near a target at longer distances, you need to know exactly how your bullet will perform. Pick a rifle and a load and stick with it. Then you can make yourself a dope sheet with distances and bullet drops that you can quickly reference. For standard survival situations, just sight in at 50 yards and leave it alone.

LOW MAGNIFICATION SCOPES

There are basically two kinds of variable power scopes that should be considered for survival situations: low and high magnification. By low magnification, I mean a 1-4x scope or a fixed 3x or 4x scope. These can be very effective, both for close-range tactical uses and mid-range applications from 300-500 yards.

One example of this is the Designated Marksman Scope from Millett, an excellent tactical scope that meets the needs of both long range and close quarters combat. The role of the designated marksman is far different than that of the sniper and calls for a different weapon system and optics. The key is to extend the capabilities of

The Weaver Tactical 5x24 Intermediate Range Optic offers great close combat support with an illuminated reticle and medium range accuracy at 5x power. *Photo: Weaver*

the rifle shooter for rapid engagements of multiple targets.

With a quickly adjustable variable 1-4x24 power, the DMS scope easily engages targets with precision out past 500 yards. The reticle has a simple 1 MOA dot surrounded by an 18 MOA donut, which can be used for range estimation. For close quarters and low light conditions, the Millett DMS features an illuminated red colored reticle with 11 levels of adjustment for intensity and is powered by an included CR2032 Lithium battery. The fully-coated optics reside inside a 30mm tube, and the scope offers a generous 3.5 inches of eye relief. Millett offers a lifetime warranty for this economically priced but high-quality optic.

The Weaver Tactical CIRT (Close-Intermediate Range Tactical) scope is another compact optic that features 1-5x24 variable power with an illuminated adjustable intensity red/green first focal plane glass-etched reticle. Glass etching the reticle ensures that there is nothing to come loose under shock or recoil. Placing

The Nikon P-223 is a super compact fixed-power 3x32 scope specifically designed for AR carbines with a built-in bullet drop compensator for fast target acquisition at various distances. *Photo: Nikon*

the reticle at the first focal plane is an added benefit, as it causes it to grow or shrink as magnification is increased or decreased. This keeps the reticle in proper perspective for use in range finding.

The horizontal crosshairs are segmented in Mils, and the center circle/dot is measured at the size of a human head at 100 yards. Another advantage to this optic is that even if the battery goes dead, the scope still functions with its standard reticle. As is to be expected from a duty optic, the Weaver Tactical CIRT features solid one-piece construction and fully multi-coated lenses. It is waterproof, shockproof, and comes with argon gas purged 30mm tubes to prevent fogging.

At 1x magnification with the illuminated reticle, it can function as a standard red or green dot CQB scope or as a both eyes open optic for rapid target engagement. Green is easier to see in daylight conditions, while red works best for low light. For more precision or intermediate range shots, you can increase magnification to 5x. In keeping with the tactical nature of the scope, the CIRT has easy adjustable turrets for windage and elevation for rapid field adjustments and no caps to drop or misplace. It's about

The Vortex Razor HD 1-4x24 CQMR-1 (Close Quarter Medium Range) with a lighted first focal plane crosshair reticle designed for the AR. *Photo: Vortex*

10 inches in length and weighs slightly more than 14 ounces.

Low magnification fixed-power scopes can be had for specific applications. An example of this is the Nikon P-223, a super compact 3x32 scope specifically designed for AR carbines with a built-in bullet drop compensator for fast target acquisition at various distances.

The tactical-style turrets adjust easily with ½ MOA adjustments and can be set to zero with a simple lift and turn. The reticle has a crosshair and two bullet drop hash marks pre-set for 200, 400, and 600 yards using a 55-grain bullet. Like all Nikon scopes, the P-233 is built tough with fully multicoated optics for maximum light transmission and has a waterproof and fog proof nitrogen-filled aluminum construction tube. It comes in an attractive matte finish.

Vortex is another company that offers top-of-the-line, Japanese made, variable power precision optics. One model specifically designed for the AR rifle is the Vortex Razor HD 1-4x24 CQMR-1 (Close Quarter Medium Range) with a lighted first focal plane crosshair reticle. The aircraft-grade aluminum body features a hard-anodized matte finish that looks like a very dark metallic gray. Each unit is waterproof, fog proof (argon gas purged) and recoil tested to 50 BMG. The Razor, however, is specifically designed to function with the 5.56mm (.223 Remington) round.

The unit features a custom BDC (Bullet Drop Compensator) turret with both green and red markings pre-calibrated to specifically compensate for the drop of the M855 62-gr. FMJ bullet (green) and the XM193 55-gr. FMJ bullet (red) at distances from 200 to 700 yards. The Razor can be had in either this version with the BDC turret or one with a BDC reticle.

While the Razor is not a compact or lightweight scope at over 10 inches long and over 20 ounces, it is designed to function on both M4 variant rifles and full-length ARs in CQB and mid-range conditions. The scope is designed to function as a sight by itself with or without a battery since the reticle remains, so backup iron sights are not a necessity.

The turrets themselves are set to ¼ MOA per click and include turret cap retaining screws that can be loosened and re-tightened once the turrets are indexed to the proper zero. The elevation turret also has a red fiber optic radius bar on top, which helps you immediately check the turret knob position. A similar fiber optic sight on the magnification adjustment knob identifies the magnification level even in low light conditions.

The lighted reticle has 11 illumination settings, with the lowest compatible for night vision devices. The reticle illumination turret has an off position between each intensity setting, a nice feature that allows you to easily shut the unit down and be able to return to the previous setting without having to completely rotate the turret. The complete package includes a battery and Vortex's killFLASH ARD (Anti-Reflection Device) unit, which screws in to replace the front lens cap.

Vortex Razor lenses are made from XD (which stands for extra low dispersion) optical glass, which improves clarity and resolution edge to edge, and are XR coated with Vortex's own anti-reflection coating, which provides for improved light transmission and brightness. Different colors focus at various distances though normal lenses in what is known as chromatic aberration. In order to help correct for this and provide maximum image quality at long range, the Vortex Razor features an apochromatic (APO) objective lens.

Mounting the Vortex Razor on a flattop AR requires high-quality 30mm rings with proper height and a cantilever mount to obtain proper (3.9-inch) eye relief. Vortex does offer a proper, American made mount with a quick-detach auto lock system.

HIGH MAGNIFICATION SCOPES

High-powered scopes offer longer range accuracy and extreme precision for closer range shots. My preference is for a 3-9x optic, which offers a wider range of versatility. My personal favorite is the Trijicon TR20-2 AccuPoint with 3-9x40 power and a Mil-Dot crosshair reticle with amber dot. The excellent fiber optics on the Trijicon scope gather ambient light to illuminate the center amber dot without batteries. This is a very welcome feature, especially for survival situations where a dead battery might otherwise render an optic ineffective.

If higher magnification is desired, I have had excellent results with the Nikon Monarch 3 with BDC (Bullet Drop Compensation). The Monarch is a variable power optic from 3-12x magnification with a 42mm objective lens. It has a first focal plane reticle, which again means that the reticle size changes with magnification to stay in proportion to the target. This allows you to use the reticle for accurate bullet drop compensation at varying distances and at any level of magnification. This tough optic is nitrogen purged and o-ring sealed, making it completely waterproof, fog proof, and shock proof. Nikon offers a free online or mobile app so you can identify your specific load and know how your bullet will drop at any distance.

A still high quality but lower cost option is the Konus 550 Ballistic Reticle 3-9x40 scope. Konus scopes feature fully coated optics, and they're built tough — fog proof, waterproof, and shock proof. The second focal plane ballistic reticle in the 550 features

The author's personal favorite is the Trijicon TR20-2 AccuPoint scope with 3-9x40 power and a Mil-Dot crosshair reticle with amber dot.

vertical aiming points to compensate for bullet drop out to 550 yards, as well as lateral hash marks for windage estimation.

There are many companies making very high-quality optics. However, there are many making low-quality optics that may not serve you well in a true survival situation. A good quality scope often will cost more than your rifle. One good way to test the quality of an optic is by "shooting the square." Once the scope is zeroed, you should be able to adjust the turrets up a couple of clicks, then right, then down, and then left the same number of clicks, and return to zero.

SCOUT RIFLE SCOPES

The scout rifle scope isn't really designed for the scout rifle. It simply means these types of scopes have an extended eye relief. On a standard scope, eye relief may be between 2.5 and 3.5 inches, meaning that your eye has to be within this range of the rear of the scope to make proper use of it. Red-dot scopes have no eye

Scout rifle scopes like this example from Bushnell are really just extended eye relief optics that have long been popular with handgun hunters.

relief requirement and can be mounted forward on a rifle or used on a pistol. Scout scopes are often called handgun scopes (mostly for use on hunting revolvers), or extended/long eye relief scopes. They tend to have less magnification than standard ones although some can go as high as 12x.

The use of extended eye relief scopes on rifles is rather uncommon. The main advocate of this was the late Jeff Cooper, founder of Gunsite Academy. He developed the scout rifle concept, one in which an optic is forward mounted. This allowed a rifle shooter to have some magnification for shots out to 500-600 yards, while allowing for both eyes open shooting, greater situational awareness and maintenance of peripheral vision.

The main optics companies that make these types of scopes include Leupold, Nikon, Bushnell, Weaver, Burris and Leatherwood. They range in power from 1.5x to 12x and in price from $200 to over $500.

RED-DOT/HOLOGRAPHIC SIGHTS

Red-dot or holographic sights have dramatically increased in popularity for the simple reason that they offer lightning fast target acquisition without the need to align front and rear sights. All you do is look through the scope with both eyes open and put the dot on the target. The colored dot does not actually appear on the target as with a laser; it is merely projected inside the objective lens of the optic.

These types of sights are 1x (meaning no magnification) and have extended eye relief, so they can be mounted farther away from the eye than a standard scope. In a survival situation, they allow you to engage targets in low light conditions much more easily, as well as quickly track multiple targets. A big advantage to being able to use a rifle effectively with both eyes open is that it preserves a wide field of view as well as peripheral vision to identify incoming threats.

Many manufacturers produce fixed-power 3x magnifiers that extend the range of the optic and can be easily deployed or removed as needed. The only downside is that these magnifiers increase the size of the dot. A large dot (which was designed for close quarters) gets even bigger at distance when magnified, limiting its precision use. Aimpoint, makers of the popular Micro T-1 and Micro H-1 red-dot sights, has responded to this issue by offering their sights with a 2 MOA dot instead of the standard 4 MOA. This means that at 100 yards with a 3x magnifier the 2 MOA dot will cover a 6-inch circle.

This is a welcome addition to those who have come to rely on Aimpoint sights, and they are pretty much a military and law enforcement standard for good reason. Both the Micro T-1 and Micro H-1 are made from high strength extruded aluminum and are waterproof to 25 meters. Both have batteries that will give you 5 years of constant "on" service and can be mounted on any Picatinny or Weaver rail with multiple risers to adapt to any weapon. They are very versatile with 12 brightness settings, including four night vision settings on the T-1.

Another option is the EOTech 512 Holographic Weapon Sight, which has a 1 MOA dot inside a 68 MOA circle, the larger circle

Aimpoint makes the Micro T-1 and Micro H-1 red-dot sights with either a 2 MOA or 4 MOA dot. *Photo: Aimpoint*

used for range estimation. For example, a 5-foot, 8-inch tall man would stand edge to edge inside the circle at 100 yards and only from the center dot to the circle edge at 200 yards. EOTech sights are built scary tough with aluminum construction and a thick hood that protects the optic. They have really easy to use on/ off and intensity adjustment buttons. The reticle will work even if broken or partially obscured, as long as any part of the glass is still visible. It comes standard with a Lithium battery that can last up to 600 hours and a built-in quick-detach lever for mounting on any Picatinny rail. For targeting at distance, add the G33.STS magnifier that easily pops out of the way when not needed and provides 3x magnification. It mounts right behind the sight for easy combined use.

The EOTech EXPS2 red-dot holographic sight features a 1 MOA dot inside a 68 MOA circle. The G33STS magnifier gives you 3x power.

All of EOTech's HWS products feature parallax-free optics with 1x magnification and unlimited eye relief. The internally sealed, fog proof, shatter resistant glass optics are coated in a non-reflective material and will operate in temperatures from minus 40 to plus 150 degrees Fahrenheit and withstand submersion in 10 feet of water. If you have to take advantage of all those features at once, you're surely having a very bad day. The standard sight includes 20 settings for brightness and an auto shutdown feature. EOTech sights with night vision capability have an additional 10 brightness settings.

The Vortex SPARC Red-Dot is another compact night vision-capable scope. Featuring an Aircraft-grade 6061-T6 aluminum nitrogen gas purged body, the SPARC is fog proof, waterproof, and shock proof. The rubberized, left-side mounted, rear facing, push-button controls provide a night vision option, which sets the dot brightness at a sufficiently low level for use with night vision equipment. The SPARC has 10 intensity settings and automatically returns to the previously set brightness level when switching between night vision and daytime modes.

The 5.3-ounce, 3-inch SPARC has a 22mm lens diameter and a 2 MOA dot size, and it comes packed with extra accessories. Obtaining proper optics mount height can often be an issue with AR rifles, so the SPARC includes a built-in modular base (no rings needed) with three risers that can be combined into four different heights. The lenses are sharp and crisp and have a slight blue tint in sunlight. The unit is parallax-free past 50 yards (eye placement is not important, and as long as you can see the dot, you will hit the target) and less than 1 inch under 50 yards. All mounting equipment and hardware is included, as is an extra CR2354 battery. Battery life is rated at 120 hours of continuous use at the highest brightness level and 3,400 hours at the lowest. The scope includes an auto shut-off after 6 hours to help preserve battery life.

The controls are well designed: one push turns the unit on, but to shut it off, you push and hold the power button for about 5 seconds (this helps prevent accidentally shutting the unit off). Another nice feature is that the battery, windage, and elevation caps are all tethered to prevent loss. Rubberized lens covers are standard. Probably the most significant extra accessory that comes included is a 2x magnifier that easily screws into the back of the unit and provides the slight magnification needed for more precision shooting. A 3x magnifier is available, as is an ARD (anti-reflection device) filter from Vortex.

The main drawback for many of these types of sights is the battery, which may be hard to find or recharge during a national crisis. For this reason, it is vitally important to have backup iron sights on your rifle and know how to use them. Some manufacturers like Aimpoint offer a five-year battery. Others, like Trijicon, combine fiber optics that are essentially powered by ambient light.

The Zeiss Z-Point Red-Dot sight actually combines its battery with a built-in solar cell to recharge. On this sight, the intensity of the illuminated reticle self-adjusts for brightness depending on the environmental conditions, although it can be manually adjusted. This feature is a great benefit that allows you to automatically maintain proper reticle intensity while entering or exiting buildings or from sunlight into shadows. The unit has an auto shutoff after four hours to help preserve battery life.

With 1x magnification and a 3.5 MOA dot, the Z-Point provides unlimited eye relief (so it can be mounted farther forward on a rifle) and an excellent field of view, especially with both eyes open operation. This makes it an optimal sight for use at combat ranges. The Zeiss Z-Point is a one-piece unit with an integral quick-detach clip for Weaver and Picatinny rails that does not stick out. It is waterproof, fog proof, and shock proof with an extremely compact aluminum housing measuring only 2.5 inches long by 1.75 inches tall and weighing just over 5 ounces.

NIGHT VISION SCOPES

Technology that allows you to see in the dark, even in a completely lightless environment, is not new, and night vision gear has been in standard military use for decades. But amplifying ambient light or using infrared illuminators is not the only way to see, and in recent years, thermal imaging technology has not only improved

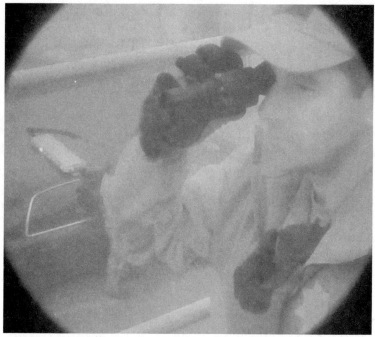

Traditional night vision devices are more properly referred to as image intensifier/near infrared systems. These gather ambient light within the visible light spectrum that can be seen by the human eye and focus that light into an intensifier, which then projects that image into a view finder. *Photo: Armasight*

in quality but become much smaller, more durable, and affordable.

Why would you want night vision in a survival situation? It can help you navigate completely dark environments, find lost objects or people, and it works in situations where a flashlight can spotlight your location to hostile parties. There are very cheap units to be had based on the oldest technology, which goes back to before the Vietnam War. These units have very low resolution. As you spend more money, you get better and better resolution.

You can purchase a dedicated night vision scope or a night vision optic that mounts in front of your standard daytime scope. The latter may be the better option, but it will add weight to your rifle.

IMAGE INTENSIFIERS

Traditional night vision devices are more properly referred to as image intensifier/near infrared systems. That means they gather ambient light within the visible light spectrum (which can be seen by the human eye) and focus that light into an intensifier which projects that image into a viewfinder.

The image, which can be viewed in any single color, is monochromatically green because that is the color which the human eye most easily processes. Just above and outside your area of vision lies the infrared spectrum. And these image intensifier devices can extend your vision into its lowest reaches, the near IR range. In total darkness, such as in a cave or closed room, there is no light to intensify, and such devices can be paired off with an IR light source that acts like a flashlight but is only visible to someone with an image intensifier/near infrared unit.

FLIR is the leading manufacturer of this technology in the U.S., and their products are not cheap, costing into the thousands of dollars and used by the military. The FLIR T90 Tactical Night Sight is a very advanced and compact unit with a high degree of resolution. It features a quick-attach/detach for any MIL-STD-1913 rail and is designed to be mounted ahead of any standard daytime optic. This includes scopes as well as red-dot or holographic sights. Again, the advantage here is that you can continue to use your day optics with their standard settings and which have been zeroed to your weapons. Plus, the T90 can be used as a standalone handheld device for nighttime observation and surveillance, unattached to a weapon.

Since image intensifiers work by gathering and focusing ambient light, the more light that is available, the better they perform, and the sharper and clearer the images become. In full daylight, however, the effect is muted, since what you see in natural light will look better. This unit can use either CR123 or AA batteries for power. The battery compartment is shaped to accept either type of battery, and the practical advantage of this can hardly be overstated. AA batteries are the most popular and common battery in the world and are easily available even in some of the most inhospitable places. Rechargeable ones can be recharged using a

Thermal devices open up a much larger section of the IR spectrum improving detection of heat radiation, but they are much more expensive. *Photo: FLIR*

solar panel. Fresh batteries will provide 20 to 30 hours of constant run time, certainly sufficient to get through several evenings of surveillance activities.

THERMAL/INFRARED

Thermal devices open up a much larger section of the IR spectrum and can detect heat radiation. However, they are much more expensive. The warmer the object, the more radiation is emitted, allowing imagers to measure the difference in radiation and present it in a visual spectrum. Any heat emitted by an object can be made visible in spite of smoke, fog, or vegetation that might otherwise block your view in daylight or even with standard night vision technology. If an enemy uses smoke to hide their movements at night, a traditional night vision device won't do you much good, but a thermal imager will let you see right through the smoke in daylight or night time conditions.

The drawback with thermal imagers is that they don't see in our visual light range. For example, they provide no image through a window, while traditional night vision will. As the technology for both types of devices has improved, they have become smaller, and they can both be used in daylight.

Soldiers are drilled on the differences between different types of cover, some of which offer physical protection from enemy fire and concealment, while others only hide the soldier but provide no actual protection. With thermal imagers, most concealment isn't even that anymore. The practical applications for engaging enemy targets has become immediately apparent, and thermal imagers are currently in use as weapon sights by U.S. Special Operations units.

These devices have tremendous tactical and lifesaving applications in domestic operations, as well as for both law enforcement and fire rescue personnel. A warm human body sticks out like a beacon against cold water, concrete, or even a wooded background, and thermal imagers can immensely help rescuers find lost and/or unconscious missing people. The ability to see through smoke aids fire and rescue personnel in locating trapped people.

Law enforcement officers use this technology to aid in fugitive and suspect searches, which can be notoriously dangerous for pursuing officers. Fleeing suspects have been known to set up ambushes for pursuing officers and hide in darkened alleys or behind cover, sometimes leaving an officer with the tough choice of either ceasing the pursuit or following blindly. A handheld thermal imaging sight can be easily carried and deployed, immediately alerting officers to hidden suspects.

WEAPON-MOUNTED LASERS AND LIGHTS

In a survival situation, lasers will have a limited but valuable use for self-defense, as they make placing accurate shots on target much easier. Tactical weapon-mounted lights make target identification possible in low light conditions. You can get dedicated lasers or lights as well as combination units.

Tactical weapon-mounted lights and lasers make target identification possible in low light conditions and show you where you will hit your target. *Photo: Crimson Trace*

With a weapon-mounted laser, you can engage a target from any position, and the shot will go where you see the dot, period. Low light and close range encounters are easiest to find that red-dot, but don't rely upon it or ignore your shooting fundamentals. Always train to focus on the fundamentals first; everything else is an aid, not a substitute.

I have been asked, "Doesn't a laser expose your position?" Yes it does, but are you using it to attack someone, or to defend yourself from an attack? If you are being attacked, then stealth is not a consideration, as your attacker clearly already knows where you are. Being able to accurately and quickly engage an attacker is the priority in this case.

RED AND GREEN LASERS

Lasers can technically be made in any color, but red has tradition-ally been the most common. This is because red is very visible, and is the easiest to produce and miniaturize. Civilian lasers have to stay below a certain power limit as mandated by federal law. In recent years, we have started to see a lot more green lasers as the technology has improved (these run hotter than red ones). Green is more visible to the human eye, and far more effective in day-light conditions. It is also more expensive.

Crimson Trace has become a leader in the area of gun-mounted and grip-activated laser sights. The main advantage is that all you have to do to activate the laser is grip your pistol — nothing else to think about. Crimson Trace makes two kinds of sights: the Lasergrip and the Laserguard. The Lasergrip, as the name implies, replaces the grips on your handgun and emits a super bright green laser from the top right side of the grip. The Laserguard series is designed to attach to the trigger guard, placing the laser directly under the barrel for most pistols. The advantage is that this adds no bulk to the grip area and does not change the overall dimen-sions of the pistol, although you will need a holster designed for the gun/laser combo.

In addition, Crimson Trace produces rail-mounted lasers such as the CMR-201 Rail Master Universal Laser Sight, which pro-vides a powerful 5mW red laser in an extremely compact pack-age. The unit features an ambidextrous rear-mounted activation switch that can be easily reached on a pistol with the trigger fin-ger. It will mount quickly on any standard Weaver and Picatinny rail for rifles and shotguns and includes four adapters for mount-ing on various handguns.

LaserMax specializes in very small, rugged laser sights and fea-tures several that take advantage of the growing number of hand-guns that have accessory rails. The new Spartan series is a com-pact and economical laser sight that fits neatly beneath almost any pistol accessory rail, from full-sized to compact. Available in red or green laser versions, the Spartan features super-fast and easy installation/removal while holding zero, ambidextrous push but-ton activation that can be easily reached with the trigger finger,

Green lasers are more visible to the human eye but tend to cost more.

and an auto-off system to preserve battery life. The bottom of the lightweight polymer unit has additional rail space so it can be combined with a tactical light if so desired, giving you the versatility of laser only or a light/laser combination.

Viridian virtually pioneered the use of green laser weapon sights and developed the first system that instantly activates the laser when you draw your pistol from its holster. It offers both an accessory rail type and a trigger guard unit. The Viridian Reactor R5 green laser is available with a red or green laser and also as a tactical light only unit that aids with target identification as well as aiming. It is built tough with a combination of 6061 aircraft grade aluminum and high-strength polymer.

LaserLyte manufactures great laser-based training aids as well as laser sights for a variety of rifles, pistols, and shotguns. In the compact handgun area, there are two standout products: the TGL (Trigger Guard Lasersight) and the Lyte Ryder compact rail-mounted laser. Both units are available as red lasers and offer durability in a very compact package. The TGL features a slick and seamless design that looks like part of the pistol and makes re-holstering easy. The Lyte Ryder is an impressively compact rail-mounted unit with a snag-free design and ambidextrous controls.

TACTICAL LIGHTS

Target identification is essential, but in low light conditions can be difficult. This is where having a hand-held flashlight or, even better, a weapon-mounted light can be extremely beneficial. Standard tactical high output flashlights project a narrow beam that is most often circular in shape. However, in real life, we don't see in circles; we scan side to side in a horizontal plane where we expect to locate objects or identify threats. Unless Spiderman is burglarizing your home, you don't need to illuminate the ceiling, and light that illuminates low threat areas is essentially wasted.

The Radiance tactical weapon light from Viridian Green Laser represents a radical breakthrough that dramatically increases the light's effectiveness in survival situations. It works by reshaping the light into a wide oval shape, narrowing the beam top to bottom

The Viridian reactor tactical pistol light is designed to cast a wide beam to aid in room searches and scanning. *Photo: Viridian*

The Viridian C5L light combines a tactical high-output flashlight and a green laser in a compact unit that can be installed on pistols or rifles with a Picatinny rail. *Photo: Viridian*

and allowing a much wider field of view — over twice the width of a normal tactical light. The game changing advantages should be immediately apparent, as the amount of time it takes to scan and clear an area is cut in half.

With a light, conducting any kind of search (from lost people to finding a blood-trail in the woods) becomes more efficient. Using the wide beam to track from side to side is more instinctive and less disorienting for the user. With a wide horizontal beam, you can avoid developing tunnel vision or having to make fast scanning movements. Even if you do, the speed of moving the light will seem muted because of the wide beam.

LASER-LIGHT COMBOS

Laser-light combination units may be the best option for long guns and large pistols. Almost all of these types of units are rail-based and can be installed on anything that has a standard rail. Many of them offer distinct versatility and an array of options, such as light only, laser only, light and laser, and strobe.

Crimson Trace has the CMR-204 Rail Master Universal Laser Sight & Tactical Light Unit. This thing combines a green laser with a compact 100 lumen tactical light. It is very small, built tough, and is waterproof with polymer construction and aluminum body. Included adapters allow it to fit most any rail-equipped handgun or Picatinny rail. The ambidextrous activation switches are easy to use but are still stiff enough to prevent unintended activation. The included CR2 Lithium battery provides one hour of continuous use, and there is a five minute auto shutoff to preserve battery life.

Crimson Trace has another unique product in their LiNQ Wireless Laser System, the first wireless grip-activated laser/light system for AR and AK rifles. The LiNQ system is revolutionary in that you get a small, forward-mounted green laser/tactical light unit that is controlled wirelessly through a custom grip that contains the controls. The unit uses a unique 256-bit encryption system to ensure near 100 percent reliability and security. The LiNQ comes already synced from the factory, so there is no need for you to manually link the laser and the grip. The grip will activate the unit up to 15-20 feet away even through barriers, and as each unit has a unique RF frequency, there is no possibility of crossover from using multiple units.

The laser unit itself combines a green laser and a 300 lumen LED white light. It has four separate settings, including laser/light, laser only, light only, and laser/light strobe with a two-hour constant use run time. These can be activated remotely using the waterproof polymer pistol grip or directly via a button at the back of the aluminum unit. Once a setting is selected, there is instant activation with a button at the front of the grip.

Another combination unit is the C5L from Viridian Green Laser Sights, which provides both a high-intensity tactical light with the green laser all in one unit. The tactical light provides 100 lumen constant on and a 140 lumen strobe that can be used independently or in combination with the green laser (which can also be set to constant on or strobe). These units are fully ambidextrous, and the controls are easy to master for on-the-fly adjustments.

During my testing, sighting the unit in for elevation and windage was easy with the included Allen wrenches, and using the pistol's sights as a guide, I was able to quickly get shots on paper. The included CR2 3V Lithium battery provides four hours of constant "on" for the light or the laser, seven hours on the strobe setting for either, and if you insist on using both simultaneously, you will get an hour of use. The unit is very compact and includes several adaptors to fit it on different pistols as well as any Picatinny rail. The whole thing weighs less than 2.5 ounces and is under 2 inches in total length. It's built tough with a combination of 6061 aircraft grade aluminum and high-strength polymer.

SURVEILLANCE

Obviously, having a scope on a rifle helps you see objects or possible game or threats from a greater distance and with more precision. However, a scoped rifle should not be used for routine surveillance except in very narrow circumstances (war for example). Instead,

The Steiner MM1050 Military-Marine 10x50 binocular is a large, military proven optic with exceptional clarity and power.
Photo: Steiner

use binoculars. Binoculars are typically found with a fixed magnification although variable power optics are available. My preference is for variable power as these can provide a much wider field of view at the lower settings for scanning and then you can zoom in for more detail, although they tend to cost more. The higher the magnification, the smaller the field of view. The larger the objective lens, the larger the field of view.

Tactical binoculars tend to be the fixed magnification variety. For fixed magnification binoculars, I would recommend no smaller than 8x with a 42mm objective lens. The Bushnell Engage 8x42mm offers a field of view of 426 feet at 1,000 yards and has fully coated lenses and is both waterproof and fog proof. The higher quality the lens the more light transmission and clarity. For a true military binocular you can't go wrong with the Steiner MM1050 Military-Marine 10x50. This is a large optic built tough (weighs over 2 pounds) and the larger objective lens lets in gobs of light so it works better in low light conditions.

In the same price range is the Leupold BX-T Tactical 10x42mm binocular, which is smaller and weighs less than the Steiner. The Leupold BX-T features a Mil-L reticle which has Mil-Dot hash marks in an upside down L shape for range estimation. Range finding reticles can be found on tactical and military binoculars but they are not the only method of range estimation.

The Bushnell Engage 8x42mm binocular gives you a field of view of 426 feet at 1,000 yards. *Photo: Bushnell*

Leupold's BX-T Tactical 10x42mm binocular has a built-in Mil-L reticle to safely range targets, without having to point your rifle at them. *Photo: Leupold*

RANGEFINDERS

There are binoculars that combine the magnification and surveillance function with a built-in laser range finder. These are extremely precise and feature a digital readout inside the reticle that provides exact distance in meters or yards. The Vortex Fury 10x42 Laser Rangefinder Binocular is one option with simple to use one-handed controls that can measure distances out to 1,600 yards. Another option is the Bushnell Fusion 1 Mile ARC 10x42mm. In addition to having coated lenses for superior clarity and light transmission, it is completely waterproof and can estimate ranges out to 1,760 yards with standard angle compensation to 90 degrees.

A less expensive option is a dedicated laser rangefinder like the Nikon ARROW ID 7000 VR. Rangefinders are an important piece of gear for many hunters who need to estimate precisely their bullet or arrow drop at distance. A missed shot is a wasted shot and a wasted opportunity. The Nikon rangefinder features an optical vibration reduction system that compensates for hand movement to provide a more accurate and precise reading. This provides a faster reading, thus less time for game to get away. It acts as a 6x magnification monocular so it can be used for surveillance and presents a lower cost and much more compact option. It can measure distances out to 1,000 yards accurately and includes angle compensation.

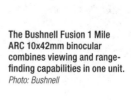

The Bushnell Fusion 1 Mile ARC 10x42mm binocular combines viewing and range-finding capabilities in one unit.
Photo: Bushnell

SURVIVAL FLASHLIGHTS

A high-quality and powerful flashlight can be a lifesaver and should be considered an essential item to have at home, in your car, and on your person for everyday carry, or EDC whenever possible. There are countless scenarios where it will come in handy. If you are walking to your car in a dark parking lot or garage, you can use the light to scan the area for anyone who might be hiding in wait. If you are in a building during a power outage or, God forbid a fire, the light will help you find your way out. If you go for a walk at night, you will be able to identify any noises. If you are assaulted, the light can be used to temporarily blind the bad guy while you run for cover or draw. I consider the tactical light among my most important and valuable pieces of everyday carry gear.

A pocket-sized flashlight like the G2X Pro from SureFire is incredibly handy and convenient. It can easily fit in your car's glove box or center console, or in a purse. This light offers a high output mode with a blinding 320 lumens, good for searching and emergency signaling, and a low output mode of 15 lumens, which is plenty to light up a room or small area as well as for basic map reading and navigation. The nice part is that at the low setting, the battery will last for 45 hours of continuous use and even in the high setting, you get over 2 hours of light.

The SureFire Y300 Ultra is a palm-sized but powerful flashlight that includes a very convenient belt clip and magnetic base. This allows the light to be attached to any metal magnetic surface for hands free operation, which can come in very handy during emergency repair work or any medical emergency that requires the use of both hands. The belt clip rotates to provide hands-free directional lighting even when metal surfaces may not be available, and it will just

The Wrist Beam flashlight from SureFire offers hands free operation and can be used in conjunction with a handgun. *Photo: SureFire*

as easily clip to clothing or a ball cap brim. The operation switch has constant on and momentary settings and two light outputs: a high of 500 lumens that is good for 2.5 hours and a low of 15 lumens that will run for 15 hours.

Another great light is the SureFire E2L AA Outdoorsman, a very powerful penlight that can be easily carried in a pants or shirt pocket. I never leave home without one. It has the added convenience of using AA batteries, which again can be found nearly everywhere. If you are ever stuck someplace overseas or in an emergency situation at home, it is a great comfort knowing that replacement batteries will be easier to find. The maximum power setting of 115 lumens lets you see objects a very good distance away, and the battery will last for 8.5 hours constant on. At the low setting of 5 lumens (which is plenty bright for the vast majority of uses), you get an amazing 100 hours of continuous use.

Another company that makes high-quality lights is StreamLight, and their ProTac 2AA is a very powerful flashlight with AA battery convenience and an unbreakable steel pocket clip. The light is quite economical to buy, so get several to keep around the house, in vehicles and bug-out bags. The aluminum construction is corrosion resistant, built tough to last, and can be submersed in water without failing. An added feature with the StreamLight ProTac AA is that it has three settings: high output with 155 lumens, low output with 11 lumens, and a high output strobe that can be used as a disorienting self-defense tool or for signaling. At the low setting, you get 36 hours of continuous use for emergencies.

The Barska 140 Lumen Zoom is a compact light that can be weapon mounted with an included Picatinny mount and offers 140 lumens with a three LED bulb. One attractive feature of the Barska light is a zoom function that allows the beam to be tightened for longer distance spotlighting or widened for a large field of view suitable for searches. The light runs on three easy to find AA batteries for convenience. There is a strobe feature, making it effective for signaling while extending the battery life, and the beveled edge at the front adds a defensive element as an impact device.

The NiteCore SRT7 may well be the Swiss Army knife of flashlights. The key feature is the SSR (Smart Selector Ring) that

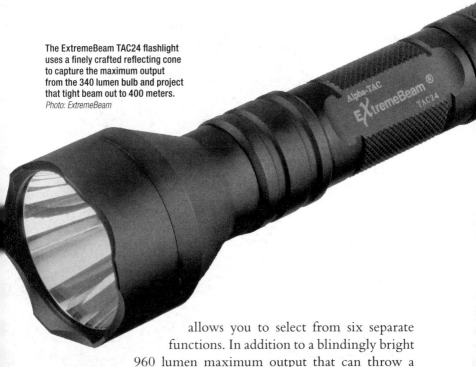

The ExtremeBeam TAC24 flashlight uses a finely crafted reflecting cone to capture the maximum output from the 340 lumen bulb and project that tight beam out to 400 meters.
Photo: ExtremeBeam

allows you to select from six separate functions. In addition to a blindingly bright 960 lumen maximum output that can throw a beam over 300 meters away, you can adjust the brightness to any point you want between 0 and the maximum output. There are integrated colored LED lights: red for tactical applications, blue for blood-trailing, and green for document or map reading. There is a low power location beacon mode (so you never have to worry about losing it in the dark) and a low battery warning signal. On the low setting, you get up to 200 hours of run time.

The ZeroHour XD flashlight is multiple emergency devices in one and perhaps most notably it can recharge your other electronic devices. In an emergency, communication is key to survival, and if your cell phone goes dead, there is little you can do — until now. This flashlight would have been considered small in the past, but by modern standards, it is large. Still, you get 1,000 lumens of light, a USB port for recharging the light as well as portable electronics, and the modular design even lets you turn part of the light into a waterproof container for emergency supplies. On the low setting, you get up to 24 hours of continuous illumination, and there is even an SOS mode that flashes a distress signal.

The ZeroHour XD flashlight is a multiple emergency device that can recharge your electronic devices.
Photo: ZeroHour

The GoalZero Torch 250 may be the most versatile survival flashlight you can get. It is even solar powered. The internal rechargeable battery can be charged with a traditional wall outlet, through the internal solar panel or via the included hand crank. Once charged, there is a USB port that can charge up your mobile devices. A front-facing spotlight produces 180 lumens, and the side floodlight has 70 lumens. Plus, there is a red emergency light. Depending on usage, it will run non-stop for 7 to 48 hours. You will never be out of power again with this light.

NIGHT VISION

Handheld night vision devices can be had inexpensively, allowing you to see much better in the dark without being seen yourself. The best systems, however, are thermal, and while costlier, they have declined in price significantly. American Technologies Network, or ATN, which specializes in high-quality optics including weapon sights, tactical flashlights, night vision, and thermal imagers, has an entry-level thermal sight that can be used as a standalone handheld device or as a weapon sight. It is even helmet mountable.

The ATN OTS-32 and OTS-64 Thermal Multi-Purpose Systems are monocular devices that can cover a wide array of survival situations. Improvements in this technology provide much better visual clarity, enabling you to more easily distinguish and identify objects (people versus animals, for example). Given that these devices operate by detecting infrared radiation, they work equally well in bright light conditions, unlike traditional night vision units.

The ATN units feature four different color reticles: red, green, black, and white, and come standard with a Picatinny rail and quick-release mounts. The screen resolution and clarity do vary slightly, with the OTS-32 resolution at 320x240 and the OTS-64 at 640x480. Both units include brightness and 2x and 4x zoom controls, as well as windage and elevation adjustments and a video output for recording and surveillance purposes.

The unit is very compact, measuring less than 8 inches and weighing little more than 1.5 pounds. The included CR123 batteries provide four hours on continuous use, and ATN provides a one year warranty.

Another company leading the way in high-tech thermal imaging devices is FLIR. Their handheld FLIR LS-Series compact thermal imager is available in two different models: standard and Scout. The FLIR-LS features compact portability, weighing only 12 ounces, and is easily belt mounted for immediate deployment. The design is very rugged and can withstand severe weather with its waterproof construction. The resolution is adjustable for various field conditions, and has up to a 4x digital zoom feature for surveillance operations from a distance. The Li-Ion battery is rechargeable, which can be done from a vehicle and eliminates the need to supply extra batteries. Simple four-button operation makes it easy to use.

Handheld night vision devices include the FLIR LS-Series, a compact thermal imager available in Standard and Scout models. *Photo: FLIR*

MOTION DETECTORS

For home protection, motion detectors can be extremely beneficial. These can be as simple as a wireless chime that sounds whenever something approaches the motion sensor or as bold as motion-activated floodlights. The benefit here is that you are immediately alerted when a vehicle or person is approaching your home or driveway. The small battery operated units last for months before requiring change and can be installed anywhere. Motion-activated floodlights are extremely effective at dissuading would-be intruders and trespassers.

SURVEILLANCE CAMERAS

There are many options when it comes to video surveillance. Closed systems provide visual notice of anyone entering your property and can be set up for recording. I prefer an online system like the one offered by Nest Camera. You can purchase as many indoor or outdoor cameras as you want, and you will need to have a Wi-Fi system to connect to the internet.

The Nest Security Camera can record continuously for seven to 30 days and includes night vision and audio that link to your cell phone. It notifies you if the camera has spotted movement. *Photo: Nest Security*

These cameras have night vision capabilities and can be set up for weekly or monthly recording, meaning they will continuously record everything for that period of time. They also have motion sensors, so you receive an alert on your smartphone when they detect activity and you can immediately see or review the source of that motion. These cameras have speakers and microphones, so you can hear what is going on and even speak to or yell at any intruders.

Even if intruders damage or steal the camera, the recording is online and can be saved and turned over to the authorities. I find this system extremely helpful when I am away from home. It alerts me to any deliveries, arrivals, or trouble.

SURVIVAL KNIVES & MULTI-TOOLS

The one tool I use more than any other and the single most important survival implement you can own is a good knife. I never go anywhere without at least a small Swiss Army knife. Fixed-blade knives are larger but also stronger, and can be used for many more tasks than can folders. However, folders are smaller and easier to carry on your person, so they tend to be what you have on you when you need a knife. Multi-tools are also extremely handy, as they have a variety of knives, saws, pliers, wire cutters, screwdrivers, can and bottle openers, and more.

A pocketknife is another distinct category and very important piece of gear. Not necessarily for self-defense, the pocketknife is ideal for everyday use. I use mine more than I use my keys or wallet.

Ideally, a self-defense knife has a quick opening feature that allows you to open it one handed. It should have a belt clip so that you can keep it easily accessible in a pants or jacket pocket. And finally, it is best to carry your knife so that you can access it with either hand; barring that, place the knife so you can grab it with your support hand. The reason you want to be able to access and deploy your knife with your support hand is in case you should ever get into a situation where your gun hand is compromised (say in a struggle over your gun). You can then access your knife with your support hand and use the blade to cut the arm or hand of your assailant to regain control of your sidearm. This involves a high level of skill and training, so you should seek out an expert in gun retention and knife combat to help you train.

If you are in an area where you cannot carry a gun, then your knife may be your primary defensive tool. Be aware that the laws on knife carry are usually very dated and have not kept pace with concealed carry laws for handguns. In many areas, knife carry is restricted even if you have a concealed carry permit for your handgun. Like the general rule for handguns, it is best to keep your carry knife concealed as much as possible and always follow the local laws.

FIXED-BLADE KNIVES

Fixed blades come in many styles and sizes and are designed for a wide variety of purposes, from kitchen knives (slicers, cleavers, and choppers) to outdoor knives with specialty uses for gutting, skinning, and deboning game. Outdoor knives can serve a variety of purposes and fulfill necessary survival tasks. A heavy blade can be used for chopping down small trees to build a shelter or for hammering stakes. It can be used for prying things open (take care not to damage the tip) and can be attached to a sturdy branch to form an impromptu spear for hunting or self-defense. Smaller fixed-blade knives can be used for more detailed work like filleting fish, sharpening smaller sticks to build a trap, cutting rope, or making a firestarter fuzz stick. A fixed blade is best kept in a vehicle or backpack, as well as in the home for use when needed.

Some fixed-blade knives are designed more for combat than for wilderness survival, but that doesn't mean they can't fit both roles. DPx Gear and Blackwater USA have teamed up to produce a pair of serious fighting blades: the Ursa and the Grizzly. DPx is the brainchild of Robert Young Pelton, a 30-year veteran of various conflict zones and wilderness environments. Pelton is the author of The World's Most Dangerous Places (Harper Collins) and has accompanied rebel forces and special operations troops from Afghanistan to Chechnya, including a four week stint with Blackwater in Iraq. The blades Pelton and DPx designed are meant for serious business.

Blackwater of course is a familiar name and is world renowned for their specialized training and security work overseas. The original Blackwater has changed its name, but the new Blackwater USA serves as an outlet for high-quality gear in the tradition of its progenitor.

Each of these two knives has its own set of distinct features that make it ideally suited for a variety of scenarios and conditions. The Blackwater Grizzly 6 has a 1.5-inch wide, 6-inch long drop point blade and is specifically designed for SERE (Survival, Evasion, Resistance and Escape) duty. The knife has in fact been selected for use by the U.S. Naval Special Warfare cadre. It is manufactured by Lionsteel in Maniago, Italy, using Niolox tool steel from Witten, Germany. This steel contains Niobium, which improves its strength and gives it the properties and edge retention of high-carbon steel but with improved corrosion resistance. The steel is tempered to 59 HRC, providing a hard and tough blade that will hold its edge despite rough use.

The steel blade is then coated with Titanium CarboNitride (TiCN) in a matte black finish using Particle Vapor Deposition (PVD). The PVD process consists of applying a thin film of a vaporized material via vacuum evaporation and condensation. TiCN adds an extremely tough layer of hardness to the metal with increased lubricity and low friction for improved corrosion resistance.

The Ursa and Grizzly, from DPx Gear and Blackwater USA, are fixed-blade knives that can pull double-duty for combat and wilderness survival. *Photo: DPx Gear*

The Ursa and Grizzly are serious fixed-blade knives for survival and useful as choppers or for tasks like making a fuzz stick.

The full tang blade is 0.2-inch thick, and the entire knife from tip to pommel measures 11.18 inches with a false edge along the spine. At 10.23 ounces and with its wide blade, the Grizzly makes for a handy chopper, and it easily downs small branches with a single swing. At the heel of the blade, there is over 1.5 inches of serration — very effective at cutting through thicker branches.

The built-in guard extends slightly below the width of the blade, but thanks to the deep-cut finger grooves in the handle, it's more than enough. The top guard has an aggressive thumb rest for precision work. Jimping grooves cut into the thumb rest are designed to be used as wire strippers for the three most common gauges. The pommel sports another welcome addition in the form of a very usable pry bar that doubles as a striker point/bone breaker and includes a lanyard hole as well.

As stated, the deep-cut finger grooves in the handle aid greatly with weapon retention in harsh conditions, and the grip is made more secure with the addition of rough checkered black G10 glass epoxy laminate scales. Despite the checkering, the handle does not bite into the hand and remains comfortable.

In another nod to the knife's intended purpose as a survival tool, the handles can be removed to reveal a sizable space measuring 2.5-inches long and almost ½-inch deep for storing emergency supplies (such as fish hooks and line, a small compass, or a fire starter). Of course, you will need a screwdriver of some sort to remove the scales, so you'll have to either bring one or use some field expedient alternative.

The Blackwater Ursa 6 carries much more of the combat/fighting knife design with a narrower, 1-inch wide dagger-type contour and a full-length (nearly 6-inch long) razor sharp uninterrupted cutting surface. In its overall length, it is both slightly larger and thicker than the Grizzly, measuring 11.38 inches total length and 0.24 inch thick.

The much more pronounced false edge of the Ursa contributes to its dagger-like appearance, as does the nearly 2 inches of Blackwater-designed serrations halfway from the tip along the spine of the blade. This knife is slightly heavier than the Grizzly at 11.1 ounces, providing for faster and stronger downward strikes with both the tip and edge of the spear point.

At the top and bottom of the integral guard lashing points are features that can be used to make a field expedient spear by affixing the blade to a branch. Like the Grizzly, the Ursa is made from identical steel and coating/finish with the same G10 grip panels and hollow space underneath for emergency supplies. The Ursa has the same wire stripper jimping on the thumb rest at the top of the guard, and the pommel has a matching pry bar and striker tip.

Both knives come standard with a tough Cordura nylon sheath with storage pocket that can easily accommodate survival supplies, a sharpening stone, or (my preference) a small multi-tool. The Kydex-lined black sheath protects the blade and has a snap closure to secure the blade in place but provide easy access when needed. There are two lanyard holes at the top and bottom of the sheath as well as polymer strap attachment points at either end. The accessory pocket features Velcro closure, and the rear of the sheath has an adjustable belt loop with a snap at the bottom. The long strap and included loops make the sheath Molle capable for added versatility.

FOLDING KNIVES

While folding knives will never be able to replicate some of the benefits of a large fixed blade (especially for chopping tasks), they are extremely handy and are the knives most likely to be at hand when you need one. Folders, by their very construction, lack the durability and strength of a fixed-blade knife. For survival, I recommend spending the extra money and getting a high-quality folder. Some can cost into the hundreds, but that is not necessary, and a good quality one that will last and serve you well can be had for as little as $50.

Being smaller, folders excel at detailed tasks like gutting and skinning game and fish, making fire-starting fuzz sticks, whittling, trap building, and general cutting chores. You will want to look for a knife with a strong lock. Many folding knives are designed for specific uses, while others have additional survival features. For in-vehicle use or in a bug-out bag, one of these multiple use larger blades is preferred. For everyday carry (EDC), I prefer more of a simple tactical knife with a plain edge, medium-sized blade, and pocket clip.

One excellent survival folder that I keep within reach inside my car is the M16-14ZER Emergency Rescue Tanto from Columbia River Knife and Tool (CRKT). This knife was designed with emergencies in mind. It has an integral seatbelt cutter that can be safely used without opening the blade. At the other end of the knife is a tungsten carbide window breaker. These two tools can be indispensable in quickly rescuing yourself or others who may be trapped in a vehicle.

The scales (sides) of the knife are bright "rescue orange" glass-filled nylon, which is highly visible in the almost certain case that you drop it at night or into water or some other hard to see spot. To add safety and strength to the liner lock design, CRKT added an additional automatic lock that keeps the blade in the open position, adding an extra pin that must be disengaged before the liner lock can be pushed out of the way to close the knife. The 3.75-inch Tanto-tipped blade design is super strong and could be used for light prying. The blade sports triple-point serrations at the rear for extra tough cutting jobs.

Another company making a full line of excellent fixed and folding blades is Kershaw, the developers of the first assisted opening folding knives. While Kershaw manufactures many of their products out of their factory in Tualatin, Oregon, their partnership with Kai Group provides them with state of the art production facilities in Japan and China. Two folders from their overseas facilities include the full-sized Scrambler and the smaller Zing SS. The Scrambler is a rock-solid folder with a 3.5-inch steel 8Cr13MoV drop-point hollow-ground blade. All the metal parts are titanium carbo-nitride coated, giving it a distinct matte gun metal grey subdued look. The finish protects the blade against corrosion. The handle is stainless steel with the front featuring a black G-10 scale with a good bit of grip.

At 5.3 ounces, this is a substantial frame lock folder. The knife is SpeedSafe-equipped with an assisted opening flipper. This protrusion on the back of the blade is smaller than most. For a

The author relies daily upon the M16-14ZER Emergency Rescue Tanto from Columbia River Knife and Tool (CRKT) as a vehicle knife.

A collection of Kershaw folders the author tested cutting everything from plastic, to nylon rope, to cardboard and wood.

pocketknife, the advantage in such a clean design is that there is nothing to get caught up in a smooth draw, and the assisted opening works well and reliably. The pocket clip is easily reversible for right- or left-handed point-up carry.

On the opposite end of the weight scale is the Zing SS at only 3.3 ounces and the thinnest overall width for very comfortable pocket carry. This matte, bead-blasted, all stainless steel knife uses the same high-quality blade steel as its larger cousin but comes across as a true gentleman's folder. Still, it carries a 3-inch blade that features small ambidextrous thumb studs for a very aggressive assisted opening. You can use the flipper protrusion to open the blade. The pocket clip has three options for carry: right-side tip-up or down, or left-side tip-up.

Two other designs come from an EMT/firefighter/rescue diver perspective and feature the Lock Bar Stabilizer, which is included on both the Thermite and Cryo II from Kershaw. This over-travel stop appears as a circular metal disk secured with a screw in the middle of the lock bar. When you are closing the blade on a frame lock knife, it's possible to force the lock bar too far out causing it to bend. If this happens, the blade will no longer lock open. The other advantage is that the stabilizer reinforces and strengthens the lock bar and prevents any unnecessary movement or wear when gripping the handle under heavy use.

The Thermite folder is a true working man's knife and has a matte finished stone-washed 3.5-inch blade with a Spanto profile, which maintains blade width and thickness toward the tip for better piercing and prying ability. All of the extra length comes from the knife's oversized handle, making it easier to get a good grip for tough jobs and is aided in turn by the textured G10 grip scale on the front. For fast opening, this blade is of stainless steel construction and has sizable ambidextrous thumb studs and an assisted opening flipper. The Thermite has a very deep pocket clip that almost completely submerges the knife in your pocket and is fully reversible for right- or left-hand carry and tip-up or tip-down, based on user preference.

SURVIVAL MULTI-TOOLS

There are a ton of different multi-tool manufacturers and styles out there, depending on your needs and intended use. These come in a variety of sizes. Leatherman is an innovator in this field and still makes among the best folding multi-tools with the largest selection.

A survival multi-tool specifically designed for the gun owner and shooter had been missing, until Crimson Trace (CTC) teamed up with Columbia River Knife & Tool (CRKT) to produce two convenient pocketknives that integrate the most commonly needed small sight tools.

Crimson Trace and CRKT teamed up to produce special knife/gun multi-tools to address many of the most common issues with guns and lasers. *Photo: CRKT*

CTC and CRKT came up with two distinct models, both of which feature CTC's rugged, grooved, non-reflective black Zytel scales and a skeletonized design. They both include lanyard holes and two CTC laser Allen wrenches (.028 and .050) firmly fitted into the scales to prevent loss.

The first and larger of the two models is the CTC Picatinny Tool, a full-sized pocketknife with belt clip designed for AR rifles. The knife has a locking 2.8-inch, 2.9mm thick blackened and partially serrated stainless steel blade, what CRKT bills as a "Plan B" weapon (although at that point, running might be a better option). Other tools include a rounded takedown pin punch that can be employed to remove cartridges stuck in the chamber, a carbon scraper for the bolt to double as a large, flat screwdriver (includes an 8mm wrench), and a small hex wrench driver with four attachment bits (flat, Phillips, Torx 20, and hex 3/32-inch) fitted into the handle.

The smaller of the two offerings is the R.B.T.-CTC Range Bag Tool. With a short, fat, rounded profile and wide pocket clip, the R.B.T. is not a handier copy of the Picatinny Tool but rather a separate knife that foresees many different uses than its larger cousin. The 1.8-inch long, 1.8mm thick, non-locking and partially serrated stainless steel blade comes razor sharp and is ground to an 8mm wide flat cut that could be used as a field expedient wrench. Two fold-out blades serve as small flat and Phillips screwdrivers, and one includes a file on one side. A handy bottle opener is included, too.

KNIFE SHARPENERS

There is hardly any feeling better than a razor sharp knife that makes quick work of boxes, packaging, leather, or game. On the other hand, there is hardly anything more frustrating than a dulled edge on your everyday carry knife that forces you to hack and saw your way through your normal cutting chores. What matters most to me is edge retention. I test knives by first using each blade to cut through a sheet of paper. A properly sharpened knife should easily slice through a sheet of office paper in one stroke with no sawing. Then the real testing begins.

I cut through stacks of cardboard and a thick leather belt, as well as length after length of heavy-duty nylon rope. I then slash thick plastic bottles to make drinking cups and funnels. Next, I use the blades on dry hardwood branches to make kindling and wood chips for fire starting material. And stab the blades repeatedly and forcefully into dried logs while twisting them to test tip and over-all durability and to gauge any play in the liner locks. Finally, I sharpen a heavy branch into a spear point for emergency hunting or self-defense. When it is all done, I go back to my office paper. A quality knife should still be able to cut through that paper just as easily as when the testing started.

The DMT Magna-Guide Kit is compact and the sharpeners can be used individually for compact travel. The Aligner Blade Guide helps you get the best angle when sharpening your blade. *Photo: DMT*

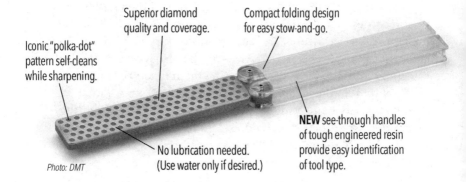

Iconic "polka-dot" pattern self-cleans while sharpening.

Superior diamond quality and coverage.

Compact folding design for easy stow-and-go.

No lubrication needed. (Use water only if desired.)

NEW see-through handles of tough engineered resin provide easy identification of tool type.

Photo: DMT

But no matter how high quality a knife may be, you will still need to sharpen it on occasion, or it will become mostly useless. There are lots of different small portable sharpeners you can use. One of these is the DMT Magna-Guide Kit. The trick to quality sharpening has always been figuring out the right angle for the blade and keeping it at that angle consistently. Sharpening a knife or other edge offhand and maintaining that consistent angle is nearly impossible. This is why the DMT kit includes a very easy to use aligner clamp, called the Aligner Blade Guide, and a magnetic angle guide.

The clamp locks onto the knife blade from the back and holds it firmly in place using an adjustable center hinge and screw tensioning knob. This will accommodate anything from a razor blade up to 3/8-inch thick tactical fixed blade. The polymer will not cause any damage to the blade itself (as can occur from metal clamps) while maintaining a solid hold for safety and consistency.

At the opposite end of the blade clamp are the adjustable guide rods. These simple but effective polymer rods have seven elevation/angle settings each. With a quarter turn, the rod can be moved up or down to the desired angle and locked into place, extending out equally on either side of the blade.

The instructions include an easy to follow guide for selecting the right angle, which number from one to seven. The highest angle, number one, produces almost a wedge-shaped edge suitable for heavy cutting tools like meat cleavers or machetes. The lowest angle, number seven, produces a very thin edge suitable for razors or craft knives. The key in selecting the best angle is based on the use of the blade. A lower angle produces a thinner and sharper edge but also one that will dull faster. A higher angle keeps the blade thicker with a less sharp edge but one that can take more of a beating. The instructions conveniently list different types of blades and the recommended angles. Not surprisingly, medium- and large-size folders (the type most often used for every day carry) fall right in the middle, providing a good strong edge with a combination of durability and sharpness.

The magnetic angle guide is a steel rod with a powerful magnet at one end that attaches to the desired Diafold sharpener; it maintains the right angle throughout the sharpening process. The steel rod goes through an opening in the polymer guide rods on the aligner clamp. This ensures that you consistently use the same angle for every pass along the blade. To sharpen the other side, reverse the process with the magnetic angle guide.

The instructions are very clear and indicate that you hold onto the blade handle and the sharpener handles, sharpening from the front of the blade to the back in one motion, then move the sharpener to the next spot along the blade and repeat until the entire blade has been covered. The final stroke simply glides the sharpener along the blade edge to smooth it out. There is an online video that spells out the process nicely.

Of course, getting the angle right is only part of the equation and having a proper sharpener to hone your blade edge is, if anything, more important. Here, DMT includes four different levels of grit with their double-sided Diafold sharpeners. These are among the most well-made and easiest to use sharpeners you can find. As the name implies, you get two sides with different grit in each sharpener, with clear plastic handles that fold out of the way butterfly-style and lock into place in the open or closed position.

The Magna Guide Kit includes two double-sided Diafold sharpeners, which range from Extra-Extra Fine (3 micron)/Extra-Fine (9 micron) to Fine (25 micron)/Coarse (45 micron) grit combination.

These are color coded, and the clear handles allow you to instantly see which grit you're selecting. The instructions include a guide that indicates which sharpener is best for the condition of the blade. The coarse grit is best for repairing damaged edges, while the finest grit will simply polish and refine an already sharp blade to a razor's edge. I find that giving my carry knife a quick touch up once a week with the Extra-Extra Fine sharpener helps maintain an ideal edge.

The sharpeners are very thin and lightweight and can be used independently of the angle guide system. They fit neatly and conveniently into a backpack or pocket for field use when needed and provide two levels of sharpening each.

The Diafold sharpeners are carefully and extensively covered with a very thin layer of diamond grit — the most diamonds per square inch in the industry, in fact. The diamond layer is extremely uniform and flat, and features extreme consistency in terms of the grit size. A steel plate with evenly spaced holes covers the diamond layer, creating a self-cleaning surface, obviating the need for any lubricants. Indeed, the instructions specifically say to use nothing more than water if necessary.

For travel or more of an outdoor field survival situation, you will want to pack light; thus, a smaller, more compact sharpener may be in order. The Smith's Consumer Products Pocket Pal X2 Sharpener and Survival Tool has a small sharpener that includes an entire off grid survival kit. This sharpener comes with three levels of sharpening for versatility, including coarse and fine pull-through slots and a tapered diamond rod. The pull-through slots are fixed angle, so there is no guesswork involved in getting a sharp edge. They easily sharpen both sides of your blade simultaneously with just a few pulls.

The coarse slot has premium carbide blades and quickly removes metal for a quick edge on very dull or damaged knives. The fine slot has ceramic stones that hone the blade to razor sharpness and are ideal for touching up a blade that just needs a bit of extra bite. Moreover, the ceramic stones work well for serrated-edge blades. Plus, Smith extended the life of this tool by making the sharpening blades replaceable.

The tapered diamond sharpening rod stores in and folds out of

The Smith's Pocket Pal X2 is a complete survival tool and knife sharpener that includes lanyard, compass, firestarter, flashlight and whistle. *Photo: Smith's*

the Pocket Pal X2 and easily hones serrated tools, gut hooks, and single-bevel blades. As mentioned, the unit includes a standard survival kit consisting of an emergency whistle to alert rescuers and a bright single bulb LED light. At night, the LED is visible for a great distance and can help rescuers locate you if needed. A fire starter is included that will cleanly spark and easily ignite kindling for warmth. A compass is standard and attached with a lanyard to the Pocket Pal X2. This is a good way to attach the unit to clothing or gear to prevent loss. It is bright orange for easy recovery if you happen to drop it. The unit is just 3 inches long and an inch wide (and it weighs less than 2 ounces), so it is light in your pack. The durable plastic construction will stand up to a fair amount of abuse.

A more traditional handheld sharpener is Smith's 4-Inch Diamond Sharpening Stone. As the name implies, it is only 4 inches in length and very flat and compact. This tool easily slips into a coat pocket or backpack for applying a quick hone when you need it. The diamond abrasive surface features a very fine grit (750) with an interrupted surface. By spacing out the small abrasive pads, the stone stays cleaner, as metal shavings are collected in the gaps and removed from the edge. This speeds up sharpening and increases the efficiency of the stone. One side has a Micro-Tool Sharpening Pad that can be used for knife blade tips (these get the most use) as well as small tools. Along the entire length of the stone, there is a groove that is designed specifically for sharpening fish hooks or other pointed objects.

The included cover protects the diamond abrasive and does double duty as a base that extends the gripping area while sharpening. Keeping your hands away from the blade while sharpening is a good idea, and this cover certainly helps. While the stone can be used dry, the manufacturer recommends using a lubricant for best results. I find that spit works well enough.

KNIFE DEFENSE TRAINING

The use of a knife for standard woodcraft and survival is not especially difficult to master; however, if you must use a knife for self-defense, it's an entirely different situation. The basic rule is that in a knife fight (where both sides are armed with a cutting tool), everyone gets cut. Just as I would never simply hand someone a gun for self-defense with no training, if you are serious about learning knife self-defense, training is imperative.

Various martial arts systems include training in defense against a knife, but few include actual knife fight training. Alessandro Padovani, a life-long martial artist and personal-defense instructor, is the founder of Safer Faster Knife Defense. Padovani's training emphasizes real world life-or-death situations where a person will have to commit themselves to using their knife in a brutal fashion in order to stop a threat.

There are five distinct Safer Faster Knife Defense courses avail-

Safer Faster Knife Defense offers five distinct courses available for civilians and military/law enforcement in basic 4- to 8-hours blocks of instruction taught in cities around the country.
Photo: Safer Faster Knife Defense

able for civilians and military/law enforcement. These are: Safer Faster Knife Defense Fundamentals (8 hours), Defending Against Multiple Assailants (8 hours), Extreme Close Quarter Knife Defense (4 hours), Fight Back Up to Standing (4 hours), and Defending Against a Gun Grab (4 hours).

Padovani starts with the basics: the draw. Ideally, he recommends that students carry a fixed-blade knife near the centerline (so it can be drawn with either hand). This eliminates any extra movements and provides the fastest access. Carrying a fixed blade may be restricted in some states and localities, and most people prefer folders with pocket clips for their convenience and size. If you carry a folder, Padovani advises carrying two, one for each

Padovani trains his students to strike the most sensitive areas for maximum effectiveness with an edged weapon.

front pocket, since access to your strong-side pocket may be restricted just when you need it the most. Effectively drawing a folder with either hand is heavily emphasized in the class.

Padovani developed his own techniques for getting a folder into action quickly. For folders with a thumb hole, he uses a simple zip tie that catches on the corner of the pants pockets and automatically opens the knife when it is drawn. On other types of folders, he has machined a cut out on the back of the blade to achieve the same effect.

Students are trained to recognize a threat and work with the body's natural survival reactions to respond more efficiently to it. They lower their center of gravity, orient themselves toward the threat, and assume a protective posture with the hands up to defend the head, mimicking the startle-flinch response. Then, they grip the knife and draw it as they make a lateral movement away from the threat. The training is based on spontaneity, not on rehearsed moves or sequences. In a real world encounter, a threat occurs dynamically and unpredictably.

Padovani trains his students on an intuitive defensive stance and shows the different grip styles, including Hammer, Filipino, and Reverse with both edge up or down. He strongly advises his students to pick one grip and stick with it. There is no use for switching grips in the middle of a fight, so practice the same grip until you are proficient with it. Stabbing, slashing moves and pommel strikes are practiced and focused on targeting anatomically sensitive areas.

Statistics show that actual knife-on-knife fights are very rare. What is more common is for a bad guy to use a knife to intimidate you into complying with his requests or, in the worst case scenario, for the bad guy to use a knife or other improvised weapon to take you by surprise and ambush you. In a fight against such a determined attacker, the defender will be at a disadvantage from the start. The attacker has already armed themselves and selected the moment of the assault and has mentally committed themselves in advance.

The best way to offset an attacker's advantage is to aim your strikes for the head and neck. These are target rich (eyes, ears, airways, carotid, jugular, brainstem), and even the most committed attacker will react instinctively and switch from offense to defense when the head and neck areas are threatened. Padovani wants his students to see these natural reactions in practice, so students are paired off in attacker/defender teams to practice targeting recognition and reaction.

Again, this is not sparring, and there are no rehearsed or choreographed moves. Dulled or polymer training knives are used for safety, and the "attackers" are provided with a variety of training weapons from bottles to crowbars. Students are also provided with face and neck guards so that strikes can be delivered in a more realistic manner while maintaining a safe and injury-free environment.

At first, these drills are practiced in slow motion to avoid flailing, but as students gain confidence, the drills are sped up. This drill achieves several objectives. First, the student receives immediate feedback on how an assailant may react and how to counter. Second, the realism of the drill helps the student to overcome any squeamishness over cutting or stabbing an assailant. Finally, students are taught to use fear management techniques to focus their aggressiveness and strengthen their resolve.

If you cannot personally attend a course, there are other options. Brian Hoffner is both a knife designer and knife fighting instructor with a black belt in the art of Goju Ryu and over 30 years of law enforcement experience as a patrol officer and firearms/defensive tactics instructor in Texas.

The Hoffner Knife Defense System is comprehensive, and he teaches it in a four-hour course: the Basic Defensive Folding Knife Operator training course. In conjunction with the knife, Hoffner has also developed a DVD of his knife defense techniques that is available independently or as part of a package with the knife and includes a red training blade. The training blade has the same handle design and blade materials as the live blade, but is 0.5 inch shorter and is rounded and dulled. It is still made from steel, so caution should be exercised when training with thrusting attacks with a live partner. It can be very effective when training at full speed against a sparring dummy.

The DVD is 60 minutes long and allows you to proceed at your own pace and review specific techniques for practice and training at home. Topics covered include a discussion of the different types of carry folders and their advantages. Hoffner tackles mindset (which is key to defensive knife use), different defensive stances to use against an assailant, and proper carry techniques, including appendix carry.

Of course, the most important aspect of carrying a defensive folder is in achieving rapid deployment. In this area, the Hoffner training DVD covers specific techniques for fast deployment, which should be practiced. These include the traditional thumb flip into the foil or sabre grip position and deployment of the blade directly into the icepick or spine pick position by gripping

Brian Hoffner is both a knife designer and knife fighting instructor. The Hoffner Knife Defense System is comprehensive and available in person or via DVD. *Photo: Brian Hoffner*

the knife handle and using the fingers to push out on the thumb stud while flicking the blade open.

The Hoffner Knife, which the man himself designed, is intended for the type of courses he teaches based on his own real world experiences. While it appears to be fairly traditional, he excludes features like flippers and levers. This liner locking folding knife carries a 3.5-inch 440C stainless steel dagger point blade with a false edge that both aids in penetration and lightens the blade itself. The Hoffner Knife has ambidextrous thumb stud opening for fast deployment. The blade is available in both standard and with a partially serrated blade, which can be especially handy in tough cutting situations with thick rope or seat belts. The knife handles are made from a black G10 in an aggressive texture for a solid grip.

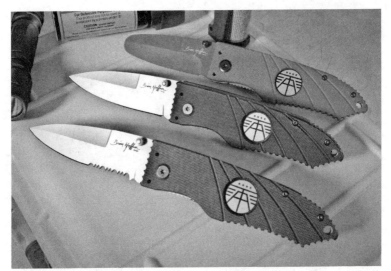

The Hoffner Knife features a 3.5-inch 440C stainless steel dagger point blade, ambidextrous thumb stud opening and is available in both standard and with a partially serrated blade. *Photo: Brian Hoffner*

You also get a reversible low carry pocket clip; however, due to the knife's design and intended use, your only option is tip down carry. The spring steel clip does allow the knife to sit low in the pocket and become almost invisible from the outside. Combine it with dark colored pants, and no one will know you are carrying it. The pommel has a lanyard hole for added retention if needed.

The blade itself is fairly conventional, but it is the handle that encompasses the most distinctive combat elements. Hoffner designed the blade to work in conjunction with his specific self-defense knife techniques. The scales have "indexing divots" — deep, round thumb-sized impressions. These are designed as tactical pivot points to allow you to more easily and quickly perform transitions and switch styles from the hammer or sabre to a reverse or spine pick grip.

The ergonomic shape of the handle and the deep and aggressive serrations along the rear outside circumference of the handle provide a very secure purchase. Combined with the textured G10 grip panels, the effect is to lock the knife in the hand even in wet conditions. When this feature is combined with the indexing divots, you get a rearward grip that extends the blade striking reach by 1.5 inches.

In an attack, you may not have time to fully deploy your defensive folder, and Hoffner has added a flat bolster at the front with sharp and very aggressive serrations. With the blade closed, these offer a less lethal striking surface and the option of using the knife as a defensive tool without having to deploy the blade. The pommel end is similarly serrated, but instead of being flat, it comes to a distinct point that provides additional striking capabilities and can be used as a compliance tool when applied to pressure points on an assailant.

In defensive applications, there are several methods that Hoffner advocates. He prefers carrying the folder on the support side front pocket. This allows for a casual thumb-hooked-in-the-pocket look while prepping the knife inconspicuously for a fast deployment if needed. This is similar to the hands-in-the-pocket with a pocket pistol method, which allows you to have your hand on the grip of your pistol for very fast draw while looking non-threatening on the outside.

In the icepick or spine pick grip, the thumb acts as a counter balance to prevent the blade from slipping out of your hand. This grip affords a strong defensive stance with the support arm up to protect the head and with the blade, facing outward, angled along the length of the forearm. Additionally, this grip is effective against any attempted grabs to sweep across the wrist or arms of an assailant while also providing for very powerful stabbing strikes. The ice pick grip has another advantage in that it is very effective against attacks from the rear, such as an assailant attempting a choke hold or arm lock.

The foil or sabre is very popular as an offensive technique that allows the maximum distance between you and an assailant for thrusting attacks while providing a high degree of mobility and speed for slashing attacks. This distance is extended by an additional 1.5 inches with the Hoffner Knife rearward grip, essentially giving you extra blade length.

AIRGUNS, BOWS & CROSSBOWS

*W*ith so many survival gun choices available today — AR-15s, concealed carry handguns, tactical shotguns, and niche ammo for each — it's easy to assume that firearms will cover every conceivable contingency.

However, there are situations in which you may want to conserve ammunition or where you simply don't have any. Or times when you need to use a weapon for hunting or self-defense, but you want to do so quietly. For these times, airguns, bows and crossbows offer an important option to diversify your survival gun arsenal. Hunters already know this and in many states there are extended or special seasons for bow hunting. Increasingly, crossbows are being allowed for hunting. Many hunters take up archery for the challenge, since range is limited and accuracy requires a lot more practice. Others simply want to be able to spend more time hunting. And in the field of airguns, new big-bore calibers and advances in projectiles have opened up options in the way of small and big game hunting with powerful pellet guns.

If you are looking for ways to hunt that do not involve firearms or direct contact with the game animal (as in the case of knives or spears), these other options deserve a look. Now, space does not permit a full, in-depth treatment here of these subjects, but after reading this chapter I hope you will look further into these essential — yet non-conventional — survival weapon choices.

AIRGUNS

There are many different types of airguns, and it is a mistake to think they are like Ralphie's official Red Ryder, carbine-action air rifle with a compass in the stock and this thing which tells time. Of course, the biggest advantage for any airgun is that you don't have to worry about gunpowder, primers, or cartridge cases. All you need is a projectile and compressed air.

This technology is not exactly new, either. The Girandoni Air Rifle was developed in 1779; it had a rifled barrel and a tubular magazine of 22 round lead balls of .46-caliber. It was one of the world's first repeating firearms and powerful enough to be adopted by the Austrian Army and used against Napoleon. A soldier could fire the entire magazine in less than a minute and quickly reload.

It functioned using a removable compressed air cylinder made of hammered and riveted iron, which took the place of the buttstock. The cylinder could contain a pressure of 800 psi, which was good for 40 shots before it started to slow down. The main drawback was that it took 1,500 strokes of a small pump to recharge the air canister. Still, a soldier could conceivably carry multiple charged canisters.

Modern air rifles can be simple BB guns with their own internal pump action that can be used for small game hunting. Professional air rifles, on the other hand, operate more like the Girandoni and are capable of taking larger game such as hogs or even deer.

Most small air guns are .17 caliber, but some can be found in .22 caliber as well. A good example of a high-quality and powerful

Most airguns are powerful enough for small game hunting and some are powerful enough for big game such as deer. *Photo: Gamo*

air rifle that is suitable for small game hunting is the Ruger Air Hawk from Umarex. The Air Hawk is a break-open single-pump pellet gun that fires at 1,000 fps. It is chambered in 0.177 caliber, or 4.5mm, with an 18.7-inch rifled steel barrel.

You can only load one pellet at a time directly into the barrel. The front and rear sights use a fiber optic insert for improved visibility, and they are adjustable for windage and elevation. The rifle has a single dove-tail mounting rail on the top, and a fixed 4x magnification scope is included. The break barrel-type action has an automatic sliding tang safety that engages upon opening of the action. The trigger weight and length of pull is 3.3 pounds and 14 inches, respectively. The cocking effort is 30 pounds. The recoil is very different from the use of an actual firearm, in that where a normal rifle would push straight into the shoulder, the airgun has

The Ruger Air Hawk from Umarex is a break-open single-pump pellet gun that fires at 1,000 fps. It is chambered in 0.177 caliber with an 18.7-inch rifled steel barrel.

a bit more drawn out recoil. It isn't straight back, rather it's almost as if the rifle is moving forward. For this reason, you have to use scopes specifically designed for air rifle use.

The single pump action fully charges the compressed air cylinder, and there is no need to worry about access to CO_2 cartridges as with some other designs. At 1,000 fps, the pellets will easily penetrate both sides of a steel can, so the rifle can be used for hunting game as large as rabbits.

AIR GUN TRAINING

Training with air handguns has become an increasingly viable alternative to improve your skills, and is something you can easily do at home. New air guns from companies like Umarex are fully licensed replicas of the most popular duty and civilian handguns on the market today. They not only look real, but have the same size, dimensions, and weight. This allows you to train using your standard carry holster.

To further increase realism and training value, many of these modern air pistols have at least some of the functional controls of the actual firearm. Even when they don't, the controls are there in appearance, and you can still train with them. The most realistic and fully functional air gun I have seen is the Umarex Colt Single Action Army Peacemaker revolver with 100 percent of the functional controls of the actual firearm. This particular all-metal revolver makes a great training aid for fans of Cowboy Action Shooting. In addition, Daisy produces a Winchester licensed 1911-style pistol with real blowback action, removable magazine, and an action that locks the slide open on the last round.

AIRGUN SAFETY

Of course, having the right airgun is only part of what you need to train; you also need a place to safely shoot it. Most CO_2-powered airguns max out at 400 to 425 fps, and you don't need too much to safely stop their projectiles (although it should be noted that these are not toys and can be very dangerous). All of the same safety rules and precautions taken with actual firearms still apply. Eye protection is especially important for everyone on the range, including non-shooters, because of the propensity for BBs to ricochet; you do not, however, need hearing protection.

If you are going to shoot indoors or in your yard, make sure of several important factors. First and foremost, identify your safe direction. You need to know where you are shooting and what is beyond. If you are shooting inside, stick with paper targets. Cans, plastic bottles, spinners, clays, and other reactive targets will make a mess and have a higher likelihood of causing a ricochet.

The first item to mention is legality. Even if it is legal for you to own an airgun (and laws vary from state to state and locality to locality), it may not be legal for you to fire it outside a formal range. Check the laws before building yourself what may be an

You can safely set up an outdoor airgun range most anywhere with either commercial foam target blocks or boxes filled with newspaper and a good backstop. *Photo: Crosman*

unusable range. Like any range, you would not want people accidentally wandering downrange where they could get injured. Ideally, your range will have only one point of access. This is easier in a fenced yard or in one room of your home. If you are shooting outside, cautionary signage can help as well as other indicators to warn anyone who wanders by.

Shooting lead pellets carries its own risks, especially indoors. As long as you keep the velocity below about 600 fps, the pellet will not break apart. As always, make sure to wash your hands after handling lead and if you drop any lead pellets pick them up rather than leave them behind for little hands to find.

Having a good backstop will ensure you don't end up with a bunch of holes in your drywall as well as help you avoid ricochets. One of the best backstops is to use a loose hanging heavy blanket or tarp behind your target. This will easily stop any escaping BBs or pellets, especially at air pistol velocities. Another option is to use a large sheet of plywood behind your target, but make sure to angle it downward.

Dirt makes a great backstop and, fortunately, there is a lot of it. It won't do you much good on the ground, however, unless it

Caution, BBs can bounce back at you with some force if they hit a hard object and should not be reused in any case. *Photo: Reiff & Bily*

is in the form of a berm or incline. If you do have a hill or berm into which you can shoot make sure it is clear of any large rocks or debris that could cause a ricochet. Again, this is less likely with pellets but happens a lot with BBs. Never shoot at a hard surface with a BB, including at trees, or they will bounce back.

If you don't want to move mounds of dirt, an easier alternative is to use hay bales. Stack them two bales deep and staggered so that there is less chance of a projectile getting through. Indoors, there are plenty of plans online for building pellet and BB traps. I have found that the absolute simplest solution is to get a medium-sized cardboard box and fill it with old newspapers. At the back, place a few old phone books for added safety.

There are plenty of commercial pellet and BB traps available (note: BBs and pellets should not be reused, as this can damage your air gun). Metal traps should only be used with pellets. Daisy and Crosman both offer easy to use pellet traps that allow you to place your target in front and safely contain your fired pellets. If you want to change the target height, you can use hay bales, cardboard boxes, or old milk crates. Read the caveats for each pellet trap, as some are rated with a maximum pellet velocity. Heavy density foam target blocks are another commercially available alternative, and these will stop BBs.

Shooting outside offers far greater versatility but comes with its own caveats. One of my top concerns when shooting outside is that my neighbors not be able to see me. Make sure to set up your backyard range somewhere inconspicuous so as not to cause alarm or create sources of complaints. As they say, high fences make for good neighbors.

BOWS AND CROSSBOWS

The two benefits of using a bow for survival are quietness and recyclable ammunition. Modern bows are highly advanced and capable of producing very flat shooting arrow trajectories. Compound bows use a series of pulleys to make the draw easier and lighter for the user and to increase the force of the arrow. Compound bows can be found in a wide price range. Arrows can be had in a variety of styles and materials from aluminum to advanced carbon composites, and with tips from simple target or "field" points to advanced broadheads for hunting. You will need to know your draw length so you can buy arrows that fit your arm length. Any modern archery shop can measure you and provide the ideal setup. Arrows, unless they get damaged, can be reused, so with care, you will have a good supply of ammunition.

With any bow, you want one in the proper draw weight for your strength. Compound bows give you the highest weight to power ratio thanks to the mechanical advantage provided by the system of cables and pullies. You also need arrows calibrated to the draw weight and length of your bow, as well as an arm guard and finger tabs or mechanical release.

Archery can be a challenging skill to develop but a very effective means of survival for hunting or even self-defense. Today, there are many types of bows.
Photo: U.S. Air Force photo/Dennis Rogers

Crossbows are more powerful and easier to master than bows and may be a better choice for the novice or part-time archer. *Photo: U.S. Marine Corps photo by Lance Cpl. Jason Jimenez*

Crossbows are prolific today, and represent an even more compact option. The crossbow was first developed because it allowed a soldier to fire a more powerful bolt with greater accuracy and minimal training. By contrast, an effective longbow archer took years to train. Modern crossbows come in a standard variety, like regular bows, and in a compound form with the pulley system. Compound crossbows make it far easier to cock the weapon and much faster, as less strength is needed. And the standard rifle stock, trigger, and ability to add optics makes modern crossbows extremely effective within 100 yards for taking any game animal with the right kind of bolt. Note that crossbows and bows do not use the same type of projectile.

TRADITIONAL ARCHERY

In extremis, you can make your own bow and arrows. Certainly, the technology and skills required are not new. In 1991, hikers discovered a 5,300 year old frozen mummy in the Alps who had a yew longbow and 14 arrows in a quiver. Likely, this was used for hunting, but the use of a traditional bow requires a lot more practice and technique.

Here are some traditional archery tips for best results:

- **Stance:** Start by standing perpendicular to the target with your support side shoulder toward the target and your strong side directly away from it. Keep your feet perpendicular to the target at a 90-degree angle about shoulder width apart.

- **Nocking:** Tilt the top of your bow slightly toward your dominant side and place an arrow so it is sitting on your bow above your support hand. If your bow does not have a shelf or arrow rest, the arrow will be resting on your fist (in which case, gloves help). Place the nock of the arrow on your string. Try to place the nock of each arrow on the same spot. If your string has a nocking point (usually a crimped brass tab), then place the arrow nock below it.

- **Finger Hook:** Using the first three fingers of your dominant hand, place your index finger above the arrow on the string and the second two fingers below it. You want to use only up to the first knuckle. If you are having to use too much of your fingers or having too hard of a time drawing the bow, use a lighter bow that requires less force to draw.

- **Set Up:** Bring the front of the bow up to the target. Keeping your shoulders down and your strong side elbow up, prepare to draw the bow. Arm position should be rotating the support arm slightly toward the bow, causing it to bend away from the path of the string to avoid it hitting the arm (which can happen even with an arm guard).

- **Draw the Bow:** Pull the string straight back along your support arm using your back muscles and keeping your strong side elbow up until you reach your anchor point.

- **Anchoring:** You should draw your bow back to the same spot on your face each and every time. This is your anchor point and helps ensure consistency. Many traditional archers find three points of contact for better consistency, such as one finger in the corner of the mouth, the arrow nock touching the nose or other part of the face, and the thumb tucked under the jowl in the same spot each time.

- **Hold:** Unlike compound bows where the bow's weight is reduced at full draw, traditional bow shooters experience the maximum weight of the bow at full draw. Holding at full draw should only be done until a proper sight picture is acquired.

- **Aim:** As most traditional bows do not have sights, the front of the arrow can serve as a reference point, and it is important to establish a proper and consistent sight picture and make adjustments as needed. There are many types of aiming you can study in-depth, including instinctive, gap shooting and hybrid gap shooting.

- **Release:** To release the arrow, smoothly roll the fingers rearward across the string until it slips loose while keeping the support arm on target. Do not "pluck" the string when releasing it, and keep the hand on your anchor point. Roll your shoulders together; use your back muscles to move your arm rather than your arm muscles.

- **Follow Through:** Once you release the arrow, continue aiming at the target and don't move until the arrow hits home.

Indeed, the modern airgun and archery setup give you additional sensible options to diversify your survival gun battery. Of course, like conventional firearms, these tools require diligent practice and preparation before things get serious. So stock up now, and practice like there's no tomorrow — because there really might not be.

EMERGENCY FOOD & WATER

T he best survival gun is worthless in the hands of a weak, malnourished person too sick to crawl out of bed. Your doomsday planning needs to be holistic, as survival requires you to be strong and at the top of your game. That's where emergency food and water factor in.

Back at the start of U.S. involvement in World War I, congress created the Council of National Defense to help organize civilian resources for support in times of national crises. By the start of World War II, the Office of Civilian Defense was established to again coordinate civilian resources and volunteers. The later advent of the Cold War again changed the mission of the Office of

SURVIVAL SNAPSHOT: EMERGENCY FOOD & WATER

PROS: An absolute necessity for short- and long-term survival.

CONS: You may be limited to what you can carry if evacuating.

STOCKPILE: Canned food lasts over 100 years. Keep a month's supply of food and water at home, plus an emergency three-day supply for evacuation, per family member.

AUTHOR'S TOP PICK: Meals Ready to Eat (MREs). **MSRP:** $59 (Case of 12)

NOTE ON WATER: For long-term water storage use sealed metal cans, not plastic containers.

Civilian Defense. The Department of Defense and the Civil Defense coordinated to turn basements in buildings across the country into fallout shelters and to properly supply them with a minimum of a two-week supply of food and water for the number of people each was rated to accommodate.

These shelters were filled with food, water, and emergency supplies. What was provided was rudimentary nutrition, consisting almost entirely of "biscuits," which were actually just crackers, like saltines. Each sealed tin can contained 434 biscuits and one cardboard box had two cans. According to the Cold War Era Civil Defense Museum, each "shelteree" was provided 10,000 calories in crackers for the entirety of their two-week sojourn, or just over 700 calories per day. Of course, physical activity was expected to be kept to a minimum during this time.

This can of Spam will be just as good and safe to eat 100 years from now as it is today, which may not be saying much about the product.

These 60-year-old cans of crackers can still be found unopened, and some people have tried them. Despite the time in storage, they are still edible — not mouthwatering good, but edible. There is some precedence for this in the form of hardtack, a simple flour, water, and salt cracker that has been around since before Roman times and is baked dry for long-term storage and transport. It was a staple of Union troops during the Civil War, and some of it had been around since the end of the Mexican-American War. Likewise, American troops got to enjoy Civil War-era surplus hardtack during the Spanish-American War.

If crackers can still be edible some 60 years later, what about other things, like canned foods? The answer is yes, and for a surprisingly long time. Expiration dates on canned foods are grossly pessimistic estimates of when the food contained inside may start to taste less fresh than a new can of food. It does not indicate that the food has gone bad. The secret of preserving food by canning is more than 200 years old and involves heating the sealed cans long enough to the point that all the bacteria inside are killed. Thus, the food cannot go bad.

In 1974, canned food recovered from a riverboat that had sunk in 1868 was tested by the National Food Processors Association (NFPA) to look for any bacteria, as well as to study the nutritional value that remained. The cans contained fruits and vegetables as well as oysters, and the chemists found zero bacteria. Nutritionally, there was significant loss of vitamins A and C, but protein and calcium levels were normal. In another test, NFPA chemists opened a can of corn that had been stored for 40 years and found that it was as fresh as a new can. The key is that the cans are not damaged.

You would think that meats may not do as well as vegetables, but you would be wrong. Canned meats do better than vegetables and keep their nutritional content and consistency longer. Some canned vegetables tend to do better than others. Tomatoes and other highly acidic vegetables are naturally anti-bacterial. Bee honey cannot go bad because of its low moisture content and high acidity. Honey has been found in 5,000-year-old tombs that is still good to eat (do not give honey to infants under one year of age, however). This is also the secret behind freeze-dried foods. No moisture means no opportunity for bacteria to grow and spoil the food.

Canned food that has been kept in a high temperature and high humidity area for long-term storage is more likely to break down faster. Subjecting canned food to fluctuating temperatures and humidity extremes is also not a good thing. These conditions may cause damage to the cans, in which case all bets are off. Since there may not be any way to know the circumstances under which very old food has been stored, make sure to check any cans for damage. Properly stored and well-maintained canned food can last well over 100 years. If you have the room, stockpile a sizable amount of a variety of foods for balanced nutrition. Don't forget to keep several manual can openers.

The amount you should be looking to store should be at minimum a month's worth per family member. More is better of course, but a one month supply should be enough to get you through all but the most severe of emergency episodes. You may not have access to a means of heating the food, so be prepared to eat it cold. I have a wood burning stove on which I can heat things, as well as an outdoor grill with a side burner and an extra propane tank, so if I need to boil water or cook something, I can.

One of my preferred emergency food sources are military MREs (Meals Ready to Eat). These are self-contained, complete, well-balanced meals neatly packed in a tough plastic bag that itself can be used for transporting water or other uses. An entire MRE contains 1,300 calories and is divided between drink and coffee powders, tea bags with creamer and sugar, crackers with butter and jelly, candy, hot sauce, a main entrée, and a dessert. These can be divided and spread throughout the day. One MRE per person per day with a lack of physical activity is enough. In the military, where troops are expected to perform significant physical activity, each soldier gets three MREs per day.

The MRE packet also includes extras such as utensils, hand wipes, toilet paper, napkins, etc. Modern MREs contain a chemical heating element that allows you to eat a hot meal in the field. The meals come 12 to a cardboard case, or they can be purchased individually. I just buy them by the case and make sure I have enough for each family member for one month. The stated shelf

Meals Ready to Eat (MREs) were developed for the military and have a decades long shelf life. That's good eating, said no one ever.

life listed (with proper storage) is 15 years, but this is just the recommendation. In reality, MREs last indefinitely.

There are other similar ready-to-eat prepackaged products out there that may be cheaper. I only prefer the MREs for their all-in-one convenience. There are freeze dried survival foods that pack lighter, but keep in mind that you will need to add water to rehydrate them before they can be eaten. If the water is cold, your meal will be, too. Make sure you are using clean water. If you use contaminated water by accident, then you will get sick and your food will be wasted. Mistakes such as this will dig into your emergency water supply.

EMERGENCY WATER

The average adult should consume about half a gallon of water per day in total. At least, that's the adage. The reality is that nearly half of all Americans consume four cups (¼ gallon) of liquid water per day or less, and no one is dying of thirst. How much water you need per day is based on your size and your level of activity. The best way to tell if you need more water is by the color of your urine. If it is bright yellow, you are dehydrated and need to drink more.

For storage purposes in an emergency survival situation, calculate at least ¼ gallon of water per person per day, plus extra for your food. For a family of four, a one month supply is going to be 30 gallons of drinking water. Again, this does not include water

For a family of four a one month supply is a minimum of 30 gallons of drinking water. Note this does not include water for washing or other purposes.

for washing or other purposes. Also, it's important to remember that even if you have natural water resources near you such as lakes, ponds, streams, rivers, or wells, and even if municipal water systems are still operational (meaning water is still coming out of your tap), they may be compromised and contaminated by the emergency with which you are dealing.

There are many economical home water testing kits you can use to test for a variety of contaminants including bacteria, lead, and other chemicals. It is well worth it to have a few of these on hand. If you must rely on contaminated water, there are many filters available that can render contaminated water safe to drink, from personal use straws to more substantial family-sized systems. Boiling the water will kill bacteria but will not remove other types of contaminants.

For short-term storage (less than a couple of years), storing water in plastic containers is OK. Typically, people will purchase 5-gallon water jugs as well as crates of individual water bottles. Remember that for a family of four for one month, you will need six of these 5-gallon plastic jugs. You don't want to store water in plastic containers long term because the plastics will eventually start to leach into the water and make it less safe to drink. You should add a few drops of bleach (4 drops per gallon) to help prevent your water from going bad and developing bacteria. I like to keep a mix of the 5-gallon water containers and individual water bottles for convenience and rotate them every two years.

For long-term water storage, you need impermeable, sealed steel cans. Major Surplus sells their Frontier Pro Inline Water Filter and 30-Year Shelf Life Emergency Canned Drinking Water (6 Can Case) for a total of 132 fluid ounces, or just over one gallon. This is a good option.

HUNTING

Every city slicker and suburban armchair warrior thinks that if things get bad, they will just head for the hills and live off the land. Well, there would presumably already be people living in the hills, and they won't take kindly to your trespassing. Another problem is that there is simply not enough wildlife to support that many people through subsistence hunting. If you think hunting is easy, you haven't done it. Hunting is a skill that must be acquired through practice. If you have never hunted for food before, you will have a very hard time doing it for survival on short notice.

All that being said, one advantage of the hunting lifestyle is that you'll tend to accumulate game meat in your freezer. Of course, that necessitates a large chest freezer, and possibly a dedicated gas generator or solar array/battery pack to keep it running during power outages. If you get busy with the procurement and storage of venison now, you can have a nice stockpile of nutritious (organic!) meat to supplement other food reserves.

The nature of this book does not permit a detailed explanation of how to hunt or how to gut, skin, and de-bone game animals or how to preserve the meat that you don't plan on eating soon. There are a lot of books available that explain and detail all of this far better than I can. I do recommend that if hunting for meat is part of your long-term survival strategy and you have never been hunting before, you need to get out there and learn exactly what it entails.

If you are a first-time hunter, you will need to learn the laws, take a state-sponsored Hunter Education class, and buy the requisite licenses. In my state of Virginia, Hunter Safety education has been required since 1988 to ensure that all hunters are safe, ethical, and responsible. On average, 14,000 people complete the course each year. States are continually looking to improve the course and to make it easier for people with busy schedules to successfully complete it.

Hunting is a skill that must be acquired. It can be made easier by hunting over bait like in this hog hunt.
Photo: Terrill Hoffman

In many places, a portion of the course can be completed online with several online quizzes and self-study guides to expedite matters. The classroom portion is an additional six hours, usually split up over two evenings or all on one Saturday. The curriculum is focused on understanding game laws, hunting ethics and gun safety, with a smaller section on wilderness survival and trapping. Typically, students are provided with a handbook that covers a wide range of topics from firearms and bows to basic hunting skills as well as survival skills and wildlife conservation. These classes are usually free of charge and are a good introduction to hunting.

I don't consider myself an expert hunter, but fortunately I have enough property that I can hunt where I live. Here's how a typical deer hunt and associated preparation recently went:

- **Pre-Hunting:** Bought a treestand at Walmart ($100) and assembled it incorrectly three times. Nearly died trying to get it attached to a random tree. Ended up calling my handyman to help ($60).

- **Day 1:** Went hunting at 6:30 Saturday morning with my son for the first day of rifle season. We got cold, bored, lasted one hour, and went home. Saw nothing but two squirrels (and they were very merry).

- **Day 2:** Went back to Walmart to buy proper cold weather hunting clothes and boots for both of us ($250). Saw more squirrels and a chipmunk. No deer. We lasted two hours this time.

- **Day 3:** Sat in the treestand for four hours. Complete bust. I have started naming the squirrels.

- **Day 4:** Saw actual deer, including one standing right by the treestand 20 feet away staring at me, but it was before legal hunting hours. The rest of the deer that I saw did not provide a clean shot. This is progress.

- **Day 5:** Still no luck. Tried watching The Deer Hunter but that only made me hungry for pho and want to play Russian roulette. Thinking of getting one of those life-sized foam deer people use for archery practice and just shooting and eating it.

- **Day 6:** Didn't hunt in the morning because it was raining, and deer go home when it rains. Went hunting in the afternoon and saw nothing. Question: Is it a bad sign if there are several large buzzards circling me? I keep hearing the occasional shot of a successful hunter, taunting me. Headed to Walmart to buy all the synthetic deer urine I can find ($30).

- **Day 7:** Lathered myself in deer urine and saw four nice deer. Took a shot at one but missed. Really starting to get hungry. This venison is going to be the world's most expensive meat by the time I get it. It would be cheaper to import beer-fed, hand-massaged Wagyu beef from Japan.

- **Day 8:** It is freezing cold, and I didn't see a single deer, I blame Obama and the DNR. I am heading back to Walmart for more deer urine and long johns ($60). I am becoming increasingly convinced that hunting is all a scam invented by Walmart to rob me of almost $500 so far.

- **Day 9:** There's nothing out here. Even the squirrels and the birds have apparently decided to sleep in. I am thinking of becoming a vegetarian.

- **Day 10:** Gloria in Excelsis Deo! Finally, after nearly 30 hours on stand, I got one. The secret is to stop trying so hard. Took it to the butcher for processing ($120).

- **Post Script:** Got the meat back (about 40 pounds of it), and the sausage was very good, as was the jerky. The meat itself tastes gamey no matter how I cook it, and it makes me think of gutting the deer, which is not appetizing. Also, now that I am done hunting for the season, three deer have made camp in my front yard.

Whole lot of nothing out here. The deer don't just show up and wait for you to shoot them. It takes years of experience to learn how to get close to wild game.

Note: For long-term life off the grid, you would ideally have a large farm where you'd produce your own meat, eggs, milk, and wool. Unfortunately, very few people today have the land, equipment, and knowledge of animal husbandry to accomplish this. While cows and sheep are wonderful, they do require lots of acreage, barn space, and labor on the part of the farmer. Smaller animals, including rabbits and poultry, are much less demanding in terms of both space and exertion. Chickens are arguably the easiest of all to raise, and they provide nutritious eggs in addition to meat. Moreover, their droppings (while less abundant than, say, a cow's) can be composted to produce fertilizer for a garden.

HUNTING TIPS

One way to improve your odds is by scouting the area where you plan on hunting and getting a feel for what animals are out there and what patterns they follow — especially when they are most active. The easiest way to do this is with a game camera, which can easily be attached to a tree and aimed at a specific area.

The Primos Proof Camera 03 is a good choice because it's not expensive and is easy to use and set up — even

One way to improve your hunting odds is by scouting the area where you plan to hunt using a game camera. The Primos Proof Camera 03 is not expensive and is easy to use and set up. *Photo: Primos*

I was able to figure it out. The battery-operated digital camera features a removable SD card and is housed inside a weatherproof camouflage plastic box, with a belt-type strap that wraps around a tree or post. The settings allow for video or still images, and it is activated with a motion sensor so anything that moves in front of the lens gets recorded. The night vision feature ensures that you capture all the action, as many animals are most active in the evening or very early morning hours. The photos provide the date and time the image was captured.

Remember, having the greatest survival guns and gear won't do you a bit of good if you're too weak to function due to dehydration and malnourishment. Take measures now, while you still can, to provide the basics for you and your family.

SHELTER
IN PLACE

HOME BUNKERS AND SAFE ROOMS

Every situation is different, and in some instances, your survival is best served by sheltering in place. This can be as a result of severe weather or some other disturbance that makes evacuation or travel too dangerous. Your solution may be as simple as staying in a well-supplied basement or as involved as a full-fledged underground dedicated bomb shelter.

The idea of a bomb shelter is really not so farfetched. In the 1950s and '60s, home bomb shelters were very popular — mostly out of fear of a Soviet attack. Many of these offered only the most rudimentary of shelter and accommodations. Today's bomb (or if you prefer, storm) shelters are significantly improved with flushing toilets, showers, queen-sized beds, and flat screen TVs.

BUNKERS/BOMB SHELTERS

If you have the land, there are plenty of companies willing to sell you pre-fabricated underground bunkers and bomb shelters (not the same thing) and install them on your property. This is the relatively cheaper option, but if you have the scratch to spare, they will custom design and build a shelter to suit your needs, even multiple family underground dwellings. These are not repurposed, moldy old leaky Cold War-era missile silos (although those do pop up for sale occasionally), but state-of-the-art shelters for you and your family. There are round steel shelters, round corrugated steel shelters, concrete shelters, square shelters, etc. Each fills a separate niche, and some are better as bomb shelters while others are better suited as storm or fallout shelters.

Atlas Survival Shelters specializes in very large, round corrugated tube shelters, which are "the only bunkers tested against the effects of a nuclear bomb," according to their website. The inside of these shelters looks like a really nice, round RV with a ton of storage space. Once you get to around 10 feet underground, the temperature stays a constant 55 degrees or so. You won't freeze, but you won't cook either. Bring a sweater.

The biggest concern in all underground shelters is air ventilation. Atlas Survival Shelters are air-tight and have CO_2 air scrubbers as well as an NBC-rated (Nuclear, Biological, and Chemical) filtration ventilation system with hand crank operation as needed. You get a separate decontamination room with shower to use before entering the shelter proper. A separate generator pod is an option. In addition to the main entrance door, Atlas includes an escape hatch that opens inward just below the ground surface for emergency egress.

Another company, Ultimate Bunker, specializes in square bunkers of various sizes and guarantees sufficient storage capacity for one year's worth of food and water per inhabitant (the smallest bunker fits two people). They also offer safe rooms and gun vaults as well as installation. Hardened Structures specializes in tornado/hurricane/fallout square steel shelters and will build them to suit

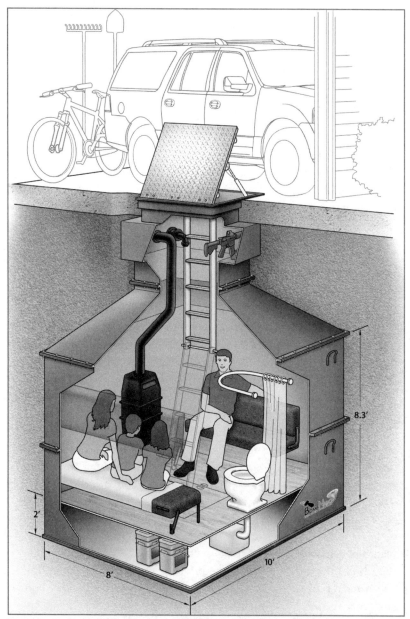

The Bombnado survival shelter is a no-nonsense bunker. *Photo: Atlas Survival Shelters*

your needs. They even have a missile silo reconditioning service with a private, above-ground runway/helicopter pad, fiber optics communications, and fully NBC-rated ventilation systems, along with five-star accommodations. Keep in mind that purchasing and installing an underground bunker can cost as much (or more) as the home above it.

SAFE ROOMS

In the movies, a safe room is usually portrayed as some elaborate hidden fortress where the heroine hides with her children from nefarious men with bad foreign accents intent on abduction or harm. If this scenario seems farfetched, that's because it is. In reality, a real safe room can provide shelter from other types of calamities, such as severe storms, tornadoes, or even earthquakes. It also represents a viable place for secure storage of firearms, valuables, and emergency supplies.

Of course, every home is different and accommodating a safe room where you live can involve some creative thinking and construction. VaultPro USA, however, has pioneered a scalable solution to this problem that provides far better security than just a large closet in your home with nothing between you and the elements other than some drywall.

The company's modular storm and tornado shelter/safe room is built to FEMA 320/361 and ICC-550 international standards for storm shelters. According to FEMA, this standard is designed to withstand winds of up to 250 miles per hour and offer the direct missile resistance of a 15-pound 2x4-inch board traveling at 100 mph. Note: this is a minimum, and VaultPro USA shelters claim to exceed this and provide other types of protection as well.

Each section is built using 1/4-inch thick reinforced steel and can be as small as a closet. Each section is bolted on using ½-inch Grade 8 bolts and Nylock nuts for superior strength, expanding the interior dimensions and adding rigidity as the flanges bolt together to make 1/2-inch steel support beams.

The front section includes the vault door, which comes with an 18-bolt locking mechanism and digital locks for fast access

VaultPro USA modular safe room/storm shelters are built to withstand winds of up to 250 mph and offer direct missile resistance against a 15-pound 2x4 board traveling at 100 mph. *Photo: VaultPro USA*

by any family member with the combination. From the inside, there is a simple release that anyone can use to exit, and the door can be designed to swing in or out, which is valuable if there is a concern with debris blocking an outward swinging door. The entire safe room/shelter can be ordered fire resistant with ceramic fireproofing rated to 2,300-deg. Fahrenheit. The vault door can be gasket-sealed to prevent gas or smoke inhalation and to add further fireproofing. Vault door sealing rated for NBC is also available. Emergency ventilation systems for interior occupants can be installed (recommended), and it is available with ballistic shielding as well.

The interior is fully customizable with lighting, electricity, and emergency backups in case of power outages. VaultPro offers complete custom carpeting, interior storage, and shelving options for occupant comfort and for the secure storage of firearms, emergency supplies, food, and water.

For anyone who may be uncomfortable in a safe room with only one way in or out, VaultPro USA manufactures custom escape hatches that can be added to any safe room. This can be especially important if the main access becomes blocked. These hatches will accommodate one person at a time and can be installed with top or bottom access via a ladder or on the sides of the safe room for horizontal egress. The hatches can be made to swing in or out and can be exit only or two way.

DIY SURVIVAL SHELTERS

It is impossible to prepare for every eventuality, and not everyone can afford to spend tens of thousands of dollars on a nuke-proof underground lair. We each do the best we can with what we have, and for many, that is simply stockpiling emergency supplies, food, and water in a basement or separate room. Basements work great because they can be fortified without much effort or cost in a storm shelter or safe room.

There are many ways to do this. In my own home, I took part of the basement that was unfinished and turned it into my own reinforced bunker. The walls were original framing and drywall, so I added half-inch thick plywood all around the interior. I also installed a combination lock steel door with reinforced frame. Inside this safe room, I have emergency food, water, and my gun safes, as well as a sizable stockpile of ammunition and other supplies.

Of course, everyone thinks of food and water first, in case you have to hunker down for an extended period, but everything you consume is going to come back sooner or later. You could simply go out into the woods and do like the bears, but what if it is not safe to go out because of weather, fallout, or marauders? Worst case scenario, you could just do your business in a plastic bag and then seal it, but there are better options. Major Surplus offers a simple Portable Folding Toilet (a toilet seat on a folding chair with a plastic bag underneath) and spare toilet bags. Their Deluxe S.I.P. Kit includes a bunch of survival items as well as a 5-gallon bucket with toilet seat and lid, plus bags and toilet paper. For the more genteel types, Sportsman's Guide sells the Reliance Flushable Loo

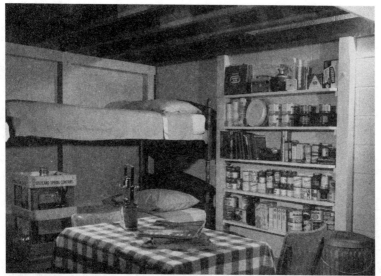
Basements can be turned into hardened survival shelters with proper planning and equipment.
Photo: Public Domain

400 Toilet. This is a self-contained unit, and you should get a least a few flushes before you have to empty it.

Most shelters, especially basement or in-home, are not air tight, so there will be some ventilation but not nearly enough. Under certain circumstances (such as radioactive fallout or chemical/biological agents), the government warns that you need to have plastic sheeting and duct tape on hand to seal all windows and vents. This will limit the entrance of contaminants but still allow you to breathe; note that plastic sheeting is not going to keep out airborne viruses. For the ultimate in clean breathable air, you need a military-grade air filtration system designed for an actual bomb shelter. These can be purchased and are typically of European or Israeli manufacture. They include full NBC filters as well as a hand crank to operate if the power goes out. The cheapest short term option is to buy a gas mask with proper filters. These are widely available (such as the popular Israeli civilian gas mask) but not comfortable for long-term use.

Small commercial or homemade solar panels can be used to provide heat to a chicken coop, recharge electronics, or power a fence or small gate.

"If high-protection-factor shelters or most other shelters that lack adequate forced ventilation were fully occupied for several days in warm or hot weather, they would become so hot and humid that the occupants would collapse from the heat if they were to remain inside," writes Cresson Kearny in Nuclear War Survival Skills. "It is important to understand that the heat and water vapor given off by the bodies of people in a crowded, long-occupied shelter could be deadly if fallout prevents leaving the shelter."

Kearny goes on to demonstrate not only how to construct very affordable expedient fallout and blast shelters, but also improvised, manually operated ventilation devices that keep the air moving and the inhabitants safe. Coincidentally, Kearny's book — which was originally published by the Oak Ridge National Laboratory (U.S. Dept. of Energy) and involved the most extensive research project ever conducted into how families can build their own nuclear fallout and blast shelters to survive a nuclear exchange — should be considered required reading for anyone concerned about survival and shelter building ... be that for nuclear war or any other contingency.

RENEWABLE ENERGY

An electrical outage, particularly one that lasts more than a few days, can have significant disruptive effects. Storms and other natural events, as well as actual physical attacks on the electrical grid from hacking or electromagnetic pulse, or EMP attack can cause power outages that can last weeks at a time. We are heavily dependent on access to electricity for basic functions of modern life. For some, being able to keep medicines refrigerated is a lifesaving necessity, as is keeping medical equipment working.

A small home generator is a sound investment, but these cannot take the strain of powering a full household, and they must be kept fueled. Generators are best suited for short-term needs for specific items that need to remain powered. More comprehensive propane-powered whole house generators are available and can be connected to a large outdoor propane tank, but such systems are expensive.

Lofty Energy makes it so you can have solar panels at a very low cost — a solar kit that you can assemble yourself. *Photo: Lofty Energy*

Renewable energy sources offer an alternative. Solar energy is clean, free, and you don't need to run a bunch of wires everywhere. Running your whole house from solar energy is not entirely feasible just yet though, even if you live where there is no tree cover and lots of sunshine. The only way solar energy becomes handy is if you use it to charge a battery bank, which in turn powers the things you need. But while the sun is free, solar panels are not.

A rooftop-mounted array of solar panels can be installed and connected to a bank of batteries. With sufficient sunlight, this can supplement your electrical needs, especially in a survival situation. Small, portable solar panels are a great way to charge personal electronics, such as cell phones, laptops, and batteries. Be aware that the larger the solar panel, the more efficient it will be, so the small portable panels will take up to 8 to 10 hours of direct sunlight to fully charge one cell phone.

Lofty Energy makes solar panels available at a very low cost, because what they sell you is a solar kit that you can assemble yourself. The kits are available in 10- and 30-watt sizes and include almost everything you need, as well as very clear DVD instructions.

You will need a voltmeter and soldering iron, as well as a screwdriver, caulk, and two Plexiglas panels. I started off with the 10-watt kit, which includes 40 solar cells, tabbing wire, bus wire, flux pen and solder, a junction box, spacers, and red/black wires. I had no experience making something like this before (and frankly, little understanding of electricity or soldering) so I went slowly and took my time. The project was completed in about 4 hours.

What I noted was that the solar cells are extremely fragile, and I broke a few during construction. I ended up only using 22 of the cells because that was all I could fit on the Plexiglas panels. Soldering took a few tries to figure out, too, but it was easy after that. It is extremely important to keep track of the negative and positive sides of the cells and to connect them properly, negative to positive all the way around to make a circuit. Finally, be sure to use the voltmeter to check that the power is flowing at each step along the way.

These types of solar cells are ideal for sheds or cabins where there is no electricity, and can charge a car or smaller battery in a matter of a few days. If you want to power an item via a wall plug, you can hook up a converter to the battery. They can also be used to power an automatic gate or provide heat for a chicken coop.

Another option is wind power. There are many companies selling and installing small- to medium-sized wind turbines. This is not an inexpensive proposition however, and really only worthwhile if you live someplace that gets plenty of wind. The latest versions are very efficient at producing electricity and can charge up a battery bank. A blended system might be the best, since you cannot guarantee sunlight or wind.

EVACUATION AND BUG-OUT VEHICLES

*I*n some situations, evacuation is necessary and may even be required by local, state or federal authorities. You may need to evacuate due to flooding or incoming severe weather events. These will be the most common causes, but evacuation can be necessary due to more serious or severely dangerous conditions, such as a nuclear reactor meltdown. When evacuating, it is vitally important to not panic, and the best way to do that is to have a plan. Of course, that plan will need to take into account your survival guns.

SURVIVAL GUNS AND EVACUATION

If you must evacuate you obviously cannot bring all of your survival preparedness gear with you. As stated, you need to have a plan and a bug-out bag for each family member ready to go with emergency supplies, food and water. But what about guns? In a home bunker, you can store sufficient guns and ammunition for a variety of contingencies, from training to self-defense to hunting. With space at

PROS: Easier to get help and coordinate with others while escaping a dangerous area.

CONS: Limited to what you can carry on your person or in your vehicle.

VEHICLE TYPES: Any 4-wheel drive is good, heavy traffic may require off road motorcycle.

AUTHOR'S TOP PICK: Military Surplus M35 6x6 truck.
MSRP: $20,000 (fully restored)

WHAT TO BRING: As much food, water and ammunition as you can carry, extra gas cans, blankets, extra clothes, important documents, survival guns.

a premium in your vehicle what should you choose to bring with you? Ideally, you should bring at least one rifle and one handgun. But if you can only bring one gun I pick the AR-15 carbine in 5.56mm or at the very minimum an AR pistol.

The AR is accurate, powerful, common, and it uses readily interchangeable parts. Plus, it's lightweight with low recoil, easy to use, and fires a very easy to find cartridge. It also breaks down easily into two parts that can be very quickly assembled and brought into use. This makes transportation and concealment much easier. If you must evacuate to a shelter or some other facility you don't want to advertise that you are armed. Showing up with a big rifle case is a clear giveaway. Fortunately, there are many off-the-shelf and DIY concealment bags.

Everyone involved in an evacuation will be expected to bring along clothes, medicines, important documents, etc. An AR carbine or an AR pistol can be easily included in a duffle bag of clothes or a side pocket to a larger duffle bag. Proper padding will protect the firearm and mask its presence.

In addition, no matter how much ammunition you may have stockpiled you will not be able to bring it all with you. Ammunition is heavy and if you are evacuating you will need to travel light. As my go-to trunk gun I use an AR pistol with an arm brace for more accurate shooting. I keep this in a Blackhawk diversion bag that looks like a tennis racket case. I also keep a sling and two full 30-round magazines. I feel for everyday emergencies this is enough. However, if I were evacuating my home, possibly for an extended period, I would want more.

Depending on how much you can carry and if you are using your own vehicle, you want a minimum of seven full 30-round magazines, or 210 rounds. To some people this may seem like a lot, but it really isn't and anyone who visits the range regularly can attest that you can go through this much ammo in an hour or less without really trying. I stress that this is a minimum per person and if you can carry more, then do so. Have all family members equipped with guns that use the same ammunition and magazines.

GUNS AND CHECKPOINTS

In an emergency evacuation there may be police patrols, checkpoints, and even home searches. This occurred during the manhunt for the Boston Bombers in 2013. Police ordered people to evacuate their homes in some areas, others to stay in their homes and, in some cases, searched homes and property door to door without warrants.

During Hurricane Katrina in 2005 an evacuation was ordered but many stayed behind. Some people stayed behind with malicious intent while most others simply did not have the means or desire to flee. In the immediate aftermath, law enforcement agencies from around the country arrived to offer assistance. But this only created a heightened sense of confusion as the order to disarm residents (in the wake of looting and violence) was unevenly enforced. Many residents that remained had armed themselves against looters and criminals and were now faced with the prospect of being disarmed by the police and then abandoned.

Emergency shelters will not allow you to bring your firearm and you may be searched before entering. Random police checkpoints may also be searching for firearms or ask about firearm possession. In the case of a fugitive situation your vehicle may be subject to searches as well, all warrantless. A state of emergency may be declared and the police may not need a warrant (or at least claim they don't).

While I'm not an attorney and can't offer legal advice, anyone who can read the Bill of Rights to the U.S. Constitution ought to know that you have the right to not consent to a search. You can simply state, "I do not consent to being searched." You are also under no obligation to answer any questions. However, the side of the road or an emergency shelter during an evacuation is not the time nor place for a discussion of constitutional law with a police officer. You should always comply with any commands or instructions given to you by law enforcement. If your rights have been violated you can address that issue later. If your guns are confiscated ask for a receipt that includes all the relevant information so that you can try to reclaim your property after the emergency has passed.

If you have no choice but to go to an emergency shelter, it may be the safest place for you and your family. Such shelters will have emergency supplies and medical personnel to assist you. Ideally, you will have already established your own evacuation zone where you can go and possibly store extra supplies. This may include a hunting cabin or second home or the home of a friend or relative outside the evacuation zone — the proverbial bug-out location.

BUG-OUT VEHICLES

Determine in advance where you will go and what resources will be available to you there. Note that your ability to bring along your emergency supplies will be limited. Plan a separate set of emergency supplies specifically for the purpose of evacuation. Transportation is key here, and if you are evacuating an area, it is likely that you will not be alone. Roadways may become clogged up very quickly, so plan alternate routes to your destination in advance. Do not rely on GPS or other electronics, as these systems may be overwhelmed or down.

Some people advocate having an off-road motorbike for each family member, which will allow you to weave in between traffic or take pedestrian paths or trails. This has its obvious drawbacks, however. It is true that small motorbikes are very fuel efficient, but your ability to carry emergency supplies is limited to one backpack per person. Each person must be comfortable riding

In 1950, the U.S. military introduced the 2.5-ton M35 "Deuce-and-a-Half" and it was produced in some form or another until 1999 when it was phased out and replaced. *Photo: Alf van Beem*

their bike for long periods of time and skilled enough to maneuver through traffic or over rough terrain.

For most people, a four-wheel drive vehicle will be the best option. Most 4x4s can effectively handle some amount of off road travel, depending on the terrain. Many people invest heavily in 4x4 Jeeps and trucks with winches in the front, lift kits, roll cages, extra-large off-road tires, etc. These vehicles are all well-suited, but there is a larger, meaner, tougher, and more affordable alternative.

Instead of a 4x4, how about a 6x6? Back in 1950, the U.S. military introduced the 2.5-ton M35 "Deuce-and-a-Half," and it was produced in some form or another until 1999 when it was phased out and replaced. The end result is that a whole lot of perfectly serviceable vehicles flooded the military surplus market. During their time in service, these trucks were the American soldier's school bus, food truck, weapons platform, and delivery van all rolled into one. My own experience with riding in the back of these is that they are big, burly, tough-as-nails, and not built for comfort.

The weight of the M35 truck (about 13,000 lbs. for a basic one) means that it doesn't require a commercial license to operate one, and they are street legal. Parking may be an issue, as these trucks are over 9-feet tall, 8-feet wide, and 23-feet long. Also, fuel efficiency is not the M35's strong suit, with an average of 8 mpg in the city and 11 mpg on the highway. You do get a 50-gallon fuel tank for an average range of almost 500 miles, though.

The M35 isn't built for speed either, topping out at 56 mph. The engine is built for power and low-end torque, with a standard turbo-charged six-cylinder, 478 cubic-inch engine producing 134 HP and 330 pounds of torque. The best part, however, especially for survival situations, is the multi-fuel capability. The M35's diesel engine will run on just about anything you put in it. The next gas crisis won't be a problem when you can fill your tank with kerosene, diesel, vegetable oil, used motor oil, heating oil, hemp oil, transmission fluid, hydraulic fluid, or high proof alcohol. The engine will run on regular unleaded gasoline, but it is recommended that you add one quart of motor oil per 15 gallons of gas.

Most M35s come with manual transmissions, especially the older models. Of course, nowadays less than 10 percent of Americans know how to drive manual. Automatic transmission models are available, and the older ones can be converted to automatic. Upgrades can include heaters, air conditioning, and power steering for the occupants in the cab. Deep water is no problem, as the M35 was purpose-built for fording. There is even an old newsreel showing an M35 driving completely submerged underwater. You will need a snorkel kit for this maneuver, and many trucks come with this already installed or it can be added. Another common feature is a 10,000-lbs. electric winch at the front. This can be easily added to trucks that don't already have them, and it allows the operator to get himself or others out of almost any jam.

Maintenance is very easy, as they were designed by the military to be almost idiot proof and easy to maintain in the field — another advantage when supply lines may be unavailable. Spare parts are readily available through surplus vendors, and many standard commercial truck parts can be used or recovered from salvage yards.

Besides its impressive off-road and underwater capabilities, the M35's other great benefit comes in its cargo capacity of over 5,000 lbs. That is a lot of supplies, or up to 20 fully equipped troops.
Photo: Alf van Beem

SPECIFICATIONS
MILITARY M35 2½-TON CARGO TRUCK

WEIGHT: 13,000 to 16,000 lbs. depending on options
LENGTH: 23 ft.
WIDTH: 8 ft.
HEIGHT: 9.3 ft.
CREW: 3 in the cab, 20 in the back
ENGINE: LDT 465 6-cylinder Turbo (134 HP)
OPERATIONAL RANGE: 400–500 miles
SPEED: 56 mph
LOAD: 5,000 lbs.
FUEL: multi-fuel diesel
GAS TANK: 50 gallons

Besides its impressive off-road and underwater capabilities, the M35's other great benefit comes with its cargo capacity of over 5,000 lbs. That is a lot of supplies or up to 20 fully equipped troops. The front cab has space for a driver and two passengers, but the rear cargo area, which measures 8 by 12 feet, can be configured in a number of ways as a flat bed or as a covered troop carrier. The rear hatch drops down for easy loading and unloading.

Over the years, many old M35s were purchased by local governments and repurposed as fire trucks, snow plows, salt spreaders, tow trucks, and police evacuation or emergency supply vehicles. Private citizens have taken a keen interest in these vehicles, and why shouldn't they? On the East Coast and Gulf States you have to worry about hurricanes. Up north, you have blizzards that can leave you stranded and without power for weeks. Down south and out west, you have the threat of tornadoes. On the Pacific coast, you have tsunamis, earthquakes, and volcanoes to contend with. That doesn't even include floods or mudslides.

You can buy an M35 right off the government surplus lot or from a reseller who may have serviced and restored the vehicle. The latter option may give the less mechanically inclined more restful sleep, plus the options are nearly limitless for customization. The most popular alteration is "bobbing" the M35 to make it smaller and more maneuverable. This involves removing an axle and installing a shorter bed, making the truck a really big 4x4 pickup.

Besides ease of driving and parking, the shorter bobbed M35 gets better fuel economy, raising it from 8-11 mpg to 12-13 mpg (which pound for pound is more efficient than a Toyota Prius). This extends your operational range from 400-550 miles to 600-650 miles and increases the maximum highway speed to 75 mph. The bobbed trucks do have smaller cargo capacity, however, but if you live in an HOA that prohibits commercial or oversized vehicles, you can get this one past them.

EQUIP YOUR TRUCK

What good is it to have 5,000 lbs. of storage capacity on your vehicle if you have nothing to store? A convenient one stop shop for all of your post-Rapture needs is Major Surplus and Survival, and they are well stocked with disaster preparedness gear, both new and military surplus.

My own personal recommendations include the following:

The 7-Day Supply for Family of Four. This kit holds a ton of emergency survival supplies, and it would cost you a lot more to put all of this together yourself. If your family is stuck and needs to shelter in place with no power, water, food, or shelter, this kit has you covered. It includes a cooking kit and stove with fuel, sufficient food (not gourmet meals, but not starvation rations either), water purification tablets, and water containers (you will need to supply your own water). Finally, you get space blankets and tents, as well as candles and first aid kits.

The Military Battalion First Aid Kit. If things really go sideways, the worst thing that can happen to you is getting injured, as there may be no medical care available in the short term. This kit has enough supplies to start a small hospital (enough to treat 50 people), and provided you have the training, it can be a lifesaver. The contents are too many to list, but you get just about every bandage, wipe, cream, glove, dressing, and (over the counter) pill known to man, as well as shears, scalpels, and sutures.

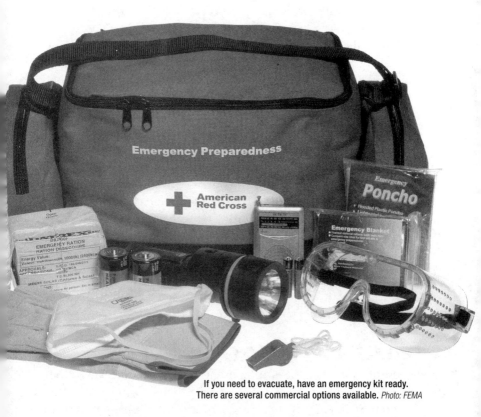

If you need to evacuate, have an emergency kit ready.
There are several commercial options available. *Photo: FEMA*

The Mil-Spec Adventure Gear Life Micro Solar Charger. The last thing you want is for your mobile and emergency devices to have a dead battery. This solar unit lets you plug in anything with a USB cable, including your cell phone and GPS. Depending on how much sun it gets, it can give you up to eight hours of run time on your devices with a day of charging.

The KA500 Voyager Dynamo Radio with hand crank and solar power. If you get stuck in some basement or in the woods with nothing to do but stare at each other, that is going to get old quick. This radio has AM/FM, shortwave, and weather alert channels, and it has a rechargeable battery that can be kept going with the included hand crank or solar panel. The radio can also be used to charge up USB devices like your cell phone or GPS and includes a flashlight. Keep up with emergency alerts, evacuation instructions, weather, and news.

The Official Swiss Army ABC System with gas mask, the Bio-Chem Personal Protection Suit, and potassium iodide capsules. Since the fall of the Soviet Union, there has been a fire sale on nukes, nuke tech, and radioactive components. Depending upon which media report you believe, it seems the North Koreans are at least a couple of years away from hitting the mainland U.S. with a nuke, but a dirty bomb could occur. Protect yourself from radiation, nerve gas, viruses, bacteria, and disease-carrying mosquitoes with this full protective gear. The Swiss Army gas mask is current issue and includes a new NATO standard filter, poncho, and gloves. The Bio-Chem Protective Suit is made from Tyvek and includes hood and booties for head to toe coverage. The iodide capsules come 90 to a box and are designed to protect your thyroid gland from damage due to radiation poisoning caused by iodine-131, a highly radioactive but thankfully short-lived product of nuclear fission.

BUG-OUT BAG

Most of us spend a lot of time in our cars (if not in them at least near them), especially when away from home. Your vehicle can be your lifeline in case of emergency and makes it easy for you to

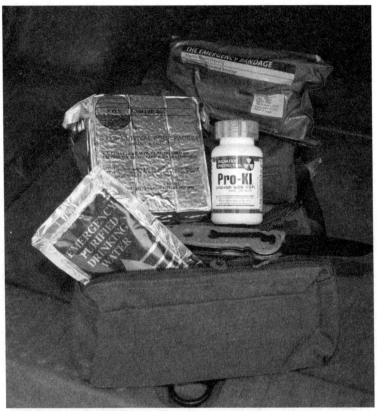

You can make your own vehicle survival kit with a minimum of three days food and water, first aid supplies and a space blanket.

carry the things you need to survive a sudden disaster. Frankly, there is no excuse not to have a small bag with a few necessary items stored in your trunk at all times.

Whether you call it a Go Bag, Bug-Out Bag, or a Three-Day Bag, there are several items you should consider having when things go badly. Three days' worth of emergency supplies is a good starting point, since it provides sufficient time for help to arrive or for you to evacuate to a safer area in most cases.

You may not find a kit that comes with everything you need, so building your own may be a necessity, but lots of companies sell basic starter kits that can serve as a foundation. First, make sure you have water and the ability to purify more. You should have emergency food rations and a way to stay warm and dry (I keep rain gear and several "space" blankets).

A good first aid kit is a must, including any medications you take and Quick-Clot in case of serious injury. In addition, include potassium iodide tablets, which block the absorption of certain types of radiation, and a surgical face mask and surgical gloves. Not essential but good to have items include a quality folding knife, emergency radio (one that is solar or hand-powered), a light source, and some cash.

COMMUNICATIONS

We all have busy schedules, and in a survival situation, it is unlikely that all of your loved ones will find themselves in one place. You will need to have a plan of action in advance and set a primary and hopefully secondary rally point where everyone knows to meet. In a real emergency, traditional landline and cell phone systems may be overwhelmed or disabled.

Modern walkie-talkies are nothing like I remember. The latest models are easy to transport, small, lightweight, rechargeable, inexpensive, and can have a range of as far as 50 miles with 22 different channels. The range estimates provided are under ideal conditions, meaning over flat open terrain and not through buildings, mountains, woods, etc. You can buy a radio for each family member and set a primary and backup channel for communications.

If the cellular system is still operational, your cell phone will be invaluable if you can keep it charged. The Scorpion II Radio from Major Surplus not only keeps you in touch with AM/FM news and emergency weather bands, but also has a solar panel and hand crank charger, so it and your cell phone can be recharged. Many handheld walkie-talkies also have NOAA weather alerts.

Other communications systems are much more direct and only work with a much shorter distance. For direct line of sight, use simple coded communications with a flashlight or a small laser that works even in daylight conditions. You can also use old military field telephones that are directly wired. The Sportsman's Guide offers US Vietnam-era field phones and cable, as well as Swedish surplus military hand crank field telephones with codes. You don't need to use military cables, either. Standard telephone cables and even speaker cables work just as well and can be used to connect phones that may be a mile apart.

Long-range walkie talkies can be purchased for each family member with pre-set channels. In addition, an emergency rechargeable radio will keep you aware of any emergency alerts.

THE DAY THE CELL PHONES DIED

WHEN ALL ELSE FAILS, TWO-WAY RADIO STILL GETS THROUGH

BY COREY GRAFF

On the afternoon of Sunday, May 22, 2011, the residents of Joplin, Missouri, learned to distrust their cell phones. On that day, the hellish winds from a maximum-strength EF5 tornado reached down from the heavens like a giant vacuum cleaner of death and touched down just east of the Kansas state line, blazing a 22-mile path of death and destruction through the town — sucking, ripping and tearing the city's structures into mangled toothpicks and violently ending the lives of 158 people.

The monster mile-wide twister caused catastrophic damage in the neighborhood of $2.2 billion. And it knocked out cell phone communications for days. When the storm passed, 1,300 people were missing. The Show Me State learned a tough lesson that day: Don't rely on cell phones. While they're a great modern convenience, they're the first to fail when high winds crush cell phone towers like pop cans.

Two-way radio was the only form of communication for many following the 2011 Joplin, Missouri tornado that flattened parts of the city, disabling cell phone networks.

Cell phone networks have been tested and retested and they routinely fail when consumption demands exceed normal levels. Industry representatives claim providers are installing additional towers and built-in network redundancy to handle the volume spike during crises. But Telecomm Analyst Gerard Hallaren paints a different picture. In the CBS News story, he revealed that networks are only designed to handle 20 to 40 percent of traffic, which includes phone calls and data modes such as wireless Internet and text messaging.

In the end, it may be business realities — as opposed to technical or infrastructure limitations — keeping cell networks lean and mean, susceptible to failure during extraordinary events. "It's just economic insanity for any carrier to try to solve the congestion problem," Hallaren said. "It's cost-prohibitive to build a network that could serve 330 million at the same time. A service like that would cost hundreds of dollars a month, and people are not willing to pay that much for cell phone service."

WHY TWO-WAY RADIO WORKS WHEN CELL PHONES FAIL

The advantage of radio lies in its ability to send and receive a signal, with no help from others. Two-way radio has come a long way since the early days of Guglielmo Marconi's historic transatlantic wireless transmission that must have struck people in those days as nothing short of magic. Today, two-way radio transceivers (transmitter-receivers) are as technologically advanced as any other "tech gadget" — with amateur or ham radio leading the march toward integration with the Internet, GPS and exotic new data modes. But at its most basic level, radio is still radio. Like the basic Marconi set that transmitted the distress signal from the sinking Titanic, it works today for the same reason it worked then: It relies on no one else to get a message out. Thus it remains the best, most reliable form of communication for emergencies. Wireless two-way allows you to be a locally operated independent radio station. You are the network, in essence, and can take advantage of built-

Electrical engineer/inventor Guglielmo Marconi operating apparatus similar to this, which he used to transmit the first documented wireless radio signal across the Atlantic. Circa 1901.

The author believes ham radio is the most versatile and effective form of two-way radio for emergency communications. Here, he operates his home-based U.S. Amateur Radio Station, W9NSE. The station operates on all bands and modes, from local and state coverage on VHF/UHF FM, to national and international on HF shortwave using the SSB and AM modes.

in network redundancy, communicating with other independent operators. If one operator loses capability, the network keeps chugging along. There is no middleman. And, other than initial equipment purchase and license fees, there is no cost, either.

Not so with commercial telecommunications systems. By their very nature, commercial communications are centralized. That means that all calls go through your service provider's network. If that system gets overloaded, which it will in the event of a widespread disaster, you're out. These systems are designed to make private companies money, not to ensure you can communicate during times of uncertainty. So fickle are they that any event that gets people talking can spark telecomm gridlock. Equally troublesome is the weather: An ice storm or a wind event such as tornado or straight-line winds can twist lines into high voltage pretzels — rendering your smartphone into nothing more than a fancy-looking paperweight.

A LOOK AT THE RADIO SERVICES:
THE AMATEUR "HAM RADIO" SERVICE

Arguably the most versatile of the radio services, amateur radio allows you to operate on all modes and bands, and push out a full legal limit of 1500 watts. You'll need an amateur radio license to transmit. There are license classes — Technician, General and Extra Class — and each require a few weeks of study and become progressively more difficult to ace. But with each new license upgrade, you attain access to more bands and modes.

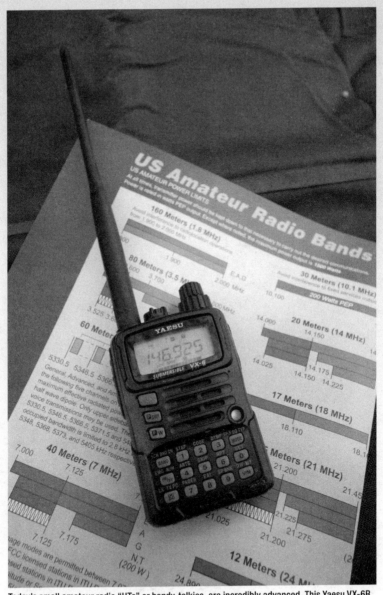

Today's small amateur radio "HTs" or handy-talkies, are incredibly advanced. This Yaesu VX-6R is a dual-band transceiver that operates in the 70cm (440 mhz) and 2m (144 mhz) bands FM. It also receives international shortwave AM transmissions and NOAA weather radio. While typically used for local emergency communications and weather spotting, it can access Internet-linked repeaters for International coverage.

The Federal Communications Commission (FCC) administers licenses, while testing is handled by certified Volunteer Examiners (VEs) through local ham radio clubs. Study manuals for each license class are available through the American Radio Relay League (www.arrl.org).

The benefits of ham radio for emergency communications include access to other local, state, national and international radio operators who are capable of staying on the air even during power outages and failures of the grid. You can operate FM, AM or Single Sideband (SSB) modes using voice, CW (Morse code) and data modes from the high frequency (shortwave) bands through the ultra-high frequency (UHF) spectrum for crystal clear local and statewide FM communications. You can find out what's happening. And you can get a signal out to get help.

PERSONAL RADIO SERVICES — CITIZENS BAND (CB)

You don't have to be a wayfaring trucker careening down the open road to realize the benefits of Citizens Band or CB radio. While described by some as a "wasteland" — a reputation gained by rampant on-air vulgarity in some parts of the country — CB radio operates in the 11-meter band (26.965 – 27.405 MHz spectrum range) on 40 designated channels, and is quite useful for emergency use. Radios can receive and transmit in FM, AM or SSB modes but are limited to 4 watts (AM) or 12 watts (SSB). Unlike some of the other radio services, Citizens Band no longer requires a license, though there are rules you need to follow. Amplifiers to boost output power are prohibited and you must observe height restrictions on antennas. You are also required to assume a "handle," though it's a safe bet that "Rubber Duck" has already been taken.

GENERAL MOBILE RADIO SERVICE (GMRS)

The General Mobile Radio Service (GMRS) requires one adult, who is the head of the household, to obtain an FCC license. The license covers your immediate family, and gives you access to local- or intermediate-range communications between family members. Some handheld GMRS radios claim up to a 36-mile range, but most units are handheld "walkie-talkie" style and are limited to 5 watts, making them much shorter distance options. While the actual power limit is 50 watts for this service, there is a loosely-scattered network of GMRS repeaters around the country (a repeater is a high-powered station that receives

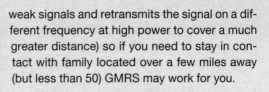

weak signals and retransmits the signal on a different frequency at high power to cover a much greater distance) so if you need to stay in contact with family located over a few miles away (but less than 50) GMRS may work for you.

FAMILY RADIO SERVICE (FRS)

Similar to the GMRS, the Family Radio Service, or FRS, is intended to keep family members in contact with one another, as its namesake implies. You do not need a license to operate a radio in this service. However, FRS is considered a close-range proposition, due to the fact that radios are limited to 1/2 watt. In practical terms, FRS radio is a one-mile or less choice. One thing to note: Many FRS radios have GMRS capability, so be sure not to operate the radio outside of the FRS limits unless you have the GMRS license. That being said, one principle of preparedness is using gear that covers more than one use. Thus, one of the handiest units I've seen in this category is the Garmin Rino — a GMRS/FRS radio with full Garmin GPS capability. Not only do you get two radio services covered with one transceiver, but you can find your way to safety (assuming the satellites are working).

LOW POWER (LPRS) AND MULTI-USE RADIO SERVICES (MURS)

Two final, less popular options are the Low Power Radio Service (LPRS) and Multi-Use Radio Service (MURS). The former uses one-way radio to transmit voice or data information to disabled persons. The latter, MURS, is a two-way service with five allocated channels in the VHF band. Radios used for this service are limited to 2 watts; a license is not required.

Another advantage of amateur radio is the option to run vintage equipment. These World War II-era radios use tubes, which allows them to keep working after an electromagnetic pulse (EMP) attack, unlike solid-state electronics.

CONCLUSION

There's only one thing you can absolutely count on when it comes to your cell phone: It will fail — probably when you need it the most. However, long-range communication is still possible if you plan now to incorporate two-way radio into your family preparedness plan. Sometimes, your ability to get a signal out is your only lifeline to outside help. Don't entrust your family's safety to a telecomm company's flimsy cell phone network. Instead, get on the air now, while you still can — and stay on the air, when all else fails.

Corey Graff is a Gun Digest Media editor and operates the U.S. Amateur Radio Station W9NSE, a two-generation station formerly owned by his father, Clarence, on the air since 1939.

SELF-DEFENSE INSIDE & OUTSIDE THE HOME

*I*n preparing to fortify your home or for self-defense, simply owning a firearm is insufficient. Even if you are experienced in the use of your survival gun, that still does not constitute being truly prepared. If you are serious about your well-being and that of your family, you need to get training. I have been fortunate to attend many different training schools and learned many high-quality techniques from each of them. It's an investment in yourself as the operator of the gun — an investment that may be the most important of all. Here's a look at modern firearms training and why you need it.

Rob Pincus developed his Combat Focus Shooting program, which is geared toward very quickly engaging close targets using your natural pointing instincts.

COMBAT FOCUS SHOOTING

There has long been a debate among defensive shooters between sighted fire and unsighted fire, or "point shooting." In general, shooters engaged in a defensive situation are taught to aim for high center mass hits, and for very good reason. First, the human torso presents the largest target, and second, this is where all the good stuff is kept: heart, lungs, major blood vessels, and assorted organs.

The key word here is aiming: focusing on the front sight, placing it on the target, and mastering trigger control to keep the front sight on the target during the trigger squeeze. On a range in a controlled environment, or even during the stress of competition with time limits, such sighted fire can take time to master. But imagine having to make a shot count in low light or while someone is advancing toward you armed or even firing at you.

Here is where the advocates of point shooting, or intuitive shooting, advance their best arguments. This style of shooting takes into account the natural tendency of people under stress to focus on the threat and lose fine motor skills. It is geared toward very quickly engaging close targets using your natural pointing instincts. It is not dissimilar from the skills that shotgun shooters employ for hitting fast-moving clay birds.

Historically, the two most famous advocates of this technique were William Fairbairn and Rex Applegate. Fairbairn's experience came from decades as a police trainer in China and later as a British Secret Service operative during World War II, specializing in close combat techniques. Applegate was also a WWII veteran and developed his close combat experience with the Office of Strategic Services (OSS), the forerunner to today's CIA.

Of course, the greater the distance to the target or the smaller the target, the more precision starts to matter and point shooting shows it weakness. In those cases, sighted fire is far preferable, even if it takes longer. This also applies when the target is much smaller, say aiming for a head shot or at a target that's only partially exposed.

This was the reality that expert firearms instructor Rob Pincus addressed when he founded the I.C.E. Firearm Training Services and developed his Combat Focus Shooting program. Pincus is a former United States Army Reserve and veteran law enforcement officer, currently serving as a training officer with the San Miguel County Sheriff's Office.

I attended an 8-hour Fundamentals of Combat Focus Shooting course taught by Evan Carson, President and Chief Instructor of Innovative Defensive Solutions, a Manassas, Virginia-based firearms training company. There is an introductory 4-hour course and a more comprehensive 16-hour course offered as well. If you attend this class, come prepared to shoot because this is not a classroom course, but rather is all range time. Students for the one-day class are expected to come prepared with gun, holster, backup magazines, and 1,000 rounds of ammunition.

Combat Focus Shooting primarily emphasizes developing intuitive shooting skills, not just marksmanship. As the instructors explained, accuracy is yes or no; either you hit the target or you

Combat Focus Shooting primarily emphasizes developing intuitive shooting skills, not just marksmanship. As the instructors explained, accuracy is yes or no, either you hit the target or you don't.

don't. Any hit in the center mass "critical area" counts; nice tight groups do not make hits better. In fact, we were reprimanded if all the shots were on target, a sign that the shooter should speed up and challenge themselves more in order to improve. Conversely, if you did not achieve hits consistently, you were told to slow down.

This is called achieving combat accuracy and self-accommodates for the skill level of the shooter. While we were told to focus on the target and not use our sights, the instructors emphasized that this is not simply a point-shooting class. The key to achieving hits lies in using and building proper technique while balancing speed and precision. A low, aggressive stance with proper grip is essential and is drilled into the students, as is a proper strong-side draw. We were drilled on the difference between unsighted fire for center mass hits at close distance and slower sighted fire for precision shots and longer distances. They key is mastering when to use the different types of fire and judging proper distances.

The training is based on an analysis of real defensive shootings, and despite the name, this is not an offensive shooting class but rather is designed to quickly deal with a threat in the most efficient manner possible. Each step of the class was explained and drilled before moving to the next step. As each step was taught, it was integrated into our shooting response so that every previous step was repeated each time.

In the real world, you don't just draw and start shooting. Threats appear without warning, and your normal initial reaction will be surprise or shock. Students were asked to simulate surprise before moving to the next step of identifying the source of the surprise and determining the presence and location of a threat before deciding to draw. Lateral motion was a key element of the course, with movement introduced before the decision to draw and fire takes place. Firing itself is static; speed reloads occur while moving and remaining target focused. "For new shooters, CFS advocates that magazines carried on the belt be staged with the bullets pointed away from the center-line, as this method requires less movement of the hands than the traditional bullets forward orientation," said Carson.

Volume of fire is another skill that is emphasized, and students were taught to get out of the double- or triple-tap mindset. Instead of always taking the same number of shots on target after each draw, we were required to mix up the number of shots. In a real-world situation, the number of shots necessary to end a threat will naturally vary, and it will not do to become stuck on firing a specific number of rounds. One-handed shooting was another aspect taught for cases that could involve injury or when a two-handed grip isn't possible.

HOME DEFENSE TRAINING

Another course taught by Innovative Defensive Solutions LLC focuses on the use of the handgun in a home defense situation. The course instructors, Evan Carson and Ben Turner, are experts in firearms handling and personal defense. The most important message to their students is: consider your own family and home

The Introduction to Home Defense Handguns Course by Innovative Defensive Solutions LLC is designed to accommodate a range of student experience levels.

situation, and develop a plan in advance for how you would respond in a home invasion scenario. Although the situation will dictate the specifics, having an idea of where to go and what to do is your best defense when you've been jolted from a deep sleep into a panic in the dark of night.

The course maps out a defensive strategy that avoids confrontation with a home invader if at all possible for the safety of yourself and your family. Consider the layout of your house and furniture when deciding where to barricade yourself in an emergency. A pre-arranged safe retreat spot with a cell phone and a gun waiting for you will prevent you from suddenly finding yourself without these necessities in a surprise invasion. Think ahead about how you can gather any children or pets in your home to keep them safe. When you call 911, describe yourself and your position in the house and avoid walking around where you might be mistaken for a burglar by the police or another family member. The course emphasizes survival and safety rather than confrontation and other risky moves.

The Introduction to Home Defense Handguns Course is designed to accommodate a range of student experience levels. Beginners, although they should know the fundamentals of gun handling before attending the class, need very little shooting experience to start developing their home defense strategies. After all, home defense is the most common reason behind most first gun purchases. More experienced shooters will appreciate the realistic training scenarios offered throughout the day. The course involves drills in firing single shots and small groups at a range of 10-12 feet. This is the distance most likely to be encountered in home defense. While longer range and more "tactical-type" training can be useful, it is still important for experienced shooters to practice the more realistic scenarios.

The first drills focused on intuitive shooting, utilizing kinesthetic alignment and threat focus (as opposed to the carefully aimed shots we normally make at the range). The former are far more relevant in short range, high-anxiety defensive situations. The class then practiced efficient weapon reloading drills, a valuable skill for any shooter.

The final drill was a one-on-one simulated break-in and covered all of the five fundamentals of home defense — Evade, Arm, Barricade, Contact and Counter. We covered contacting the police and what to tell the dispatcher, which included: what is happening, your home address and where you are in the house, if you are armed and if the intruder is armed, a description of yourself and family members and of the intruder. The instructors caught each student by surprise and added some of the urgency and alarm that would be felt during a real burglary. The target was announced suddenly, and students had to react quickly. We also practiced calling 911 and handling both a phone and gun at the same time. This drill can produce some surprising reactions, even from very experienced shooters. The post-scenario analysis was very enlightening, allowing students to discuss and evaluate with the instructors their individual execution of skills.

Regarding storage, Turner stated the preferred method is keeping your home defense gun loaded but with no round in the chamber. That way, the gun is ready to use but won't go off if you negligently grab the trigger when you reach for it. This also forces you to bring the gun into the "high compressed ready" position to rack the slide before moving to your barricade location. If you prefer to store your gun unloaded, have a full magazine close at hand and practice reloading while not looking at the gun and continuing to take in and process information. The course covers various storage options and strategies; your preference will be greatly dependent on the number and ages of the people in your home. The end goal is that the gun be readily available to you yet secured from unauthorized individuals.

The class discussed the strategic location of defensive handguns in the home, which goes hand in hand with choosing a preferred spot to barricade. While the instructors touched on the legal ramifications of defensive shooting, it was neither a comprehensive discussion nor legal advice of any sort. The instructors were clear that anyone concerned with personal protection either in the home or out should consult with an attorney licensed to practice and familiar with self-defense law in their home state, as these laws vary greatly from state to state. They did, however, give each student a handbook from the Armed Citizens' Legal Defense Network for further information and referrals.

REALITY-BASED TRAINING

Rob Pincus is a busy man and is constantly looking to improve the training he offers and to challenge his instructors. In an effort to make his defensive training as realistic as possible (while maintaining an absolute level of safety), he designed a reality-based training program offered though his I.C.E Training Company.

Essentially, the course combines safety gear and non-lethal marking ammunition with reality-based scenarios such as home invasions and carjackings to test student training and reactions. I.C.E. partnered with Practical Defense Training Technologies (PDT), a reality-based training solutions and protective equipment manufacturer, to provide the required gear in one complete package to instructors who successfully complete the course.

Of course, this type of hands-on, force-on-force scenario-based

Rob Pincus designed a training program offered though his I.C.E. Training Company, which combines safety gear and non-lethal marking ammunition with reality-based scenarios.

training requires very specific safety guidelines to increase the realism and ensure that neither students nor instructors are injured. Scenarios need to be strictly scripted with a lot of "what if" reactions, and only instructors should run the drills. Students should never participate as part of the scenario, i.e.: pretending to be an assailant, etc.

Safety equipment is an important consideration, and ATK/Federal has developed special non-lethal training ammunition branded Force-on-Force that is used in the scenarios. As was demonstrated by a company representative, the ammunition is available in .223 or 9mm and has an accurate range of about 50 feet. The marking rounds can be had in several colors and are water-based for very easy clean up and no staining. They have far less force than comparable training ammunition and will not cause pain to anyone hit. Blank firing ammunition is also available that is non-lethal. The instructor fired a blank round into his palm at almost contact distance with no harm or pain to demonstrate.

Protective gear from PDT is used extensively by all participants in the scenarios. This includes the PDT Force 1 Helmet, which features a wide-angle no-fog dual lens, heavily padded face and head protection, and a padded hood. A separate neck protector offers improved safety while the chest protector affords breathable comfort and mobility. The groin protector is made from molded foam core to allow for free movement. Finally, as self-defense students and instructors know, shooters tend to become threat-focused, and shots can often hit the target's hands. PDT's hand armor gloves prevent painful hits to the hands with a proprietary foam filling that still allows for the dexterity needed for weapon manipulation.

No real firearms or other weapons are allowed in the training area where scenarios are run. Every person entering the training area must empty their pockets and undergo two separate pat downs by two individuals. This was done without exception during training, and proper safety protocols were heavily emphasized.

Five separate scenarios were presented for the instructor candidates: home defense, vehicle incident, armed robbery, spree attack, and violent personal attack. Each of these can be tailored in myriad different ways to suit each trainer's needs for their students. Instructors emphasized that each scenario should last from 30 seconds to no more than 2 minutes. Scenarios that are allowed to drag on can lose their training value for the students and are less useful as a tool for instructors to gauge student reaction.

In the vehicle scenario, an armed assailant attacks a motorist who must defend himself. In the scenario I witnessed, drawing from concealment and firing through the open driver's side window at the assailant while taking a defensive position was on the menu. The home defense scenario involves a sleeping homeowner awakened by a loud crash and a yelling intruder in another part of their home. The armed robbery scenario takes place in a park, emphasizing situational awareness and effective reaction.

ISRAELI COMBAT SHOOTING

The real-world experiences of Israeli law enforcement and military personnel are vastly different than that of American soldiers and police. Likewise, the skills and tactics developed under fire and constant threat have been fine tuned to deal with this divergent reality. While we do not face these same obstacles in the U.S. (and hopefully never will), the hard-earned success of the Israeli military and security forces is undeniable, and there is much to learn from their experiences.

That was the goal of Tzviel Blankchtein (or BK as he is more colloquially known) when he founded Masada Tactical in 2007. BK immigrated to the United States following a four-year stint (1993-1997) with the Israeli Defense Forces (IDF), and he remains an active IDF instructor. He was the lead Defensive Tactics Instructor for the Maryland Police and Correctional Training Commission from 2008-2012.

I attended a law enforcement two-day Tactical Urban Handgun Class held at Bollinger Gunsmithing & Sales in Taneytown, Maryland taught by BK and Masada Tactical instructors who were all IDF veterans. The basis of this course is to teach the specific Israeli Combat shooting system, and it is indeed far different than what most American law enforcement and civilian shooters are used to.

The first difference is that the IDF use a point-shooting system with handguns. Based on videos of defensive shootings as well as shooter interviews, it quickly became very obvious that in the real world, defensive shooters don't use their sights; they just point and shoot. This happens even with highly trained professionals. In the IDF, those who are provided pistols are specialized operators who must undergo a five-week course. The goal was to develop a system in which beginners could quickly be trained to place hits center mass without using the sights. The Israeli combat shooting system works just as well for experts, however.

It can be difficult at first for someone who has consistently trained using their sights to stop looking at them. However, if you come to view the target as a legitimate threat, it gets a lot easier to become target-focused and not use your sights. The key to accurate point shooting is to get your muzzle pointed to the

The distinctively styled Israeli Combat Shooting is available in the U.S. as the Tactical Urban Handgun Class taught by Masada Tactical.

target as you would point your finger. That part is easy. The hard part is doing it quickly, and that is where the Israeli system poses another major difference for Americans.

What the IDF developed is a drawing technique that avoids the upward arm swing of the American technique. When Americans draw, keeping the gun low and then pushing outward to full extension, the gun path follows an upward arc, and under stress, it is easy to over extend and shoot high. The Israelis instead bring both hands to the face when they draw, with elbows extended outward and angled upward, gun hand to the cheek, and gun on top of the support hand. From this position, both hands are extended straight toward the target, locking them into a firm two-handed grip as full extension is reached. With both eyes focused on the target, this technique brings the pistol straight forward with no arc or overcompensation. Point shooting has a limited

The Israeli Defense Forces (IDF) developed a drawing technique that avoids the upward swing of the arm common to the American technique. Instead, they bring both hands to the face with elbows extended outward and angled upward, and handgun hand to the cheek and gun on top of the support hand.

effectiveness to no more than 7 yards distance, but since the vast majority of defensive encounters occur well within this range, it is well suited for the task.

Historically and to this day, Israelis carry handguns in Condition Two: empty chamber and full magazine. They train to rack the slide on the draw. Once the pistol slide is under the chin, they use a thumb grip with the support hand to grab the slide and push the gun forward, chambering a round and firing one handed. The historical reason for this was that the IDF had long been equipped with a wide array of handgun makes and models (mostly war surplus), and this technique simplified the training process and promoted safety.

Masada Tactical has modified their course for American Condition One carry (loaded chamber and full magazine). However, the pinching-the-slide technique remains and is used for reloads. This is an adjustment for American shooters who have long become accustomed to the cup technique for operating the slide. The pinch technique is weaker and requires finer motor skills, but it does work well with the peculiar Israeli draw.

The entire process for engaging a target seems at first exaggerated and very choreographed. First, shooters take a wide-legged, squatting stance squared to the threat with back upright and shoulders back. The gun is drawn with both hands coming to the face and with elbows out. Finally, the handgun is pushed forward toward the target while the arms rotate inward to prevent any movement off target and to secure a firm two-handed grip.

If there is more than one threat, the process must be completed again. First, bring the gun and hands back to the face, then identify the second threat and take a step forward to square yourself in the same wide, low stance toward the threat. Engage by driving the hands forward. This system is certainly slower than simply swinging the gun to the new threat, but it does avoid overcompensating and missing.

After engaging a threat and running empty, shooters are taught to move laterally and vertically, taking a knee to help avoid return fire. Of course, if actual cover is available, use that. Upon taking a knee, the pistol is brought back in front of the face, muzzle up for a speed reload, keeping target-focused the entire time. Once a new magazine is inserted, elbows go back up, gun hand to the cheek, and the support hand pinches the slide. Push the pistol forward and re-engage any remaining threats one-handed. On the reload, threats are engaged one-handed for speed, and at the distances mentioned the decrease in accuracy is not material. Another very important part of the training is support hand techniques. This is something that few shooters ever practice. Despite hundreds of hours of firearms training, this was in fact my first time. Students trained on drawing their handgun with the support hand, rotating the grip for a firm support hand hold, and engaging one-handed. Officers using their duty retention holsters had a harder time with this than I did with my standard Safariland belt holster, but everyone managed. The importance of this type of training was certainly highlighted, especially considering that an officer or CCW holder may be injured and unable to use their strong hand.

Next, we trained on one-handed reloads using only the support hand. Taking a knee, the empty pistol was placed behind the knee and held in place while a fresh magazine was inserted. Next, using the belt or shoe against the rear sight, the pistol slide was racked to chamber a round, and the target re-engaged. Needless to say, muzzle awareness and finger off the trigger safety was paramount.

The last thing you want to do in a gun fight is just stand there, and like American shooters, the IDF trains in moving and shooting drills, though with one big difference. The Israelis do not move and shoot at the same time; they do one or the other. Moving and shooting at the same time is a good way to miss a lot, they believe. Instead, operators are taught to run toward the threat, stop, and then engage. This provides both faster movement and better accuracy.

In order to more closely simulate firing under stress, students were required to identify different targets before engaging and were subject to physical challenges, such as running, push-ups, and having to reassemble a handgun and load before moving to engage a target. All of this was done with added stress inducers, courtesy of the instructors.

Given how much time we tend to spend in our vehicles, and with more and more people facing long commutes, vehicle tactics are another essential aspect of the Masada Tactical course.

Team and vehicle tactics were also a part of the law enforcement version of this class and mostly took place on day two. Communication between team members is essential, and each team of two shooters had to vocalize specific commands indicating when they were at slide lock (Dry), when they took a knee to reload (Reload), and to announce when they were ready to stand back up (Standing). This last command was essential for safety, as the second team member may still be engaging his target. Only when the second team member gave the command (verbal and physical) to stand could the first team member do so.

Given how much time we tend to spend in our vehicles and with more and more people facing long commutes, vehicle tactics are another essential aspect of this course. When driving as a team, the driver is in command and lets the passengers know of threats outside and if they need to evacuate the vehicle. We drove as targets presented on both sides, and both the driver and passenger engaged. We also drove to targets on the driver's side, and he engaged while the passenger exited. Once the passenger was out and using the engine block for cover, the passenger could engage and give the driver time to exit out the passenger side. In addition, we trained for a passenger to hang out of the window while the vehicle was driven toward the target and then engage.

Civilians and CCW holders, of course, don't have much need for team tactics. The civilian class is one 8-hour day instead of two, and the vehicle training is limited to carjacking-type scenarios where the driver must engage a target. One very important note of caution when firing from inside a vehicle is to keep the muzzle outside when firing; otherwise, the noise and concussive effect is extremely disorienting.

LOW LIGHT SELF-DEFENSE

Many negative encounters occur when the sun goes down, so training to survive in such conditions is paramount. Very few people train in low light, but they should. Tactical lights and lasers on your gun help a lot, but you still need to learn how to make the best use of them.

Fortunately, Gunsite Academy teamed up with Crimson Trace to design such a class. Gunsite has taken their standard 250 Pistol course and integrated specialized training on the use of weapon-mounted lasers and flashlights. This is a comprehensive five-day course with the vast majority of your time spent on the range.

This is not an "everyone-gets-a-trophy" class. You are evaluated and graded, and you must perform well to pass and receive a certificate. Marksmanship and speed are emphasized at various distances with timed targets and from challenging positions. On my carry gun, I use a laser, but before I went through this training, I had a limited concept of how to best use it. In bright daylight, the red laser dot has a tendency to wash out against the target, and the farther the distance, the more profound the effect.

Realistically, any farther than 7 yards and the red laser gets a lot

Gunsite Academy teamed up with Crimson Trace to design a class that offers specialized training on the use of weapon-mounted lasers and flashlights. *Photo: Crimson Trace*

harder to see. Crimson Trace has a green laser unit for the Glock that is much easier to see. Green laser units have been traditionally hard to produce in miniaturized packages because of the way the lenses need to be designed. They also use more energy. That problem has now been resolved, and the green light is far more visible to the human eye than red.

I did find one drawback to the use of a weapon-mounted laser. In the beginning, once I saw how visible the laser was against the target, I had a tendency to become overly target-focused. Instead of sticking to proper form, I ended up looking over the gun trying to find the laser dot before engaging. At close range, this isn't problematic, but it is a very bad habit, especially if you get into a situation where you can't see or find the dot. The first lesson is that the laser is not a replacement for proper technique. Without proper training, it can be easy to develop bad habits. The key is to follow through on your correct draw and presentation, driving the front sight forward toward the target, aligned with your eyes. If you do this correctly, the laser dot will appear on the target and greatly improve your hit probability with both eyes open.

When you don't want your laser to be visible, keep your trigger finger along the frame of the gun.
Photo: Crimson Trace

On the range, we practiced drawing and hitting the targets at distances out to 15 yards from different positions including standing, kneeling, and rollover prone. We practiced identifying and engaging targets from different directions using combat turns, including having to identify a target behind you, turn, draw, and accurately engage in just a few seconds. Indeed, most all of the shooting drills are timed, and accurate hits are expected. We also practiced malfunction clearing drills, engaging multiple targets, as well as tactical reloads (removing a partial magazine and replacing it with a full mag during a lull in the fight) and speed reloads (shooting until slide locks and then inserting a fresh magazine).

There may be times when you do not want the laser to be visible. With the Crimson Trace grip lasers, the easiest solution is to have your trigger finger off the trigger and alongside the frame of the gun. Bringing your finger up into a slightly higher position will block the laser. Left-handed shooters can use a high thumb to accomplish the same thing.

We were guided one at a time through each of two onsite shoot houses. This exercise was conducted during the day, but inside the covered and enclosed area, conditions provided a low light experience. It should be noted, however, that house clearing is extremely dangerous even when done in teams with well-trained professionals, and it should only be attempted by a lone individual in the most extreme of circumstances.

Indeed, my first go around was not successful. I completely failed to find one bad guy target altogether that was waiting in ambush, and I failed to neutralize another that had a child held hostage. I blame nerves and bad habits. I experienced significant improvement in the second shoot house exercise. By using the lasers indoors, it was certainly much easier to get faster and more accurate hits, especially considering the use of small iron sights against dark targets while trying to differentiate friend from foe. The fact that some of the targets were armed and some were not emphasized the significant importance of proper target identification. The laser won't help you do this, but it will help you engage a bad guy much faster once you do identify him or her.

During the night range session, we focused on the use of the tactical flashlight and the various techniques for identifying targets and engaging. It should go without saying that if you have a weapon-mounted flashlight, do not use it for searching since that means that you are pointing a loaded gun at a lot of things you probably don't want to shoot. This may include family members. A handheld flashlight is the proper tool for searching and can be used in conjunction with your handgun.

The Harries technique involves locking your hands together back to back with the flashlight in one and your pistol in the other. This allows you to engage the target quickly and provides better support to the shooting hand than a pure one-handed technique. The FBI hold involves keeping the flashlight hand away from the body to prevent an assailant from easily targeting you. Since the light and gun do not have to point in the same direction, this is a better technique for room searching.

At night on the range, we practiced using the lasers in combination with flashlights. With the flashlight alone, it was still extremely difficult to line up my sights quickly and engage the targets. With the combined use of the laser, I was able to do so almost as quickly as during the day. Of course, the lasers are much more visible at night. We also trained in the use of awkward positions and barricades at night with both lights and lasers. Using a barricade at night with a flashlight can be especially challenging, since it is easy for the light to bounce off the barricade and reflect back at you, causing a loss of night vision. You have to make sure to place the front of the light forward of the barricade to avoid this.

Adding accessories to your gun is something most of us like to do, but training with those accessories and learning their best use is extremely important. With weapon-mounted lasers, make sure to sight them in properly and install them solidly. For this class, you need a reliable semi-auto pistol, a solid strong-side holster, at least three (preferably six) magazines, a good tactical flashlight, and obviously, a weapon-mounted laser. You also need to bring 1,000 rounds of ammunition for your handgun and an additional 50 rounds of frangible ammo (which is available onsite for purchase). The shop will have anything else you may need but forgot to bring.

HOME SECURITY

There are worse things that can happen to you than getting your stuff stolen, but nevertheless when it does happens, it feels like a horrible violation. In times of societal collapse, looting of your home can mean losing not only your survival guns, but backup food and water reserves — things that are extremely valuable when the national distribution system goes offline. I once had the hubcaps stolen off my vehicle, which was parked in the shopping mall I was guarding at the time. That just made it even more insulting. But having your home burglarized is so much worse, so much more personal.

Your home is your castle, and when someone violates that, it is not just your property that goes missing, but your sense of security as well. To make matters worse, a home that has been burglarized once is much more likely to be broken into again. It could be that your neighborhood is going to the dogs, or that burglars know you will be replacing your old junk with brand new and more expensive items that they can steal.

Replacing the items you have lost is one thing, but you will also need to repair damage to your home, since most burglars lack the finesse needed to gently pick your locks. Depending on your insurance policy, you may be out hundreds of dollars in repair costs alone, especially to door jambs. But fixing the damage is only the first part. You also want to make sure it doesn't happen again. You can install security cameras around your house with motion sensors and night vision that can be monitored from anywhere with Internet access. You could install a monitored alarm system, but most thieves know they have several minutes to grab what they can before police are able to respond and, frankly, home and business alarms do not get the highest priority, especially in high crime areas where police tend to be busiest.

Home break-ins occur with alarming regularity in the United States, approximately 2,000,000 annually in fact, and account for 66 percent of all burglaries. *Photo: Armor Concepts*

Motion sensitive floodlights on the outside of your home can be an effective deterrent. If things are really bad, you could install steel bars on doors and windows, although that seems extreme (not to mention expensive). A large dog is a solution for some, but that carries its own upsides and downsides.

Homeowners who have been victimized by a burglary or who just want to make sure to prevent one in the future should take note not to forget one of the simplest and most cost effective methods available: to reinforce their door jambs. A solid lock and deadbolt won't do you much good if the only thing securing them to the house is some old dried up wood and a dime store fastener. The vast majority of break-ins occur though an outside door, and it only takes a few seconds for someone to kick your poorly secured door wide open.

Securing the entrance to your home and reinforcing it does several things to help you. First, it will keep out all but the most determined burglars, and they will have to make a lot more noise, which can alert the neighbors. Second, if you are home, you will have a lot more time to react by arming yourself and calling the police. Third, keeping someone out of your home in the first place is a lot more valuable that scaring them off with an alarm or getting some nice HD video of them stealing your stuff. Finally, think of it as a home improvement that can add value to your house.

One company producing high quality and effective fixes to help you secure your exterior doors is Armor Concepts. The company owner takes security seriously, having been the victim of multiple break-ins on a property he was renovating, which led him to develop the system he uses and sells. Necessity is truly the mother of invention, as the frustration and expense of the damage led to the company's product line.

Door Armor is available in individual parts or as a complete kit and reinforces the jamb, locks, and hinges. All of the weak points on your door and door frame are reinforced with galvanized powder-coated steel strips for superior strength, long-lasting durability, and corrosion resistance. The EZ Armor Basic Kit is very simple for anyone with a drill to install and does not require that you remove your door. It can be completely installed in less than half

The EZ Armor Basic Kit from Armor Concepts is very simple for anyone with a drill to install and does not require that you remove your door. This completely secures your door and door jamb from being kicked in.

an hour and includes all of the parts you need. The steel shields are very long for a reason: this allows them to be made thinner while retaining a lot of strength, redistributing any force applied to the outside of the door along the entire length of the wall stud.

Another nice feature of the shields is that when the door is closed, they remain largely invisible, so it doesn't look like you live in Beirut. Protecting the area around the lock itself is important because if the jamb is reinforced, the weak point becomes the door itself, which will split. The idea to reinforce the hinges came about through trial and error. As the other parts of the door were reinforced, the hinges became the weak point and can be kicked in.

If your home has already been broken into and the jamb badly damaged, a repair can be costly, but Armor Concepts also produces Fix-A-Jamb II. This L-shaped, long steel plate can be installed right over the damage and repairs the jamb, fixing the door

The author was impressed with Ruger's pepper sprays. The Tornado 3-in-1 and the Ruger Stealth are law enforcement-strength sprays with 2 million Scoville heat units.

frame while reinforcing it against future break-in attempts.

Another product, Door Jamb Armor, requires professional installation and some trim removal for a proper fit. It is, however, the strongest and best reinforcement system you can get for your door, hinges, locks, and jamb. It is actually the original product the company made before introducing the simpler DIY kit.

Armor Concepts' newest product is an extremely innovative deadbolt for your sliding glass door. Sliding doors are especially vulnerable, since they are typically located at the back of the home and away from passersby and traffic where the noises of a break-in are more easily shielded. Most sliding door locks are pretty pitiful and easily defeated by burglars. Placing a dowel or other block inside the door so it cannot be slid open is not especially effective either, since the entire door can be lifted off its tracks. The only real solution is a better lock.

The Armor Latch is a sliding door deadbolt that keeps your old lock in place but adds a new and stronger lock above it. A covered lock attaches to the door and is secured to the jamb with dual steel rods, top and bottom, while remaining unobtrusive. Installation is very easy with basic tools and takes no more than 10 minutes.

There are plenty of downloadable installation instructions for all of these security devices and DIY step-by-step videos on their website. The kits and parts are reasonably priced and are available online or at many popular home improvement stores. Indeed, this is one easy and inexpensive home improvement for anyone, and it pays off immediately in peace of mind.

DEFENSIVE SPRAYS AND STUN GUNS

In some areas, you are not allowed to carry a gun. Some people may not be comfortable with a gun, and others may not be old enough to be able to carry one legally. Even if you do carry, there may be situations where you need to defend yourself but in a proportional manner where lethal force is not appropriate. For these reasons, self-defense sprays (mostly pepper-based) are extremely popular, but they do require some training.

Ruger has developed an excellent line of pepper sprays and stun guns to meet this need. The company's standard model of pepper spray is sold as both the Tornado 3-in-1 and Ruger Stealth (stealth in the sense that it doesn't flash or make noise). This is a law enforcement-strength pepper spray that rates at 2 million Scoville heat units — about a thousand times hotter than Sriracha sauce. It has a 15-foot spray range and includes a convenient belt clip for easy carry. This model comes in a unique safety holder designed to reduce the chances of accidental discharge. To access the spray, slide the safety door down and push a release button. The sprayer pops free in your hand, already in firing position. The mechanism becomes second nature after a bit of practice, but you will definitely need to familiarize yourself with it to avoid fumbling in a true emergency. If you prefer a simple point-and-spray model, Ruger's Armor Case should fit the bill. It has the same potent liquid but in a classic pepper spray container.

To move one step up from its standard model, Ruger has introduced the Tornado 5-in-1, also sold as the Ruger Ultra. This has the same setup as the 3-in-1 but includes a strobe light and a 125dB alarm that activates automatically whenever the safety is released. The strobe is designed to spook or confuse an attacker, and the alarm draws the attention of anyone else in the area, making it a great option for joggers and anyone out after dark. There are instructions for deactivating the alarm to allow you to practice drawing the spray.

Ruger even makes convenient spray holders if you want to keep your pepper spray at home or in the car rather than on your person. The Home Defense Wall Unit attaches to any surface (for example, the wall next to your bed) and acts as a holster for your spray. In an emergency, this can save precious seconds spent searching and fumbling around in the dark. The similar Vehicle Defense Unit mounts on the power outlet of your car, holding your spray at the ready.

If you're seeking an extra-discreet option, Ruger created the lipstick pepper spray. This clever design looks just like a tube of lipstick and even comes in a variety of colors including red, pink, black, silver, and blue. Even when opened, the spray nozzle looks just like a perfume spritzer.

Stun guns are another less lethal self-defense option offered by

Ruger, but they are more heavily regulated than pepper sprays, so be sure to check the laws in your area before you carry one. Also keep in mind that stun guns are not Tasers and cannot be fired from a distance, but rather must actually be touching the attacker to work. Having made those disclaimers, stun guns are one of the most effective defenses you can carry without resorting to lethal force. Ruger produces stun guns in three levels of size and strength.

The Ruger 650V (which fires at 650,000 volts) is the smallest model, a square unit that fits in your hand and can be easily carried in a pocket or a purse. It has a soft rubber outer coating and a finger-contoured grip. The safety switch, which prevents you from accidently setting it off on yourself, has an LED light so it can be easily located in the dark. The unit even comes with its own carrying case and batteries included.

The Ruger 800V (800,000 volts) has many of the same features as its smaller sibling — rubber coating, grip, LED light, batteries

Stun guns can be very effective but you have to actually make contact with an assailant to use most of the ones that are commercially available. *Photo: Ruger*

included. However, it's longer and shaped more like a flashlight, so it's not as easily carried in a pocket. Instead, it comes with a wrist strap so it can be carried like one of those collapsible umbrellas, either on your wrist, belt, or in a bag. Both the 650V and 800V are available in black or pink, making them look even more like an umbrella or personal flashlight. The 800V features electrodes that are pointed so they can pierce through clothes to reach skin — a handy feature when an attacker's bare skin is out of reach.

The ultimate Ruger stun gun is the 1MV Flashlight (that's 1 million volts). As the name suggests, it is an ultra-bright LED flashlight that also happens to have a built-in stun gun. Its electrodes are pointed like those on the 800V for maximum effectiveness through clothing. It comes with a carrying case, rechargeable battery, and wrist strap if you want to take it out and about, as well as a wall charger for when you're at home.

Sabre Pepper Spray Products has a 3-in-1 formula that includes both tear gas and a UV marking dye in addition to the traditional pepper spray for added effectiveness. And they have recently introduced the Stop Strap, an ingenious device that instantly deactivates the spray if it's yanked off a carrier's wrist, thus preventing a criminal from using it against his victim.

In addition, the company makes water-filled trainer sprays to practice drawing from a pocket, deactivating the safety, and aiming the spray at a target. I was surprised to find that working the safety often altered the aim of my spray, to the point that it went off in a completely different direction. You get a good feel for the range and coverage area of the spray, an important aspect to be able to visualize in an emergency. You may be surprised at the limited number of "squirts" a canister will dispense before running out.

Kimber's solution is the Pepperblaster II. Pull the trigger on this little guy, and it fires a dose of powerful gel up to 13 feet at over 100 miles per hour. A blast like that easily penetrates through any mask, bandanna, or around any type of glasses an attacker might be wearing. Since the formulation is a gel rather than the usual aerosol, there is much less blowback and wind dispersal, making this weapon much safer for its carrier and any bystanders who would otherwise be at risk of catching a whiff of spray. This is very lucky, because Kimber has formulated its gel with 10 percent capsaicin (made from cayenne peppers) to produce a potent blend that instantly causes severe coughing, nausea, and blindness, and lasts up to 45 minutes. At its full range of 13 feet, the gel disperses to cover only about a two-foot wide zone; it will coat the attacker, but not much else. At its minimum distance of two feet, the gel zone is only a few inches wide — perfect for zeroing in on someone's face.

Pepperblaster uses a unique firing system that sets it apart from other defensive sprays. Instead of storing the spray under pressure and releasing it when fired, the Pepperblaster's gel is not pressurized. When the trigger is pulled, a power-driven piston expels the gel at high speed, resulting in a much more powerful blast than regular pepper spray. Each Pepperblaster unit contains two capsules of gel, and pulling the trigger expels the entire capsule. You therefore get two shots per unit, but they're powerful shots, capable of completely coating and disabling an attacker. Best of all, since the spray

Kimber's Pepperblaster II. Pulling the trigger offers two shots of a powerful gel up to 13 feet at over 100 mph!
Photo: Kimber

isn't pressurized, its lifetime is much longer than ordinary pepper spray. Pressurized sprays tend to go bad due to gradual loss of pressure over time or due to temperature swings. By eliminating pressurization, Kimber extended the Pepperblaster's lifetime to about four years. Of course, if you're practicing your technique regularly, you'll probably replace it much more often, but it's nice to know that an older unit will still do its job when called upon.

The Pepperblaster II has a small pistol grip that makes it second nature to orient in your hand and hold. This is particularly valuable if you carry your spray in a purse or backpack where it might flip over or get turned around. The grip instantly tells you which way to hold the spray so it faces the attacker. After all, fumbling around in an emergency can easily create a life-threatening delay. The pistol grip is more ergonomic for those with arthritis or other hand problems. Its trigger has about 6.5 pounds of pull, so it should be a relatively easy action, even for those who have difficulty firing a gun. The Pepperblaster II features small sights on the top of the spray. While these may be unnecessary at very close range, they can be helpful when aiming 10-12 feet away at an attacker's face.

The Pepperblaster is only about the size of a deck of cards, so it fits easily in your pocket or purse. For joggers or anyone else who might not have a pocket, Kimber sells inexpensive clips to hang on waistbands or belt. Pepper sprays are particularly valuable for walkers and joggers because, in addition to human threats, they can be used against aggressive dogs without causing any permanent damage. The unit weighs only 4 ounces, so it is very comfortable to carry, and it won't weigh you down or make your waistband sag. Kimber has taken measures to reduce the risk of accidental discharge, too. The trigger has a small plastic tab that prevents it from being pressed unintentionally. When your finger goes to the trigger, the tab swings out of the way naturally.

When a unit is fresh and has never been fired, a white stripe is displayed on the side of the trigger. However, if one or both capsules inside have been discharged, the stripe is hidden. In this way, you can never mistake an old, used spray for a new one and find yourself defenseless when it counts.

Training is important when using any self-defense device and many companies like Kimber make training versions of their defense sprays.

Most people who carry pepper spray neglect to practice with their sprays, assuming that the devices are so easy to use that there's no need to train with them. In reality, they would be much better prepared if they trained every year or two. A training day provides an opportunity to role play various scenarios, become familiar with the trigger mechanism on the spray unit, and get a feel for exactly how far the blast goes and how widely it disperses. Reading that your spray is effective out to 10 feet is fine, but do you have a good sense of exactly how far away a person has to be before they're outside that zone?

To that end, Kimber sells Pepperblaster II training units that are filled with a washable blue liquid instead of pepper spray. Training units are orange, while real Pepperblasters come in red or a more subtle gray. With the trainer unit, you can get a feel for the trigger and the spray's range with no ill effects. Of course, you can also train with the real spray and use up an old unit whenever it's time to replace it with a new one. It is best to train using a face-sized target such as a paper plate mounted at eye level outside.

There are many pepper spray training classes all over the country; there's a good chance that one is offered near you. Good resources for class information include your local police department, shooting range, and self-defense trainers. They may offer classes specifically on pepper spray techniques, or the use of pepper sprays may be covered as part of a more general self-defense course. Either one is well worth your time and money. Local instructors should be familiar with any local laws and regulations concerning the carrying of pepper spray. Unfortunately, some jurisdictions limit pepper sprays or ban them outright (and these tend to be the types of places where you feel the most need to carry such a spray). If you live in such an area, a self-defense class will be all the more important for you to take.

Finally, keep in mind that 10 to 15 percent of the population is unaffected by pepper sprays, so they are not a panacea.

MEDICAL EMERGENCIES: EQUIPMENT & TRAINING

*T*his book recognizes that life itself is quite fragile, and the need for self-sufficient medical care a real possibility during times of calamity. Thus, in addition to your survival gun readiness, it is critical that you stock up on the supplies and knowledge required to overcome any number of life-threatening medical conditions should regular access to medical care become unavailable, or hospitals overwhelmed.

DISEASE OUTBREAKS

Disease and contagion have always been facts of life for humanity and most likely always will be, in spite of all our medical advancements. Although much has been made in recent years of bioweapons and genetically modified superbugs, the most likely scenario for encountering a disease outbreak is the naturally occurring pathogens that appear after natural disasters.

WATERBORNE OUTBREAKS

The most likely route of infection following a natural disaster is via the water supply. Storms and floods can backup or overwhelm any sewage system, contaminating your drinking water with waste — a certain recipe for disease. Any emergency that disrupts the water supply (hurricane, earthquake, power outage, etc.) jeopardizes access to clean water.

Your best preparation is to stock bottles of clean water in your home before any emergency occurs. However, if you run out or you're caught away from home, you can still disinfect unpurified water to make it safe to drink. If the water is cloudy or dirty, filter out the sediment by pouring the water through several layers of cloth. Then, disinfect the water by boiling it for one minute or adding a small amount of bleach (6 drops per gallon/2 drops per liter) and let it sit for 30 minutes. Although it might taste a little funny, the water is now safe for drinking.

The most feared waterborne contagion is cholera. This bacterial disease is rarely seen now in wealthy countries, but it caused mass fatalities in the days before sewage treatment and continues to do so in the developing world. Cholera infection results in "rice water" diarrhea, a gray liquid with tiny flecks of mucus that look like fragments of rice. An infected person can produce 3-5 gallons of this diarrhea each day. Obviously, this can lead very rapidly to death by dehydration. The first line of treatment is drinking large quantities of an electrolyte drink (such as PediaLyte or a sports drink such as Gatorade) to replenish what is lost. In many cases, this is enough to allow an individual to recover, but more severe cases may require

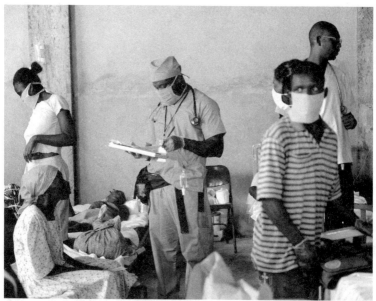

Cholera outbreaks can occur anywhere there is contaminated water, or if municipal water systems are compromised from flooding. *Photo: Kendra Helmer, USAID*

a saline IV drip and treatment with the antibiotic doxycycline. Cholera sufferers do not usually develop a fever.

Another commonly encountered but much less serious waterborne infection is Giardia. Hikers and campers often acquire this parasite by drinking out of streams (an example of water that looks pristine but still needs disinfection). Luckily, Giardia is a relatively mild infection, resulting in flatulence and very smelly diarrhea, but nothing severe enough to require urgent treatment. Persistent symptoms are treated with metronidazole or a related drug.

There are several gastrointestinal viruses that are waterborne, but most cause only short-lived diarrhea. The most serious and rarest virus, however, is polio. Polio was eliminated from the Western Hemisphere in 1994, but it can still be found overseas. Although most polio cases are asymptomatic, in rare cases it can cause paralysis and can be fatal if the paralysis affects the lungs. Unfortunately, the only treatment is supportive care, so the best preventive measure you can take is to get yourself vaccinated for it before an outbreak occurs.

One serious disease that often follows a flood is malaria. The malaria parasite is transmitted by mosquitos, which can breed uncontrollably in the standing waters left behind by a flood or hurricane. Infection with malaria leads to bad headaches, muscle aches, and a fever that ebbs and flows in an unusual cyclical pattern. The exact timing of the pattern depends on which species of the malarial parasite you have. And although malaria is always miserable, the severity of the disease varies from species to species. It is treated with doxycycline or a drug in the quinine family. Keep in mind that if the drug is not taken for the full recommended period, the parasite can develop resistance and become untreatable.

FOODBORNE PATHOGENS

While food poisoning is generally seen as an unpleasant but relatively minor illness, the stakes become much higher in emergency situations where medical help might not be readily available. The likelihood of ingesting a foodborne pathogen increases greatly when the power goes out and refrigeration is no longer an option. Meat and other vulnerable foods should be cooked well if they've been sitting at room temperature for more than an hour or two. If you're hunting your own food, assume that all wild game meat is carrying parasites and cook it accordingly.

Food poisoning generally causes diarrhea and/or vomiting within a couple hours to a few days after ingestion. The most common type is a watery diarrhea without a fever, usually caused by a virus or a mild bacterial infection. Fortunately, this form often resolves itself after a couple days and does not require any treatment beyond keeping hydrated and maybe taking some probiotic capsules or yogurt (keep in mind that yogurt requires refrigeration, unlike probiotic capsules). A more serious type of food poisoning is dysentery, a condition where blood is present in the diarrhea, often accompanied by a fever. The blood might resemble black tar rather than normal bright red blood, because it has passed through the digestive tract and has been partially digested. The presence of

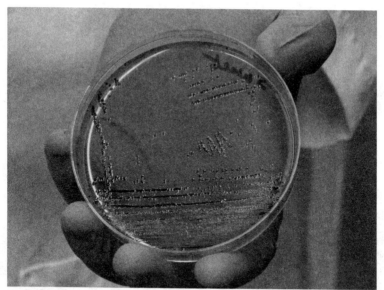

Salmonella bacteria, shown here in a petri dish, are a major cause of foodborne illnesses.
Photo: U.S. Food and Drug Administration

blood indicates that the offending bacteria are actually attacking and invading the lining of the intestines. This can eventually lead to serious damage in the intestines and to the bacteria getting into the blood stream and migrating to other parts of the body. It must therefore be treated more aggressively, usually with antibiotics and followed up with probiotics after the antibiotic course is completed.

There are two schools of thought regarding the use of antidiarrheal medications. Some people swear by them, and there are clearly situations where they can be a godsend. Others, though, take a "better out than in" approach to intestinal pathogens and eschew antidiarrheals. In general, these medications are safe to use for simple, watery diarrhea. However, if the diarrhea is bloody, stopping the bowel movements just gives the bacteria more time to invade the intestinal lining and cause more damage. Dysentery victims are therefore generally advised to avoid anti-diarrheals beyond simple Pepto-Bismol. Be sure to wash your hands constantly when dealing with diarrhea, as it can be highly contagious.

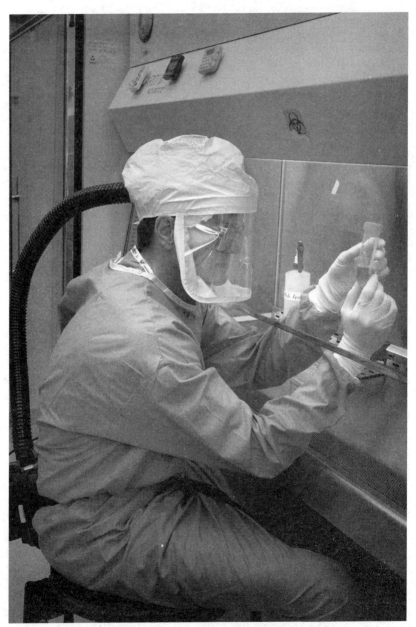

Centers for Disease Control and Prevention's staff microbiologists examining reconstructed 1918 pandemic influenza virus in a Biosafety Level 3-enhanced laboratory. *Photo: James Gathany CDC*

EPIDEMICS

There have been numerous terrible epidemics in the course of human history: the Plague, smallpox with its 30 percent mortality rate, yellow fever, and most recently, influenza in 1918 when somewhere between 3 and 5 percent of the world's population died. Now that the most recent severe pandemic has passed out of living memory, we are well overdue for another. The 1918 flu was facilitated by the movement of troops all over the world during World War I, but its travel was glacial compared to the possible course of a pandemic today, when travelers can cross the globe in mere hours.

Although these historical epidemics include both viruses (influenza, smallpox, yellow fever) and bacteria (plague), the advent of antibiotics has made bacteria much less of a threat. There are far fewer airborne bacteria than there are airborne viruses. For example, tuberculosis is caused by an airborne bacterium, but it takes months or years to cause symptoms, and it is treatable. Anthrax is an airborne bacterium of great interest as a potential bioweapon, but it can also be treated with antibiotics. Most importantly, anthrax is not contagious from person to person. Only those present at the initial release of the bacteria would be infected, with no further infections beyond those.

Viruses, in contrast, are much more likely to be transmitted from person to person by aerosol in an uncontrollable chain of infections, and they are much less likely to be easily treatable. Influenza is an ever-present threat because it mutates easily, with new strains appearing frequently. This happens particularly in places where different species live close together, such as farms occupied by pigs, chickens, and humans. Such farms have been the source of several outbreaks of bird flu in recent years that have killed large numbers of poultry but proved far less contagious in humans.

Swine flu, on the other hand, has shown itself to be very contagious in people. Since pigs can simultaneously harbor swine, avian, and human flu strains, scientists are very concerned that pigs could serve as a mixing bowl of flu viruses, eventually producing a strain that melds the deadliness of bird flu with the rapid spread of swine flu. Thus a new pandemic would be born. More exotic viruses, such as Ebola, are emerging each year as humans become more numerous, more crowded, and more internationally mobile. Unfortunately, antiviral medications are far less common and less affordable than the antibiotics for bacterial infections. With nothing more than supportive care to offer for many viral infections, we rely heavily on vaccines to prevent and control the spread of viruses.

Historically, the only effective defense against an epidemic was to isolate your village or farm as much as possible. Roads were blocked, ports closed, and visitors turned away. American Samoa successfully avoided the 1918 flu outbreak by refusing to let any ships dock at its ports. Of course, that level of isolation can itself create major problems unless you are highly self-sufficient. The best modern defense, therefore, is to take advantage of all the vaccines that have been developed over the past century and are now available to us to prevent disease. The commonly available vaccines include: measles, mumps, German measles (Rubella), diphtheria, tetanus, whooping cough (pertussis), meningococcus (for bacterial meningitis), hepatitis A, hepatitis B, chickenpox, polio, rotavirus (a diarrhea virus that is dangerous for babies but not for adults), Haemophilus (causes pneumonia and meningitis), pneumococcus (causes pneumonia in older adults), and influenza. Influenza mutates so easily that the vaccine is usually given each year to account for newly emerging strains.

Take advantage of all these vaccines to protect yourself against infections that were historically often a death sentence but which are now preventable. Less common vaccines include rabies (available to those who work with animals), anthrax (given to military), smallpox (occasionally available), and typhoid, yellow fever, and cholera (these three available to international travelers). If you have an opportunity to receive any of these vaccines, seize your chance to protect yourself.

A slower type of epidemic involves pathogens spread by mosquitoes rather than by aerosol. Examples include malaria (a parasite) and viruses such as yellow fever, dengue, zika, and the many encephalitis viruses. Malaria is treatable with medications, but many of the mosquito-borne viruses have no treatments or vaccines available. Stock up on mosquito netting and bug repellants to keep these infections out of your home.

Regardless of the exact circumstances of the epidemic, you will need to be prepared to disinfect items in your home and to protect yourself from outside exposure. The best way to clean off your body is simply a good wash with hot water and soap. If a particular area of the body has been heavily contaminated, rubbing alcohol adds an extra measure of decontamination. Don't scrub too hard — doing so creates tiny breaks in the skin that can become portals for germs to enter the body. Household surfaces and objects can be disinfected using a variety of chemicals. The best is bleach, diluted to make a 5-10 percent solution. Alternatives to bleach include alcohol (ethanol, isopropanol, or any grain alcohol will work) and ammonia-based cleaners. Be sure not to mix ammonia-based cleaners (like Lysol) with bleach, as doing so releases toxic chlorine gas. As mentioned previously, water can be purified by boiling for one minute or by adding bleach at the rate of 6 drops per gallon.

BIOHAZARD SUITS

Leaving your home during an epidemic is risky, but often very necessary. Stocking up on a few biohazard suits in case of this type of emergency may sound a bit paranoid, but they can be lifesavers. The very best biohazard suits are full-body plastic casings with faceplates and a battery-powered blower that supplies filtered air. Unfortunately, the blower's battery packs require recharging every few hours, and if the battery dies, the suit becomes nothing more than a big plastic bag over your head.

There are simpler biohazard suits that require no electricity to run, but they aren't considered quite as good at excluding germs as the plastic ones. The simpler suits are usually designed to be single-use disposables and are made of a paper-like material that is both tough and water resistant (such as Tyvek). The suit usually includes a hood to cover the hair and is worn with rubber boots and gloves, since the hands and feet are the body parts that are most in contact with the world. To protect the face, wear glasses (the type used for shooting are fine) and a face mask.

Although we often see people wearing simple surgical masks to

Gas masks with good filters can protect the wearer against many airborne toxins and diseases.
Photo: Sgt. Mark Fayloga, USMC

The simpler biohazard suits are usually designed to be single-use disposables and are made of a paper-like material that is both tough and water resistant (such as Tyvek).

prevent the spread of germs, the best respiratory masks are tighter fitting and have the designation N95 (meaning they exclude 95% of small airborne particles). N95 masks are designed to press tightly against the skin, so they are somewhat compromised by the presence of facial hair. The N95 masks are also a bit laborious to breathe through, so those with respiratory problems may be better off with regular surgical masks. Biohazard suits in general can be quite uncomfortable to wear if the weather is even slightly warm, since they tend to act as a personal insulator and greenhouse. In a long-term epidemic, you may find that you cannot treat any suit as disposable without risking running out of them, so even these "single use" suits must be reused repeatedly. If you must re-wear your biohazard gear, be sure to thoroughly spray the outside of your suit, gloves, boots, glasses, and mask with a disinfectant (bleach is best) before taking them off.

Basic, readily available supplies for combating infections include bottled water, peroxide, bleach, mosquito netting, bug repellant,

Pepto-Bismol, electrolyte drink (PediaLyte or sports drink or you can make your own by mixing small amounts of salt with water), antibiotic ointment, Epsom salts, probiotic capsules, and rubber gloves. More advanced supplies that may be harder to obtain include antibiotic eye and ear drops, biohazard suit, N95 masks, IV lines and bags of sterile saline, oral antibiotics.

Obtaining antibiotics other than topical ointments can be an exercise in compromise. Since they can only be obtained in the United States by prescription, acquiring pharmacy-grade antibiotics usually involves a trip to another country with laxer medication laws. Unfortunately, these countries often have looser quality control laws as well. Some people have opted instead to stockpile antibiotics that are intended for veterinary use. Some veterinary antibiotics are available at farm stores, with recommended dosages based on the weight of the animal. In general, medications intended for farm mammals (cows, sheep, etc.) are a safer choice than those intended for fish (although fish medications are sold at all pet

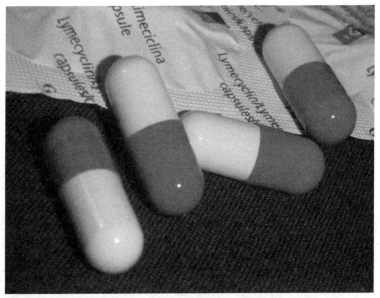

Know when to administer antibiotics to avoid wasting your supply and potentially creating drug-resistant bugs. Viruses do not respond to antibiotics at all. *Photo: Obli*

stores). Fish antibiotics undergo very little quality control testing and are designed to be dissolved in large amounts of water rather than swallowed intact. That said, if your situation is truly desperate, even an antibiotic meant for fish could potentially be helpful. Antiviral medications are much less common than antibiotics for bacterial infections. Most antivirals on the market are for the control of chronic infections (like herpes), but there are a couple that are used against influenza which might be useful in the case of a flu epidemic. Tamiflu and Relenza can reduce the length and severity of a flu case (but won't cure it completely) if taken within the first couple days after symptoms begin. Unfortunately, these are not medications that you can find easily in a farm store or even at a foreign tourist shop. If you locate a source, it's worthwhile to stock up, but only if you feel confident that the source is legitimate. Real antivirals are not cheap; a single course of Tamiflu retails for over $100 in the States.

It is strongly recommended that if you decide to acquire some antibiotics or antivirals for your medical preparedness kit, you also invest in a pharmacology guide that lists the uses, dosages, and lengths of treatment for each medication. There are dozens of commonly used antibiotics, and the drug of choice for a particular infection often depends on the exact site of the infection in the body and the species of bacteria causing the infection. Since identifying the species of bacteria can be impossible in an emergency, you may have to use trial and error to find a medication for which the infection responds (don't feel too badly about this — doctors do it all the time!) Be sure to always take the antibiotic for the full recommended length of treatment, even if you're feeling completely well again. Ending the treatment early may lead to the infection returning in a more resistant form that proves impossible to cure.

Know when to administer antibiotics to avoid wasting your supply and potentially creating drug-resistant bugs. Viruses do not respond to antibiotics at all. For viral diseases like colds, flu, chickenpox, measles, and mumps, you simply have to wait it out until you recover. As mentioned in the foodborne pathogens section, simple watery diarrhea is another condition where antibiotics aren't usually necessary and can do more harm than good.

Bloody diarrhea, on the other hand, calls for immediate treatment with antibiotics, as does a severe sore throat (Strep throat), whooping cough, and any wound involving pus, swelling, redness, or a high fever. Influenza causes a high fever, but don't bother trying to treat it with antibiotics unless you have an antiviral like Tamiflu. Do watch, though, for a second fever spike as the flu patient is beginning to recover. Often, bacteria set in as secondary infections in the waning days of a flu case. These secondary infections should be treated immediately with antibiotics, as they can become very serious.

Some situations require treatment that is more specialized. Pinkeye and other eye infections should be given antibiotic eye drops (optic drops). Ear infections can be treated with antibiotic ear drops (otic drops). For urinary tract infections, consult your pharmacy guide to see which of your oral antibiotics will be able to reach the bladder effectively. Wounds, especially those contaminated with dirt or saliva, should be cleaned well with soap and peroxide (or another disinfectant) before applying antibiotic ointment. Antibiotic ointment should be tried first, since it's readily obtained and has no side effects. If the wound becomes infected anyway, an oral antibiotic may be required. Abscesses often drain when submerged in an Epsom salts bath. Burns are very vulnerable to infection and require close monitoring. There are also many situations that are simply beyond the reach of at-home medical care: sepsis and meningitis require specialized, intensive therapy that is most likely not achievable even for the most well-prepared home medic. Appendicitis and gangrene require surgery. And cases of tetanus and botulism require special antitoxins (not regular antibiotics) that are unlikely to be found anywhere but a hospital.

As you can see, home-based emergency medical treatment requires a great deal of knowledge and preparation. If you are interested, you should take a class that covers emergency medical techniques for civilians. I recommend the following resources:

The Survival Medicine Handbook: A Guide for when Help is NOT on the Way by Joseph D. Alton, MD and Amy E. Alton, RN

Prepper's Survival Medicine Handbook: A Lifesaving Collection of Emergency Procedures from US Army Field Manuals by Scott Finazzo

SHTF Antibiotics: The Antibiotics that Could Save your Life When Disaster Strikes – And How to Get Them by John Williams

The Doomsday Book of Medicine by Ralph La Guardia, MD

NUCLEAR RADIATION RESPONSE

A nuclear or radiation attack is the starkest example of the apocalyptic doomsday for which we try to prepare. Although you can try your best to organize shelter and supplies, the biggest factor for survival in this situation is pure and simple luck. Living in a rural area away from attractive military or terrorism targets is the best preventive measure that you can take to protect yourself from a nuclear blast. Unfortunately, many of us have to live in or near cities to find work, and that puts us at higher risk. Let's examine what happens after a radiation attack and how to protect ourselves.

TYPES OF RADIATION ATTACKS

The very worst case scenario is a nuclear weapon detonation. This type of bomb sets off a true nuclear reaction that generates a tremendous amount of energy, heat, and radiation. Typically, a single nuclear weapon is sufficient to destroy or damage an entire city. These weapons require very specialized knowledge and resources to construct, and they are typically guarded very closely by the militaries that possess them. Unfortunately, it is still possible that one could be stolen or used by a rogue state.

A dirty bomb is a much less destructive weapon. Dirty bombs use regular explosives to spread radioactive material over an area, but there's no actual nuclear reaction (so there's much less destruction). Dirty bombs are not used by any military, but a terrorist group

FALLOUT SHELTER

Radiation damages DNA, and this damage particularly affects dividing cells, such as those in the bone marrow and digestive tract. *Photo: Public Domain*

could theoretically build one using stolen radioactive material or nuclear waste, which is not guarded as closely as nuclear weapons. Since dirty bombs use only regular explosives, design and construction would be relatively straightforward. The effects of a dirty bomb would be highly dependent on the exact type of radioactive material used. The strength and lifespan of radiation varies widely depending on the exact chemical involved. Since we have no historical data of a dirty bomb explosion to examine, scientists have tried to make predictions about possible outcomes. Happily, they've determined that it would actually be quite difficult to create fatal or even injurious levels of radiation using a dirty bomb. It would be more of a psychological weapon to create panic than a physical threat, but it would still be very disruptive.

A third concern is a radiation exposure device, which contains no explosives at all. Such a device simply emits large doses of radiation, like an overpowered X-ray machine. A terrorist who hides one of these on, say, public transportation could harm the people nearby, but the effect would not spread beyond the immediate area.

A final area of trouble is the electromagnetic pulse, or EMP. In an EMP, electromagnetic waves silently knock out solid-state electronics, which are found in nearly everything we use today — from the electrical grid to our vehicles. Such an attack could send society back into the dark ages overnight.

RADIATION SICKNESS

What happens after exposure to radiation? Radiation damages our DNA, and this damage particularly affects dividing cells, such as those in the bone marrow and digestive tract. The effect depends very much on the dosage of the radiation you've received. Even a relatively low dose of radiation can severely affect the bone marrow, producing anemia that makes one feel weak and tired. The immune system becomes compromised, leading to recurring infections. Finally, platelet production is impaired, so victims may bruise easily and bleed from the nose and gums. These symptoms take several weeks to develop, so exposure is not immediately apparent. Bone marrow failure is treated with blood transfusions and carefully selected antibiotics; it cannot be treated at home.

A higher dose of radiation produces symptoms that are much more apparent, usually in the form of nausea and vomiting. Victims may also develop a sunburn-like reaction to the radiation on their skin. This radiation burn can appear quickly or after a few days. Very strong doses of radiation can affect the brain, causing headaches, dizziness, and even seizures. The appearance of these brain damage symptoms within a few hours of the exposure indicate that the radiation dosage was very high and will most likely be fatal. Victims usually die within a couple weeks, and very little can be done medically to prevent their deaths.

The length of time that it takes for symptoms to appear is a strong indicator of the level of radiation exposure. A fatal exposure will produce immediate dizziness and disorientation, with nausea and vomiting developing within a few minutes. If the nausea and vomiting take a couple hours to appear, the radiation dosage is serious but not 100% fatal. For milder exposures, nausea may take several hours to appear or may not develop at all.

The typical course of radiation sickness produces short-term symptoms (like nausea and vomiting) that subside after a few days. The victim then feels much better for a couple weeks before the symptoms of bone marrow failure appear: fatigue, fever, and mild bleeding. Those lucky enough to survive radiation exposure may not be free of all consequences. Even if no symptoms appear initially, survivors still face a lifelong increased risk of cancer and infertility.

SHELTERING AND DECONTAMINATION

The single most important response to an attack involving radiation is to find shelter as quickly as possible. A basement is an OK option for many, but any interior room will do. The idea is to put as many walls and as much concrete and soil between you and the radiation as possible. Windows and doors can allow radioactive dust through the cracks, so avoid outer rooms and tape plastic sheeting over the inside of doors, windows, and air vents. Shut the chimney flue and turn off the central air system. You're trying to exclude anything from the outside, even the air. Ideally, you would have a 1950s-style fallout shelter prepared in your home, complete with food, water, blankets, first aid kit, and radio. If you're caught at work or somewhere else, head for a basement. Since radioactive dust settles rapidly, it's generally better to wait in place for a day or two than to risk evacuating though the worst of the radiation. The time you'll be stuck there is highly variable, depending on the type of radioactive material used and your proximity to the blast. Listen to a radio or watch TV or Internet for official information. Wait times could range from one day up to a month (this would be a worst-case scenario where you're very close to the blast site). Even those who are outside the blast zone should seek shelter, since radioactive fallout can be carried for hundreds of miles by the wind.

If you're caught outside when a blast occurs, immediately cover your mouth and nose with cloth to avoid inhaling any radioactive dust. Once you find shelter, strip off your outer clothes and shoes and leave them outside the door. They're covered with radioactive dust, and you should avoid bringing any dust inside the shelter (luckily, undergarments should be uncontaminated). Immediately take a shower to thoroughly rinse off any dust clinging to your skin and hair. Use plenty of soap but no oils or hair conditioner, which would just make the dust adhere to your skin. Unlike the decontamination showers you may have seen in the movies, you should avoid severe scrubbing, which can break the skin and allow radiation into the body. If the shelter does not have a shower, try using any faucet available for a makeshift one. If there's no running water, wipe yourself down thoroughly with

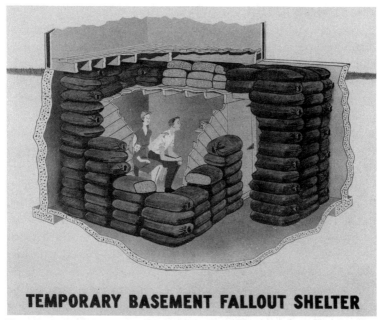

TEMPORARY BASEMENT FALLOUT SHELTER

The single most important response to an attack involving radiation is to find shelter as quickly as possible. A basement is better than nothing, as are interior rooms. *Photo: Public Domain*

a wet cloth. Treat the dust on your skin and hair like the deadly contaminant that it is.

One more note on shelters. Back in 1979, Cresson H. Kearny published the book, *Nuclear War Survival Skills*, through the Oak Ridge National Laboratory, a facility of the U.S. Department of Energy. Kearny's eye-opening research is a must-read today, for he revealed how communities in the U.S.S.R. at the time — and in Russia today, following the collapse of the Soviet Union — routinely teach their citizens how to build simple, "family expedient" fallout shelters below ground. Plans and step-by-step instructions for constructing the shelters are found throughout the book and tests proved that a typical family could dig the trench, cover it with earth (critical) create the entrance and exit holes, stock it and ventilate it in a matter of days and for relatively little money.

POTASSIUM IODIDE

Potassium iodide tablets are frequently touted as a treatment for radiation exposure, but their action is actually rather limited. Iodide tablets protect the thyroid gland in your neck from any radioactive iodine particles that you might absorb that could cause thyroid cancer in the future. That is iodide's sole function — to prevent potential future thyroid cancer. It doesn't treat radiation sickness at all. But since it's one of the very few proactive measures you can take in this type of emergency, you may as well keep some iodide tablets in your preparedness kit. In a radiation emergency, they must be taken on the first day of exposure to have the best effect, so you must stock them ahead of time and have them at the ready. Iodized salt does not contain enough iodine to be used as a substitute. A 130mg iodide tablet floods the body with 100x the normal iodine intake. With the body saturated, any radioactive iodine that you happen to absorb will be quickly excreted. The dose is repeated daily until the threat of radiation decreases.

Unfortunately, high doses of iodide can themselves cause adverse effects by over-stimulating or under stimulating the thyroid gland. Repeated doses of iodide are therefore a bit risky. You'll need to take the first dose immediately after the blast, but wait to take follow-up doses until you have more information. Most dirty bombs

Iodide tablets protect the thyroid gland in your neck from any radioactive iodine particles that you might absorb that could cause thyroid cancer in the future.

would not produce any radioactive iodine, so you would be exposing your thyroid gland to unnecessary risk. People over age 40 are most likely to experience adverse side effects from iodide tablets and least likely to develop thyroid cancer, so use caution if you fall into this group, particularly if you already have issues with your thyroid function. Children, in contrast, are most likely to develop thyroid cancer after radiation exposure, so they should be given iodide tablets unless they have an allergy to iodine.

HAZMAT SUITS

Hazmat suits (similar but not the same as biohazard suits touched upon elsewhere in this book) provide little to no protection from a nuclear blast. However, they can be useful if you afterward have to evacuate or move from one shelter to another. Although some models include a radiation shield lining, their most valuable function is to serve as a removable covering that prevents radioactive dust from getting on your skin and hair. Peeling off the hazmat suit before entering a shelter effectively excludes most of the radioactive dust from coming inside with you. To be effective, the suit must cover your whole body — feet, hands, face, and head. A tank of compressed air connected to a respirator prevents the wearer from inhaling radioactive particles. Although hazmat suits are valuable if you must go out, the best practice is to remain sheltered until the threat of radiation has decreased.

RADIATION DETECTORS

Both new and vintage Cold War radiation detectors are available on the market at a wide range of prices. Although many are designed for professional laboratory use, these tend to be larger and more expensive than is necessary for personal home use. Dose rate meters (including traditional Geiger counters) detect ionizing radiation in the environment. They can be used to monitor the level of contamination in your area after a radiation emergency, but tend to be somewhat bulky to carry around.

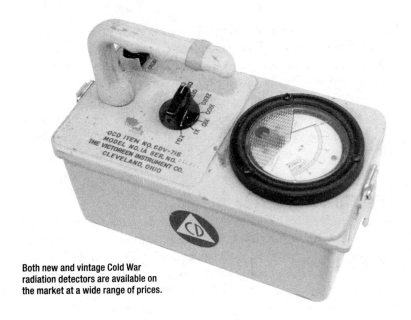

Both new and vintage Cold War radiation detectors are available on the market at a wide range of prices.

A smaller personal dosimeter is a radiation detector that is worn on your person to measure your radiation exposure as you go about your day (they're normally worn by such professions as nuclear workers and x-ray technicians). Traditionally, these detectors were film badges that could be developed like camera film to show your exposure level. Unfortunately, film can be sensitive to temperature and humidity conditions while in storage, so there's a chance it might not be usable when brought out in an emergency. Luckily, the new electronic dosimeters are much less delicate and are easier to use. Electronic dosimeters display their readings in real-time and without any processing needed. You can even set them to alarm at a radiation level of your choice, which is very useful if you need to go outside after a radiation attack for any reason. Some models are designed for first responders and are appropriately built to be tough and unbreakable.

Electronic dosimeters can be easily donned after an emergency occurs, but you're unlikely to be wearing one at the outset and therefore won't know your initial radiation exposure. RAD Triage has developed a radiation-detecting card that can easily be carried in a wallet, all but forgotten until an emergency occurs. The card can then show your total radiation exposure from the very moment of detonation. These cards are inexpensive, require no battery, and can be carried in a wallet for two years. Extra cards can be kept frozen for up to 10 years before use.

DISASTER FIRST AID

It is certainly not difficult to imagine a catastrophic event that results in mass casualties, loss of communications, or disruptions in transportation that might prevent medical assistance or evacuation. Simply turn on your TV news and (in between cats playing the piano, runaway llamas, and friendship-ending arguments over the color of a wedding dress) you will get plenty of scenes of tragedy and despair from all over the world.

Such deprivations may be more common in places with high poverty and little infrastructure, but they can be just as severe, if shorter-lived, in developed countries like ours. Some may say that we are even less prepared than people in poor countries because we don't expect it, whereas they live with it all the time.

In Nicaragua (where my family is from), you had better be prepared for earthquakes, volcanoes, and frequent power and water outages. In the United States, more common sources of catastrophe involve tornadoes, blizzards, hurricanes, flash floods, landslides, power outages, terrorism, and civil unrest.

We are fortunate that when these events do occur, we recover quickly. It is extremely unlikely that anyone in this country will have to go more than a few days without assistance or evacuation of any sort. However, if you or a loved one is injured, you may not have a few days, or even one day. Emergency medical treatment may need to be performed immediately.

Most of us have little to no medical training or experience and are not prepared mentally or in terms of equipment to treat anything but the most minor of injuries. My own limited medical experience is already better than most people. I learned a lot in the military, such as the use of tourniquets to stop uncontrollable bleeding, the use of plastic to seal lung injuries, basic splints and bandages, and how to handle the effects of nerve gas. As a security guard working my way through college, I was certified in basic CPR, but that is a class that needs to be retaken every few years.

In an emergency, your lack of preparedness does not mean you are out of luck. The average home is full of field-expedient materials that can be repurposed for medical necessity. The first and often the most obvious injuries involve bleeding. Most trauma-related deaths are a result of blood loss, and the simplest way to reduce blood loss is through pressure. A bandage can consist of a T-shirt or towel and some duct tape or packing tape. The bandage should only be tight enough to stop the bleeding.

If the bleeding continues and the injury is to an appendage, you may have to apply a tourniquet to cut off the blood supply above the injury. It has to be tight enough to do this, and one field expedient method involves some rope or strong twine and a stick (pen, kitchen utensil, etc.). Tie the rope tightly above the injury and use the stick to wind it tighter until the bleeding stops. Use a second piece of rope or duct tape to secure the stick.

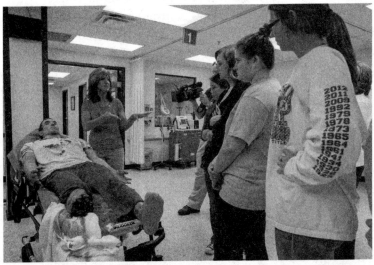

Bleeding that is severe enough to be potentially fatal can be stopped by means of a tourniquet. However, tourniquets should not be left on for more than 2 hours at a time, or the limb might die completely. *Photo: Benjamin Crossley*

If someone is not breathing or is having difficulty breathing, their airway must remain clear. One way to do this is the head tilt: chin lifted to keep the head tilted up with their chin up. Using pillows and duct tape or a belt, the head can be secured in this position. If the person is unconscious, monitor them and place them on their side to prevent choking if they vomit. Depending on the severity of the event, it is possible that a person may have suffered an amputation. The best chance to preserve and reattach the limb is to wrap it in a damp cloth, place it in a plastic bag, and set it on ice. Do not place human tissue directly in ice or water.

Impalements are not uncommon and can result from vehicle accidents, falls, explosions, and even from high winds and debris. Any person who still has an object sticking out of them should be assisted by first trying to control and stop the bleeding. The object should never be removed (unless it is blocking an airway) but should be stabilized so it doesn't move around and cause more damage.

An impalement that occurs in the chest can perforate a lung, causing the chest cavity to fill with air, resulting in a collapsed lung and difficulty breathing. It can be identified by an entrance wound making a distinct sucking sound. This puncture needs to be sealed ASAP, and this can be done with a large sheet of plastic, such as a trash bag, large zip lock bag, or any similar material, which is taped down to create a seal. This keeps air from entering the chest cavity, but any air already built up inside the chest also has to be released. Monitor the person and if they have continued or worsening shortness of breath or their chest appears larger on one side than the other, release the seal to let air out and then reapply.

In a natural or manmade disaster, injuries will undoubtedly include fractures and broken bones. A broken bone where there is no external bleeding should be placed in the most comfortable position, splinted, and immobilized. Fortunately, splints are just about the easiest thing you can make, and you can use any sturdy item (or preferably two). A splint can be made from rolled up magazines, sticks, broom or mop handles, etc. Then all you need is to secure them with rope, belts, or duct tape.

With any injury, especially one that breaks the skin, there is a chance of infection, and the worse the injury, the greater the risk.

Injuries should be cleaned as best you can to prevent infection. Clean water works well, but in a disaster the water supply may be non-existent or contaminated. In cases of floods or earthquakes where there is any chance of water contamination, stick to bottled water instead. Grain alcohol will work as well.

If you take medications, always try to keep a minimum of one month's supply on hand. However, the typical medicines we all keep in the house can serve multiple uses as well. Aspirin is a pain reliever and fever reducer, but it's also a blood thinner, so it should not be used for someone who has a lot of bleeding.

Finally, it is essential to stay calm and keep injured people warm and comfortable. Blankets are essential, but do not give food or water to anyone who is suffering from shock or possible internal injuries.

BASIC FIRST AID TECHNIQUES

CUTS AND WOUNDS

Small cuts and injuries should be washed well with soap and water, then covered with antibiotic ointment and bandaged. Deeper cuts may require that you hold pressure on the wound with gauze or a bandage until it stops bleeding, which can take up to an hour. The cut can then be very carefully washed (avoid disrupting the blood clot) and bandaged. If a wound does not stop bleeding, or if the person appears to be in danger of rapidly bleeding out, call for medical assistance by whatever means are available. Bleeding that is severe enough to be potentially fatal can be stopped by means of a tourniquet. However, tourniquets should not be left on for more than 2 hours at a time, or the limb can die completely.

Prompt washing and application of antibiotic ointment is the best defense against infection in a wound. Should an infection develop anyway, the abscess must be lanced, drained, rinsed out with hydrogen peroxide, and the ointment and bandage reapplied. You may have to repeat this daily (always using fresh bandages) until the infection clears. Burns and animal bites are particularly prone to becoming infected. If the victim develops a fever or red streaks on the skin leading away from the wound, call for medical aid. If help is not forthcoming, start a course of oral antibiotics if there are any available.

Some cuts are too severe to heal properly on their own and require stitches to hold the edges of the wound together. Ideally, this stitching is performed by a medical professional. If that is impossible, the home medic can use butterfly closures to achieve the same effect without stitches. Unfortunately, butterfly closures can pop open and are not really adequate for very large wounds. If you are able to get training in suturing or stapling skin, you can handle these situations. Skin staples are relatively simple to perform, but require a special stapler. Sutures are a little more complicated, but only need a needle and thread. Silk or nylon thread is preferred, as ordinary thread can wick moisture and contaminants under the skin, leading to infection. The needle can be sterilized by dipping it in alcohol and passing it through a flame, then allowing it to cool. There is surgical glue that can be used to close a wound, but it requires specialized training. Glue should not be used in wounds that are prone to infection, as it limits the wound's ability to drain.

First and second degree burns can be handled at home by applying a pain-relieving burn spray or ointment to the area, and then lightly bandaging it so that the bandage does not press too hard on the burn. When the bandage is changed, apply an antibiotic ointment to prevent infection. Third degree burns should be treated by a medical professional.

ALLERGY AND SHOCK

Minor allergic reactions (such as hives) can be treated with antihistamines (like Benadryl). Always do your best to determine the cause of the reaction and remove it from the area. Ideally, a doctor should be consulted as soon as possible. Anaphylactic reactions, which are severe constrictions of the airway, should be treated with an Epi-pen and nasopharyngeal airway if necessary. The insertion of a nasopharyngeal airway requires some training,

Shock arises from low blood pressure after an injury or trauma. Victims can have cool, pale skin, rapid pulse and breathing, and may feel faint, anxious, or nauseous. *Photo: Jocelyn Augustino*

but finding a class is worthwhile if a family member is prone to anaphylaxis. Anyone with an allergy of this type should keep an Epi-pen on hand at all times.

Shock is a state of low blood pressure due to an injury or other medical emergency. Victims may have cool, pale skin, rapid pulse and breathing, and can feel faint, anxious, or nauseous. Shock is not a condition that can be treated at home, but you can help by having the victim lie down with their legs elevated and wrap them in a blanket for warmth. Summon medical assistance by any means available.

STINGS AND POISONS

Animal and insect stings often occur in remote areas where medical help is not easily accessible. Packing a small first aid kit whenever you hike or swim can buy you the time you need to get help. For insect stings, gently remove the stinger (if it's been left in the skin) and apply pain cream and a cold compress. Spider bites should be washed well to prevent infection, then treated with a cold compress. Some spider bites (such as those of black widows and brown recluses) should be seen by a doctor as soon as possible. For jellyfish stings, wear a glove while removing any attached tentacles. The area can be washed with saltwater or vinegar to remove any residual stingers. An antihistamine (such as Benadryl) will provide pain relief. Venomous snakebites are always a very serious situation, and require immediate medical attention. The best first aid involves keeping the victim calm (easier said than done), removing clothes and jewelry from the affected limb, which will swell badly, and keeping the limb below the level of the heart. Medical attention and the prompt administration of antivenin are the only true treatments for venomous snakebites. Don't bother with "snake bite kits" containing scalpels, tourniquets, and suction devices. Trying to drain or suck the venom out of the wound is ineffective and wastes precious time.

Accidental poisonings from medications and household cleaners are very common with small children. Since every chemical is different, it's difficult to learn the treatments for all of them. Instead, keep the number of your local poison control hotline posted or programmed into your phone. Their operators can guide you through first aid for your particular situation. In case of a phone service outage, keep a poison control guidebook in your home as a backup. Although inducing vomiting was once a mainstay of poison treatment, it is seldom recommended anymore. In fact, ipecac syrup is no longer being produced for home use. Many poisons, particularly those that are caustic or petroleum-based, can burn the skin and cause severe injury when vomited back up. Instead, keep a bottle of activated charcoal suspension on hand. Based on the guidance of the poison control authorities, drinking activated charcoal within an hour of poisoning can often prevent the poison from being absorbed into the bloodstream.

EYES AND TEETH

Injuries to the eye can easily lead to loss of vision without prompt medical treatment. If home treatment is the only option, permanent damage is unfortunately likely. Eyes that have been splashed by chemicals should be rinsed thoroughly with eyewash or sterile saline for at least 15 minutes. Embedded objects and scratches to the eye surface should be treated by a professional. Home treatment with antibiotic eye drops and an eye patch might help, but they are not likely to be completely effective.

Dental first aid supplies are often overlooked when preparing a home kit. Oral pain relief gel can be a godsend when a dentist is not immediately available. Save-A-Tooth kits can preserve a knocked-out tooth for 24 hours, potentially enabling its return to service. Temporary filling kits can replace lost fillings until dental help is available. They come with good instructions and are easy to use, especially if someone is able to help you place the filling.

MORE SERIOUS SITUATIONS

Many medical emergencies simply cannot be handled at home. Still, stopgap measures can prevent the injury from worsening while you wait for aid. Keep a splint roll on hand at home and while hiking. In case of a broken bone, this thin band of aluminum can be rolled out and cut at the necessary length, then curved along its width, rendering it instantly rigid. The splint is then bandaged onto the affected limb, allowing moderate use until medical help is available. Carrying a splint roll is much easier than stocking splints in various sizes for every bone in every individual. Like broken bones, dislocated joints really need professional intervention, although you'll hear stories of people who managed to pop their joints back into place. Barring that much luck, the joint should be immobilized, elevated, and chilled with a cold compress to prevent swelling. Medical evaluation is necessary for proper healing that allows continued full use of the joint.

Treatment of heart attacks and strokes is clearly beyond the reach of home medicine. Chewing a 325mg aspirin can help greatly in recovering from heart attacks and some types of strokes,

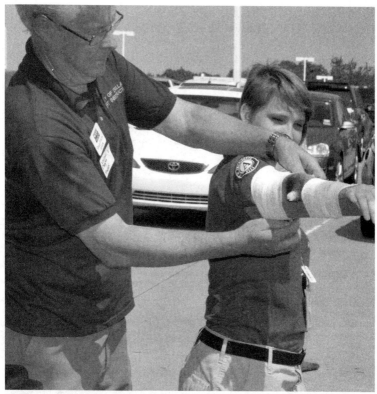

In case of a broken bone a splint is bandaged onto the affected limb, allowing moderate use until medical help is available. *Photo: Earl Armstrong*

and aspirin should be administered as soon as possible after symptoms appear (even if professional help is on the way). Other than aspirin and CPR if necessary, there is not much else for a non-professional to do in these situations. Seizures, shock, snake bites, and anaphylactic reactions are the same — unlikely to recover without hospital-level care. Anyone who has pre-existing medical problems and prescriptions should create a little stockpile of all their meds to tide them over in case care becomes unavailable. Depending on your prescription drug insurance, it may be possible to obtain 6-12 months' worth of pills at a time, creating a cushion in case refills become scarce.

FIRST AID SUPPLIES

Organize a well-stocked first aid drawer in your home and keep it updated. Have a smaller, more basic kit in each vehicle. If you are worried that your kit is lacking an essential component, here's a list to ensure you're well prepared:

GENERAL SUPPLIES:

- [ ] Blunt-ended trauma shears, sharp enough to cut through clothing
- [ ] Latex or nitrile disposable gloves
- [ ] Acetaminophen pain reliever (aspirin is not safe for children)
- [ ] 325mg chewable aspirin, in case of chest pains
- [ ] Cold medicine
- [ ] Flashlight and batteries
- [ ] Hand sanitizer gel or wipes
- [ ] Hot and cold instant compresses
- [ ] Space blanket
- [ ] Cotton sheets to use for carrying someone or to cut up
- [ ] Duct tape

WOUND TREATMENTS:

- [ ] Trauma pack with QuikClot
- [ ] Emergency tourniquet
- [ ] Band-Aids in a variety of sizes and shapes
- [ ] Absorbent compress dressings
- [ ] Cotton balls and cotton swabs
- [ ] Tweezers
- [ ] Sterile gauze
- [ ] Antibiotic ointment
- [ ] Bandage wrap, with clips or the self-sticking type
- [ ] Thermometer – digital type is easiest to use, but the battery will eventually die. Glass thermometers last longer and now contain alcohol instead of mercury, but they break easily so have a backup on hand.

Every household needs a well-stocked first aid drawer or closet. Most of us have one, although we may not always keep up on restocking it. *Photo: U.S. Air Force photo/Staff Sgt. Jonathan Fowler*

- ☐ Rubbing alcohol
- ☐ Hydrogen peroxide
- ☐ Topical pain cream, such as benzocaine
- ☐ Sewing needles, to remove splinters and perform sutures if necessary
- ☐ Sterile scalpel
- ☐ Butterfly closures
- ☐ Large syringe for wound irrigation
- ☐ Pain-relieving burn spray or ointment
- ☐ Skin stapler or nylon/silk suture thread (requires training for use)
- ☐ Allergy and Sting Treatment:
- ☐ Hydrocortisone cream
- ☐ Calamine lotion
- ☐ Antihistamine, such as Benadryl
- ☐ Nasopharyngeal airway (requires training for use)

DIGESTIVE TREATMENTS:
- ☐ Electrolyte drink or sports drink
- ☐ Anti-nausea medication
- ☐ Activated charcoal suspension

DENTAL TREATMENT:
- ☐ Oral pain relief gel
- ☐ Dental mirror
- ☐ Temporary filling kit with instructions
- ☐ Save-A-Tooth kit (preserves knocked-out teeth)

MISCELLANEOUS:
- ☐ Sterile eye wash
- ☐ Splint roll, can be cut to size
- ☐ N95 masks
- ☐ Supply of all prescription medications, at least 1-month doses

REFERENCES:
- ☐ CPR instruction chart
- ☐ Heimlich maneuver chart
- ☐ Poison control guide
- ☐ Book on poisonous plants and insects
- ☐ Book on first aid
- ☐ List of your doctors' phone numbers
- ☐ List of your allergies, current prescriptions, and dosages

MEDICAL TRAINING

To better prepare yourself for medical emergencies, take as many classes as possible on first aid and home medical treatment. Most communities offer classes on CPR and the treatment of medical emergencies in children. Check with your local fire department or hospital for availability. Also check redcross.org for Red Cross-sponsored classes nearby. You might even decide to become an emergency medical technician and volunteer in your neighborhood, which benefits both your own knowledge and your community.

Once you've taken the classes, keep the knowledge readily on hand by stocking up on first aid guides and books. You can find easy-to-follow, laminated sheets describing how to perform CPR and the Heimlich maneuver. Having these on hand can provide welcome reassurance during an emergency. As previously noted, guides to poison control and local poisonous plants and insects can be valuable tools for dealing with scenarios that are both hard to anticipate and require very specific treatment. Some examples:

A Field Guide to Venomous Animals and Poisonous Plants: North America North of Mexico (Petersen Field Guides) by Roger Caras

Deadly Daffodils, Toxic Caterpillars: The Family Guide to Preventing and Treating Accidental Poisoning Inside and Outside by Dr. Christopher Holstege and Carol Ann Turkinton

Survival Medicine & First Aid: The Leading Prepper's Guide to Surviving Medical Emergencies in Tough Survival Situations by Beau Griffin

The American Red Cross First Aid and Safety Handbook by American Red Cross and Kathleen Handal

Prepper's Survival Medicine Handbook by Timothy Morris

First Aid Guide: Basic First Aid Skills Everyone Should Know! by Daniel Hopkins

Survival Medicine: Prepper's Guide to Emergency First Aid & Safety by Josh McCoy

TRAINING COURSES

When it comes to emergency medical training, we are not dealing with the unlikely but rather with the inevitable. You or a person near you could be injured at any time as a result of a car crash or household accident. It is important to have some idea what to do in addition to calling 911. You don't have to go through full

Other emergency medical kits may be more involved and include sutures, tourniquets, breathing tubes and QuickClot for severe bleeding.

EMT training, however, and there are several extremely well-qualified instructors who offer weekend courses to at least get you familiar with the basics of trauma care. These instructors include registered nurses, paramedics, military medics, and law enforcement professionals, all of whom have seen and treated traumatic injuries first hand.

Tactical First Aid and "System Collapse" Medicine is a one- or two-day course offered by Active Response Training and taught by Greg Ellifritz. This course covers all of the basics, including self-care, and expands into injection prevention and minor suturing with hands-on training (using chicken parts).

According to Ellifritz, "The majority in my class are regular citizens who are concerned about a short- or long-term breakdown in our current medical system. I also get a large number of shooters who are concerned with emergency gunshot wound treatment in the context of a range accident or criminal violence. The remainder of the students are interested in third world travel or outdoor recreation where medical care is limited or non-existent."

The use of improvised medical equipment is also covered. "I think it is very important to teach students how to improvise from common household goods. No matter how much anyone stockpiles, if a disaster lasts long enough, supplies will run out. I teach how to improvise a tourniquet using a key chain and how to improvise airway management using a safety pin. There are also a whole lot of injuries that can be treated with a triangular bandage and some duct tape," said Ellifritz.

Another option is the Tactical Aid Course from Dark Angel Medical, which offers a more emergency- and combat-oriented class for traumatic injuries, including stabbings and shootings. The more intense portions of the class deal with severe injuries as

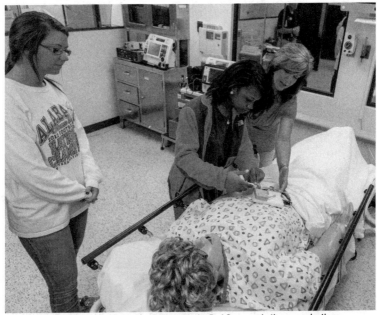

Basic first aid training is available locally through the Red Cross and other organizations.
Photo Benjamin Crossley

a result of explosions. This course offers tactical advice in providing medical care in dangerous or hostile situations. It's a two-day 16-hour course, and each student is provided with an easily portable CAT (Combat Application Tourniquet) and the D.A.R.K. (Direct Action Response Kit) emergency medical supply package, which fits onto Molle gear. This course splits the difference between standard EMS training and military first aid.

In addition to the usual advice on controlling bleeding, ensuring breathing and circulation, and treating shock and fractures, the class envisions scenarios in which rendering medical care may not be immediately possible or safe. Combat scenarios, as well as terrorism, civil unrest, active shooter, or criminal situations, may present an ongoing threat that must be dealt with or worked around before aid can be provided. For example, the class discussed the use of cover and concealment, and the differences between them.

The medical kit provided and the training on the use of its contents alone is worth the price of admission. Included are the CAT tourniquet, trauma shears for cutting away clothing in order to gain access to injuries, and several vacuum-sealed components.

Common household items can be used for emergency first aid treatment when necessary.

The Tactical Aid Course from Dark Angel Medical offers a more emergency- and combat-oriented class for traumatic injuries, including stabbings and shootings. *Photo: Firelance Media-Dark Angel*

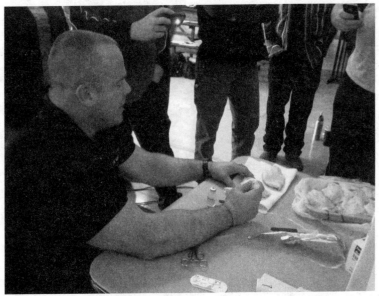

Tactical First Aid and "System Collapse" Medicine is a one- or two-day course offered by Active Response Training and taught by Greg Ellifritz. *Photo: Greg Ellifritz*

These include gloves (note that anything with rubber in it should be checked periodically and rotated out), HALO Seals for sucking chest wounds, a Nasal Airway to be inserted into the nose to ensure a clear breathing channel, Israeli Bandage, QuikClot Combat Gauze to stop bleeding, PriMed Compressed Gauze to treat heavy blood loss, and a Mylar Space Blanket for shock treatment.

Neither of these classes has any pre-requisite or offers any certification. They are geared toward the beginner with basic information and hands-on training for emergencies only when medical personnel are not available.

Remember, survival guns are only part of the equation as it relates to stopping a threat or obtaining food. The ability to keep yourself and family members healthy and in the fight is a recognition that this is real life of which we speak, not the movies. Good guys get shot and stabbed. We bleed, we get sick. If emergency medical systems go down, your preparedness in terms of first aid supplies and tactical medical training can help you live to fight another day.

SUPPRESSORS,
SHORT-BARRELED ARMS, MACHINE GUNS & IMPROVISED WEAPONS

SUPPRESSORS

The basic suppressor is not exactly new technology and was originally invented and marketed back in 1902 by Hiram Percy Maxim, whose father invented the Maxim Machine Gun. It basically works like the muffler on a car. Arguably America's most famous hunter, President Theodore Roosevelt, had a suppressed Model 1894 lever-action .30-30 rifle, which he used in his upstate New York backyard for hunting varmints without disturbing his neighbors. I myself have eliminated several aggressive raccoons this way.

Regardless, and for whatever reason, suppressors became associated in the public's mind with crime and, as a result, were eventually highly regulated by the National Firearms Act (NFA) of 1934. But "regulated" does not mean that they are banned, for if you submit the proper paperwork, pay the transfer tax, and wait, you too can legally own one in almost every state. It is very important, however, to always have a copy of any paperwork and the federal tax stamp with the suppressor at all times.

The American attitude toward suppressor use is not shared by the many European countries where suppressors are not regulated and

Suppressors don't silence your gun, per se, but lower the decibel level to a safe, or near safe level to avoid hearing damage. The gunshot will still be heard.

SURVIVAL SNAPSHOT: SUPPRESSORS

PROS: Reduces noise and recoil, improves accuracy.

CONS: Makes weapon longer and heavier, legal hassle to obtain.

WHAT TO STOCKPILE: One .22-caliber suppressor for rifles and pistols, one .30-caliber for rifles.

AUTHOR'S TOP PICK:
AAC Element 2 in .22.
MSRP: $499

AUTHOR'S TIP: Subsonic ammunition will further reduce noise.

Suppressors use internal baffles surrounded by a tube to suppress and redirect escaping gas just like a car muffler. *Photo: Gemtech*

simply are treated as an accessory or rifle part. In fact, their use is encouraged while hunting to reduce noise complaints. There is legislation pending in the U.S. to remove suppressors from the NFA and treat them as firearms — still regulated but much less so.

Suppressors don't silence your gun; that is why I resist using the term "silencer" because it is not accurate. Suppressors lower the decibel level of firearms to a safe, or near safe, level to avoid hearing damage; the gunshot will still be heard. There are generally two types of suppressors: direct thread, which attach directly to a threaded barrel, and Quick Detach (QD), where the suppressor is attached to a muzzle device. A direct thread suppressor will most often result in the maximum sound suppression, but the convenience of a QD mount makes these a popular choice.

A decibel is the commonly used term in acoustics to quantify sound levels relative to a 0dB reference point, which is where the average person will begin to hear any sound. A good quality suppressor can deliver 30 to 40dB of noise reduction. This is a bit better than your average hearing protection, which provides between 20 and 33dB of noise reduction.

A good way to think about noise level is by comparing everyday sounds. Normal conversation is 40 to 60dB; at 85 decibels, it is possible to sustain hearing damage with continuous noise. A gas-powered chainsaw reaches about 110dB, and at 120dB, hearing damage can occur from a single occurrence. Your ears will hurt at 130dB, and a high-powered rifle will produce 160 to 170dB. Even the best suppressors will only reduce the sound level to the comfortable range — but not necessarily the safe range.

The hearing protection benefits of suppressors are not lost on law enforcement. Increasingly, SWAT teams are equipped with them. This allows members to give each other alerts and instructions when working as a team, to be able to hear any suspicious or threatening activity, and to be able to engage a threat (often indoors) without losing their ability to hear. Electronic hearing protection does the same thing but does not protect bystanders who may not have hearing protection.

Besides the benefits to hearing and the ability to operate indoors and coordinate with others, there are many other survival-related reasons to check out suppressors.

SUPPRESSORS PRESERVE NIGHT VISION

A suppressor means no muzzle flash, and that means you preserve your night vision when shooting in low light conditions. The suppressor body itself is just a hollow metal tube that attaches to

Besides noise reduction, suppressors improve accuracy and reduce recoil.
Photo: DeadAir

the muzzle of the firearm. Internally, it contains multiple, separate gas expansion chambers or baffles. Since the baffles are temporarily trapping the escaping gas, any unburned powder that would otherwise exit the barrel and create a muzzle flash is also trapped, and it burns inside the baffles.

SUPPRESSORS HIDE YOUR POSITION

In addition to hiding the muzzle flash and thus helping to conceal your location, the firearm's normal sound signature is disrupted so that identifying where the sound of the shot came from is more difficult. This occurs because the sound of the shot's impact is louder than the sound of the muzzle blast and will be heard coming from a different direction. In a rifle using supersonic ammunition, the bullet will make a sonic boom, which a person will hear as the bullet passes, and they will think the shot came from a different direction than where it originated. Subsonic ammunition eliminates the sonic boom (the crack of the bullet breaking the speed of sound) and can further reduce the muzzle sound levels by as much as 10dB.

SUPPRESSORS REDUCE RECOIL

Suppressors reduce recoil in an interesting way. We all know that force equals mass multiplied by acceleration, and that for every action there is an equal and opposite reaction. This is the very substance of the cause of recoil. The bigger and faster the bullet and the smaller the gun, the more recoil. But it isn't just the bullet exiting the front of the barrel; there is also a stream of hot propellant gas that is traveling faster than the bullet and contributes to recoil.

This gas doesn't have much mass, but it does have a lot of acceleration (which has about a threefold effect on force), so reducing the velocity has a disproportionate effect on reducing the rearward recoil. Thus, by trapping and slowing the release of escaping gas, recoil reduction is achieved. Another factor that contributes to reduced perceived recoil comes from the added weight of the suppressor to the rifle. Also, the baffles themselves act as a muzzle brake and reduce recoil by diverting gas rearward and "pulling" the rifle forward. Depending on the size of the cartridge, a good suppressor can reduce recoil by as much a 30 percent. The more powerful the cartridge, the more pronounced the effect.

SUPPRESSORS IMPROVE ACCURACY

Suppressors can make your rifle shoot better by improving the harmonic stabilization of the barrel and by reducing the effect of atmospheric instability on the bullet caused by the escaping gas. Most notably, however, a suppressor will affect the point of impact, so if you are using a suppressor to hunt make sure you have sighted your rifle in with the suppressor installed.

SUPPRESSED HUNTING

Most hunting involves a lot more waiting around than it does shooting. It also involves being aware of your surroundings and being able to hear game or other hunters. As a result, hunters don't usually wear hearing protection, but even limited exposure to gunfire will cause hearing damage and loss, which is compounded over time. Fortunately, 39 states currently allow the private ownership of suppressors, and at least 29 of these allow them to be used for hunting.

In the U.S., most states allow the use of suppressors for hunting any game or nuisance species. These include: AK, AR, AZ, CO, ID, KS, KY, MD, MO, MS, NC, ND, NE, NM, NV, OR, PA, SC, SD, TN, TX, UT, VA, WA, WI , WV, and WY. In addition, LA and MT allow suppressed hunting for non-game and nuisance species.

Of course, laws do change, and it is always best to check ahead of time (preferably getting a response in writing) before venturing into the wilderness. Again, bring your paperwork with you to prove legal ownership, and print out the relevant state laws that allow you to hunt with a suppressor. Federal lands that allow hunting primarily follow the regulations of the states in which they are located, but again, check ahead of time. Also, many hunting areas, especially on the east coast, can straddle state boundaries, so make sure you know where you are.

SUPPRESSOR SELECTION

There are pistol, shotgun, and rifle suppressors for different calibers. Pistol suppressors are direct thread, while rifle suppressors can be either direct thread or quick detach. Suppressors also come in different sizes, with the larger ones being more effective as a rule. A .22 LR suppressor can be used on a rifle or a pistol, so it is a good choice to have. For rifle suppressors, and given the current hassle in owning one, I recommend getting a .30-caliber suppressor. This can be used on both a .223 and a .308 rifle with little difference in effectiveness.

Note that QD suppressors must be paired off with the right muzzle device. If you buy a suppressor from one company, you should also buy their muzzle device to make sure the two fit together. For the most part, suppressors do not need to be cleaned. In fact, rifle suppressors work better if you don't clean them. Pistol suppressors should, however, be cleaned on occasion.

When using .223, there is a note of caution, however, regarding barrel length. Most manufacturers will recommend a minimum length of 10 inches in order to adequately stabilize the bullet. A shorter barrel may result in a baffle strike from an un-stabilized bullet. This is not the case with some other calibers, such as .300 Blackout.

SUPPRESSED RIMFIRE

The .22 Long Rifle rimfire cartridge is already well established as ideal for first time shooters because of its low recoil. Its availability, low cost, and high fun coefficient make it the most popular all-around cartridge. Adding a suppressor makes it even better, and a growing number of manufacturers are including threaded barrels as a standard option on their .22 pistols for this reason.

I own a Walther P22 and recently acquired the excellent AAC Element 2 suppressor. This adds just 4 ounces to the pistol, thanks to its titanium construction, which keeps it very light and easy to handle. The bit of extra weight soaks up some of the already light recoil, and since the extra weight is all at the front, it keeps the muzzle on target with virtually zero climb. This makes shooting fast and staying on target extremely easy.

The extra length the Element 2 adds to the front of the pistol (just over 5 inches) helps emphasize muzzle awareness for beginners and the importance of keeping the pistol pointed in a safe

A rimfire suppressor, especially when combined with subsonic ammunition, can reduce decibel levels to the airgun range.

direction. This suppressor is only an inch in diameter, so it stays very compact and has a tough Cerakote black finish and stainless steel baffles for durability and ultimate corrosion resistance. It can be disassembled for cleaning, which is not something you need to do very often, but the .22 LR does shoot pretty dirty, so the occasional cleaning is a good idea.

Of course, the main advantage is in reducing the noise levels associated with shooting. Here, the Element 2 is superb with a rated sound reduction of 41dB. The .22 LR cartridge is not a major noise maker normally, and decibel levels unsuppressed can range from 90 to 120dB, depending on a variety of factors such as ammunition and type of firearms used. A 40dB reduction brings the sound level down to that of normal conversation. Indeed, when I shoot my suppressed P22, I have no need for hearing protection at all, and it sounds like you are shooting a CO2-powered pellet gun instead of a firearm.

The only other factor to consider in the sound of the suppressed .22 LR is the velocity of the bullet. Rimfire ammunition in this caliber can range in velocity from standard cartridges at just over 1,100 fps to hyper-velocity rounds that exceed 1,400 fps. The speed of sound is about 1,140 fps, depending on elevation and atmospheric conditions. When a bullet breaks the sound barrier, you get a sonic boom, which defeats sound suppression.

As a result, those who want the ultimate in sound suppression should use subsonic ammunition. However, in a pistol this isn't really necessary. The shorter barrel length means that the bullets do not reach their maximum velocity (which is rated using longer rifle barrels). Pretty much all .22 LR will shoot subsonic out of a pistol (at about 1,000 fps). I also tested this out using high velocity and subsonic ammunition and could not notice any difference.

I fired a .22 rifle suppressed and there was a significant difference between high velocity and subsonic ammunition. The high velocity stuff remained within comfort levels, but the sonic boom could certainly be heard. With the subsonic ammo, I could hear the sound of the bullet hitting the paper target and the sound of the action cycling but little else.

Many manufacturers make .22 LR suppressors, and there are many choices for the consumer. The commonality of the threads on the barrels allow the same suppressor to be used on a variety of rimfire pistols and rifles, and most rimfire suppressors will work with .22 LR, .17HMR, and .22 Magnum cartridges.

SHORT-BARRELED WEAPONS

Short-barreled rifles (SBRs) and shotguns, like suppressors, are NFA weapons, and you have to go through the same paperwork hassles, the overly long waiting period, and pay the same tax. For this reason, many people are simply opting for AR and AK pistols with an attached arm brace. The Bureau of Alcohol Tobacco and Firearms (BATF) is the regulatory agency enforcing the NFA and other federal gun laws. Initially, they approved the use of

arm braces on pistols, then they saw that people were using the braces as makeshift stocks, and the number of people applying to register SBRs went down. So, BATF decided that you could still keep the arm brace on your AR pistol but that "shouldering" it was a violation of the NFA and a felony. Now, they have changed their minds again and state that you can shoulder an arm brace-equipped pistol. Tomorrow, they may change their mind yet again, but who cares? We are talking about life or death survival

The main advantage of an SBR, or short-barreled rifle, is convenience and portability especially in tight quarters. The main drawback is that the shorter the barrel the more velocity and effectiveness you lose from your ammunition. *Photo: SIG Sauer*

situations, not the intricacies of federal bureaucracy.

The main advantage of an SBR is convenience and portability, especially in tight quarters. The main drawback is that the shorter the barrel, the more velocity and effectiveness you lose from your ammunition. For a survival situation, I would say that an SBR is nice to have, but not an absolute necessity.

FULL-AUTO

Fully automatic weapons, or machine guns, are perfectly legal to own but also NFA weapons. Prior to 1986, you could register new machine guns; they were plentiful, and prices were reasonable, but then everything changed. The Firearm Owners' Protection Act of 1986 (FOPA) brought about many much-needed reforms and protections for gun owners, but there was also a so-called compromise regarding machine guns. After a specific date in 1986, no more machine guns could be registered. This permanently froze the supply and immediately drove prices sky high.

The primary benefit of full-auto fire is to engage an adversary with overwhelming force. However, in a survival situation, this is

Forget about full-auto ARs. What you want is a crew-served weapon like the Vietnam-era M60 machine gun, which fires the 7.62mm NATO.
Photo: SSGT Timothy Cook, USAF

unlikely to be necessary. If you feel that you need this level of support, then don't waste your time with individual weapon systems like a full-auto AR. A full-auto AR or AK will mostly just cause you to waste ammunition, which is not recommended. What you want is a crew-served weapon like the Vietnam-era M60 machine gun. Getting a machine gun made after 1986 will be extremely difficult (only dealer samples are allowed).

The M60 is a belt-fed machine gun firing the 7.62mm NATO cartridge. It is very effective against equipment and a good area weapon. In a standard platoon, the two M60s provided 70 percent of the unit's firepower. The M60 is supposed to have a three-man crew, but I was issued one and had to handle it alone. That just meant that I ditched the tripod, extra barrel, and associated gear and carried less ammunition.

IMPROVISED WEAPONS

In any survival situation, the need may arise to improvise weapons. This is beyond my level of expertise, but I do recommend one very good source: the U.S. Army. Having a library of survival methods, first aid techniques, and other information will be extremely handy, and when it comes to information on improvised weapons, I turn to the U.S. Army Improvised Munitions Handbook (TM 31-210). This book is easily available online, and it was designed originally for special operators and insurgent forces behind enemy lines.

It features simple instructions and lots of illustrations for using commonly found civilian products to make everything from firearms to various explosives. Do not attempt to manufacture any of the explosives listed in this book. That would be a felony (assuming you don't kill yourself in the process). It is intended only for the direst of circumstances.

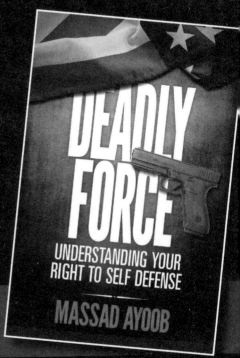